Social Movements

Social Movements and Transformative Dissent

Series Editors: **Savyasaachi**, Department of Sociology, Jamia Millia Islamia, New Delhi and **Ravi Kumar**, Department of Sociology, South Asian University, New Delhi

The emergence of new forms of dissent, protest, resistance and political mobilizations in South Asia in recent times has rendered several analytical frameworks in social movement studies obsolete. The books in this Series bring together perspectives from across the world, current debates, life, examples and works of activist thinkers associated with progressive social movements.

The volumes discuss social movements in relation to globalization, neoliberalism, civil society, labour movements, democracy, technology, feminism, new media, and the role of state, economy, politics and market in the face of rapid social transformations. Dealing with questions of justice, equality and reciprocity, they aim to create synergies between critical thinking, transformative action and creativity.

Addressing the diversity of social movements from trans-disciplinary intersections, the Series will appeal to students, scholars and interested readers.

Social Movements

Transformative Shifts and Turning Points

Editors

Savyasaachi

Ravi Kumar

Routledge
Taylor & Francis Group
LONDON AND NEW YORK

First published 2014 by Routledge

2 Park Square, Milton Park, Abingdon, Oxfordshire OX14 4RN
52 Vanderbilt Avenue, New York, NY 10017

Routledge is an imprint of the Taylor & Francis Group, an informa business

First issued in paperback 2019

Typeset by
Solution Graphics
A-14, Indira Puri, Loni Road
Ghaziabad, Uttar Pradesh 201 102

British Library Cataloguing-in-Publication Data
A catalogue record of this book is available from the British Library

ISBN 978-0-415-71736-6 (hbk)
ISBN 978-0-367-17675-4 (pbk)

Contents

Acknowledgements

The inspiration for this series comes from our students — their inquisitiveness to explore the potential of creative labour of dissent. We express our gratitude to Bhumika, Labanya, Ipshita, Antaranga, Paromita, and Nafis for their work in preparing the documents of the chapters included in this volume.

We want to thank all contributors to this first volume for their generosity to share their work. This is in fact a critique of today's madness for copyrights. A special thanks to Ana Cecelia Dinerstein, Maitrayee Chaudhuri and John Holloway for writing specifically for this volume.

We are grateful to Omita Goyal for doing the necessary groundwork with Routledge, New Delhi, and for encouraging us to put together this series. We owe thanks to Routledge's commissioning team for helping us keep track of the different tasks involved in bringing out such a collection. Often the last part of the journey in editing such books is very demanding and the energy level is not quite up to the mark. At such a moment the editorial team stood steadfast and tied up all loose ends. Their eye for publication detail, procedure, structure, content, and presentation is a contribution to the creative labour of dissent.

Introduction

The Emerging Contours of a Transformative Act

Savyasaachi and *Ravi Kumar*

Indeed, at the turn of the century we are reminded of what Aesop said — 'after all that is said and done, more is said than done'.[1]

The fall of the Berlin Wall and the Soviet Union in 1989 announced the downfall of the communist regime and the spread of neoliberal economy and democracy across the world. This was an occasion to introspect. Those with Marxist persuasion, and people at large, who had historically experienced transformative action and dissent, got the fillip to rigorously undertake a closer examination of the neoliberal ideology and worldview.

The history of neoliberalism can be traced back to the post-war reconstruction agenda formulated by the Bretton Woods institutions. Margaret Thatcher proclaimed that

> [t]here is 'no other alternative' (TINA)[2] to the neo-liberal alliance between the corporate open free market and the State; to growth rates; biotechnological advances, information revolution, infrastructure development; growing purchasing power of people, inflation, indebtedness . . . etc and Francis Fukuyama declared 'the end of history'.

What was becoming of the subject, its human will, its right to self-determination, human volition, the use of reason, and the relation of all these to human labour? What was becoming of the idea of freedom and responsibility? Susan George, a critic of neoliberal globalization, pointed out that another world is possible.[3] People no longer believe that the unjust world order is inevitable. Their reply to Margaret Thatcher's TINA is 'there are thousand alternatives' (TATA). Fukuyama's assertion is insensitive to the emerging contours of a transformative act! The public debates between New Social Movements (NSMs) and Classical Labour Movements

(CLMs) after 1989 have deepened our understandings about differences, society, labour, history, politics, justice, rights, protest, resistance, struggle, capital, language . . . etc., and of the transformative act.

Gunnar Olofsson's chapter in this volume written in 1986, three years before the fall of the Berlin Wall and the Soviet Union, points out that many social theorists have viewed NSMs as 'authentic representatives of post-industrial social forces . . . the historical role of labour movements is beginning to fade away; that the NSMs are the natural and self-evident successors of the labour movements' and 'hold up the promise of relevancy for the post-industrial age'. In his understanding, however, many NSMs were 'remakes of the old ones' (CLMs) and the social basis of NSM is 'students, intellectuals, white-collar employees within social work, education, health services . . . and professionals especially those in public employment'.

According to Olofsson, the societal relations and changes around which the NSMs organize themselves — gender contradictions, socialization of reproduction, contradictions in the forms of modern urban living, nature society — do not single out a new social force as their 'natural' counterpart. They are both more encompassing in their reach and more non-partisan in character. The most likely centre for a possible coalescence of a multitude of NSMs into a major social movement, if not in the class formative sense, is the societal basic relationship of nature–society.

Can the themes and issues raised by the NSMs be enunciated by existing political institutions and social forces? Similarly, do these forces have the capacity to absorb the issues raised by the NSMs? Are the matters taken up by NSMs incommensurate with those taken up by CLMs? What have the CLMs and NSMs contributed to the transformative processes?

The issues NSMs are concerned with are (physical) territory, space of action, or life world, such as body, health, and sexual identity; the neighbourhood, the city and the physical environment; cultural and ethnic, national, and linguistic heritage and identity; physical conditions of life and the survival for humankind in general. The NSMs comprise ecological and environment movements (including the natural and built urban environment); human rights movements for equitable treatment of those defined by gender, age, race, language, and region; feminist movements; those for identity and dignity; the pacifist and peace movements; anti-nuclear energy movements; those against mega hydroelectric dams; and for communal modes of production and distribution of goods.

From NSMs has emerged 'prominent values of autonomy and identity (with organizational correlates such as decentralization, self-government, and self-help) and opposition to manipulation, control, dependence, bureaucratization, regulation, etc. (Offe 1985: 829).

Is there sufficient ground for NSMs and CLMs to work together? Are the issues of NSMs not connected with labour–capital conflict? Are not the questions of identity, race, environment, decentralization, etc. (issues NSMs are concerned with), impacting labour–capital conflicts and struggles with which CLMs are concerned. Is not the loss of dignity and identity, the discrimination by gender, age, language, and region, the making of nuclear power plants, and the construction of dams determined by the logic of capital accumulation? Are these works of capital not anti-labour? Is not the struggle looking towards autonomy of labour the basis of cooperation against capital and commodification of work?

The innovations in information technology today determine the character of post-industrial capitalism and the process of commodification. These technologies

> produce by an increasing integration of the economic, political and cultural structures. Material goods are produced and consumed with the mediation of huge informational and symbolic systems. Social conflicts move from the traditional economic/industrial to cultural grounds; they affect personal identity, the time and space in everyday life, the motivation and the cultural patterns of individual action.
>
> The possibility of unifying individual experience beyond the operational rationality becomes more and more difficult: there is no place for questions concerning individual destiny and choices, life, birth, death, love (Melucci 1985: 805).

What is being suggested is that the struggle against commodification includes that for jobs, wages, conditions of work, and also for social and cultural values. For without these values and their organizational correlates, a job is another form of servitude — to time, capital and the employer.

With the coming of post-industrial capitalism, capital–labour conflicts have multiplied and diversified as well as spread to all spheres and all levels of social life, inside and outside the place of work along the entire value chain. The workplace is not just a factory floor, but is distributed all along the value chain across the primary, secondary and tertiary sectors of the economy — places for customary work (festivals, rituals and ceremonies); creative production of cultural goods and services (the works or art and crafts); intellectual work in schools, colleges and research institutions; the production and reproduction of leisure goods and services; play and sports. All this is necessary for the accumulation and reproduction of capital.

In other words, capital has hegemonized and commodified all spheres and levels of social and cultural life. It is very difficult to say what lies outside. It is for this reason capital–labour conflicts are part of all aspects of life. This total subsumption of society and labour under capital has dissolved the divisions between the public and the private, as well as between the subjective and the objective. Capital has expanded to absorb and consume all of society and labour. It has been commodifying goods, services and identity, and more than this, 'life' as well as life processes.

Today the struggles are not just against commodification of work, but also commodification of life-world as well as of life processes. Everyone has the right to work irrespective of gender, race and language; in the workplace no one can be overworked and should be given protection from occupational hazards. Peace movements draw attention to the production of armament that takes away valuable resources that need to be invested in the production of food, improving health services and education. The environmental and ecological struggle is against commodification of human and non-human nature that makes our life-world.

The 'thousand voices' draw attention to the interconnections between NSM's and CLM's struggles. It is worthwhile to explore not only the extent to which the differences in their modes of struggle are complementary, but also how the relationship between their respective social bases, namely the radical section of petit bourgeoisie and the working class (industrial workers, peasant and agricultural workers), is shaping up.

The 'thousand voices' are outlining the emerging contours of determination and necessity of labour to constitute the significant transformative act to say TATA to TINA. This emerging act has three elements, viz., necessity of theoretical thinking, dissent and negotiation. The chapters in this volume discuss some aspects of these elements.

Thinking Theoretically

Where is the potential of labour power, its capacity for work and its determination to struggle against the subsumption of society and labour under capital and to create political opportunity for thousand alternatives? In what way do the voices that have emerged from the struggles enrich this potential as well draw out its creative energy?

Michael Hardt in his Introduction to Christian Marazzi's *Capital and Language* writes:

> Marazzi analyzes how, as labor becomes increasingly defined by linguistic performance, work-time has generally increased and, in fact, the traditional barriers that divide work-time from non-work-time, that divide work from life, are progressively breaking down, a fact which carries with it a series of important consequences. Labor produces social life and, in turn, all social life is put to work (Hardt 2008: 10).

This is a very important aspect of neoliberal capital — it brings language, linguistic performance, knowledge production, and capacities for communication under control. In this way capital takes away the capacity of labour power to think independently of capital. It continuously engages the mind with vocabularies of finance, money, investments, debts, costs, prices, and so on. In this regard Marazzi argues

> that in the New Economy *language* and communication are structurally and contemporaneously present throughout both the sphere of production and distribution of goods and services and the sphere of finance, and that it is for *this very reason* that changes in the world of work and the modification in financial markets must be seen as two sides of the same coin (2008: 14).

The question is how can language and linguistic performance and the production of knowledge and the capacities for communication be liberated from the control of capital. This is an important component of the struggle against commodification of life-world and, in fact, of life itself.

The importance of autonomy and identity that has emerged from these struggles underlines the necessity for each voice to think theoretically. This has two interdependent facets — intellectual self-reliance and thinking responsibly, for this is the basis for autonomy and identity. The potential of labour power is embedded in the necessity for theoretical thinking — that is to say, by thinking theoretically labour power can become intellectually self-reliant and responsible. In these voices there is the recognition that thinking theoretically will bring forth the determination for work that is necessary to create political opportunity. This recognition, that work loses its autonomy and identity in the absence of theoretical thinking, comes from the history of commodification of work — the process of commodification compels a worker to labour like Sisyphus, caught in an endless routine of meaningless toil. Instead of being a means to self-discovery work becomes drudgery, leading to alienation and reification.

Further, these voices struggle to bring the notion of responsibility to thinking, taking it beyond pure logic, enhancing its capacity to return to itself and be accountable to itself in relation to the larger social and historical context. The labour (hard work) of returning to itself requires thinking to revisit not only the logic (its principles and procedures) but also the language(s) selected and critically examine the appropriateness of words (verbal and non-verbal concepts, categories of reference) and the grammar of language (principles and theories of meaning and orientation) that shape the sense of ratio and reason to arrange labour in a structure to express meaning on the one hand, and deepen the capacity for volition of human agency, discretion of human will and resolve of human determination on the other. All these theoretical elements of thinking enhance the quality of self-criticality in labour and equip it with the capacity to return to itself. There is labour of language and a practice of the language of labour, in the place of work and outside. Together they constitute labour power. In the same way, as the act of parole (speech) makes use of the potentialities of the generic faculty of language to hold, structure and express thoughts, the necessity of theoretical thinking makes use of the faculties of labour power. Similarly, the faculty of labour power makes use of the different elements of language.

We learn from these voices that labour power is the potential (capacities and capabilities) of the physical body, of the intellect, of the mind, of cultural practices, as well as of conscious and unconscious dispositions, and of the determination of the spirit. All this determines its productive capacity which is inclusive of its ability to reproduce. The absence of mindfulness deprives labour power of its orientation and impoverishes its spirit and determination. Disempowerment of language over time disempowers labour and makes labour power dead. This potential is 'held-up' or 'realised' within the verbal and non-verbal language(s), available to labour power in the place of work and outside.

As thinking gets embedded in labour and language, labour power gets the energy to counter the subsumption of labour and society under capital. It is this that makes labour resilient. Can capital transform its personhood into a commodity? So far, it has not. Labour will continue to have the potential to not only rebel, but also to create other possible worlds. The thousand voices that have emerged in relation to, and from within, these struggles are expressions of such labour power. What language frames are available to labour power to learn about the determination of capitalism in its neoliberal incarnation, and for the determination necessary to work out a thousand alternatives? The determination of capitalism is manifest in the use of force for primitive accumulation.

In this volume Pratyush Chandra and Deepankar Basu point out that 'primitiveness' of 'primitive accumulation' (see also Perelman 2000) is not a historically dated aspect of initial stage of capitalism, rather it is 'constitutive' of the capitalist system and process. It perpetuates its foundation — the separation between producers and means of production. The core of capitalism is this 'primitiveness', that is, capitalism cannot free itself of primitiveness because this is what determines capital accumulation. Under neoliberalism primitive accumulation operates through the market: 'capital accumulation is the extension of primitive accumulation, enforced through the market'. In India, they point out, the state intervenes with all its might to secure control over resources — both non-human (natural) and human. When on its intrusive march, capital encounters other modes of production — property and social relations that have been in operation before capitalism. Hence, primitive accumulation comes into play and, more often than not, direct use of force is necessary to effect this separation. Primitive accumulation, therefore, is at the base of capital–labour conflict and the subsumption of society and labour under capital.

What is this primitiveness? It is the use of force to separate the producer from means of production all along the commodity value chain, beginning with the extraction of natural resources in the primary sector, going on to the production as well as reproduction of goods and services in the secondary and the tertiary sector, respectively. This is true of India as well of other parts of the world. The primitiveness of capitalism is universal — it is a global phenomenon. We know about this from the struggles across the world against neoliberal capitalism. These range from those against price rise, consumerism, ecocide, genocide, libricide, large dams, displacement and forced migration, racism, market fundamentalism, gender discrimination, ethnic cleansing and so on.

The language of primitive accumulation, that is its vocabulary, categories, principles and theories, includes the theories of sustainable development, progress, per capita income, debts, gross national product, distributive justice, and entrepreneurship. These undermine the producer and their means of production.

A producer is defined by labour power, that is, by the productive capacity to produce use values in the form of real goods. This labour power is a worker's means of production. The mind, body and spirit along with the language frames embedded in the necessity for theoretical thinking together shape the means of production, namely the determination of labour power to create its will, volition and agency.

What is required to forcibly separate the producer from the means of production? This is determined by the conflict between capital and labour. In the capitalist system, the preconditions are natural resources (to begin with land), free labour and capital. To get free labour, capital will forcibly take away or separate the producer from the means of production, for as long as the producer has control over the means of production free labour will not be available. This separation of the producer from means of production is the basis of transforming use value into exchange value, and is at the origin of a value chain and becomes a presupposition for all stages of capitalism. The market perpetuates this separation by luring people to invest in speculative markets and disconnecting them from real economy, thus increasing the propensity to indebtedness and impoverishment of productive capacity.

Post-1989, the market has sped up the rate at which resources and other means of production are being taken away from the producer to keep up with the demands for quicker availability of more. There is a disconnect between the real economy, where material and immaterial goods are produced and sold, and the monetary-financial economy where the speculative dimension dominates the investors' decisions. This disconnect is a manifestation of the presupposition of capitalism, and it carries forward the task of separating the producer from the means of production. Over time this has severely impoverished the productive capacity of labour power.

It is worthwhile to reflect on what Fedrico Rampini says about the crisis of the New Economy:

> Because of the singular disconnect between the real economy and finance, the year 2000 was at one and the same time the last year of the great magic spell and the first year of brutal disillusionment. The world economy grew by 5%, the strongest growth rate in the last 16 years, still driven by an American economy in perfect health: 4% unemployment, the lowest since the Vietnam War. In the meantime, the Wall Street was heading towards collapse ... at the end of 2000 American investors discovered first time in 55 years ... that they were actually poor (Marazzi 2008: 15).

To this Marazzi adds,

> [t]he 1920's had also witnessed a New Economy that had given rise to great innovation and changed the face of modern industry: the advent of the automobile, the wide spread availability of electrical energy, the invention of cinema. But when the crash came, between 1929 and 1932, the Wall Street lost 90% of its capitalization ... what drove the expansion phase of financial markets to the point of collapse were the tech stocks.[4]

This disconnect is an integral part of primitive accumulation.

The problem is that this does not convince an economic investor to change his/her mind to shift the savings to less remunerative but safer securities (Marazzi 2008: 135). The addiction to risks of high return in the monetary economy is the contribution of the market to the processes of primitive capital accumulation. The productivity is measured with respect to production of real goods. The market economy has been compelling producers to become investors. Their capacities are now being determined by the language of finance of markets. The producer of use value in real goods is compelled to generate exchange value. The addiction is deepening the vulnerability, anguish and dreaded risks, due to the realization that there is no possibility of getting out of this vortex. It is this that fuels TINA, and makes the separation of the 'producer from the means of production by use of force' primitive. Underlying this addiction is the suppression of real economy, by the speculative monetary-financial economy of investors. This is an investors' fetish — a standpoint that it is impossible to create value without domination.

With this disconnect between real and speculative economy, labour and society get totally subsumed under capital and are thus dominated by it, consequently reducing use value (of real economy) to exchange value (abstracted from real goods).

What happens to the producer and to the means of production in the course of this separation? For the producer, this undermines the ground for initiative and volition and impoverishes the capacity to think critically. It deprives them of agency, suffocates their will and suppresses their determination to take charge of their lives, be responsible and accountable. This de-theorizes work, its existence and relation to social life for each. The time and space for initiative and for the exercise of volition shrinks — the speed at which capital reproduces and transforms use value leaves little time. This increases the propensity for differences and inequalities to speedily generate conflicts, for conflicts to escalate into violence, to degenerate into war and terrorism. The intellect, culture and social relations are structured by capital's need for porous borders. This porosity leaves no space for intellectual and spiritual buffers and insulations between fields of human activities.

From multiple sufferings on account of ecocide, genocide and libricide on diverse fronts, people have been afflicted by an 'acquired immunity syndrome' that gnaws and corrodes inner resilience and sense of dignity; thus rendering human condition vulnerable, on account of risks from disasters. Fear and anguish get situated inside the community and overtake the sense of belonging and being in the world. Underlying this is the process of commodification and subsumption of labour and society under capital. With the separation of the producer from means of production, the being of a producer is pushed to become an investor — uprooted from real economy and displaced into the speculative financial economy.

Vulnerability is a condition of 'being-in-the-world' of an individual fixed in a perpetual angst from being de-theorized, progressively deprived of means for thinking theoretically that are necessary to understand, regulate and have a hold over the material means of production. In all sectors of the speculative monetary economy, wage-earners are trained in technical skills to do the job well. This is, in fact, training in only terminologies and procedures for particular tasks. All other attributes of thinking theoretically (that come from culture, art, literature, and philosophy) that are necessary to make sense of work and its relation to the world are separated from these terminologies and procedures. The neoliberal ideology holds that culture, language and reflexivity do not keep pace with the technological change. These are fetters that slow down the pace of change; the rate at which languages change is not as fast as technological change.

Dissent

From the perspective of dissent and resistance, this slowness of the rate of change discussed earlier is in fact a manifestation of the 'angst' language does not yield to the speculative monetary economy, of which technological change is only one aspect. Further, dissent holds that the neoliberal ideology de-theorizes work by not letting language, culture and philosophy address questions of survival, dignity, justice, and existence as these emerge on the horizon of history and confront the diverse ways of being-in-the-world.

Furthermore, as a producer is driven to become an investor, the language of the real economy of use value is undermined. For instance, the idea of freedom that comes with the freedom to use time is weakened — the meaning of freedom changes to that of choices in the market. Thus, time is commodified, that means there is little free time for family and friends.

Language shows resilience — it resists being pushed. It struggles to attend to the necessities of thinking theoretically by means of social sciences, art, philosophy, literature, and theatre. It seeks to create political opportunity in the face of 'primitive accumulation', and reaches out to people who want to express their anguish. Language works towards formulating questions concerning responsibility and responding to fear and dread. It engages with questions such as what kind of theoretical thinking is necessary, and what is the role of volition, discretion and resolve. All this constitutes the language of dissent.

Dissent is a mode of radical insistence; it is the determination to hold on to thinking theoretically as the means to live the life of a producer (and not become an investor). It is the resilience of language (discussed earlier) in the face of dread generated by the speculative monetary market that can hold back the producer from becoming an investor and not succumb to this fear. Dissent is anti-systemic way of life that upholds the foundational position of use value and the producers' right to means of production, as well as the space for volition and discretion, all along the value chain of the real economy. It thus constitutes labour power — the body, mind and spirit, and the language necessary for theoretical thinking. This foundational position of the use value is the non-negotiable terms of reference in the struggle against neoliberal capitalism.

John Holloway's chapter in this volume points out that it is fundamental not to accept the 'mad logic of capitalist system' and to 'go a different direction'. 'Revolution is no longer about taking power, but about breaking the insane dynamic that is embedded in the social cohesion of capitalism. Revolution is a puncturing of that cohesion, it is the creation of cracks in the texture of capitalist relations. This cohesion is constituted by abstract labour.' It can be cracked by 'a different activity that is not abstract labour, by ceasing to allow the daily transformation of our doing, our concrete activity that does not create capitalist social relations, an activity that does not fit the logic of the social cohesion of capitalism'. He argues that in everyday life concrete labour which is concrete doing is in perpetual struggle to not be absorbed by the logic of abstract labour — for instance 'when we refuse to work that we can play with the children, when we choose something not because it brings money but because we enjoy it. In these choices we oppose use value to exchange value and concrete doing to abstract doing. With these revolts in everyday life and 'not from the struggles of activists and political parties' the possibility of ceasing to create capitalism and 'creating a different sort of society needs to be posed'. Life is a constant struggle to break through the connections forged by abstract labour.

An important dimension of this struggle is to counter the determinations of operational rationality that place value on efficiency, consistency and logical coherence. These ideas have a resonance with Antonio Negri's views:

> If you are looking for use value, you will not find it in naturalness but rather in history, in struggles, in the continual transformations of ways

> of life. *Use value is always reconstructed; it is always to the 'nth' power* (2008: 84).

This is a way to express what we learnt from Marx that use value is living labour. The struggle questions the form and content of means of production, modes of thinking, the language and the semantics of investors in the speculative monetary economy. The awareness that these means of production are destructive (for instance, techno-stocks led to the crash of stocks and to the undermining of real economy) generates resistance to the inner necessity of primitive capital accumulation to reduce producer individuals to numbers of homogenous groups, such as class, mass, collection of wage-earners, income groups, and so on. In this regard, Negri points out:

> In 'anti-systemic' thought, the scope of class struggle was in reality greatly reduced in favor of Third Worldism. Synthesis only occurred on a superior, completely ideological level, according to a classical deterministic conception of the development of struggles and of capitalism itself: the predetermination of crisis, the tendency towards falling rates of profit.etc. What could antisystemic still mean to a realist conception of the class struggle (2008: 62–63).

Anti-systemic thinking is an expression of teleology of labour that comes from within labour power to realize itself with its own means. Negri calls this 'materialist teleology':

> When we speak of 'materialist teleology' we never imply — contrary to all transcendental teleologies and to all metaphysics of history — a predetermined *telos*, preexisting the material conditions of historical development. Rather, we are speaking of a *telos* that is permanently redefined, reformulated, reopened, and revived by social, political, economic and — *last but not the least* — historically antagonistic determinations (ibid.: 41).

There are creative possibilities in contradiction, in not looking for consistency and coherence.

Marieke de Goede in her chapter argues that

> understanding global resistance in terms of a coherent programme entails a limited definition of contemporary political possibilities of dissent. By defining and delineating not just the new global movements

> but also their goals and ideals, some authors tend to read each dissenting voice in the context of a larger global purpose, while devaluing those, often complex and contradictory, political practices of festivals, laughter and everyday coping strategies that cannot be seen to contribute to this purpose.

She shows that carnival and laughter are forms of dissent in an era of globalizing finance, that do not aspire to culminate in a new world order but transform people's everyday experiences of money and finance in important ways.

> Laughing about financial practices is more than a helpless gesture in the face of financial power, but has the potential to challenge its rationality and expose its contingency. These cultural practices are ways in which people cope with the seemingly overwhelming power of finance in everyday life, and create space for imagining financial alternatives.

These strategies transform and challenge dominant discourses and create spaces for alternative imaginations, and contribute to overcoming the fear and hopelessness generated by monolithic accounts of neoliberal project — they do transform people's experience of monetary instruments and financial discourses.

Further in this volume Ana Cecilia Dinerstein argues that hope is embedded in 'how autonomous practices create alternative symbolic and/or territorial spaces. The 'practice of autonomy', across the world, has increasingly become a mode of mobilizing resistance. 'Hope is a political category, which must not be understood as a 'wish' or 'a form of romantic return to the (indigenous) past, it is rather a form of anticipating the future'. She argues that in 'radical democracy, the idea of individuals who delegate power is rejected on behalf of women and men governing themselves'.

Dissent, as women and men govern themselves, is inclusive of different modes of insistence, modes of being and thinking theoretically. As partners in the materialist teleology to create alternatives to development, they bring in different understandings of agency, volition, will, and self-consciousness. The task for dissent is not to change the world but to create a new one.

What is common to this partnership? Between whom is this partnership?

One way is to see the common from the standpoint of labour. That is to say, on one hand dissent constitutes the labour force that resists being bought and sold as a commodity, and on the other it positions itself against the constant (the presence of constant capital undermines the possibility of creating a common). This prepares the ground for a new world.[5]

In this new world created there is space for children's point of view and perceptions as well for the radical petit bourgeoisie, the peasant, the agricultural worker, the forest dweller, and the dalits and other minorities.

Janette Habashi argues in her chapter that 'to the extent that power discourse attempts to objectify socio-political reality as a tool of domination the voices of the children serve as an experiential countermeasure to the power of greater forces operating in their lives'. Further,

> children's refusal to be objectified by the global discourse is, in itself, an act of liberation. Global discourse tends to objectify the discourse and create a singular meaning of resistance; on the other hand, children in local settings create shades of meaning that reflect their realities.

Her study shows that socio-political circumstances of life constitute the current language usage of Palestinian children. Language usage and presentation are a power structure and power discourse where meaning is generated. Thereby, the contested usage of language encompasses language meaning in the context of global hegemony. Language innovativeness counters global discourses. Janette underlines language as a very important aspect of resilience, resistance and transformation on the one hand, and a very powerful tool for hegemony and dominance on the other.

The language innovativeness referred to by Janette is not possible as long as labour is subsumed under (dependent on) constant capital and is directed by the operational rationality of exchange value. It will not allow the vocabularies of political resistance to reach children. There are several studies showing that the censorship by parents, schools, state agencies of children's books, plays, and theatre keeps children away from these languages. They push towards the use of terms and categories that favour the market (and the production of exchange value).

Included in this partnership is the peasant as well. For long their contribution to everydayness of resistance has not been recognized. In this volume, Sivaramakrishnan draws attention to everyday struggles of agrarian people. He traces the genealogy of the concept of everyday resistances and shows that the agency and ideology of the poor and lower classes is quiet independent of the conscientization programmes of mass organizations, political parties and others. It is constitutive of a moral economy that legitimately allowed the negotiation of rights and obligations, which was made increasingly difficult by rational impersonal regulations. He points out that

> it is correct to say that everyday forms of resistance are about custom and usage. On the one hand, as a means, such resistance is anarchic: spontaneous, non-hierarchical, and loosely organized. On the other hand . . . it seeks not the overthrow of the state or even its policies but merely to mitigate or subvert their effects.

What then are the origins of their everyday struggles? Around this question, the debate between Ranjit Guha (1983) and Mridula Mukherjee (2004) is interesting. It is concerned with whether the language and consciousness for resistance and struggle come from within everyday life or from the outside introduced by the elites? Ranjit Guha shows that the inspiration to struggle comes from within the cultural traditions of peasants, agricultural workers and forest dwellers. Mridula Mukherjee points out that the outside has a very important role to play as well. The resistances that both these historians study are in the context of primitive accumulation. We can now reformulate the question — do the peasants, forest dwellers and other people living in the frame of the cycles of nature need outsiders to tell them that they are being separated from their means of production? This question is important to understand the dynamics of children acquiring the language of resistance as well. It is important to recollect here the colonial construction that classified peasants and forest dwellers and others as children — like *tabula rasa*.

The society and labour of producers, such as peasants and forest dwellers, is grounded in use value and real goods. This is the basis of their sense of dignity. Their being-in-the-world is determined by a materialist teleology that is continuously creating the commons. The resistances to different types of domination — slavery, feudalism and capitalism — that have attempted to separate them from the production of real goods of use value have taken different forms, such as inversion of dominant social practices, silence, migration, and aggression.

This throws light on the nature of dissent. It is embedded in use value and the sense of dignity that comes from it. This is a foundational element, an inner attribute of being and of labour power. Resistance is an expression of assertion of one's own dignity, when being is denied the means for manifestation. This common element of the new world brings together children's point of view and perceptions as well as that of the radical petit bourgeoisie, the peasant, agricultural worker, forest dweller, the dalits and other minorities.

Negotiation

An important aspect of dissent is 'to negotiate'. Jane Mansbridge in her chapter in this volume is in disagreement with 'difference feminism' with regard to their anti-Statism and their holding on to the gender difference. She is of the view that 'we still need both states and international institutions to help solve collective action problems and to give scope to the human capacity for justice'. For instance, she argues

> state power can serve both as a brake on the negative externalities of capitalism and as a positive force for material redistribution. Particularly when patriarchal power takes violent forms in the private sphere, state power can help women struggle against that violence as well as other non-state evils. The question, then, is how far to carry wariness of state power and of theories of state universalism and impartiality.

She points out that the state as a tool is dangerous and flawed and we need to use it with caution. As regards 'stress on women's differences from men, it reinforces the tendency of dominant groups such as white or middle-class women to interpret women's experiences primarily in the light of their own'.

Maitrayee Chaudhuri says that 'women's movement and the dalit movement are inextricably engaged with not just the state but also international institutions'. An understanding of the transformed nature of capital, functioning increasingly at a global level, provides insights into changes in the nature of social movements. Her study of the women and dalit movements suggest that negotiation with the state remains a key site and mode of social movements. She argues that here the middle class has a critical ideological role to play. Jane Mansbridge and Maitrayee Chaudhuri state that negotiation is concerned with what can be got from the state. Mansbridge takes care to not overdo gender differences and Chaudhuri cautions to not overlook class inequalities.

The state is not likely to wither away and thus it is important to neither under- nor over-estimate its character. In reaction to thousand voices, a counterinsurgency state has emerged post-1989 to ensure the promotion of neoliberal markets. Each of these thousand dissenting voices is now seen as constituting insurgency and correspondingly sophisticated means for counterinsurgency are being developed. Development programmes are now emerging as an integral part of the counterinsurgency strategies supported by the use of military, paramilitary and police forces, both overt and covert (intelligence). Post-industrial capitalism is in fact an industrial-military complex, which is the true face of development from its very inception. It is now clear that primitive accumulation is not possible without this complex.

Ian Roxborough has argued that counterinsurgency efforts have contributed to the emergence of the Global State. He gives a working definition of counterinsurgency: 'Counterinsurgency refers to the policies of a state facing internal war. It is the effort on the part of the state to defeat insurgency. Insurgency and counterinsurgency form the two faces of a couplet of contention' (Roxborough 2008: 5). Counterinsurgency seeks to shrink political and social spaces for expressing differences.

Post-1989 there has been an augmentation of modes of mass mobilizations that have creatively combined litigation, lobbying and protest. This has enriched dissent to negotiate the non-negotiable foundational position of use value and strive to make available the means of production to producers all along the value chain. It has to contend with a counterinsurgency State. 'Thousand voices' have worked out creative combinations of litigation, lobbying and protest to continue the work of augmenting labour power and the materialist teleology. These modes are now available to more people, have contributed to political literacy, have created space in the public domain, and empowered multiple resistances at all levels of social life. What kind of space in the public domain do litigation, lobbying and protest determine? This space is outside the formal parliamentary political process shaped by processes of consensual democracy and deliberative democracy.

In this volume, D. L. Sheth discusses the 'micro-movements in India', referred to as 'grass roots movements', social movements, non-party political formations, social-action groups and movement-groups. These movements became visible and acquired political salience in the mid-1970s and have since been active on a variety of issues, which in their own perception are — directly or indirectly — related to what they see as their long-term goal of democratising development and transforming. These organizations self-consciously and sharply differentiate themselves from the welfare, philanthropic and other such non-political non-governmental organizations (NGOs). He points out that these movement organizations lead political struggles on issues that were articulated by people themselves. Further, with their emergence there was a clear shift from representative to participatory democracy. They dissented against meritocracy, decision-making that relied on experts and specialists, and against elected representatives. The participatory democracy that emerged was shaped by empowerment of people through everyday struggles as well as by collective action.

Today litigation, lobbying and protest shape the dynamics of non-party political processes. Christopher J. Hilson in his chapter states that a 'lack of political opportunity may influence the adoption of litigation as a strategy in place of lobbying, and that the choice of protest as a strategy may be influenced by poor political and legal opportunities'. He takes the example of four movements — environmental, animal welfare, lesbian and gay, and women's movements in the United Kingdom (UK) to show that resources, identity, ideas, and values influence the choice of strategy.

Further, the creative use of these modes has prepared the ground for new alternative logics and modes of organization, namely networks. It is being argued that the logic of networks is different from that of order, centralization and hierarchy-building.

Information and Communication Technologies (ICTs) and cyberspaces be included in party consensual political processes? Arturo Escobar suggests that ICTs and cyberspace tend to promote the creation of networked cultures without the homogenized identities assumed by the mass media; they foster routes for the circulation of ideas that are not so subject to centralized controls, and the eruption of sub-cultures that are aware of the need to re-invent social and political orders. As a space for intercultural exchange and for the construction of shared artistic and political strategies, cyberspace affords unprecedented opportunities to build shared visions with peoples from all over the world.

He further argues that 'in its utopian conception, cyberspace can thus be seen as enacting a decentralized, non-hierarchical logic of self-organization. Self-organization is also at the heart of complexity in biological and social life. Ants, swarming moulds, cities, and certain markets are among the entities that show what scientists call 'complex adaptive behaviour.' This alternative logic of social organization, Escobar points out, allows for decentralization for communities can create their own media and process their own information with it.

Chris Atton in this volume says 'internet-based network of independent media Centres (IMCs) emerged as coalition of anti-capitalist social justice groups over 30 years after November protests in Seattle against the WTO in 1999'. In Seattle the IMC made available 'hundreds of hours of audio and video footage and hundreds of thousands of eyewitness reports, analyses and commentary became available to activists, supporters, detractors — to "global citizens" at large'. No prior approval was needed from the core group, neither was that group responsible for editing the content of reports in any way. Another example is the use of internet by the Zapatistas in their struggle for land, and for political and cultural recognition. Dialogic praxis through internet sought a 'radical internationalization' from the available technology. Further, he points out that this network embeds internet practices in a 'wider socio-economic struggle against the internationalization of capital can be considered as a globalized, radical-democratic struggle against globalized finance'.

Harry Cleaver's chapter in this volume deepens our understanding of networks and their significance. He points out that in the '1960s the Marxist sociologist Romano Alquati in his studies of workers conflicts with the Italian auto giant FIAT enmeshed his analysis of class composition with that of networks at factory, national and international levels'. The concept of networks today describes that the interconnections among proliferating struggles against capitalism is a shift away from the classical project of socialism, towards emergence of several thousands of distinct projects that underline no need for universal rules. Most importantly, networks of these struggles show resilience against the military and paramilitary force that try to co-opt and destroy these projects on the one hand and a better capability to attack when the need be.

Cleaver describes 'swarming' as a sustainable and structured way to strike from all directions — as a way networks can attack.

The dynamics of bottom-up networks is shaping a civil society. Sangeeta Kamat's chapter argues that '[c]ivil society has emerged only recently as a distinct political actor within international development discourse, and its ascendancy can be traced to the end of the Cold War and the launch of the global free market'. She points out that

> the state, today, is represented as fragmented by private interests (otherwise referred to as corruption), and hence inept at representing the will of the people, whereas civil society is seen as the honest broker of "the people's interests" ... In advancing this proposition, the role of NGOs is provided as evidence of the new capacities of civil society, mediating the excesses of the state. This new conception of civil society does not fit neatly with neoliberal conceptions of state and civil society either. Liberal democratic theory understands civil society as constituted by competing private interests and individual desires that are stabilised by free interactions in the market place.

She draws attention to the fact that events in Seattle, Genoa and Washington, DC demonstrate that the grassroots advocate NGOs supported by social movements and trade unions, and are in a position to disrupt and stall the formation of global capitalist market. These grassroots-level NGOs work with marginalized people — poor women, landless peasants, urban street children, and civil society. They are witness to the devastations of privatization and markets fundamentalism. In some countries these NGOs have allied with Left parties and radical movements to challenge the policies of international institutions.

The Necessities and Determination Transforming Subjectivities

The necessity to creat another world comes with the determination to transform subjectivities.

The theoretical thinking in the chapters in this volume reaches out to grasp the many sides of struggles and outline the emerging contours of the transformative act, enrich its dissenting imaginations with terms, categories, principles, and theories that emerge from transformative social processes and the dynamics of litigation, lobbying and protest.

A creative combination of litigation, lobbying and protest against TINA shapes the vocabularies and language frames of theoretical thinking and the contours of the 'determination' of the emerging public intellect to negotiate the non-negotiable terms of reference and give expression to anti-systemic struggles. The foundational position of use value, the real economy of labour power and the producer right to means of production as well as to the space for volition and discretion, all along the value chain is non-negotiable.

These terms of reference go beyond what legal provisions provide for in Acts, to include everyday experiences, indigenous knowledge systems and cultural practices in the work place and outside it. This allows for a greater awareness of the necessity of theoretical thinking to frame, understand and know what to do, and brings new energy to non-party political processes, networks and new grassroots-level civil society for radical insistence against de-theorizing, for the production of use value and enriching labour power. This has over time made people's democracy a strong contender against liberal parliamentary democracy. It does not seek to take over the State and control capital, but to make sure that labour and society are not subsumed under these and create a new world.

Further, the emergence of network coalitions has been viewed as a critique of necessity of the 'vanguard' for radical systemic transformation (Graeber 2004); it enriches the process to build a deliberative democracy to transcend the limitations of liberal democracy, to strengthen political process with persuasion, build consensus to agree to disagree and evolve a democracy for anti-systemic struggles. This is central to the emerging politics of inclusion.

After 1989, conflicts that are based on structural contradictions have contributed to discriminations. The transformative act seeks to create political opportunity for people from all walks life — the rich and the poor, the old middle class and the new middle class, the industrial working class, peasants and landless people, people of all religion, caste and race. Amongst other things this act is constituted by the labour power to produce use value and resist becoming part of the investors exchange regime. This transforms the subjectivities of people resisting in all walks of life. Finally, common to the determinations of transforming subjectivities is the necessity to create another world.

Notes

1. http://thinkexist.com/quotation/after_all_is_said_and_done-more_is_said_than_done/221866.html (accessed 13 September 2013).
2. Maranon points out that 'those who worked shoulder to shoulder with her called her TINA, obviously not to her face . . . Thatcher received this nickname because she repeated this sentence to her collobo-ators'. See Munck (2003).
3. For her biography see http://www.tni.org/susangeorge (accessed 13 September 2013).
4. See Marazzi (2008: 14–15). According to Marazzi Fedrico, Rampini is a West Coast correspondent for the Rome daily 'La Pepublica'.
5. In this regard Negri points out, 'the common is the sum of everything that the labor force (V) produces independently of C (constant capital, total capital) and against it' (2008: 67).

References

George, Susan. 2002. 'Another World is Possible', *The Nation*, 18 February, http://www.thenation.com/article/another-world-possible (accessed 28 February 2013).

Graeber, David. 2004. 'The Twilight of Vanguardism', in Jai Sen, Anita Anand, Arturo Escobar and Peter Waterman (eds), *World Social Forum: Challenging Empires*. New Delhi: Viveka.

Guha, Ranjit. 1983. *Elementary Aspects of Peasant Insurgency in Colonial India*. New Delhi: Oxford University Press.

Marazzi, Christian. 2008. *Capital and Language from the New Economy to the War Economy*, trans. Georgory Conti. Los Angeles, CA: Semiotext(e).

Melucci, Alberto. 1985. 'The Symbolic Challenge of Contemporary Social Movements', *Social Research*, 52(4): 795–96.

Hardt, Michael. 2008. 'Introduction', in Christian Marazzi (ed.), *Capital and Language: From the New Economy to the War Economy* trans. Georgory Conti. Los Angeles, CA: Semiotext(e).

Mukherjee, Mridula. 2004. *Peasants in India's Non-violent Revolution: Practice and Theory*. New Delhi: Sage Publications.

Munck, Ronaldo. 2003. 'Neoliberalism, Necessitarianism and Alternatives in Latin America: There are no Alternatives', *Third World Quarterly*, 24(3): 495–511.

Negri, Antonio. 2008. *The Porcelain Workshop: For a New Grammer of Politics*. Los Angeles, CA: Semiotext(e).
Offe, Claus. 1985. 'New Social Movements: Challenging the Boundaries of Institutional Politics', *Social Research*, 52(4): 828–29.
Roxborough, Ian. 2008. 'Counterinsurgency and the Rise of the Global State System'. Paper for the Stony Brook Initiative for Historical Social Sciences, 16 October 2008.
Perelman, Michael. 2000. *The Invention of Capitalism: Classical Political Economy and the Secret History of Primitive Accumulation*. London: Duke University Press.

1

New Anti-Capitalist Movements

Beyond the Questions of Taking Power

*John Holloway**

At the heart of the social movements of recent years, at least in their more radical variants, is a drive against the logic of capitalist society. The so-called social movements are not organized as political parties. Their aim is not to win state power, rather to reverse the movement of a society gone mad, systematically mad. The movements say in effect: 'No, we refuse to go in that direction, we refuse to accept the mad logic of the capitalist system, we shall go in a different direction, or in different directions'.

The anti-capitalist movements of recent years give a new meaning to revolution. It is no longer about taking power but breaking the insane dynamic that is embedded in the social cohesion of capitalism. The only way of thinking of this is as a movement from the particular, as the puncturing of that cohesion, as the creation of cracks in the texture of capitalist social relations, spaces or moments of refusal-and-creation. Revolution, then, becomes the creation, expansion, multiplication, and confluence of these cracks (for a development of this argument, see Holloway 2010). How does one conceptualize this sort of revolution? By going back to a category that was of central importance for Marx, but has been almost completely forgotten by his followers? This is the dual character of labour.

One can distinguish between two kinds of labour — abstract and concrete. Abstract labour comprises the social cohesion of capitalism against which we revolt, which is not constituted by money or value, but by the activity that generates money forms. To crack the social cohesion of capitalism is to confront the cohesive force of abstract labour with a different sort of activity — something that does not fit in to, and is not wholly contained within, abstract labour.

This is not a dry theoretical point, as the starting point for considering the relationship between abstract and concrete labour is, and must be, rage, the scream. This is empirically true — the place where the reader actually starts from. Moreover, rage is the key to theory. It is rage which turns complaint into critique because it reminds us all the time that we do not fit, that we are not exhausted in that which we criticise. Rage is the voice of non-identity, of those who do not fit. The criticism of capitalism is absolutely boring if it is not critique *ad hominem*: if we do not open the categories and try to understand them, not just as fetishized expressions of human creative power, but as categories in which we do not fit and from which we overflow. Sometimes our creativity is contained, and sometimes it is not, in the social forms that negate it. The form is never adequate and the content does not always fit with it: that is our expression of rage, and is also our hope. This is crucial theoretically as well as politically.

In recent years, it has become more common to cite Karl Marx's key statement in the opening pages of his *Capital*: [T]his point [the two-fold nature of the labour contained in commodities] is the pivot on which a clear comprehension of Political Economy turns' (Marx 1965: 41). After the publication of the first volume, he wrote to Friedrich Engels:

> The best points in my book are: 1) the two-fold character of labour, according to whether it is expressed as use value or exchange value. (*All* understanding of the facts depends upon *this*. It is emphasised immediately in the *first* chapter) (ibid.: 407; emphasis added).

It is important to emphasize this statement that went against the Marxist tradition and buried it for so long, with quite extraordinary success. Moreover, it takes us to the core of Marx's critique *ad hominem*, understanding the world in terms of human action and its contradictions.

The two-fold nature of labour refers to abstract and concrete or useful labour. Concrete labour, according to Marx, is the activity that exists in all kinds of society and is necessary for human reproduction. Arguably, Marx was mistaken when he referred to this as labour, since labour as an activity distinct from other activities is not common to all societies. So it seems more accurate to speak of concrete action rather than concrete labour. In capitalist society, concrete doing (what Marx calls concrete labour) exists in the historically specific form of abstract labour. Concrete labours are brought into relation with other concrete labours through a process which abstracts a process of quantitative commensuration from their concrete characteristics, normally effected through the medium of money, and this process of abstraction rebounds upon the concrete labour, transforming it into an activity abstracted from (or alienated from) the person performing it.

Thus, it is the abstraction of our activity into abstract labour that constitutes the social cohesion of capitalist society. This is an important advancement in the concept of alienated labour developed in the 1844 manuscripts: capitalist labour is not only an activity alienated from us, but it is this alienation that constitutes the social nexus in capitalism. The key to understanding the cohesion (and functioning) of capitalist society is not money or value, but that which constitutes these factors, namely abstract labour. In other words, we create the society that is destroying us, and this is what makes us think that we can stop building it.

Abstract labour as a form of activity did not always exist. It is a historically specific form of concrete doing that has been established as a socially dominant form through the historical process generally referred to as primitive accumulation. The metamorphosis of human activity into abstract labour is not restricted to the workplace but involves the reorganization of all aspects of human sociality: essentially, the objectification of nature, homogenization of time, de-morphization of sexuality, separation of the political from the economic and the constitution of the state, and so on.

If we say that revolution is the breaking of the social cohesion of capitalism and that cohesion is constituted by abstract labour, the question then arises how we understand the solidity of this cohesion. In other words, how opaque is the social form of abstract labour? Or, in other words, is primitive accumulation to be understood simply as a historical phase that preceded capitalism? If we say (as Postone [1996] does) that labour is the central fetish of capitalist society, then how do we understand that fetish?

Marx, in the passage quoted earlier, refers to the dual character of labour as the key to an understanding of political economy. He does not refer to just abstract labour but to the twofold nature of labour as abstract and concrete labour. Yet the commentaries that focus on this point concentrate almost exclusively on abstract labour, assuming that concrete labour (concrete doing) is unproblematic since it is entirely subsumed within abstract labour, and can simply be discussed as productivity. This entails that primitive accumulation is to be understood as a historical phase that was completed in the past, effectively establishing abstract labour as the dominant form of concrete labour, and thus separating the constitution of capitalism from its existence. It implies the understanding of form and content as related to identity, in which content is completely subordinated to form until the moment of revolution. This establishes a clear separation between the past (in which concrete doing existed independent of its abstraction) and the present (in which doing is entirely subsumed within its form), effectively enclosing the analysis of the relation between concrete doing and abstract labour within the homogenous concept of time, that is itself a moment of abstract labour. This inevitably takes us to a view of capital as related to domination (rather than a contested relationship of struggle), and therefore to perceive revolution as something that would have to come from outside the capital relation (from the political party, for example).

However, it is not adequate to understand the relationship between abstract labour and concrete doing as one of domination. Rather, abstract labour is a constant struggle to contain concrete doing, and to subject our daily activity to the logic of capital. Concrete doing not only exists in, but also against and beyond abstract labour, which is constantly revolting against abstract labour. This is not to say that there is some trans-historical entity called concrete doing, but that in a capitalist society concrete doing is constituted by its not fitting and non-identity with abstract labour, as well as its opposition to and overflowing from abstract labour.

This means that there can be no clear separation between the constitution and existence of capitalist social relations. It is not the case that capitalist social relations were first constituted in the period of primitive accumulation or during the transition from feudalism, or that then they simply existed as closed social relations. If concrete doing constantly rebels against and overflows beyond abstract labour, if (in other words) our attempt to live like humans constantly clashes with and ruptures the logic of capitalist cohesion, then it means that the existence of capitalist social relations depends on their constant reconstitution and, therefore, primitive accumulation is not just an episode in the past. If capitalism exists today, it is because of what it constitutes now, not because what it comprised two or three hundred years ago. If this is so, then the question of revolution is radically transformed. It is not how we abolish capitalism, but rather how we cease to reconstitute and stop creating it. The answer is clear (but not easy): by ceasing to allow the daily transformation of our doing, our concrete activity, into abstract labour, by developing an activity that does not recreate capitalist social relations, and does not fit in with the logic of social cohesion of capitalism.

This might seem absurd were it not for the fact that the revolt of concrete doing against abstract labour is all around us. Sometimes it takes dramatic proportions when, for instance, a group such as the Zapatistas says 'no, we will not act according to the logic of capital, we shall do what we consider important at the rhythm that we consider appropriate'. But of course it does not have to be on such a large scale: the revolt of action against abstract labour and the determinations and rhythms that it imposes upon us is deeply rooted in our everyday lives. Anton Pannekoek commented about the workplace that 'every shop, every enterprise, even outside of times of sharp conflict, of strikes and wage reductions, is the scene of a constant silent war, of a perpetual struggle, of pressure and counter-pressure' (quoted in Shukaitis 2009: 15). But it is not just in the workplace, life itself is a constant struggle to break through the connections forged by abstract labour to create other sorts of social relations — when we refuse to go to work so that we can stay and play with the children, when we read (or write) an such as this, when we choose to do something not because it will bring us money but just because we enjoy it or consider it important. All the time we oppose use value against value, and concrete doing against abstract labour. It is from these revolts of everyday existence, and not from the struggles of activists or parties, that we must pose the question of the possibility of ceasing to create capitalism and building a different sort of society.

Not only is there a constant revolt of concrete against abstract labour, but now there is a crisis of abstract labour. Abstract labour cannot be understood as something stable: its rhythms are shaped by socially necessary labour time. Since abstract labour is value-producing labour and value production is determined by socially necessary labour time, there is a constant redefinition of abstract labour — as a constant compulsion to go faster and faster. Abstract labour constantly undermines its own existence; it is an activity that produced value a 100 (or 10, or five) years ago but no longer produces it today. The process of abstraction becomes more and more exigent, and harder for people to keep pace with it; leaving many as misfits and consciously revolting against abstract labour. Abstraction becomes an ever greater pressure, but at the same time it is a more inadequate form of organizing human activity — it is not able to effectively channel the activities of a large part of humanity.

The dynamic of abstraction increasingly comes up against a resistance that splits open the apparently unitary concept of labour and poses the struggle against abstract labour at the centre of anti-capitalist struggle. Anti-capitalist struggle becomes the assertion of a different way of doing and living; or rather, the simple assertion of a different way of doing (I want to spend time with my friends, my children, or I want to be a good teacher, carpenter, doctor, and work at a slower pace, I want to cultivate my garden) is converted into anti-capitalist struggle. The survival of capital depends on its ability to impose (and constantly redefine) abstract labour, whereas the survival of humanity depends on our ability to stop performing abstract labour and do something sensible instead. Humanity is simply the struggle of action against labour.

It is in the context of this crisis that the discussion of abstract labour acquires importance. It is important when we focus not just on abstract labour but on the dual character of labour, and the antagonism between doing and labour. If we focus just on abstract labour and forget concrete doing, then we only develop a more sophisticated picture of capitalist domination, of how capitalism works. Our problem, however, is not to understand how capitalism works but to stop creating and recreating it. And that means strengthening action in its struggle against labour.

It is not theory that brings about the splitting of the unitary concept of labour. It has been the result of a multitude of struggles, large and small, that have made it clear that it makes little sense to speak just of 'labour', that we have to open it up and see that the category conceals the constant tension and antagonism between concrete doing (doing what we want, what we consider necessary or enjoyable) and abstract labour (value- and capital-producing labour). It is struggle that splits open the category, but theoretical reflection (understood as a moment of struggle) has an important role to play in keeping the distinction open.

This is important at the moment when there are so many pressures to close the category, to forget about the antagonism the category conceals, and to dismiss the notion that there could be some form of activity other than abstract labour as silly, romantic or irresponsible. In a capitalist society, access to the means of production and survival usually depends upon our converting our activity, our doing, into labour in the service of capital, abstract labour. We are now at a moment in the entire world where capital is unable to convert the activity of millions and millions of people (especially young people) into labour, other than on a very precarious basis. Given that exclusion from labour is generally associated with material poverty, do we now ask capital to 'please give us more employment, please convert our doing into labour, we will happily labour faster-faster-faster'? This is the position of the trade unions and many left political parties, as it must be, for they are organizations based on abstract labour, and on the suppression of the distinction between labour and doing. Or do we say

> no, we cannot go that way (and we do not ask anything of capital). We know that the logic of faster-faster-faster will lead to ever bigger crises, and we know that, if it continues, it will probably destroy human existence altogether. For this reason we see crisis and unemployment and precariousness as a stimulus to strengthen other forms of doing, to strengthen the struggle of doing against labour.

There is no easy answer here, and no pure solution, because our material survival depends, for most of us, on subordinating our activity to some degree to the logic of abstraction. But it is essential to keep the distinction open and find ways forward, to strengthen the in submission of doing to labour, to extend the rupture of labour by doing. That is the only way in which we can stop reproducing the system that is killing us.

Note

* This chapter is a revised version of the article 'Doing In-Against-and-Beyond Labour', *Radical Notes*, 31 May 2010, http://radicalnotes.com/2010/05/31/doing-in-against-and-beyond-labour/ (accessed 20 December 2013). Reproduced with permission.

References

Holloway, John. 2010. *Crack Capitalism*. London: Pluto Press.
Marx, Karl. 1965 [1867]. *Capital*, vol. 1. Moscow: Progress Publishers.
Marx, Karl. 1987 [1867]. 'Letter of Marx to Engels, 24.8.1867', in Karl Marx, Frederick Engels, *Collected Works*, vol. 42. p. 407. London: Lawrence & Wishart.
Pannekoek, Anton. 2005. *Workers' Councils*. Oakland: AK Press.
Postone, Moishe. 1996. *Time, Labour, and Social Domination: A Reinterpretation of Marx's Critical Theory*. Cambridge: Cambridge University Press.
Shukaitis, Stevphen. 2009. *Imaginal Machines: Autonomy and Self-Organisation in the Revolutions of Everyday Life*. New York: Autonomedia.

2

From the Working-Class Movement to the New Social Movements

*Gunnar Olofsson**

In 1986, many social theorists regarded the 'New Social Movements' (NSMs) as possible and relevant agents of social transformation, as well as authentic representatives of post-industrial social forces. This idea of an ascending primacy of the NSMs as a subject for historical change can be found in the works of several (radical) sociologists and philosophers. Alain Touraine (1981) has given the boldest exposition of this theme, but the idea can be found in many fascinating and different varieties (Anderson 1983; Gorz 1980, 1983; Habermas 1981a, 1981b; Offe 1984; Williams 1983). In Scandinavia, similar themes have been echoed, applied and developed by sociologists (cf. CVS 1986; Friberg and Galtung 1984). This discussion takes place in the context of a shift within the intellectual left-wing discussion, especially in Denmark (E. Christensen 1985, 1986; Gundelach 1986; Thomsen 1986).

The basic argument in the NSM thesis deals with the relationship between the 'new' and the 'old' Social Movements. It implies two interconnected propositions:

(*a*) The historical role of the labour movement is beginning to fade away. The labour movement is too imbricated in the structures, institutions and dilemmas of the past, defending old interests and social relations, and standing in the way of a 'new project'. It is fettered by its commitment to economic growth, to the state (in its Keynesian welfare variety), and to the reality, ideals and norms of industrialism.

(*b*) The NSMs are the natural and self-evident successors of the labour movement. Their goals and ideas, their forms of

> struggle and organization, are perceived to be in tune with the modern age, its development trajectory and its contradictions. They hold up the promise of relevancy for the post-industrial age. The labour movement, in all its organizational and political forms — unions and parties, communism and social democracy — is perceived as that 'old' social movement that the NSMs are projected to transcend and replace.

The critical thrust in this chapter is directed against the claims of the social and theoretical centrality of the NSMs, by asking what is new and what is social in them. The major features of two old social movements will be recapitulated, focusing on the relationship between these movements and basic societal structures and processes. The implicit argument is that social movements worth their name are intrinsically related to central aspects of transformative social processes.

European and American Conceptions of Social Movements

In sociology and social history there are different concepts of 'social movement'. We can broadly distinguish between a European and an American conception. In the classical European tradition, from von Stein, Marx, Sombart and others, 'social movement' has meant organizations, focusing on major social issues, related to major social forces (or classes). In American sociology 'social movement' has been used much more empirically, meaning voluntary groups organizing around a social, political or cultural issue. If they become large or popular enough they can be regarded as a 'movement' (IESS 1968). In the modern debate there is interplay between the 'European' and 'American' conceptualizations, often fruitful but sometimes confusing (Rammstedt 1978). A good example can be found in Castells' analyses of the urban social movements in the United States (US) (1977: Chapter 14). Such groups abound in European cities too, fighting against landlords and housing authorities, the town and traffic planners, demanding better schools, nursery and hospital facilities, better collective communication, less pollution and noise.

This conceptual duality, designated here by the dichotomy 'European–American', comprises several analytical dimensions:

- Type of issue (central–marginal)
- Goal/issue-relation (comprehensive–single-issue)
- Organization (permanent representation of interest) versus campaign (momentary mobilization)

Scandinavian sociology and social history have adopted the category 'popular movement' as a common label for the whole complex of organizations born in the late 19th century. These include the trade unions and the labour movement, the temperance movement, the consumer cooperatives, the agrarian producer cooperatives, the non-conformist churches, and sometimes the sports movement (N. F. Christiansen 1985; Lundkvist 1977; Olofsson 1979: Chapter 9). This concept is a regional variety of the European conceptual tradition. The popular aspect is important (cf. the next section).

Classical Social Movements

To characterize certain forms of struggle and organization as 'social movements', the European conceptual tradition presupposes a definite relationship between a social process and an organized–organizing social collectivity. Social movements are the mediating links between basic societal processes and/or contradictions and the individual/collective reactions to these.

The social character of the social movements can be located on three separate, but tightly interconnected levels:

- Their roots in social processes and contradictions
- Their own social existence
- Their programs and goals

There is yet another decisive characteristic of social movements, namely, their popular character. Social movements are expressions of protest and programmes for change from below, that is, from social groups, strata and classes that in one way or another are repressed, marginalized, exploited, or disrespected. The social action of the nobility or the upper classes in general, or of the modern bourgeoisie, takes other political and social forms. The nascent bourgeoisie had its own distinctive forms of organization, epitomized in the literature on the bourgeois revolutions and in the theory of 'public sphere' (Habermas 1961). In 19th-century Denmark it was the organizational efforts of the peasants and the farmers that came to be labelled as 'social movements', not the strong and efficient, albeit much smaller and tighter organization of big landowners.

Two major and classical social movements in the European pattern have had a decisive influence on the Scandinavian societies, i.e., the farmers and peasants movement and the labour movement. Their character as social movements will be sketched in order to serve as a background, comparison and contrast to the NSMs.

Agrarian Social Movements in Scandinavia — The Case of Denmark

Starting in Denmark in the latter half of the 19th century, the organizational efforts of farmers and peasants brought about the constitution of agrarian social movements in Scandinavia. These acquired a distinctive character compared with peasant movements in Eastern and Central Europe (not to mention Asia). There the peasants' major goal was land, and the struggle was fought by a large, landless and poor agrarian proletariat. The peasant movements were organized around the land reform issues, directed against feudal social relations. The peasant parties which developed in Russia and in Eastern Europe, ranging from the Socialist Revolutionaries in Russia to the peasant parties in the Balkans and to the peasant struggle in China, became the social base for the communists. The rapid growth and the rural penetration of Finnish Social Democracy after 1900, with the poor crofters constituting the social backbone of the Reds in the Civil War 1918–19, had an 'eastern' character.

In the three Scandinavian countries the peasant movements were the outcome of a radically different situation. Their fundamental energy did not come from a land-hungry proletariat fighting their noble masters. Instead the agrarian social movements in Scandinavia, most evident in the Danish case, were part of the emergence of a rural petty bourgeoisie, of peasants and farmers in possession of their land, successfully adapting to (an increasing) dependence on the market. The change in the market relations meant both a growing entanglement in the networks of the world market, mainly the

English, and the growing internal Danish market, due to industrialization and urbanization. This economic reorientation concurred with political modernization, with a protracted struggle for democracy.

Towards the end of the 19th century, the farmers and peasants in Denmark built up an impressive array of strong, efficient and encompassing organizations. The cooperative organizations in both production and distribution of agricultural products formed the solid nucleus in the peasant movement. They developed dairies as well as slaughterhouses; wholesale and marketing associations within the sphere of distribution, including a rurally-based consumers' co-op; credit associations for mortgages and loans as well as rural savings banks; a major political party — the liberal *Venstre* party — representing the interests of the farmer class; the people's high schools as an instrument for civic and cultural training; and a string of newspapers.

What made this set of often prosaic organizational activities into a social movement? They were all focused around the conditions of living and reproduction of the farmers, as individuals and families, in their neighbourhood, communities and localities. In this process the farmers were constituted into a social class. A social, political and cultural identity of a farmer class took form. The different organizations and activities complemented each other. The members, as well as the leadership and activists, cut across the whole spectrum.

At the heart of the movement were, from one perspective, those cooperatives that made the farmers' production more efficient and profitable. Modernization and the switch from cereals to animal husbandry, i.e., an adaption to the changing demand patterns in England and the intensified competition in the wheat and rye markets were combined with aggressive marketing of standardized high-quality bacon and butter. By reshaping their production, Danish farmers could survive and expand. This development was conditioned by and in turn conducive to political organization through parties. Mobilization was necessary both for the spread of cooperatives and for political organizing. In this process the cultural and ideological formation of the farmers, both as producers acting on different economic markets and as citizens in the political world of parliamentary elections and the self-government of localities, was important. Sturdy individualist producers and landowners were formed into a strong, cohesive and class-conscious social force. Their organizational activities were the formal side of the process of 'making a Danish farmer class'. The social situation of the individual farmer, and the farmer class as a whole, were bound together by a richly differentiated pattern of social relations and obligations, actions and organizations.

The Danish farmers' movement was a social movement in the full European sense, being a comprehensive and differentiated class project, inseparable from the constitution of the (farmer) class itself. As a class project it has been influential and effective during a long historical epoch. It has been efficient precisely because the farmers at the decisive point in time chose to fight the battle of today and tomorrow, not that of yesterday trying to recapture or resurrect a golden past. Through their successful modernization, the Danish farmers came to work along the path of development opened up by world market forces in production, distribution and consumption of food products. Their economic and cooperative organizations were at one and the same time instruments for protecting the individual farmer and the class as a whole from the vicissitudes of the market and making them able to exploit its expansionary possibilities, to surf on the crest of expansion and change. A creative reliance on the expanding export market was the driving force beneath the growth of the (then) new social movement of the farmers, an economic dilemma that made their organizational complex possible/necessary.

The Labour Movement

The labour movement is a social movement that is specific to and characteristic of capitalist societies (for this part, cf. Olofsson 1979; Thompson 1966; Vester 1970). Labour movements exist in several different ideological and organizational configurations, richly varied in the historical trajectories of national states.

When capital through industrial expansion entered and gradually subsumed production and distribution of goods, the already existing 'lower classes' were transformed. Out of the 'people' or 'popular classes' — poor peasants, destitute artisans, and the landless poor — an industrial working class gradually evolved and became a social force. These individuals and groups of workers developed a specific mode of existence, basically due to their wage-dependency. By selling their labour power in the market they acquired a money wage. With the money they could and had to buy goods and services in different markets, in order to reproduce themselves (and their families). The following sequence became established as their form of reproduction:

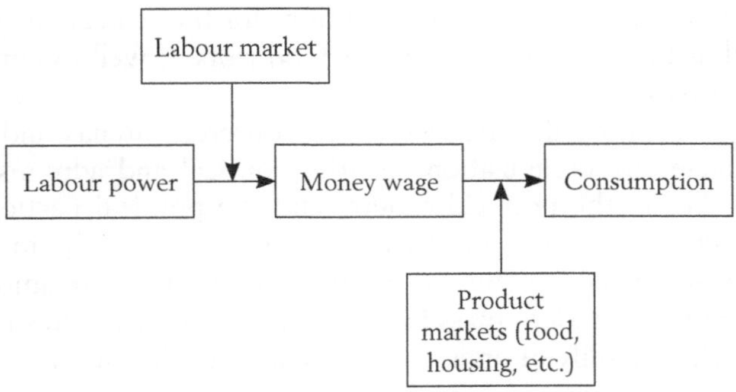

The basic forms for struggle and organization for workers have developed around the wage nexus. The transformation of a worker's potential labour power into a money wage makes at least three arenas strategic to struggle and organization: employment, wage level and working conditions. Historically, we can observe the sequence:

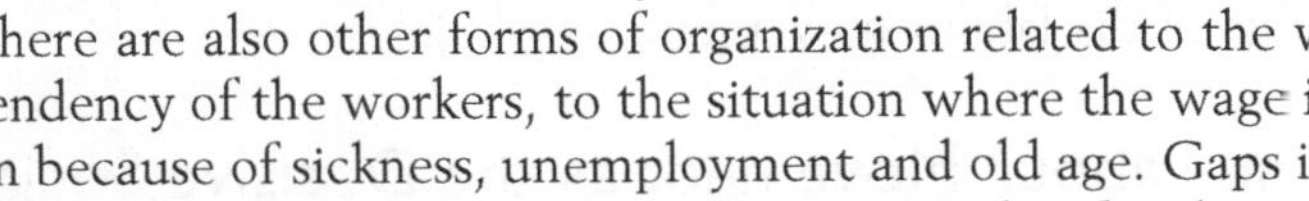

The unions try in most cases to connect the interests of workers in the labour market and on the job, i.e., in the factory/workplace.

There are also other forms of organization related to the wage-dependency of the workers, to the situation where the wage is not given because of sickness, unemployment and old age. Gaps in the wage-earning capacity are potentially catastrophic for the worker (and/or his family). The resultant poverty can partly be avoided by compensatory, often insurance-based organizations (friendly societies, sickness insurance schemes). The 'solutions' to these poverty risks basically have gone the way of either self-organization (i.e., insurance-based in the form of friendly societies) or through the political agencies at state or local level (*Social policy* in the

German sense). Through time, more and more of these compensatory mechanisms have been transformed into state-regulated or state-run social insurance schemes.

The transformation of money wage into means of existence — food, clothing, housing, heating, and so on — is yet another structurally given focus of organization. Sharp rises in housing costs or food prices have been the preconditions for the struggle of tenants as well as housing associations, for food riots as well as consumer cooperatives.

The mediating link between these different arenas and forms of struggle and organization and the political and administrative power, lies in the political sphere, and the political parties. This characteristic aspect of modern societies is particularly important for the labour movements, whose political parties were among the first genuinely modern mass parties in many countries. In short, we find a whole family of organizations related to the emergent working class: trade unions, labour and social democratic parties (and later communist), consumer cooperatives, tenants' movements, friendly societies, and cultural organizations. What makes this set of organizations, and the practices they incorporate, into a labour movement? The different forms of struggle and organization are all various aspects of a class movement, and have been instrumental in the formation of the working class, in its 'making'. In one way or another, they all have their structural roots in the specific life form of dependent wage labour, characterized by the subjugation, exploitation and precarious living that apply to the working class under capitalist forms of production and social existence. The existential dilemmas of the wage-dependent classes — and perforce to its nucleus, the industrial working class — are the basic and structural roots and foci for the goals as well as for the strength and cohesion of the labour movements as wholes.

The Labour Movement as the Decisive Social Movement in the Modern Epoch

Why did the labour movement become the major social movement in Europe? Because it springs directly from the heart of the modern social order. Wage labour is the precondition for the accumulation of capital. Through processes of growth, change and crisis peculiar to capitalism, the working class in its formation was continually being challenged by processes, outcomes and changes that fostered and sometimes necessitated the kinds of struggle and organization sketched earlier in the discussion. The rise of industrial capitalism gave birth to the labour movement, and also gave it the social setting to work within.

Industrialism and its emergent new social order gave rise to a whole set of other social movements, for example, the temperance movement, the non-conformist churches, consumer cooperatives, and later the sports movement. In Scandinavia they became known as 'popular movements'. Quantitatively, these movements overshadowed the labour movement for a long time; the temperance movement was larger than the unions in Sweden (Lundkvist 1977).

Functionally, these movements can be seen as social reactions to the storms of change introduced by the transforming power of capital. The movements redirected and institutionalized reactions of despair and bewilderment in the face of the new society. They expressed the predicament of the modern capitalist society, each defining certain aspects of life as the major key to understanding, changing or accommodating the emergent social order. But, they were not as such strategically related to basic social or economic processes, in the way the labour movement was with its defining sequence:

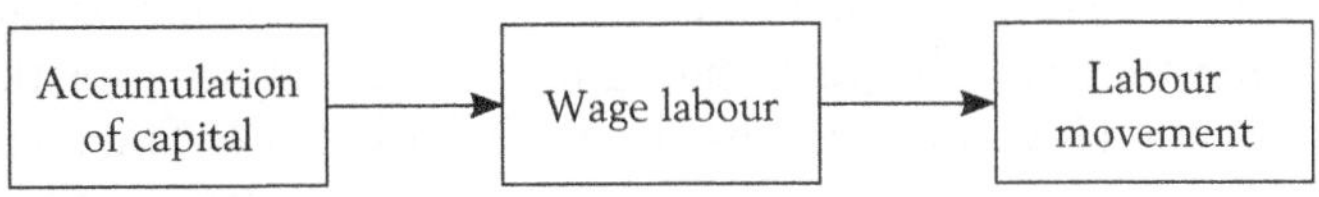

The axis between unions and the party was the defining focus for the ancillary organizations in the labour movement 'family', and the whole complex of organizations and practices was related to a class in formation, expressing a basic societal process. The labour movement has become the decisive social movement due to the role of wage labour in the basic socio-economic process — and contradiction — in modern capitalist society. It has not become the actual major social movement in every capitalist society, even though structurally it has been the possible pretender to that role.

Social Movements as Class Projects

The 'peasant movement' and the 'labour movement' became important and influential social movements because they organizationally and culturally transformed, in a class formative manner, reactions to decisive social changes. For the Danish farmers it was modifications in the demand for foodstuffs and changing market conditions that led to a redirection of their production — from corn to dairy — and to new methods of marketing. For the labour movement it was the expansion of capital and its demand for wage labour, and the ensuing commoditization of labour, that became the structural possibility for wage struggle and for the organization of unions.

Both movements were 'families' of interrelated and interconnected practices and organizations, to a large extent organically complementary in their nature. They were equally tied to an identifiable social force. They were class projects, both in the sense of being an expression of a distinctive class situation, and at the same time being part of the class-constituting process. These two movements had their roots in fundamental social processes and relations. The classes and 'their' movements thereby acquired a crucial position in society. As social movements they linked decisive shifts and crises in the social order with the basic interests and reproduction problems of 'their' class through a comprehensive political programme that took the form of a 'class project'. The Danish farmers and the Swedish workers (and Social Democracy) have been two typical examples.

When the NSMs are hailed as the (possible) new historical subject, then they are obviously thought of as substituting for the old movements. How do they measure up to this claim? The recapitulation mentioned earlier, which summarizes the major aspects of two old social movements, can serve as a baseline when asking for the credentials of the NSMs as social movements in the European meaning of the concept.

Movement and Institution

The difference between old and new social movements partly overlaps a famous conceptual pair in social theory, the polarity movement–institution (cf. Alberoni 1984). Movement (or *bewegung, mouvement, rörelse*) implies that something happens — it is where the action is. Activity, participation, engagement, and responsible and conscious action are key concepts that characterize a movement. They cover the socio-psychological and inter-organizational aspects, i.e., the relations between the participants/activists, and the struggle and goals, as well as the sociological aspects, their relation to society and its institutions at large. Institution here is the inversion of movement, its antidote. The dimension movement–institution can be used as a conceptual grid in analysing empirical social movements. The distinction can be more salient if other conceptual pairs, which usually coalesce in the movement–institution divide, are made explicit (see Table 2.1).

Table 2.1: Aspects of Movement–Institution

Area	*Movement*	*Institution*
Leadership quality	Agitator	Administrator
Legitimacy	Charisma	Bureaucracy
Forms of relations	Emotional	Rational
Object for struggle	Radical breaks	Consolidation of gains
Relation to goals	Ideals	Realization, even partial
Model age	Youth	Middle age

There are parallels between this series of oppositions and other conceptual pairs in social and political theory. Reform and revolution in the Marxist and labour tradition is one obvious case. Sartre's analysis of collectivity, with the pair *series/groupe-en-fusion*, is another parallel in social theory (Sartre 1976).

Any new collectivity, group or organization has, as such, more of the movement qualities than old, established organizations. Both Sartre and Alberoni have convincingly argued that 'the movement stage' cannot be perpetuated for ever. 'The nascent state' with all its accompanying emotional intensity does end (Alberoni 1984). A new movement will always have a comparative advantage with regard to the existential quality of a movement, the attraction of the not yet petrified. The movement quality of the NSMs per se is not a relevant criterion for the evaluation of new movements. It does not make them more relevant as social forces, even if they might evoke more emotional sympathy.

One crucial aspect of the dimension movement–institution deserves to be taken seriously. Real social movements take shape between the poles of 'the nascent state' and institutionalization (Alberoni 1984). The 'nascent state' of the movement, its goals, hopes and aspirations, tends to remain as a yardstick for the institution. The institution stands in relation to the movement as a realization to the programmatic ideal.

Traditional organizations have been criticized by activists and theoreticians of the NSM on two counts. First, institutions have been condemned for not being movements. Second, the organizational forms of 'old' movements, i.e., institutions, have been criticized for not being adequate in relation to their stated goals. When the proponents of the NSMs ask for an open and broader type of organization, not hierarchic, laying more stress on participation and responsibility, less on efficient expertise, this can either be an expression of a dream to eternalize the phase of 'the nascent state' of movements, or wanting another form of institutionalization. From the perspective of social movements as major social forces, only the latter type of critique is relevant. In the ongoing debate these two forms of assessment are typically mixed.

Movement–institution illustrates yet another distinction, between mobilization/articulation of new interests, of social forces in formation and institutionally reproduced representation of already structured and organized interests and social forces. This distinction points to the major theoretical issue in the discussion on NSMs, i.e., to the postulated confluence of social structural changes, in class structures as well as the type of dilemmas that characterize a given social formation, and the 'corresponding' social movements.

New social forces and strata have developed, and at the same time new social contradictions and predicaments have also seen the light. The emergence of the NSMs raises the question of the relation between these two sets of changes. Empirically, there is overwhelming evidence for a close relationship between the NSMs and the new social strata (the new middle-class in the public sector, especially in the welfare apparatuses) (cf. Brand 1985). Members and activists in the different NSMs are students, intellectuals and white-collar employees within social work, education, health services, and others. Since the NSMs are relatively small, we cannot turn the argument the other way and say that they are the typical organization of these strata. The argument that the NSMs are part of a process of class-formation has to rest on other than empirical arguments. As a challenge, however, it reopens a major sociological debate on the relationship between social forces and their (political) organization.

The New Social Movements

'NSMs' has become a recognized common label for a complex and widely varied set of organizations and struggles. Several of them emerged in the wake of the students' movements of the 1960s.

They include the women's liberation movement, the peace movement, the anti-nuclear movements, the whole alternative scene (*Alternativszene*), urban squatters and house occupations, cooperatives and collectives, regionalist movements, the environmentalist and green organizations, and others. The wide variations among nations over time are evident in the Scandinavian as well as American, French and German literature (Brand 1983, 1985; Friberg and Galtung 1984; Paris 1981; Roth 1984; Rucht 1982; *Social Research* 1985; Touraine 1981).

The Social Roots of the 'New Social Movements'

The social and historical background for the NSMs is usually constructed and analysed on two different levels. The first is to look for predecessors in the 'biographical' sense, i.e., to try to find the roots of the NSM among the earlier protest and alternative movements in the 1950s and 1960s (cf. the essays in Brand [1985] for systematic trajectories of West Germany, United Kingdom, France, USA, and Sweden). These were predecessors in political style, opening up the protest and alternative sphere, with regard to both themes and models of organization. The social categories active in these early protest movements were largely the same as those populating the modern NSMs. The decisive shift from forerunners to the actual NSMs came in the wake of the students' movement of the late 1960s (ibid.).

The second approach, complementary to the first, digs deeper into the social background and relates the emergence of the NSMs to societal changes during the post-war period, especially from the 1950s onwards. The 'grand theory' of the NSMs is located on this level. The crisis of civilization, the passage from industrial to post-industrial society, with the emergence of the programmed society, reactions to the colonization of the life-world have been some of the larger contexts where the coming of the NSMs has been located (Friberg and Galtung 1984; Habermas 1981a, 1981b; Touraine 1981).

The Contradiction Pre-modern–Modern

There are two analytically different strands in this argument, both relating to the modernization of society. The post-war capitalist societies in Western Europe have only recently become genuinely modern societies, in the sense that capitalist social relations have marginalized pre-capitalist relations, forms of production and social classes. *Durchkapitalisierung* is, with the exception of the UK, a recent phenomenon. The capitalist economic process no longer exists within the framework of a social formation permeated with pre-capitalist relations, habits and institutions. The rapid reduction and the radical reshaping of the peasants and the classical urban petty bourgeoisie have led to a radical transformation of the middle-class. These archaic middle-classes were often seen as the social base of the bourgeois/capitalist forces in the political arena (cf. Schumpeter 1976).

Certain parts of the protest or alternative movements can be analyzed as reactions to enforced modernization, and as reactions on the part of the pre-industrial classes or elites. Cases given are regionalist and parts of the environmentalist movements. In several European countries there has been a resurgence of regional movements, combining the interests of the cultural, political and economic peripheries in their fight for survival.

In Sweden there have been cases of resistance in the economic periphery, against the effects of not only industrialization but also against the effects of deindustrialization. Rationalization in agriculture, forestry and the traditional staple industries (steel and iron, sawmills, paper and pulp, and mining) have had serious effects on earlier major industrial areas (in the north and the mid-central Sweden). The protest (and adaption) to this situation has in some cases been channelled outside the political parties.

In Scandinavia, and especially in Sweden, another kind of reaction against enforced modernization was the much-publicized 'green wave' in the 1970s. Many young people moved out of the cities, sometimes to take up farming, often on a part-time basis, combined with reshaping everyday life (collectives), and/or artistic or political ambitions. That was part of a broader 'alternative movement', criticizing urban-industrial ways of alienated living. The commuting wage-earner existence in the newly built suburbs was contrasted with other, in a sense more traditional, images of what a good life and a decent living implied. The 'green wave' never became a mass exodus from the cities — its importance instead came to lie in the ideological resonance it evoked, as a baseline for the critique of the way of living, among broader social groups. Together with the mobilization around the referendum on the future of nuclear power in Sweden, held in spring 1980, it might illustrate the fusion of the protest reaction of pre- and post-industrial elites and sentiments alluded to by K. W. Brand (1983).

Contradictions within Modernity

These protests took part of their energy from the confrontation between modern and traditional life-forms. Within the most modernized parts of society a new major arena for articulation of interests developed in response to the reshaping of the conditions for reproduction of the urban wage-earning population. The protests have been 'politicized' as an effect of the growth of welfare state apparatuses and have highlighted problems such as the quality of dwellings and of urban life in general, housing rents and other costs, the organization of collective provision of day-care, public communications, parks and recreational facilities, the devastating effects of urban change and renewal through the building of highways, zoning regulations, etc. All these dilemmas and changes in the urban scene have shaped distinct possibilities for the emergence, articulation, mobilization and organization of new interests. These have been analyzed by authors on the 'new urban social movements', M. Castells (1977), among others.

In Scandinavia it is in the first place the reorganization and reshaping of the life situation for the emerging new middle-class of state employees, students, etc., that has ushered in new urban forms of protest and new political allegiances (in red and green directions). This kind of mobilization and organization, that in more than one sense is the product of the expansion of the welfare state, can be regarded as part of the NSMs.

Concurrent with this restructuration has been a radical change in the ways of living. The labour force participation rate for women increased dramatically in Scandinavia between 1960 and 1980. In Sweden this rate increased from 50 to 74 per cent, in Denmark from 43 to 71 per cent (OECD 1985). The preconditions for familial existence have as a consequence been 'socialized'. Expansion of certain welfare services, such as nurseries, school meals, institutionalized care for the elderly, and so on, is related to this development. Increasing female employment in the welfare apparatuses is both cause and effect, fuelling further expansion and constituting an expansionary development bloc of its own.

This radical change within the post-war capitalist societies has given birth to two analytically different sets of interests, struggles and organized activities of a movement kind. The first set focuses on the effects of the formation of individuals/subjects, roles, attitudes, and forms of social relations, especially around the constitution of gender. The second relates to interests, struggles and organization in the field of the 'socialization' of familial and individual reproduction. A growing part of the 'consumption fund', the goods and services constituting a given level-of-living, is channelled through the public sector in the form of social services. The provision of certain social services is, in the given social order, an important, growing and necessary part of the non-monetary 'social wage'. Two Danish sociologists have conceptualized the first set of movements and interests as cultural revolutionary, and the second as defence of the real social consumption (Jensen and von Nordheim Nielsen 1985).

The Women's Movement: The Major Cultural Revolutionary Movement

The immediate background for the women's liberation movement was the students' movements in the 1960s (Brand 1985). More generally, the background was the new social situation for young, educated urban women, and the changing conditions of family life. The cultural revolutionary impact of the women's movement, on values and norms for what are normal or desirable ways of living, for changes in family relations, and in the sexual division of labour in households, if not on the labour market, has been pervasive within the Scandinavian new urban middle-class. The impact has not (yet) reached the basic economic and political institutions, processes and structures.

The socialist-feminist current had wider socio-political goals. Their hopes have not yet materialized. The reason for this can be explained in two ways. One explanation points to the specific kinds of dilemma and contradictions upon which the feminist movement has worked. They are, it can be argued, of such an art that they can be complementary to a whole series of socio-political options.

There is no relation of necessity between feminism as a cultural revolutionary option and any other definite political or ideological position. Feminism can, according to this interpretation, become articulated with forms of practices and organizations already existing. Another, much more radical conception, would argue the other way round. Feminism is the antidote to patriarchy, the latter being a fundamental principle and form of oppression so basic that it prefigures the shaping of modern, capitalist society as such.

In any case the women's movement of the 1960s had traits and characteristics that were new, compared with the old liberal and socialist women's movements. These were basically oriented towards formal-juridical and political equality (the vote, discrimination in the labour market, marriage and inheritance laws). The modern women's movement incorporated part of the programme and practice of its predecessors. (It also re-established the symbolic day of the socialist women's movement — 8 March.) Politically and symbolically there has been some continuity with the old European traditions of feminist organizations, but as a social force the modern women's movement has been much more a response to the new situation of urban, especially academic women.

The main impetus came from militant American feminism, including the cultural-revolutionary aspects of consciousness-raising, a critique of received notions of femininity, which was in tune with the real changes in the lives of students and young urban middle-class women in Europe too. It was a profoundly modern movement, working along, and not against, inexorable and rapidly modernizing development processes in the restructuring of relations between family, market and the state. The self-sufficiency of the family not only as an economic unit but also as the main agent in upbringing and socialization rapidly eroded, public institutions filling the gap.

'Real Consumption' Movements

Housing facilities, traffic and planning, schools and nurseries became increasingly politicized at the same time as their role became more important. Their public character lies in the fact that they are mostly run and/or controlled by the localities, and paid through taxes. The imbrications of individual and familial existence with the sphere of welfare agencies as well as their increasing dependence upon labour and housing markets 'politicize' their social reproduction.

The level-of-living is not decided by market forces alone. The quantity and quality of (public) services become increasingly strategic.

For the wage-earners, and for the labour movement, the ancillary organizations of consumer cooperatives, tenants' associations, building societies, etc., made the transformation of money wages into real consumption more efficient (cf. Olofsson 1979: Chapter 8). The struggle for the living standard, that is, the real wage, was on two fronts: getting a wage, and getting the most out of it. The growth of public services as a component in the real consumption makes a whole array of urban social movements a part of the struggle in the area of 'real consumption' for the modern urban wage-earners. During the last 10–15 years we have witnessed a mushrooming of new campaign groups, local, often short-lived organizations, pressure groups and even local parties fighting in the field of public provisions. In a sense they belong more to an 'American' rather than a 'European' tradition with their typical focus on single issues. Nonetheless, they can be regarded as making up a 'family' of pressure and activist groups, merging traditional middle-class pressure-group politics with the wider concerns of emergent social strata, propelled by rapidly changing economic and social relations. It is their combination of issues and social base that gives them the form of a social movement.

The New Social Movements between Class and Politics

What relationship exists between the emergence of a new social force, the growth of a wage-dependent middle-class in public employment, and the NSMs? In this chapter, it has been argued that both the social group (public employed white-collars) and some of the most important new movements have grown out of the new contradictions in modernizing capitalist social formations, especially out of the dilemmas in the existence and reproduction for precisely the new urban wage-dependent middle-class.

Empirical investigations have shown that the social bases of the different NSMs are students, white-collars and professionals, especially those in public employment (or out of employment — cf. the German '*Alternativszene*' [Brand 1985]; Gidlund 1978). This case is amply demonstrated for the Greens in Germany, but also for other Green parties (Müller-Rommel 1985; Schmollinger 1984). On the other hand, only a small part of this new middle-class is engaged, as activists, sympathizers or voters, on the side of the NSMs (and parties taking up their causes).

Two hypotheses on the relation between social base and kind of politics can be formulated with regard to the NSMs in general. The first begins in the middle-class character of the voters/activists, and argues along the lines of a broadly materialist political sociology, where the right–left dimension more or less expresses the social division between bourgeois–labour, rich–poor. In this light the NSMs would be regarded as a new formation in the middle, perhaps a variety of the radical-liberal kind. (The transformation of the Italian *Partito Radicale* from a classical radical-liberal formation to a force giving voice to the NSMs would be an argument in reverse.) The proponents for the Green parties in Sweden, Denmark and Finland argue for the irrelevance of the right–left dimension, and could reasonably be said to be a part of a changing centre position. The Swedish Greens are represented in several local councils and seem to locate themselves in the political middle, both negatively (refusing to enter the game of 'bloc politics', with the socialist bloc confronting the bourgeois) and positively (in support of the centre or liberal parties).

This picture is far from the one the NSMs make of themselves, and those constructed by their theoreticians. It is also too crude a social reductionism. Through their background, both as movements and among their leaders and activists, they could justifiably be regarded as radical left movements, albeit transcending the traditional delimitations of left-wing politics. In the case of the German Green party, the left-wing antecedents of many of its leading spokesmen are obvious (cf. the illuminating biography of Joschka Fischer, Green minister in Hessen, in *Der Spiegel* 1985). In Germany the student movement in the 1960s gave birth to the revival of orthodox left-wing currents, developing into several minuscule parties and organizations in the early 1970s, carrying one or another communist/socialist label (for a fascinating account, cf. *War warred der stärkste der K-partien* 1977). Most of them collapsed, as have their counterparts among the *groupuscules* in the rest of Europe. The militants and activists from this phase of the students' movements have spread in many directions, and some have entered the NSMs. In many countries this generation of radical activists has entered the traditional parties of the left, especially if they were of an open and receptive character. Labour, socialist, communist, social democratic, and left socialist parties have all received their share. In some countries the threshold has been higher, due to national political traditions. In Germany the political system was more closed (Brand 1985).

The traditional interpretation of the second hypothesis is to analyze it in the terms of new alternative elites. The development of the 1960s, through the expansion of higher education and an explosion among university graduates, gave birth to new organizations of potential elites, vying for support in the population. First they tried to resurrect old political formulas from within the working-class and communist traditions. Sometimes they had success (as in the case of the French Socialist Party) and sometimes they failed (the *groupuscule* strategy). When they failed, they tried new ways, among them NSMs and/or Green parties. This 'elite reductionism' is as problematic as the sociological reductionism referred to earlier. But they give elements of an explanation, with their one-sided accentuation of the structural and actor perspectives.

NSMs and the New Middle Class — Keys to the Politics of the Future?

Up until now there have been few signs that an alternative NSM or Green position as such has taken the place of the right/bourgeois–left/socialist axis as structuring the field of European politics. The strength and saliency of the new issues and the impact of the NSMs can nonetheless be decisive in the tug-of-war between left and right political forces in the battle over the new dilemmas and issues as well as over the allegiance of the new employee middle-class. Both the issues and the new social force will play a major role in the ongoing reconstitution of political formations.

The old middle-classes of farmers and urban petty bourgeoisie, as well as the industrial working class, the traditional social bases of the right and left political formations, have rapidly diminished. The new middle-class of employees is growing. Politically they are divided along expected lines. Higher salaried employees tend to the right, lower more to the left. Other lines of division, between sexes and sectors (public–private) are also of importance (J. G. Andersen 1979; Holmberg 1981, 1984).

Strictly speaking, the new middle-class is not so much a clearly delineated and well-organized class as a set of interrelated social strata. What they have in common has aptly been described as a 'contradictory class location' (Wright 1978, 1985). The different parts of the 'new middle class' have different combinations of privileged/dispossessed positions with regard to qualifications, property ownership, income level, power in work organizations/hierarchies, status, etc. The appeal of the right (bourgeois, conservative and liberal forces) lies in the different forms of privilege, while the appeal of the left lies in the different forms of subordination, dispossession and powerlessness.

In Scandinavia the social democratic orthodoxy has stressed the common interests of workers and white-collars as wage-earners, by designing policies and institutions expressing and incorporating that identity. Pensions, employment policies, sick pay and expansion of education and health services have been successful policy areas. The design of the superannuation pension scheme in Sweden, Allmän tjänstepension (ATP), is a famous case. Unionization of the white-collar workers can also be interpreted in this light. The practice of trade unionism defines both politically and organizationally a set of common interests between workers and white-collars. The rate of unionization is exceptionally high among Swedish white-collar workers. Unionization establishes a possible affinity that can be expressed in non-monetary union action (safety and health organizations at the workplace, co-determination schemes, and so on).

The left outside traditional social democracy can build upon traditions of working-class militancy in appealing to radicalized sections of the new middle-class, referring to the common practice of extra-parliamentary militancy. The left formulates a general apprehension of an impending crisis of capitalism, or even the industrial civilization, requiring new political formulas. In the most successful New Left political formation in Europe — the Danish Socialist People's Party — there is an obvious coexistence of old and new radical traditions, incorporating the radical wing of the labour movement (militant trade unionism) and the NSMs, especially the feminist movement. This party is now trying to merge the Red and Green strands, the radical traditions from both the old and new social movements (Christensen 1985).

The relative attraction and saliency of these alternatives for different parts of the new urban middle-classes will have a decisive impact on the political divisions in the future, because of centrality of the white-collar constituency. The way these new strata are interpellated from existing social forces and politico-ideological formations will mean a lot for the way the cleavages will run. The social-democratic/traditional bourgeois cleavage runs mainly along the axis of relative privilege and redistribution through public services, taxes and social security. The radical neoliberal, left–liberal and 'Green socialist' positions are pushing other issues into the foreground, and new cleavage lines may emerge, when they become articulated with existing positions, thereby transforming them (Laclau 1977; Laclau and Mouffe 1985; Fryklund and Peterson 1983).

Conclusions: Making a Mountain Out of a Mole Hill?

The NSMs have been a major and much publicized component in the political landscape of the 1970s and the early 1980s. Sociologists and social theorists try to explain these movements as the outcomes of and new answers to the present crisis of Western European societies or of modern civilization as a whole (Friberg and Galtung 1984; Touraine 1981). The dilemmas and contradictions of the modern world have been painted in broad strokes on a wide canvas. The movements that are said to be the relevant solutions to a crisis of this magnitude are, in contrast, small, unstable and even ephemeral organizations. It looks like a paradox to claim that this flickering organizational structure is the authentic answer to a deep crisis of a whole civilization.

This paradox, which is a discrepancy between an ideal historical agent, posited by a social theory, and the existing manifestation of that agent, is familiar to any student of the labour movement. In the *Communist Manifesto* we can find a similar discrepancy between the diagnosis of an era and the social class and movement that was designated as the privileged agent of change. It was more than 50 years from the publication of the Manifesto until the first socialist minister arrived, and even longer before social transformations in accordance with the analysis. The decisive analytical point in the *Manifesto* — and its further development and refinement in Marx's later works — was that it showed how the processes of capitalist growth and crisis were directly related to the struggle and organization of the working class into a labour movement, the social movement for which Marxism was valid. The issue was not whether the labour movement was the noblest or morally most high-standing alternative to the emergent capitalist social order — there were more natural candidates for that medal among the social movements in the 19th century.

Capitalist societies reshape, as an integral part of their development, the existing poor and dependent social classes. Wherever there are capitalist social relations there is a struggle over wages, and some kind of union organization. In their fight for existence, for a better life, these classes constituted themselves into a working class and labour movement that fostered goals and organizations which could, and in many cases did, transcend the given social order. The relation between fundamental processes in capitalist social orders and a set of social movements springing directly from the heart of its contradictions and dilemmas is very intimate. It was embodied in the labour movement and resonates in the formulation of a 'scientific' as opposed to a utopian socialism.

Are the new and old social movements comparable on this account? So far this question cannot be settled. Many of the so-called new movements are remakes of older ones. The impressive peace movement activities in the early 1980s have their parallels in earlier upsurges (before 1914, in the inter-war period in the anti-nuclear movement around 1960), although the agenda has changed. The feminist movement since the 1960s continues but drastically transforms the focus of the early women's movement. In a formal sense, there is continuity between Bohemian cultures of earlier epochs and the modern pop and youth culture, but the mass character makes a decisive difference.

A point argued in this chapter is that the field of operation and the validity of the cultural revolutionary activities are politically indeterminate. They can be articulated with very different politico-ideological formations, social groups and classes. As they are related to the constitution of individuals as subjects, and the micro-social relations, their transformative energy can coexist with very different macro-social trajectories. In earlier social movements there was a series of activities and organizations that could be labelled 'sub-cultural', forming consciousness and movements around class issues and organizations. The modern cultural revolutionary activities are more open and indeterminate, more generally counter-cultural than specifically sub-cultural.

The defining quality of the old social movements was the close relation between the fate and existential situation of individuals and families and the major social and economic processes of an emerging, and later victorious social order. This relation was not only, or even primarily, of an ideological or normative kind, but one of socio-economic necessity. The fates of individuals, families and 'their' social class were closely linked. Along with C. W. Mills (1959) we can also say that through the social movements personal problems and social issues were connected.

Which contradiction and dilemma in modern society can give rise to a similar connection between problems and issues and to the rise of a social movement comparable to the classical? Among the existing pretenders, the most probable candidate seems to be the environmental, 'Green' movement. The relation between nature and society has become increasingly central, conflicting and complex, covering the whole field of resources, pollution, deforestation, and the nuclear issue. These questions directly relate to the personal-individual situation and behaviour and the reproductive capacity of a society and economy at large. But their effects are not specific or limited to a definite social group or even to a class-in-being. Its general and non-partisan character makes the environmental question (the Green dimension) possible to articulate with different socio-political formations, not least for the socio-political centre.

In some countries there has been a successful 'Red–Green' constellation, evident in the Green Party in West Germany but also present in the Danish Socialist People's Party. This has been able to mobilize and constitute a loose 'family' of struggles and organization and goals, connecting the social wage-oriented urban social movements (including the alternative 'scene') with the feminist and ecological aspects, all of which are closely related to definite segments of the white-collar strata.

The threshold for constituting new and surviving social movements depends on the character of national political traditions and political systems. The more open, flexible and adaptable a political system, the less chance there is for an autonomous new major social movement to develop, and the greater the possibility of selective acceptance of new themes and issues among the already given political forces (Brand 1985). Social movements of the 'American', single-issue campaign character may be able to coalesce around the nexus ecology — urban social wage defence — cultural revolutionary (feminist) new middle-class base, and form a new variety of social movement in the European tradition. But it is equally probable that different parts of these new organizing potentials can become allied to already given socio-political formations, through their reshaping and interpellative capacity.

Note

* This is a revised version of the chapter that was written for the 1985 Aalborg Conference of the Danish 'Centre for Welfare State Studies', and published in CVS (1986). In the mid-1980s I was an associate professor at the Sociological institute, University of Copenhagen and this text was written from within the Danish intellectual discussion at that time. I benefitted greatly from the many suggestions and comments made by Per H. Jensen, Sven E. Olsson and the editorial team of *Zenit*, where this version, in a Swedish translation, was published in an issue of *Zenit* (see Olofsson 1986: 3).

References

Alberoni, F. 1984. *Movement and Institution.* New York: Cambridge University Press.

Anderson, J. G. 1979. *Mellemlagene i Danmark.* Århus: Politica.

Andersen, P. 1983. *In the Tracks of Historical Materialism.* London: Verso.

Brand, K-W. (ed.). 1985. *Neue Soziale Bewegungen in Westeuropa und den USA. Ein Internationaler Vergleich.* Frankfurt: Campus.

Brand, K-W, D. Büsser and D. Rucht. 1983. *Aufbruch in eine Andere Gesellschafi.* Frankfurt: Campus.

Castells, M. 1977. *The Urban Question.* London: Edward Arnold.

Christensen, E. 1985. 'Socialistisk Folkeparti — Ett danskt vänsterparti med parlamentarisk framgång', *Zenit,* no. 89: 55–73.

———. 1986. 'De nye sociale bevaegelser som svar/lösninger på velfaerdsstatens problemer', Center for Velfaerdsstatsstudier (CVS), pp. 143–67.

Christiansen, N. F. 1985. 'Klassebevaegelser og folkebevaegelser'. Paper presented at the CVS seminar, May, Aalborg.

CVS. 1986. A-D. Christensen et al. (eds.) 'Velfaerdsstaten i krise i — Sociale og politiske bevaegelser', *Gloder* 8, Aalborg.

Der Spiegel. 1985. *Dossier: Biography of Joschka Fischer,* no. 45.

Die Zeit 1985. Dossier: 'Die Grünen vor der Zerreissprobe' (22–24 Mai).

Friberg, M. and J. Galtung (eds). 1984. *Rörelserna*. Stockholm: Akademilitteratur.
Fryklund, B. and T. Peterson. 1983. 'Klass och folklighet', *Sociologisk Forskning*, no. 2: 64– 78.
Gidlund, J. 1978. *Aktionsgrupper och lokala partier*. Lund: CWK Gleerup.
Gorz, A. 1980. *Adieux au Proletariat*. Paris: Editions Galilée.
———. 1983. *Les Chemins du Paradis*. Paris: Editions Galilée.
Gundelach, P. 1986. 'Nye og gamle bevaegelser, nye og gamle teorier', *CVS 1986*, pp. 55–82.
Habermas, J. 1961. *Strukturwandel der Öffentlichkeit*. Neuwied: Luchterhand.
———. 1981a. *Theorie des kommunikativen Handelns*. Frankfurt: Suhrkamp.
———. 1981b. 'An Interview with Jürgen Habermas', *Telos*, no. 49, pp. 5–31.
Holmberg, S. 1981. *Svenska Väljare*. Stockholm: Liber.
———. 1984. *Väljare I Förändring*. Stockholm: Liber.
International Encyclopedia of the Social Sciences (IESS). 1968. 'Social Movements', *International Encyclopedia of the Social Sciences*, vol. 14: 438–45. New York and London: Macmillan.
Jensen, Per H. and Fritz von Nordheim Nielsen. 1985. *Nye og gamle bevaegelser I relation til velfaerdsstatskomplekset*, PAW Arbejdspapir, no. 8. Copenhagen: Sociological Institute.
Laclau, E. 1977. *Politics and Ideology in Marxist Theory*. London: NLB.
Laclau, E. and C. Mouffe. 1985. *Hegemony and Socialist Strategy*. London: Verso.
Lundkvist, S. 1977. *Folkrörelserna i det soenska samhället 1850–1970*. Stockholm: Sober.
Mills, C. W. 1959. *The Sociological Imagination*. New York: Oxford University Press.
Müller-Rommel, F. 1985. 'The Greens in Europe', *International Political Science Review*, 6(4): 48–99.
Organisation for Economic Co-operation and Development (OECD). 1985. *Historical Statistics 1960–1983*. Paris: OECD.
Offe, C. 1984. *Contradictions of the Welfare State*. London: Hutchinson.
Olofsson, G. 1979. *Mellan klass och stat*. Lund: Arkiv.
———. 1986. 'Efter arbetarrörelsen? Om vad som är "nytt" och "socialt" i de nya sociala rörelserna', *Zenit*, 3: 24–40
Paris, R. 1981. 'Soziale Bewegung und Öffentlichkeit', *Prokla*, 43(2): 103–28, Berlin.
Rammstedt, O. 1978. *Soziale Bewegung*. Frankfurt: Suhrkamp.
Roth, R. 1984. 'Analysen af nye sociale bevaegelser — Teorier og begreber', *Kurasje*, 34: 49–68, Copenhagen.
Rucht, D., 1982. 'Neue soziale Bewegungen oder: Die Grenzen bürokratischer Modernisierung', in *Politische Viertelsjahresschrift*, Sonderheft, 13: 272–91.

Sartre, J. P. 1976. *Critique of Dialectical Reason.* London: NLB.
Schmollinger, S. 1984. 'Bundestagswahlen und soziale Basis politischer Parteien in der Bundersrepublik, *Prokla,* 56(September): 21–50.
Schumpeter, J. 1976. *Capitalism, Socialism and Democracy.* London: Allen & Unwin.
Social Research. 1985. Winter issue on 'Social Movements', 52(4).
Thompson, E. P. 1966. *The Making of the English Working Class.* New York: Vintage.
Thomsen, L. 1986. 'Sociale bevaegelser og social forandring', *CVS,* pp. 9–32.
Touraine, A. 1981. *The Voice and the Eye: An Analysis of Social Movements.* Cambridge: Cambridge University Press.
Vester, M. 1970. *Die Entstehung des Prolatariats als Lernprozess.* Frankfurt: EVA.
Williams, R. 1983. *Towards 2000.* London: Chatto & Windus.
Anon. 1977. *Wir waren die stärkste der Parteien ... Erfahrungsberichte am der Welt der K-parteien.* Berlin: Rotbuch Verlag.
Wright, E. O. 1985. *Classes.* London: Verso.
———. 1978. *Class, Crisis and the State.* London: NLB.

3

Some Intellectual Genealogies for the Concept of Everyday Resistance

*K. Sivaramakrishnan**

Given the range and variety of debates and scholarship inspired by the urge to emulate or criticize James Scott's contributions, I eschew two temptations in this chapter and, thus, hopefully avoid the inevitable defeat of efforts to be comprehensive in their treatment. First, I will not try to summarize the arguments of each of the four major books by James Scott that I have already discussed in the editorial introduction. Second, I will not try to review all the work done in critical engagement with them. Rather, I will try to map a tour through Scott's writing that takes into account some of the key ideas that appear as central pillars and beams in the architecture of Scott's work, reaching from moral economy to resistance and power to his critiques of high modernism and the working of modern states across the world. Inasmuch as the elucidation of power, hegemony, and resistance as one of the main conceptual pillars, I will also direct most of my attention to that cluster of concepts, focusing on how they are worked out in *Weapons of the Weak* (Scott 1985) and some seminal essays.

My choice of emphasis is in part shaped by Joan Vincent's report that anthropologists in the 1970s and 1980s were greatly interested in the devastation being caused by global capitalism in the remotest rural areas they habitually visited. They were also puzzled by what appeared to be a failure of class-based mobilization in these communities.[1] Vincent further notes that to investigate this puzzle anthropologists drew on the work of E. P. Thompson and Scott (Vincent 1990).[2] In addition to paying attention to that which the definitive history of political anthropology denotes as important, I believe my approach will provide a measure of coherence to what is admittedly a selective treatment. Last, by focusing more on *Weapons of the Weak* (Scott 1985), I hope to lay the groundwork for the other articles in this 'In Focus', each of which provides a more sustained engagement with *The Moral Economy of the Peasant* (Scott 1976), *Domination and the Arts of Resistance* (Scott 1990), or *Seeing Like a State* (Scott 1998).

Between 1977 and 1989 — following the publication of *The Moral Economy of the Peasant* (Scott 1976) and preceding the publication of *Domination and the Arts of Resistance* (Scott 1990) — anthropological literature on agricultural development and social change in postcolonial Asia, Africa and Latin America began to grow.[3] This growth paralleled and yet followed emerging literature in Marxism-influenced development studies and, more broadly, economic history, which was concerned with transitions to capitalism in agrarian social relations.[4] Scholars writing on these transitions were initially economic historians working on industrialized Europe, but others — economists and anthropologists interested in the political economy of development — soon joined the debate.[5]

We can consider the ramification of Scott's ideas, and the general turn toward cultural dimensions of rural social conflict, in two ways that are complementary for scholars of agrarian social change. One way is to remember that Scott greatly admired the work of Eric Hobsbawm and Raymond Williams. So, it is significant that we can see, in the early 1980s, New Left Marxists gathering around the work of Hobsbawm to reflect on the relationship of ideology and politics in contexts of rural social change. Equally, Williams had, in a series of influential essays and books, brought the formation of cultural hegemony and its role in social change to the centre of debate in Marxist theory during the 1970s. The other way is to note work by anthropologists on Europe that brought the study of cultural aspects of such change back from postcolonial settings to the very European contexts in which earlier transition debates had eschewed cultural analysis.[6]

Culture, Class and Hegemony

I should clarify that the focus on cultural dimensions of class relations in Scott's work comes with a specific set of interests. These interests are not akin to those of structural functional, or even just structural, anthropologists trying to explain the organization of economic relations in terms of a social structure or a system of deeply embedded culture-shaping ideas. As I note in the Introduction, Scott's anthropological peers at the time were the Manchester school and a small group of cultural Marxists. But Scott is interested in recovering the agency and ideologies of poor and lower-class rural people to show how their political actions in contexts of rapid agrarian change 'limited the types of economic relations and the intensity of exploitation that elites were able to impose' (Edelman and Haugerud 2004: 38). This required him to develop a new understanding of hegemony. He did so in an intellectual context in which post-structuralists, post-Marxists, and scholars in cultural studies were drawing on Gramsci to understand how consent was manufactured in society in the absence of coercion and raw or brutal domination. Having completed and published *The Moral Economy of the Peasant* (Scott 1976), Scott wrote his first major piece on hegemony (1977) soon after.

Ultimately, Scott arrives at a position about hegemony that parallels and resembles influential formulations emerging within historical anthropology during the 1980s. For instance, one such key synthesis notes:

> Since it is possible, indeed inevitable, for some symbols and meanings not to be hegemonic — and impossible that any hegemony can claim all the signs in the world for its own — culture cannot be subsumed within hegemony, however the terms may be conceived. Meaning may never be innocent, but it is also not merely reducible to the postures of power (Comaroff and Comaroff 1991: 20).[7]

A more omnipotent view of hegemony had been developed by Pierre Bourdieu (1977), who is closer to Raymond Williams in his reading of hegemony across dominant cultural forms. But inside and outside anthropology, in the broader field of cultural studies, a more unstable and contested understanding of hegemony was developing. Scott provides a unique perspective to this debate with his distinctive, limited reading of the notion of 'ideological' or 'cultural' hegemony.[8]

Therefore, in this chapter, my substantive engagements with Scott's work begin with an excursus into ideas about the concept of 'hegemony'. I then examine Thompson's influence on Scott and the study of everyday forms of resistance. The last of these items became a major preoccupation of anthropologists from the mid-1980s to more than a decade thereafter. Scott was a big fan of

Thompson, a New Left historian, and we can, therefore, appropriately start with Thompson's well-known definition of 'hegemony' — a concept Scott deals with extensively, in both *Weapons of the Weak* (Scott 1985) and *Domination and the Arts of Resistance* (Scott 1990). Thompson disagreed with the idea that hegemony entailed acceptance by the poor of the gentry's paternalism in any uncontested sense. 'The deference of the poor could be seen from below as one part necessary self-preservation and one part calculated extraction of whatever could be extracted. Both parties to the equation were constrained within a common field of force' (Thompson 1971).[9]

This formulation considerably influenced and was acknowledged by Scott (1985) in his discussion of patterns of peasant resistance and the nature of social change in a Malaysian village undergoing the 'Green Revolution'. For Scott, the fundamental problem is inequities and the exploitative relationships that they breed in the social structure. He notes, '[t]he kinds of resistance and the kinds of compliance we find in Sedaka cannot be understood without reference to the larger context of real and anticipated coercion' (Scott 1985: 244).[10] This suggests a strong sense of boundaries inhibiting certain forms of protest and defiance at the pragmatic level. Scott, in his definition of social change, also indicates experientially drawn boundaries to social transformation in action and imagination. Such a definition is in keeping with Thompson's 'field of force' idea.[11]

Scott's analysis of everyday forms of resistance — as opposed to spectacular outbreaks of revolutionary protest and the rejection of the categorization of such resistance by criteria seeking to assess its relative selflessness — is based on his understanding of class relationships. His ideas about class can be summarized as follows: (*a*) class formation is mediated by human experience and interpretation of that experience in determinate productive relations;[12] (*b*) class does not exhaust the total explanatory space of social action, because 'the messy reality of multiple identities will continue to be the experience out of which social relations are conducted' (Scott 1985: 43); and (*c*) such a concept of 'class' is embedded in particular histories of social relations, gaining, thus, its unique power and meaning.[13] Scott argues that much of the politics of subordinate groups falls into the category of everyday forms of resistance. He asserts further that this is definitely a form of class struggle because it requires a high level of tacit cooperation among classes of resisters. Finally, he points out that the everyday forms of resistance, being loosely coordinated, have to rely on venerable popular cultures of resistance.[14]

With this culturally inflected theory of class formation in hand, let us turn to the concept of 'ideological hegemony' and Scott's discontent with it. Hegemony theory originated in the Hegelian formulation of the dialectical relationship between the consciousness of the master and the consciousness of the oppressed, with the former independent and the latter dependent (Hegel 1977). Gramsci (1971) dilated on the concept and developed a body of theory that essentially retained the description of the hegemonic process as something that excluded alternatives to the current structure of power and status.[15] It was Williams (1977) who expanded the notion to include a whole body of practices and expectation. He spoke of hegemony as a constellation of lived meanings and values that, when expressed in forms of social and political practice, appeared as reciprocally confirming — with specific and changing pressures and limits.

In his study of 18th-century English society, Thompson (1978) highlighted how much these pressures are exerted from below and the constant flux in which hegemonic discourses remain. Scott deals with such hegemony as has been created in prior struggle and how this hegemony is constantly being tested and modified (Scott 1985: 336 n.). His understanding of hegemony, briefly put, is a comprehensive rejection of false consciousness and the attempts to infer the ideological persuasion of the poor from observed acts of routine compliance.[16] Returning to this theme in *Domination and the Arts of Resistance* (1990), Scott asserts that the presence of social conflict in various historical periods in agrarian and industrial civilizations demonstrates the considerable overestimation of ideological hegemony in the work of the people he dubs the successors of Gramsci.[17]

Routine resistance, then, is the resort. Its performance is visible in exchanges like the curtailed deference shown by peasants to their landlords on the village footpath, or cursory attendance by the poor at feasts hosted by an influential Haji. Scott is interested in the declining force of such symbolic appeal to the conscience of the rich farmer, especially when couched in what he terms as pre-capitalist notions of 'moral obligation'. He explains the diminishing efficacy of such performed reproach as an outcome of the marginalization of the peasantry in agricultural production.[18] This change emanates from the capitalist transformation of productive relations in agriculture. One consequence is the weakening of symbiotic interdependence among classes in village society. When the need for 'euphemization of economic power' by symbolic means diminishes for the rich, the efficacy of similar strategies is also reduced for the poor.[19] Scott (1985) underlines the instability of their shared symbolic universe when he describes the different aspects that the various social groups in Sedaka pick to buttress their claims of cultural legitimacy for political aspirations. As Marc Bloch (1961) points out, selective use of tradition is indicative of disorder. This, too, is borne out by Scott's description of the normative environment as one filled with conflict and divergent interpretations (Scott 1985: 303).

Dyads and Networks

In his own way, Scott (1985) has contributed to strengthening the argument for small-scale, close-to-the-ground approaches to social science inquiry. In the process, he puts himself in the mixed company of revisionists, critical theorists, postmodernists, and even sociologists who, in the mid-1980s, felt that attempts to abstract large processes from big systems must be seriously tempered. More attention, many scholars argued, should be paid to the 'cat nets' and other such mutual interconnections in which people were enmeshed — as individuals and members of social groups (Tilly 1984). It is important to note here that such webs of connection are important to two major, and often divergent, streams of thought in anthropology during the 1970s and 1980s. One that may be characterized as a more historical materialist stream is represented by the work of Eric Wolf.

The other stream of thought, better portrayed as interpretive and symbolic in its emphasis, benefited from the influential contributions of Clifford Geertz (1973). We know that Scott read Geertz closely and interacted with him extensively at the Institute for Advanced Studies at Princeton while still writing *Weapons of the Weak* (Scott 1985) and allied articles. Geertz, of course, has famously argued for keeping the analysis of symbolic forms closely tied to concrete social events and occasions. To this end, Geertz has called the perspective of the anthropologist one of extended acquaintance with extremely small matters. He has gone further to advocate a narrative approach in the interpretative quest of the ethnographer, to keep the connections between theoretical formulation and thick description unobscured by appeals to dark sciences (Geertz 1973).

Scott was always a great admirer of Wolf and often used Wolf's valuable monograph, *Peasants* (Wolf 1966), in classes he taught.[20] But it is important to distinguish how their shared interest in the origins of, and courses of action taken by, peasant revolt or resistance manifested very differently in the study of relations of domination and resistance. Wolf, as Roseberry argues, always wanted to place 'the constitution of particular anthropological subjects at the confluence of global, regional, and local currents of state making, empire building, market expansion and contraction, migration and so on' (Roseberry 1995: 56).[21] Scott is no less interested in this process; however, in individual works like *The Moral Economy of the Peasant* (Scott 1976) or *Weapons of the Weak* (Scott 1985), he chooses a level of interaction to focus on and presents the class conflicts he examines primarily in the form of a dialectical binary, an approach that was widely popularized in *Subaltern Studies*.[22] It should be clear to a reader acquainted with Scott and *Subaltern Studies* that he, Ranajit Guha, and the early *Subaltern Studies* volumes, 1982–87, are mutually influenced in formulating this mode of studying peasant resistance.[23]

In some contrast to a focus on the dyadic relationship between domination and resistance, Wolf suggested that 'the decisive factor in making a peasant rebellion possible lies in the relation of the peasantry to the field of power which surrounds it' (Wolf 1969: 290).[24] Here, Wolf was drawing on a tradition of scholarship that saw the social field as made up of web like and netlike connections that also revealed historically shaped asymmetries of power.[25] Such an approach undermined anthropological bounding of villages and clans, but it also questioned sociological taxonomy of states and regions that facilitated large comparisons. Wolf is clear that dominant figures — landlords, merchants, government officials, and priests — stand at a crucial point between the lives of peasants and the world beyond the villages they inhabit. These intermediaries are the nodes in the webs and nets of connection.

One key distinction emerges, then, in comparing Scott or Guha to Wolf. This appears to be that Wolf, even for purposes of expository efficacy, is reluctant to reduce the number of antagonistic groups described in his ethnography. And he is keen to show the layered social groups discussed in his work as historically emergent formations always interacting in the context of wider social and economic processes. Scott, on the other hand, works with riveting contrasts, and distils from notions of 'custom' the elements that endure in providing political energy to peasant aspirations Without denying that customs are a dynamic set of culturally specified practices, Scott is most interested in them as markers of group identity. In both *The Moral Economy of the Peasant* (Scott 1976) and *Weapons of the Weak* (Scott 1985), he explores those spatial and historical identities that have to be constructed and maintained to prevent class antagonism from shattering the necessary predictability of poor rural lives in changing agrarian conditions.

But what is present, in both Wolf and Scott, is an acute awareness of what becomes more popularly studied after Foucault as the microphysics of power. Here, Scott can be distinguished to his advantage from Geertz and others in the hermeneutic tradition less attentive to questions of power, social inequality, and injustice. To take only one influential example, I will take a brief detour through the work of Paul Ricoeur. In the realm of theory interested in the symbolic mediation of action, Ricoeur (1986) builds a framework juxtaposing ideology and utopia. He wishes to facilitate exploratory development of the symbolic structure of action for a description of the effects of economic ideas in a motivational frame, emphasizing real people under definite conditions. Thus Ricoeur, by placing together the symbolic mediation of action and the determinate context of history, is attempting, arguably, a fusion of Marx and Geertz. This brings into view his notion of 'ideology' as a legitimating mechanism that never fully closes the credibility gap between claim and belief. Ricoeur describes the social space in which Utopia — that which would shatter dominant ideology — can exist and become the focus for challenges to constituted authority and its incomplete power. This formulation of the relationship between ideology and utopia bears a strong resemblance to the one Scott posits for the relationship between the indomitable hidden transcript and the public transcript: the former existing precisely in the space created for it by the latter. What is striking in this strongly dialectical model is the complete absence of any conception of 'inequality' — and, therefore, of hegemony. It is in this vital respect that Scott differs from the Ricoeur–Geertz approaches to particularity and interpretation of social texts. As Scott shows us in *Seeing Like a State* (1998), the careful analysis of power, admittedly in a dyadic scheme, makes Scott's unique version of the emphasis on 'local knowledge' more incisive and better connected to larger structures.

Rethinking Hegemony

I would now like to offer a few questions that might give us pause in accepting the complete dismantling of theories of hegemony that Scott pursues in both *Weapons of the Weak* (1985) and *Domination and the Arts of Resistance* (1990). The main thrust of *Weapons of the Weak* is to prove the fallaciousness of explaining the quiescence and overt complicity of the poor in exploitative situations as the predictable outcome of the hegemonic control exercised by dominant ideologies. Decoding the language of deference reveals dissimulation. The obdurate persistence of hidden transcripts and their role in everyday forms of peasant resistance is the impeccable evidence produced in support. This is adequately argued for the critical implication of hegemony — that class rule is perpetuated not so much by sanctions and coercion as by the consent and passive compliance of subordinate classes. However, as he points out, hegemony has also been treated as political control that may lack consent.[26]

The answer appears to alter radically if we take Scott at his word when he says, '[h]egemony, of course, may be used to refer to the entire complex of social domination' (Scott 1985: 316). Why is that so? The following argument and examples are offered illustratively, to keep the debate open. A millenarian vision, a utopian dream, may set in motion an inversionary discourse that, in turn, sustains the hidden transcript. However, the overcoming project imagined in such revolutionary discourse being couched in the language of prevalent ideology must be a hegemonic constraint. The participants in, and creators of, this subversive narrative seem to desire nothing more than a restoration of an idealized past or the upending of present power relations, placing those now at the bottom later on top of the heap. This is, in another sense, entirely consistent with the model of dialogic and dialectic tension between ideology and utopia, or between public and hidden transcripts. For the model to work, it has to define 'the common field of force' in which it operates, to return to the metaphor with which we began.[27]

What is this field? From a Geertzian perspective, it could be a cultural tradition; from a Gramscian one, it could be hegemony. In the multilayered political domain consisting of interconnected social spaces traversing the continuum from local to global arenas of political action — the sort for which Wolf argues — the distinction between cultural and hegemonic tradition may become blurred. If the distinction were dissolved, the analytical frame may comprise a symbolic universe of discourse grounded in material relations of production and exchange that are originally and historically unequal — hence, likely to instrument discordant symbolizations. Certain symbolizations take centre stage because they coincide with the greater political power and have a hegemonic advantage. This gives them a preeminent position in crafting emergent dominant traditions.[28]

To ground this tentative argument in *Weapons of the Weak* (Scott 1985), let us examine village partisanship and how it changed in Sedaka, was criticized by the villagers, and was influenced by the state. As Scott notes, '[t]he pattern of village partisanship has its roots in older, family based factions that existed well before the formation of political parties' (Scott 1985: 133). As party politics entered the scene and battened on these structures of vertical affiliation, protest came to be expressed primarily in the religious metaphor of the requirements of Islam for pious conduct. Can this not be viewed as a restatement of religious identity? In rejecting secular coalitions that were being built in party politics and experienced as collusive with the economic marginalization of the poor, protest could express a 'new' need for class identity, couched in 'old' discourses of religious sentiment.

After all, the excesses of partisanship that affronted 'traditional ritual decencies' (Scott 1985: 224) were perceived in conjunction with new directions in contesting, negotiating, and defining the state in village society. This was a process compounded by government-sponsored development projects like the village improvement scheme. Scott has described how this scheme was divisive and disruptive in Sedaka. The division of the village by political party is important because it delineates the channels by which active state efforts are instituted to weaken residual insularities; they thus create a qualitatively different hegemonic discourse that does not simply batten on the old hierarchies and relationships of dependence. There is a qualitative difference between the use of traditional political elites as local political agents and the more comprehensive recruitment of large sections of the village into party affiliations.

The former can be seen as a simple extension of existing hegemonic arrangements to larger power structures. A group of elites provide the link by leading a dual existence in two systems of power. The latter emerges out of the deconstruction of older, local hegemonies and their replacement by newer, larger, and more organically connected discourse communities in regional hegemonic formations. The tensions and struggles inherent in such a process are captured by Scott when he says, '[i]t is difficult in Sedaka even to raise with anyone the question of party affiliation, without provoking a disclaimer that when it comes to marriage, sickness, funerals, or even helping to move house, party makes no difference at all' (Scott 1985: 225).

Situating Resistance

Scott is a self-acknowledged admirer of several anarchist thinkers. His sympathies lie with Rosa Luxembourg and not with Lenin. He believes Jane Jacobs was right and Le Corbusier was wrong.[29] We should note, however, the ambiguous connection of everyday forms of resistance to anarchism. On the one hand, as a means, such resistance is anarchic: spontaneous, non-hierarchical, and loosely organized. On the other hand, as a programme it is very modest and most unanarchic: It seeks not the overthrow of the state or even its policies but merely to mitigate or subvert their effects. This quality of everyday resistance is, I believe, an appropriate point to enter a discussion of the relationship between everyday protest, power, hegemony, and moral economy. I shall do so by raising a series of hopefully provocative questions and some comments.

The argument for everyday protest seems to rest on the valid assumption that the peasantry and the landlord class (or the state), mutually, perceive the advantage of avoiding open confrontation. But this says as much about power as it does about resistance. It becomes all the more important to know why then both sides get involved in escalated conflicts like social movements. Are violent confrontations the unintended consequences of everyday struggles, or do they reveal a particular interest striking to consolidate at a moment of perceived opportunity? Everyday resistance emphasizes a constant strategic alertness on the part of those involved that places a lot of weight on agency and calculation. On the contrary, at times social structures, roles, statuses, and contingent factors modify agency and its consequences. For example, if our actors are individuals, they may engage in everyday acts of resistance or desist from them under the structural pressures of local leadership roles, parenthood, or status derived from political positions or offices taken. If the actors are groups, then there is the problem of how consensus, or even a modicum of coordination, is created within the group.

If hegemony is the tolerable level of appropriation as naturalized, or at least acquiesced in, and if hegemony is constantly negotiated and altered through both covert and overt protest, this approach suggests a mutualistic, dialectical process in which the state is integrally involved. *Hegemony*, as T. J. Jackson Lears recovers it, is relevant here. Lears writes, '[a]s Gramsci understood, the hegemonic culture depends not on brainwashing the "masses" but on the tendency of public discourse to make some form of experience readily available to consciousness, while ignoring or suppressing others' (Lears 1985: 577). Thompson (1975a) reminds us that crime as resistance was carried out in the framework of a law that was never fully adapted to narrow class purposes. When standards of procedure and fairness were set, they sometimes ran counter to dominant interests, and this was done in the larger spirit of rule of law. Because law promised a reign of universal norms with utopian implications, the meaning could be contested; as Thompson suggests, hegemony could be negotiated through a fund of values that the poor drew from the law.

I would then suggest that although the concept of 'everyday forms of resistance' provides a welcome redefinition of *protest* and enlarges the field of vision in a most valuable manner, a fuller picture will emerge from an equally careful discussion of everyday exercise of power — what Douglas Haynes and Gyan Prakash have called the 'intersection of power and resistance, and the complex processes in which the two are constantly enmeshed' (Haynes and Prakash 1992: 19). The 'In Focus' articles other provide many clues and helpful pointers for such a project. Different levels of the state can work at cross-purposes, even when dealing with things as basic to the interests of the state as taxes, agricultural loans, and rural labour relations. Everyday forms of resistance to one level of the state may well play into the hands of another level. Again, to take an example, let us consider a situation in which the state may consist of a loose coalition of kulaks, industrialists, and an urban professional bourgeoisie — a typology that Pranab Bardhan (1984) uses for the Indian state. It often becomes difficult for small farmers to figure out who is responsible for what policy out of a confusing array that impinges on their lives. Thus, it is also difficult to have a cogent plan of resistance that traces a reliable line between resistive act and ameliorative outcome.

This conclusion has implications for the all-knowing, strategizing, everyday resistor as a model subaltern. It also rests on the logic that specific modes of resistance (especially when they are cloaked in the apparent innocuousness of everyday forms) are effective only in relation to particular forms of domination. Thompson nicely illustrates this very point in his analysis of anonymous letters. He shows how the letters related to industrial conflict, agrarian contexts, and food riots of a particular type 'where they gave publicity to a curious kind of dialogue between the authorities and the crowd' (Thompson 1975a: 270). Although it is right to stress that everyday resistance focuses on the point of enforcement to minimize domination, the precise strategy does depend on knowing where domination is coming from — that is, a reading of the intentions inherent in domination. Take the case of poaching or squatting and the distinctions Douglas Hay (1975) makes between poaching and thieving. The definition of these acts as crimes presupposes a framework in which power holders have reallocated the natural resources involved as exclusively the property of specific classes, or prescribed a scale of rights to which the crimes must be matched as repudiation, in defining them as *resistance*.

On this matter, Foucault and Thompson converge.[30] Foucault (1979: 85) points out that more and more restrictive pressure was exerted on accepted illegalities with the intensification of agriculture, moving customary usufructs into the category of 'theft'. Illegality of rights was separated from another class of illegality that Foucault calls the 'illegality of property' (Foucault 1979: 87). Although the former remained a privilege of the upper classes, the latter became the heinous offence of the lower strata. In a similar vein, Thompson (1975b) discusses the redefinition of *crime* and *punishment*. He places the Black Act of 1723 in the context of a more generally repressive legal framework that was emerging and writes, 'What was now to be punished was not an offence between [men] … but an offence against property' (ibid.: 207). He also argues that law, strategies of domination, and appropriation emerge out of specific contingent situations and out of the way they intersect with elite ideologies, interests, and perceptions of these contingencies (ibid.: 214). Towards the end of Thompson's book, in an extended discussion of law, its creation and legitimation, Thompson pithily states the point I wish to make about the inseparability of resistance and power: 'Law was often a definition of actual agrarian practice … deeply imbricated within the very basis of productive relations' (ibid.:261). This is a claim that can be made about protest when it is rooted in everyday resistance.

It is correct to say that everyday forms of resistance are about custom and usage. But as Sally Falk Moore (1986) cautions, custom is not a fixed entity. She rightly points out that just looking at cases might highlight continuity when the act of stepping back and viewing the wider political economy reveals the changes in custom, because 'the peculiar place of any system of official institutions can only become visible in relation to life outside them' (Moore 1986: 209). Describing the installation of secular law in Kilimanjaro, Moore shows how the magistrates developed a judicial discourse predicated on narrow definition of cases, formal interpretation of rules, and a bureaucratic standardization of the customary domain (ibid.: 302–5). It was precisely the intent of modern law to confine the room for negotiation that custom always implied. The contest over customary right is often not so much about the quantities or character of the privileges in question as it is about the very contingent negotiability of custom that is in danger when more formal legal arrangements threaten to replace or reify it.

Another example from Scott's work (1987) can be used to illustrate this point. Consider his discussion of the way Malay peasantry stressed the fitful and voluntary nature of *zakat peribadi* payments to local poor and imam, before *zakat raja* became a state levy. What additionally becomes clear from Scott (1987: 428, n. 18) is that inflexible demands of the state have adverse material consequences when there is a cost-price squeeze on agricultural profits, real incomes are declining, and yields are falling. But they are culturally experienced through a world of peasant–state relations, in which the state has become more directly involved in the agricultural production process. However, the same state is less willing to share in the vicissitudes of the process and this undermines the negotiability of the moral economy. This commentary on the notion of 'moral economy' is something critics of the idea frequently overlook. I submit that the valuable aspect of moral economy is not the imagined benign reciprocity aspect that people have chosen to attack (cf. Desan 1989), thus taking their critique down an unimportant byway. Instead, what is important is that, within limits, moral economy legitimately allowed the negotiation of rights and obligations, which rational impersonal regulation made increasingly difficult. Crime and other forms of everyday resistance must be seen in this light of the 'moral economy' concept. I believe I am not redefining *moral economy* at will, because Thompson (1991) provides such careful re-specification of the concept.[31]

Green revolution agriculture, high-modernist city planning, or industrial forestry — all of which have been vehicles in which the developmental state has ridden roughshod over the lives of peasants, poor people, and ethnic or racial minorities across Asia and Africa — received the considered attention of Scott in *Seeing Like a State* (1998). In this work, Scott returned to a recurrent theme: The conditions under which moral economies collapse and the consequences of such collapse. But in *Seeing Like a State,* he does so from the perspective of why modern states must necessarily break the ties of mutualism between its aspirations and those of its citizens or subjects. He wonders what in the pathology of modern-state systems makes them work not so much to reweave the fabric of dependence between the powerful and the subaltern but, instead, to shred it. I do not provide an extended discussion of this last book because several of the other articles in this 'In Focus' section have done so with great elegance and insight.

Acknowledgments

A venture such as this conjures up the possibility of thanking everyone I ever studied with or learned from. The list would be too long. I should just thank all of those whose paths crossed mine at Agrarian Studies, for the conversations that resulted from those encounters were surely the stimulus for this chapter and my Introduction to this collection. My dialogues with James Scott began because of his extraordinary generosity as scholar, mentor and friend. Those are not gifts I can reciprocally return. I am grateful to two anonymous *AA* reviewers, and the editors of *American Anthropologist,* for their comments on the draft of this chapter. Responding to them has certainly made it better. I wish also to record my gratitude to a Fellowship from the American Council of Learned Societies, New York, and the College of Arts and Sciences, University of Washington, Seattle, for supplemental support. All of that enabled me to take a year of release from multifarious teaching and administrative duties and complete this work. I remain, of course, solely responsible for its remaining shortcomings.

Notes

* This chapter has been reproduced with permission of the American Anthropological Association from *American Anthropologist,* 107(3): 346–55, 2005.

1. See Vincent (1990: 400–5) for a pithy treatment of politics from below and the importance of ideas about moral economy in peasant society for agrarian scholarship in the last quarter of the 20th century.
2. Almost as quickly as Scott helped focus attention of anthropologists on the plight of peasantries, his work drew out challenges, notably by feminist scholars, that helped construct alternate histories, not only of peasants and their struggles but also of the very making of the 'peasant' category. These revisionist studies recount how the peasantry as an identity was populated and how peasant households came to be recognized and reified in scholarly and development discourse. For an excellent review and original analysis of these trends, see Tsing (2003).
3. A few notable examples of key works that contributed a Marxism-influenced anthropological perspective on agrarian class relations would include Berry (1985), Gough (1981), Kahn (1980), Roseberry (1983), and Watts (1983). A widely read survey of the relations between Marxism and social anthropology had been conducted in the early 1970s at St John's College, Oxford University, and was published as *Marxist Analyses and Social Anthropology* (1975). Many anthropologists found a venue for this kind of work in the pages of *Peasant Studies,* a journal that started publication in the United States in 1976, and the *Journal of Peasant Studies,* first published in 1973 in England.
4. The best review of transition debates remains Aston and Philpin (1987). See also Hart et al. (1989) who, in some respects, brought the debate

to Southeast Asia and who also took great interest in debating Scott's work (1976, 1985). A broader appreciation of Scott's work for the field of historical anthropology can be found in Roseberry (1989: 55–79).

5. Edelman and Haugerud (2004) provide an excellent survey of the emergence of development studies and the role played by anthropology, and by Scott, in infusing cultural perspectives into the study of agrarian transitions and class relations.
6. For the discussion of Hobsbawn, see Samuel and Jones (1983); Hobsbawm (1981) and Hobsbawm and Rude´ (1968) were particularly important to Scott. Some works of Williams are most relevant here (1973a, 1973b, and 1977). For the focus on cultural aspects in contexts of agrarian change in Europe, see Blok (1972), Herzfeld (1985) and Holmes (1989) — a few examples that relate rural identity formation to both rural and urban transformations.
7. Other important historical anthropologists who have also addressed this question of hegemony being insecure and unstable include Cohn and Dirks (1988).
8. For discussions of hegemony in cultural studies during the 1980s, see Nelson and Grossberg (1988).
9. Thompson goes on to explain his 'field of force' metaphor elsewhere (1991: 73), referring to a school experiment with a magnet and iron filings. Like the filings clustered at two poles, with a few distributed in the middle but most oriented in one or other direction, Thompson finds gentry and crowd at opposite ends with professional groups and merchants alternating between dependency on rulers and common action with the crowd.
10. By dealing with the historical emergence of differentiation and the way cultural meaning is refracted from the asymmetries of power and status, Scott avoids the criticism leveled at Geertz by Roseberry (1989) and Scholte (1986), respectively, about a historicism and the neglect of totalizing conditions.
11. See Scott's comment, for instance, that 'the main point is that the peasants of Sedaka do not simply react to objective conditions per se but rather to the interpretation that they place on these conditions as mediated by values embedded in concrete practices' (Scott 1985: 305). This leads him to a definition of resistance, which is based on self-interested material need, congruent with the historically experienced nature of class consciousness. This places Scott in agreement with Thompson (1978).
12. Citing the extreme cases of the 'greedy rich' and 'shiftless poor' images that characterized the discussion of class relations in Sedaka, Scott writes: 'Haji Broom and Razak gain much of their power as symbols by virtue of their reality as concrete human examples of the behavior they have come to signify . . . what one chooses to make of these living

legends — precisely what they signify — is another matter, but they originate in social facts ... the stories that swirl around these two men must also be recognized as cornerstones of an ideological edifice under construction ... such stories can be read as a kind of social text on the subject of human decency' (Scott 1985: 23).

13. This follows closely on Thompson (1978), for whom class eventuates as men and women live their productive relations, experience determined social relations within frameworks of meaning historically available to them, and as they handle these experiences in culturally informed political actions.
14. See Scott (1993: 2–7) for one of the most succinct expositions of what he counts as 'everyday resistance' and why it is important both as a class-based social struggle and a cultural–historical event in the life of agrarian societies.
15. For a useful survey of how the concept of 'hegemony' was formulated by Gramsci and then further developed and deployed in cultural studies and anthropology, see Smith (2003).
16. As Scott says, 'Hamzah has no difficulty recognizing when he has been exploited or shabbily treated, his effort and his achievement has been to swallow his anger lest it endanger his livelihood' (1985: 279).
17. A survey of several historical cases leads Scott to emphatically declare that 'the attempt to turn a thin theory of naturalization into a fat theory of hegemony seems, in my view, clearly unwarranted' (1990: 79).
18. See the discussion of 'commercialization' and the erosive influence on institutions of redistribution and social solidarity (Scott 1985: 173), the later consideration of existential constraints on the ideological struggle (ibid.: 240), or the decreased sanctioning power of the 'war of words', as poor households became superfluous to paddy cultivation (ibid.:284).
19. The finding that ties of obedience and protection held disparate groups together in a situation of fragmented authority, typically in feudal societies, is amply documented. See, for instance, the classic account by Bloch (1961).
20. Wolf's works (1966 and 1969), the latter cited extensively in *The Moral Economy of the Peasant* (1976) when developing definitions of *peasantries* to be used in the argument, remain key texts in peasant studies and the study of agrarian unrest throughout the 1990s. Wolf (1969) included a chapter on Vietnam, the region of interest in *The Moral Economy of the Peasant* (1976). But it is also interesting to note that Wolf was at pains to locate peasants in regionally specific histories even as he tried to develop comparisons across those histories. This has led some of his interpreters to view his work at odds with notions of 'moral economy', in service of which Scott (1976) draws on Wolf (1969). As Scott (1976) and Schneider (1995) have noted, Wolf's

peasants were risk averse and fond of the limited autonomy afforded by subsistence cultivation.

21. In this article, Roseberry discusses Wolf's cultural historical project as particularly interested in the intermediation of global and local relations by key classes that straddled the two arenas of power and production.
22. I have discussed the dualistic mode of analysis and its pitfalls in *Subaltern Studies* elsewhere (see Sivaramakrishnan 1995). Other critical engagements with the work of this important collective and its work during the 1980s and 1990s, a period when Scott was also closely engaged with its principal scholars, include various essays in Ludden (2001) and Chaturvedi (2000).
23. In his Foreword to the new edition of Ranajit Guha's classic work on peasant insurgency (Guha 1983), Scott elaborates on this dialectical relation between the dyad of domination and resistance. He notes, '[o]n Guha's reading, insurgency and domination are the two voices in an adversarial conversation composed of gestures, violence, symbolic claims negation' (Scott 1999: xiii). Read with Scott's skepticism for ideological hegemony, and thereby his belief in the relative autonomy of peasant (subaltern) consciousness, this sharply dyadic presentation generates two important points of confluence in the theoretical frameworks of Scott and Guha.
24. It is not that wider networks of power are not present in Scott's analysis. They get pushed to the background as he focuses on the face-to-face interactions in which individuals and small groups encounter domination and practice resistance.
25. I refer here to the historicism of Alexander Lesser and the pioneering role he played in challenging functionalism and synchronicity while promoting the study of political change over time, with a keen eye to the injustices enabled by governments against minorities and disenfranchised groups in society. See Vincent (1990: 191–94) for an account of the battles Lesser fought against hegemonic anthropological theories of the 1930s and 1940s, and the role he played in keeping an interest in Marxism alive in the universe of US anthropology.
26. See note 17 on page 315, where he cites the article by Perry Anderson. We have no reason to believe that this formidable figure of the New Left, contemporary of E. P. Thompson and core member of the Gramscian tradition, erred in understanding 'hegemony'. On the contrary, his definition flows logically out of his comprehensive study of medieval state-making processes (Anderson 1977). In fact, as suggested briefly in this chapter, a more sensitive consideration of the state in village politics and the processes of state making, in which localities are invariably embroiled, would have enabled a wider notion

of 'hegemony' that eludes extinction. For example, see Siu (1989) and Sivaramakrishnan (1999).

27. In an important article, Partha Chatterjee (2004) suggests that nationalisms prevalent in 20th-century anticolonial struggles are likely being reinscribed in contemporary wars against US hegemony; thus, he reminds us of the historically constrained nature of political possibilities available in subaltern politics. He cautions against an overly disconnected analysis of new empires from the history of empires; however, for my purposes, he does illustrate the working of a field of force on an international scale. To that extent, we learn that even newer forms of domination cannot escape historical determination by older forms; this is an element of hegemony as an institutionally embedded aspect of domination that cannot ever be fully dismantled.
28. For example, at their most successful level, hidden transcripts may found a new religion; in doing so, though, they largely rewrite old ones in terms of removing blemishes, as the study of comparative religion is apt to reveal (ideas of 'heaven' and 'hell' seem inescapable in organized religion).
29. See Scott (1998), in which his arguments against 'high modernism' and for 'metis' are underscored by a sympathetic reading of anarchist theory.
30. This is not an easy point to make. I also do not have space here to elaborate it and defend it against some surprised glances that will be cast at this claim. I am aware, even as I assert this point, that there are substantial philosophical differences in the way Foucault and Thompson — who, in this regard, is part of the same group as Gramsci, Bourdieu, and Scott — understand power. Mitchell (1991) discusses these differences at length in his extended criticism of *Weapons of the Weak* (1985). But I am not entirely convinced of the incompatibility of the approaches. Ultimately, Scott focused relentlessly on political action; furthermore, when micropolitics is the object of study, cultural Marxist and poststructuralist approaches are not incommensurable in their descriptions of power, its flows, and its repudiations.
31. E. P. Thompson actually comes down heavily on people like Paul Greenough (1982), who, in his view, make more static use of the concept.

References

Anderson, Perry. 1977. *Transitions from Antiquity to Feudalism.* London: New Left Books.

Aston, T. H., and C. H. E. Philpin. 1987. *The Brenner: Agrarian Class Structure and Economic Development in Pre-Industrial Europe.* Cambridge: Cambridge University Press.

Bardhan, Pranab. 1984. *The Political Economy of Development in India*. Delhi: Oxford University Press.

Berry, Sara. 1985. *Fathers Work for Their Sons: Accumulation, Mobility, and Class Formation in an Extended Yorù bá Community*. Berkeley: University of California Press.

Bloch, Marc. 1961. *Feudal Society, vol.1: The Growth of Ties of Dependence*. Chicago: Chicago University Press.

Bloch, Maurice. 1975. *Marxist Analyses and Social Anthropology*. London: Malaby Press.

Blok, Anton. 1972. *The Mafia of a Sicilian Village (1860–1960): An Anthropological Study of Political Middlemen*. Amsterdam: University of Amsterdam Press.

Bourdieu, Pierre. 1977. *Outline of a Theory of Practice*. Cambridge: Cambridge University Press.

Chatterjee, Partha. 2004. 'Empire after Globalization', *Economic and Political Weekly*, 39(37): 4155–64.

Chaturvedi, Vinayak (ed.). 2000. *Mapping Subaltern Studies and the Postcolonial*. London: Verso.

Cohn, Bernard, and Nicholas Dirks. 1988. 'Beyond the Fringe: The Nation-State, Colonialism and the Technologies of Power', *Journal of Historical Sociology*, 1(2): 224–29.

Comaroff, Jean, and John Comaroff. 1991. *Of Revelation and Revolution, vol. 1: Christianity, Colonialism, and Consciousness in South Africa*. Chicago: University of Chicago Press.

Desan, Suzanne. 1989. 'Crowds, Community and Ritual in the Work of E. P. Thompson and Natalie Davis', in Lynn Hunt (ed.), *The New Cultural History*, pp. 47–71. Berkeley: University of California Press.

Edelman, Marc, and Angelique Haugerud. 2004. 'Introduction: The Anthropology of Development and Globalization, in Marc Edelman and Angelique Haugerud (eds), *The Anthropology of Development and Globalization: From Classical Political Economy to Contemporary Neoliberalism*, pp. 1–74. Oxford: Blackwell.

Foucault, Michel. 1979. *Discipline and Punish: The Birth of the Prison*, A. Sheridan (trans.). New York: Vintage/Random House.

Geertz, Clifford. 1973. *The Interpretation of Cultures*. New York: Basic Books.

Gramsci, Antonio. 1971. *Selections from the Prison Notebooks*, Q. Hoare and G. N. Smith (eds). London: Lawrence and Wishart.

Greenough, Paul. 1982. *Prosperity and Misery in Modern Bengal: The Famine of 1943–1944*. New York: Oxford University Press.

Gough, Kathleen. 1981. *Rural Society in Southeast India*. Cambridge: Cambridge University Press.

Guha, Ranajit. 1983. *Elementary Aspects of Peasant Insurgency in Colonial India*. Delhi: Oxford University Press.

Guha, Ranajit. (ed.). 1982–87. *Subaltern Studies: Writings on South Asian History and Society*, vols. 1–5. Delhi: Oxford University Press.

Hart, Gillian, Andrew Turton, and Benjamin White (eds). 1989. *Agrarian Transformations: Local Processes and the State in Southeast Asia*. Berkeley: University of California Press.

Hay, Douglas. 1975. 'Poaching and the Game Laws on Cannock Chase', in Douglas Hay, Peter Linebaugh, John G. Rule, E. P. Thompson, and Cal Winslow (eds), *Albion's Fatal Tree: Crime and Society in Eighteenth Century England*. New York: Pantheon.

Haynes, Douglas, and Gyan Prakash. 1992. 'Introduction: The Entanglement of Power and Resistance', in Douglas Haynes and Gyan Prakash (eds), *Contesting Power: Resistance and Everyday Social Relations in South Asia*, pp. 1–22. Berkeley: University of California Press.

Hegel, G. W. F. 1977. *The Phenomenology of the Spirit*. Oxford: Clarendon Press.

Herzfeld, Michael. 1985. *The Poetics of Manhood: Contest and Identity in a Cretan Mountain Village*. Princeton: Princeton University Press.

Hobsbawm, Eric. 1981. *Bandits*. New York: Pantheon Books.

Hobsbawm, Eric, and George Rude´. 1968. *Captain Swing*. New York: Pantheon Books.

Holmes, Douglas. 1989. *Cultural Disenchantments: Worker Peasantries in Northeast Italy*. Princeton: Princeton University Press.

Kahn, Joel. 1980. *Minangkabau Social Formations: Indonesian Peasants and the World Economy*. Cambridge: Cambridge University Press.

Lears, T. J. Jackson. 1985. 'The Concept of Cultural Hegemony: Problems and Possibilities', *American Historical Review*, 9: 567–93.

Ludden, David (ed.). 2001. *Reading Subaltern Studies: Critical History, Contesting Meaning, and the Globalization of South Asia*. New Delhi: Permanent Black.

Mitchell, Timothy. 1991. 'Everyday Metaphors of Power', *Theory and Society*, 19: 545–77.

Moore, Sally Falk. 1986. *Social Facts and Fabrications: 'Customary' Law on Kilimanjaro, 1880–1980*. Cambridge, MA: Harvard University Press.

Nelson, Cary, and Lawrence Grossberg (eds). 1988. *Marxism and the Interpretation of Culture*. Urbana: University of Illinois Press.

Ricoeur, Paul. 1986. *Lectures on Ideology and Utopia*, G. H. Taylor (ed.). New York: Columbia University Press.

Roseberry, William. 1983. *Coffee and Capitalism in the Venezuelan Andes*. Austin: University of Texas Press.

———. 1989. *Anthropologies and Histories: Essays in Culture, History and Political Economy*. New Brunswick, NJ: Rutgers University Press.

———. 1995. 'The Cultural History of Peasantries', in Jane Schneider and Rayna Rapp (eds), *Articulating Hidden Histories: Exploring the Influence of Eric R. Wolf*, pp. 51–66. Berkeley: University of California Press.

Samuel, Raphael, and Gareth Stedman Jones (eds). 1983. *Culture, Ideology and Politics: Essays for Eric Hobsbawm*. Boston: Routledge and Kegan Paul.

Schneider, Jane. 1995. 'Introduction: The Analytical Strategies of Eric Wolf', in Jane Schneider and Rayna Rapp (eds), *Articulating Hidden Histories: Exploring the Influence of Eric R. Wolf*, pp. 3–30. Berkeley: University of California Press.

Scholte, Bob. 1986. 'The Charmed Circle of Geertz's Hermeneutics: A Neo-Marxist Critique', *Critique of Anthropology*, 6(1): 5–15.

Scott, James C. 1976. *The Moral Economy of the Peasant: Rebellion and Subsistence in Southeast Asia*. New Haven, CT: Yale University Press.

———. 1977. 'Hegemony and the Peasantry', *Politics and Society*, 7(3): 267–96.

———. 1985. *Weapons of the Weak: Everyday Forms of Peasant Resistance*. New Haven, CT: Yale University Press.

———. 1987. 'Resistance without Protest and without Organization: Peasant Opposition to the Islamic Zakat and the Christian Tithe', *Comparative Studies, Society and History*, 29: 417–52.

———. 1990. *Domination and the Arts of Resistance: Hidden Transcripts*. New Haven, CT: Yale University Press.

———. 1993. *Everyday Forms of Resistance*. PRIME Occasional Papers, 15. Meigaku: International Peace Research Institute.

———. 1998. *Seeing Like a State: How Certain Schemes to Improve the Human Condition Have Failed*. New Haven, CT: Yale University Press.

———. 1999. 'Foreword', in Ranajit Guha (ed.), *Elementary Aspects of Peasant Insurgency in Colonial India*. Durham, NC: Duke University Press.

Siu, Helen F. 1989. *Agents and Victims in South China: Accomplices in Rural Revolt*. New Haven, CT: Yale University Press.

Sivaramakrishnan, K. 1995. 'Situating the Subaltern: History and Anthropology in the Subaltern Studies Project', *Journal of Historical Sociology*, 8(4): 395–429.

———. 1999. *Modern Forests: Statemaking and Environmental Change in Colonial Eastern India*. Stanford: Stanford University Press.

Smith, Gavin. 2003. 'Hegemony', in David Nugent and Joan Vincent (eds), *A Companion to the Anthropology of Politics*, pp. 216–30. Oxford: Blackwell.

Thompson, E. P. 1971. 'The Moral Economy of the English Crowd in the Eighteenth Century', *Past and Present*, 50: 76–136.

———. 1975a. 'The Crime of Anonymity', in Douglas Hay, Peter Linebaugh, John G. Rule, E. P. Thompson, and Cal Winslow (eds), *Albion's Fatal Tree: Crime and Society in Eighteenth Century England*, pp. 255–308. New York: Pantheon.

Thompson, E. P. 1975b. *Whigs and Hunters: The Origins of the Black Act*. New York: Pantheon.

———. 1978. 'Eighteenth Century English Society: Class Struggle without Class', *Social History*, 3(2): 133–65.

———. 1991. *Customs in Common: Studies in Traditional Popular Culture*. New York: New Press.

Tilly, Charles. 1984. *Big Structures, Large Processes, Huge Comparisons*. New York: Russell Sage Foundation.

Tsing, Anna Lowenhaupt. 2003. 'Agrarian Allegory and Global Futures', in Paul Greenough and Anna Lowenhaupt Tsing (eds), *Nature in the Global South: Environmental Projects in South and Southeast Asia*, pp. 124–69. Durham, NC: Duke University Press.

Vincent, Joan. 1990. *Anthropology and Politics: Visions, Traditions, and Trends*. Tucson: University of Arizona Press.

Watts, Michael. 1983. *Silent Violence: Food, Famine, and Peasantry in Northern Nigeria*. Berkeley: University of California Press.

Williams, Raymond. 1973a. 'Base and Superstructure in Marxist Cultural Theory', *New Left Review*, 82: 3–16.

———. 1973b. *The Country and the City*. New York: Oxford University Press.

———. 1977. *Marxism and Literature*. London: Penguin.

Wolf, Eric. 1966. *Peasants*. Englewood Cliffs, NJ: Prentice Hall.

———. 1969. *Peasant Wars of the Twentieth Century*. New York: Harper and Row.

4

Carnival of Money

Politics of Dissent in an Era of Globalizing Finance

*Marieke de Goede**

Introduction: Ethical Inconsistency

In the recent Radcliffe Harvard Lecture, Zadie Smith (2003: 2) celebrates the work of E. M. Forster as a novelist whose 'deliberate rejection of controlled style reflects the messy complexities of the human heart'. Smith holds up Forster as an author whose muddled stories and inconsistent characters are not literarily flawed but closer to the bewildering realities of life while opening up an ethical space. Forster's style has been often criticized and ridiculed, but why, argues Smith, do we value consistency and rationality so much? Clarity and consistency in literary characters and plots are not just *unreal* — does everyday life ever adhere to such structure? — but can also be morally problematic: 'The lesson of the comic novel', Smith writes, 'is that our moral enthusiasms make us inflexible, one-dimensional, flat ... we lose a vital dimension when we embrace the *esprit des serieux*' (2003: 3). Indeed, Smith argues, 'there might be some ethical advantage in not always pursuing a perfect and unyielding rationality' (ibid.: 4). Smith's analysis emphasizes the ethical and political dimensions of comedy and ambiguity: instead of moral certainty and consistency, a comic literary muddle opens up an ethical space in which we as readers 'find ourselves caring about people who are various, muddled, uncertain and not quite like us' (ibid.: 4).

This chapter theorizes the politics of dissent and resistance in an era of globalizing finance, when nothing short of broad-based and internally consistent global movements seem to be able to challenge the power of financial institutions. Smith's suggestion that there might be ethical advantage in not always pursuing an unyielding rationality is relevant in light of the increasing call for global resistance movements to develop coherent, rational programmes for reform in order to be taken seriously. This call comes from those unsympathetic to global dissent movements, but increasingly also from within the movements themselves. British journalist and activist George Monbiot (2003), for example, has recently launched a comprehensive proposal for global governance, seeking consensus and unity. 'For until we have a programme behind which we can unite', Monbiot writes, 'we will neither present a viable threat to the current rulers of the world, nor seize the revolutionary moment which their miscalculation affords us' (ibid.). Monbiot sees political divergence as a weakness to be conquered on the road to a revolution in global governance, the proper end goal of protests like those in Seattle (cf. Cox 1999; Gill 2000; Kaldor 2000; Scholte 2002).

I will argue that understanding global resistance in terms of a coherent programme entails a limited definition of contemporary political possibilities of dissent. By defining and delineating not just the new global movements but also their goals and ideals, some authors tend to read each dissenting voice in the context of a larger global purpose, while devaluing those, often complex and contradictory, political practices of festivals, laughter and everyday coping strategies that cannot be seen to contribute to this purpose. Here, I build on existing critiques of global civil society in order to offer a reading of the multiple possibilities of the politics of dissent in an era of globalizing finance which do not aspire to culminate in a new world order, but which *do* transform people's everyday experiences of money and finance in important ways. Carnival and laughter play a special role in the examples offered here: I argue that laughing about financial practices is more than a helpless gesture in the face of financial power, but has the potential to challenge its rationality and expose its contingency. These cultural practices are ways in which people cope with the seemingly overwhelming power of finance in everyday life, and create space for imagining financial alternatives.

The Politics of 'Making Strange'

In their drive to detect a common programme behind the many possible acts and movements of resistance, theorists of civil society may erase the ambiguities and contradictions inherent in the contemporary politics of dissent. It is easily assumed, for example, that the manifold movements protesting at Seattle had a commonality. 'Look a little closer', writes Naomi Klein for example, 'and it's clear that these smaller targeted movements are indeed battling the same forces' (quoted in Amoore and Langley 2004: 107–8). In their article 'Ambiguities of Global Civil Society', Amoore and Langley argue that civil society theory 'celebrates diversity and difference within settled, defined and clearly delimited boundaries' (ibid.: 107). Amoore and Langley instead emphasize the conceptual and political ambiguity of civil society, and encourage thinking about the contradictions within the global political economy. 'Within existing conceptions of [Global Civil Society]', Amoore and Langley ask,

> do we have ways of thinking about the individual who is a member of Amnesty International while simultaneously holding portfolio investments in a number of large multination corporations; the Visa holder who joins Reclaim the Streets?; or the report from the Seattle protests that asked: 'did the protester who was filmed kicking lumps off the Nike sign while wearing Nike shoes see the irony?' For it is in such contradictory relationships with the global political economy that we all find ourselves (2004: 106).

Dissolving the contradictions and ambiguities of global protest is not just a conceptual weakness of civil society theory, but it is politically problematic. Mostly, finding commonalities in diverse movements and practices of opposition is held out as the road to political strength (Cox 1999; Monbiot 2003). However, eliminating ambiguity in favour of unity can also be interpreted as a political weakness. First, reducing the multiplicity of possible refusals and resistances to a single force or movement can be seen as an exclusionary political project in itself. Civil society organizations, Scholte notes rightly, are not always democratic organizations themselves, and they 'may purport to speak on behalf of certain constituencies without adequately consulting them' (2002: 28). Put differently, global protest movements may be dominated by elite participants who have access to networks of communication and travel but who nonetheless claim to speak for a disenfranchised mass. The danger becomes, according to Pasha and Blaney, that 'the vision of Global Civil Society itself . . . appears as a hegemonic project; as the imposition of a particular norm of civility in the name of global values and democracy' (1998: 435). Without outrightly rejecting existing proposals for reform, these criticisms suggest that it may not always be desirable to transform a plurality of protest into a unity of programme.

Second, ambiguity, laughter and *making strange* can be important political practices *in their own right*, which may not add up to a revolutionary politics of global change, but may constitute important transformations of people's experiences of money and finance. According to Bleiker, dissent is too often understood 'in romantic and masculine terms, as heroic rebellions against authority, exemplified by demonstrating masses, striking workers, brick-throwing students and fasting dissidents' (2000: 256). For Bleiker, however, dissent can work more slowly, more insidiously but also ambiguously, for example, through poetry and other practices of discursive dissent. In the place of the heroic act or singular programme against domination, it is possible to observe manifold discursive practices that transform and challenge dominant discourses and create space for alternative imaginations.

The practice of criticism, according to Michel Foucault, begins by denaturalizing, or *making strange*, political practices that appear as natural or common sense. Criticism, writes Foucault, 'is a matter of pointing out on what kinds of assumptions, what kinds of familiar, unchallenged, unconsidered modes of thought the practices that we accept rest' (1988: 154). It is in this way that space for transformation and the imagination of alternatives is opened, according to Foucault. '[A]s soon as one can no longer think things as one formerly thought them, transformation becomes both very urgent, very difficult and quite possible', Foucault continues, '[i]t not therefore a question of there being a time for criticism and a time for transformation' (ibid.: 155). In other words, social transformation does not need necessarily critique *first*, and the development of effective political programmes second, but requires 'a *permanent* criticism' or 'making strange' (ibid., emphasis added).

Comedy and carnival can be important ways of practising *financial* criticism precisely because the authority and legitimacy of financial practices is underpinned by their rationality and differentiation from emotion. When in the 18th and 19th centuries the emerging *Bourses* were accused of being little more than gambling houses, and thus morally and socially corrupt, defenders of the

Bourses argued that the new credit practices provided security in the face of the uncertain business future through the rational calculation and hedging of future scenarios (de Goede 2004). Graphical and statistical methods, borrowed from physics, contributed to the image of scientific objectivity of financial practices and rendered possible their legal and moral — albeit unstable — separation from gambling (cf. Poovey 1998; Preda 2001). In this sense, financial discourse is profoundly *modern*, influenced by an Enlightenment thinking which sought to effect 'the disenchantment of the world; the dissolution of myths and the substitution of knowledge for fancy' (Adorno and Horkheimer quoted in Odysseos 2001: 709). The comical narrative lost its political function and educative role in Enlightenment society, and, according to Bakhtin, joking became relegated to the private sphere because '[t]hat which is important and essential cannot be comical' (1968: 67).

Because the calculative rationality of finance is not a logical corollary of its practices, but a conscious political move to foster its moral legitimacy, the disturbance of this rationality, through jokes or gambling, can form a threat to its existence. Indeed, precisely *because* in the modern worldview the important cannot be comical, it became crucial for financial institutions — attacked in pamphlets, poems and plays — to assert their seriousness with the help of the scientific method. Laughter, then, is more than a superficial attack or helpless gesture in the face of the power of financial institutions: it has a potential to shake the discursive foundations of modern financial rationality. 'Comedy', Odysseos writes, 'highlights the limits of rational discourse . . . it allows critical reflection to render the commonplace strange' (2001: 730). Comedy and carnival — by virtue of being both emotive and populist — have the potential to 'make strange' the unquestioned rationality of money and finance.

Carnival is characterized by a reversal of the 'normal' social order and an atmosphere of licentiousness during which prohibitions are challenged. 'What is most interesting about carnival', writes Scott, 'is the way it allows certain things to be said, certain forms of social power to be exercised that are muted or suppressed outside this social sphere' (1990: 173). Carnival moreover involves the appropriation of, for example, symbols, clothes and language by those to whom these practices are normally barred — cross-dressing and the adornments of Prince Carnival being traditional examples.

But these festive appropriations of the symbols and practices of power can have important political meanings. According to Scott, they 'play an important imaginative function . . . They . . . create an imaginative breathing space in which the normal categories of order and hierarchy seem less than completely inevitable' (1990: 168).

According to Appadurai, moreover, festive appropriations of dominant practices can contribute to more democratic and inclusive forms of dissent than what he calls 'the politics of charity, training and projectisation' (2002: 43). Appadurai discusses the housing and toilet festivals organized by a slum dwellers' coalition in Mumbai (Bombay) as both a 'creative hijacking of an upper-class form' and as a way in which slum dwellers' own knowledge and expertise to build 'adequate housing out of the flimsiest of materials and in the most insecure of circumstances' became visible (ibid.: 37). The slum dwellers alliance theorized by Appadurai has an explicitly 'populist and anti-expert . . . strategy and flavour' and is committed to building on 'what poor persons already know and understand' (ibid.: 28). Anti-expert dissent is of crucial importance to financial politics, where non-experts are easily disqualified, while experts tend to share similar assumptions about the nature of the financial system (even if they do not always agree on policy proposals) (see de Goede 2005, chapter 1). In financial politics, the Jubilee 2000 coalition campaigning for debt relief has most notably called for a popularization of financial knowledge. Jubilee's policies were anti-expert and according to campaign President Ann Pettifor '*all* can understand and grapple with supposedly complex financial matters' (Barrett 2000, emphasis added).

Through carnivalesque dissent, the contingency and vulnerability of financial power may be exposed — in contrast to the serious and expert demeanour that underpins financial exclusion. Such dissent moreover enables a different conception of *agency* than prevalent in calls for programmatic resistance. In Monbiot's world order, for example, one *either* belongs to the elite *or* the disenfranchised, one either governs from the institutions of global, capitalism or articulates alternative — but consistent — programmes, one either profits from capital's power or is swallowed up by it. There is little space, as Amoore and Langley (2004) point out, to consider the many contradictions of the global political economy within which we all find ourselves. In carnivalesque politics, the figure of

Capital itself — and the divisions it gives rise to — appears much less stable and secure: its rationality is laughed at, its power is disturbed and the contradictions within the global political economy become apparent (cf. Gibson-Graham 1996). In the examples that follow, we encounter a financial advisor who jokes with investment practice; a group of artists who appropriate financial discourse; a rural carnival that laughs at its money but still uses it. These agents neither *can* nor *wish* to overthrow global Capital; however, they disturb the assumed unity of capital, question its rationality, and reappropriate its language.

Appropriating the Images and Rituals of Money

There are numerous examples of the appropriation of money and financial symbols in art and carnival: Agnew, for example, documents that medieval carnival was a marketplace festival in which 'mock coinage passed from hand to hand' (1986: 35). Money itself provides a rich canvas for political dissent, precisely because of the icons of state, religion and authority that are portrayed on paper money (Goux 1999). On the one hand, the images of authority and national greatness which, at least since the 19th century, circulate on paper money are a way of educating the masses in the national history and, according to one 19th-century US government official, 'imbuing them with a National feeling' (quoted in Helleiner 2003: 106). On the other hand, these images of authority are precisely the way in which the value and reliability of the note are communicated and even generated (Goggin 2003; Shell 1999). Thus, the imagery on paper money can be understood as not just an adornment of pre-existing value, but the *very way* in which modern monetary value emerges. The iconography of paper money, according to Goggin, is 'universally recognised yet overlooked' in everyday life (2003: 273).

Precisely because the functioning of paper money in everyday life depends upon a forgetting of its contestability, the iconography of paper money is an important site for financial dissent. As lawyer Stapel (1995) argues in her examination of the legal conflict between US counterfeiting law and the First Amendment, the 'tremendous symbolic value' of the image of money in general and the American dollar bill in particular makes it 'a rich symbol in the vocabulary of those seeking to express thoughts lying at the heart of the First Amendment's protection'. That making fun of money and the appropriation of its iconography and rituals are important sites of financial dissent is underlined by the monetary authorities' often harsh reactions to money art, as for instance in their persecution of 19th-century *trompe d'oeil* painters who worked with images of money (Wenschler 1999: 85–91). Stapel concludes that US counterfeiting law is used regularly for pursuing those whose money paintings do *not* have the intention to defraud (1995: 13). Thus counterfeiting law can be seen as having less to do with the state's desire to maintain the currency's buying power, and more with its desire to maintain 'control over the currency's image'.

It is the very *circulation* of currency that gives defacing or reappropriating money its political potential, according to Wambui Mwangi's study of the iconography of East African colonial money. This iconography included a depiction of a lion in an empty, wild African landscape, until — to the horror of the British rulers — a five shilling note was signalled with the words 'Mau Mau Very Good' scrawled upon it. According to Mwangi, the anxiety of the British was less to do with the question whether banks would still accept the note — as was argued by one British official — and more to do with fear that 'this five-shilling note, and possibly countless others like it, all inscribed with "Mau Mau" propaganda, were circulating freely among the Africans' (Mwangi 2002: 49). The Mau Mau insurrection in Kenya appropriated not just the colonial currency to spread its political message, but also translated Christian songs and parables in ways that gave them new, subversive meanings, which, according to one British official, were nonetheless 'so cleverly worded that it would be impossible to prove in a court of law that this was their meaning used' (ibid.: 51). In the case of the symbols on paper money, Mwangi concludes, '[t]he Mau Mau had put Africans back into the empty landscape'(2002: 49). The reappropriation of the (cultural) symbols of power is a carnivalesque form of dissent — not just because it can be funny, but also because it is based on a 'ritual of reversal' in which subordinate groups use the language, symbols and songs that *are not theirs to use* (Scott 1990).

A recent example of the reappropriation of money — which straddles the divide between dissent and counterfeiting — is a $200 bill featuring a smiling President Bush which was successfully used to pay for groceries in Kentucky in January 2001.[1] This 'Moral Reserve Note' (instead of Federal Reserve Note) has replaced the seal of the Federal Reserve System with the words 'The Right to Bear Arms', and depicts a number of protest signs on the White House lawn, including an image of an oil crane and the slogan 'No More Scandals'. Another sign on the lawn reads 'We like Broccoli', apparently a reference to George Bush Sr.'s profound dislike of the vegetable (BBC 2001). The combination of amusing alternative symbols on the note can be read as a political commentary on the Bush government's close connections to the oil industry and the arms lobby. The note draws the image of money into the moral domain, and provides a funny but ambiguous voice of dissent. The bill moreover managed to skirt the counterfeiting issue in a comical way. 'Because there is no $200 bill', a Kentucky police detective told the BBC (2001), 'the perpetrator is likely to face a charge of theft by deception, but not counterfeiting'.

An artist who has not only redesigned money for more than 20 years, but whose performances open questions of value and faith in paper money on an every day level is JSG Boggs. Boggs never sells his painted banknotes to collectors, but spends them in 'proper' economic transactions, where he asks people — waiters, hotel managers, shop assistants — to accept his art notes instead of banknotes and to give him the correct change and receipts for the transactions. By doing so, Boggs provokes a moment of thought in naturalized economic practices: according to journalist Wenschler, he 'is engaged in philosophical disruptions, in provoking brief, momentary tears in the ordinarily seamless fabric of taken-for-granted mundanity' (1999: 49). One of Boggs' most striking bills is the 1999 Josie bill. On it, the traditional monetary iconography of a figure of authority — usually a (male) head of state or a (male) nationally renowned artist — has been replaced by the portrait of a young girl. If the portrait of the elder statesmen can be seen as a way of infusing the bill with authority and projecting its reliability, the Josie bill effects a complete reversal of the masculine discourse of value and authority. Boggs has furthermore replaced the words on the 'Federal Reserve Bank of America' seal with the words 'Fedreal Reverse Kunstbank' and he reverses the ownership of the note's iconography by replacing the words 'this note is legal tender' with the words 'this note is legal art so keep your sticky fingers off!' The latter is important in the context of Boggs' ongoing legal battles with the Federal Reserve, which in 1992 confiscated a number of his works on charges of counterfeiting.

Appropriating the images and rituals of money in a way that causes both questions and laughter on an everyday level, is also at the heart of the work of British-based art group *foreign investment*. The performances of *foreign investment* play with the corporate language, image and dress code, partly in order to challenge the commercialization of the art world which transforms the art object and the image of the individual artist into investment tools. *Foreign investment*, according to its press release, 'devises and sets up performances in public places which involve the passer-by in familiar, unfamiliar and almost familiar exchange'. The performances of *foreign investment* include carefully staged rituals, which accord new value to everyday objects — eggs, nuts, objects that visitors find in their pockets — by submitting them to the capitalist practices of measuring, weighing, registering, transcribing and, in one show, gilding. These performances on the one hand make visible and demystify the capitalist rituals, but on the other hand seek to accord value to things that are not generally valued in late-modern capitalist practices. 'It's not adding value, but it's making visible an inherent value of these things', one *foreign investment* member explains of a show involving the re-importation of Brazil nuts (packaged in the West) into Brazil and their weighing, measuring and gilding.[2] *Foreign investment*'s business-like objectives, such as the realization of the 'eggsess dividend' in the Breeding show, and the slogans in its *operational review* ('providing tomorrow's solutions today' and 'spontaneity cannot be underestimated. It is a vital part of our work and therefore executed with meticulous care') moreover ridicule the corporate language, while making us think twice about its actual content. As one *foreign investment* member explains: 'it's a kind of interference, like almost sending another wavelength into a certain jargon . . . Appropriation is always getting hold of something which is threatening to get hold of you'.[3]

One performance by *foreign investment* which is of particular relevance to the argument developed here is its 1998 *Laughing Stock Exchange*. This performance incorporates the elements of appropriating and ridiculing financial language and rituals, while according new value to the ephemeral object of jokes. 'Your joke and your laughter are an important contribution to the archive of laughter and jokes for the generations of the coming millennium', a flyer for the *laughing stock exchange* reads, 'visit us at the laughing stock exchange and trade in your laughter/all you need is a joke'. The show invited people to tell their jokes or listen to pre-recorded jokes, while members of *foreign investment* recorded both jokes and laughter. The staging of the show was very formal, offering a ritual involving headphones, a choice of languages, recording equipment and transcription of the jokes, which turned the joke into a commercialized product. Thus, the *laughing stock exchange* played with the way in which abstract notions of value and security (in the form of stocks, options, futures) are turned into objects to be traded on financial exchanges. As one member of *foreign investment* explained:

> It was yet another quasi-ephemeral product we were using . . . [J]okes and laughter are a kind of currency that passes around people, and somehow don't belong to anyone. They are being retold, and appear throughout different languages, and there's no-one who actually made them. The interesting thing is, can you tell them well, at this moment in time? Can you remember them and tell them well?[4]

The idea of jokes and laughter being a precious resource for the future which needs to be carefully collected, taped and stored, however, is the anathema of the logic of financial exchange, whose risk-trading, I argued, *depends upon* its differentiation from irrationality and comedy. The particular setting of the *laughing stock exchange*, which invited people off the streets of Berlin and Liverpool to participate, moreover confronted an unsuspecting public with questions of ownership and exchange. *Foreign investment*'s shows and products, in its name, make fun of the seriousness of the actual exchanges. More generally, all examples discussed here involve the appropriation of images and discourses of money that are, normally, not for the wider public to use, and the authority of which depends precisely on its possession by experts.

Carnival and April Fool's Day

On 1 April 2000, the respected Dutch investment website iex.nl announced: 'F/Rite Air IPO [Initial Public Offering] Will Be Big Hit'. The press release announced the stock offering of the Californian biotech company F/Rite Air, which had registered patents for the 'ionisation' of normal air with a positive effect on the human nervous system, leading to 'increased physical resistance, stress resistance, and ability to concentrate'. It was further reported that this product was used in secret by fighter pilots of the Israeli army and 'Top Gun squadrons', and that Pfizer could be behind the development of these patents. The report announced that F/Rite Air would be noted on the exchanges with the ticker symbol FRYD, that the share price of the IPO would be $25–28, and that George Soros and Bill Gates had already invested (Kraland 2000a). Within hours, iex.nl received pledges of 15 million Dutch guilders (around €7 million) from interested investors, so eager to grab the chance to invest in F/Rite Air that none of them asked for a company brochure. Later the same day, iex.nl released the message 'Fried Air Offering is Cancelled', explaining:

> We have good and bad news for our dear readers. The bad news is that the April 1 offering of F/Rite Air (pronounced Fried Air), the wondercompany that ionises microwaves, with a euphoric effect surpassing Prozac and Viagra, is cancelled. The reason is that the company does not exist. The good news is that we have collected 15 million guilders in a few hours (Kraland 2000b).

Fried Air — *gebakken lucht* — is Dutch for hot air, and the F/Rite Air April fool's joke provided a sharp and comical critique of the investment climate during the so-called dotcom boom. 'The joke was so obvious, it's unbelievable that people actually went for it', says F/Rite Air inventor and investment manager Michael Kraland, 'it showed how gullible people are. Fear and greed are the driving forces on the exchanges'. According to Kraland, there is not enough fun and laughter on the exchanges and this demeanour of seriousness underlies people's credulity because, wrapped in numbers and statistics, nonsense stories will be believed. 'Only laughter is not yet taxed', concludes Kraland jokingly, 'it has an anti-oxydating effect and is one of the few pleasures that does not make you fat or is bad for the environment'.[5] Although the joke elicited some angry responses from iex.nl readers, it received wide international media attention as a warning against investor optimism during the dotcom boom.

It was no coincidence, then, that F/Rite Air was a Californian-based biotech company, designing products similar to Prozac and Viagra: the story was carefully designed to include the buzz words of the new economy. A second parody of the new economy is the website iTulip.com, launched in 1998 and dedicated to nothing but selling its own stock certificates for US$10 each. iTulip.com defines itself as

> a corporation that relies on the Internet to deliver products or services to its customers at a loss; a. requires private or public capital to maintain unprofitable operations indefinitely; b. raises capital through the public markets to achieve an historically unprecedented market capitalisation induced by the stock performance of similar companies, none of which are profitable.[6]

The site named itself after the famous Dutch 17th-century tulip bubble, and provides accounts of past financial crises juxtaposed with recent quotes of business and government leaders heralding a new age of unprecedented wealth and profit. 'Now you too can enjoy the thrill of owning an uneconomical Internet company's stock certificate without fear of losing all your money', the site announces, '[b]uy an ilulip.com Stock Certificate. Not only does iTulip.com not have any assets, revenues or profits, *it doesn't even exist*. Of course, some Internet companies won't exist either after the Internet stock speculative mania ends'.[7]

These new economy jokes — F/Rite Air and iTulip.com — play with what have been identified as the most important aspects of the new economy, namely the 'extension of the financial audience', through romanticized tales of limitless profit-opportunities and a culture of entrepreneurialism (Thrift 2001: 422). The extension of the financial audience was bound up with an explosion of financial media — magazines, websites, special news-channels — where the new economy story was told by financial analysts and business gurus and affirmed by political leaders. 'Running the new economy story through this financial machine had enormous benefits for a number of actors', writes Thrift, 'it added value to particular shares . . . it proved analysts' worth and made media stars of some of them, it demonstrated the worth of the system as a whole and so on' (2001: 425). It is precisely this connection between the media, the extension of the financial audience and the very real effects on financial entitlements that is subject of the F/Rite Air and the iTulip satires. Both jokes provide sharp commentary on the eagerness and greed of investors; both spoof the culture of financial media and expertise by offering a product for sale that follows the logic of the new economy to absurdity. And just as the dotcom boom has permanently transformed financial practices and entitlements (Feng et al. 2001; Thrift 2001), these jokes maintain their satirical — albeit ambiguous — political message, even though now the bubble is pronounced burst.

Carnivalesque dissent cannot be observed just within the channels of the new economy itself (the internet), but also in the more traditional space of the carnival. In the Wasungen carnival in former East Germany in February 2003, for example, the new European currency proved a rich topic for satire. The introduction of the Euro in European states in 2000 had been preceded by protracted, complex and mystifying negotiations at EU level, largely invisible to the European populations. Two years after its introduction, the Euro came under increasing popular criticism, especially for having made daily life more expensive. Participants in the Wasungen carnival turned the Euro into a comic monster, through images of hell and vultures. 'Zum Teufel mit dem T€uro' ('To hell with the expensive Euro'), one float with a massive papier-mâché devil read (Figure 4.1). The Euro-demon was surrounded by small torches,

Figure 4.1: Euro-devil at Wasungen carnival, Germany, 2003. Photograph by the Author.

a pitchfork and people in costumes with the sun on one side and rain on the other — a comment on the instability of the economic climate. One of the other Euro floats was a massive vulture, surrounded by people in shiny costumes of old German pennies, with the comment 'The €uro trick: Our pennies are being destroyed by the vulture' (Figure 4.2). 'We express what everybody is thinking', says Heiner Kampf, one of the makers of the Euro-floats, 'the Euro makes the poor poorer within the EU, and other values, like ecological values, are forgotten about. We use a kind of black humour to get people to think about these things'.[8]

The significance of Medieval laughter, according to Bakhtin (1968) lies in its 'victory over fear':

> We always find [in Medieval comic images] the defeat of fear presented in a droll and monstrous form, the symbols of power and violence turned inside out . . . All that was terrifying becomes grotesque . . . The people play with terror and laugh at it; *the awesome becomes a comic monster* (ibid.: 91; emphasis added).

The Wasungen carnival provides examples of how the serious but mystifying power of finance is turned into a comic monster. Images

Figure 4.2: Euro-vulture at Wasungen carnival, Germany, 2003. Photograph courtesy of Lorenz Grimm.

of hell, demons and death in carnival rituals, for Bakhtin, were precisely the means through which fear and intimidation could be overcome. The set of hell, which was a traditional part of the Medieval carnival, 'was solemnly burned at the peak of the festivities' (ibid.). In financial discourse, the association between money and the devil moreover is a historically important one, from medieval prohibitions on usury — making interest and speculation the work of the devil — to the way in which critics made sense of 'devilish' credit money (Shell 1995: 63–72). The incomprehensible and at times unreliable magic of credit-creation gave rise to a whole series of money-devils which were used to make sense of, for example, the tulip bubble in Holland and the 1720 Mississippi bubble in France. The Euro devil of the Wasungen carnival then, has a long historical lineage while providing a rare popular and comical comment on the highly technical and depoliticized Euro debate. This carnivalesque critique of the new European currency provokes thought on an everyday level, and opens space for alternative imaginations.

Conclusions: Carnival through the Year

Clearly, neither laughter nor irony are inherent forces for good. Bakhtin's enthusiasms for 'images of the material bodily lower stratum', as Bleiker points out, 'never touches upon the issue of gender relations and related systems of exclusion. He never asks *who laughs at whom* in Rabelais' world' (Bleiker 2000: 205, emphasis added). Still, I argue that joking, laughter and carnival *can be* important politics of dissent in an era when the political legitimacy of financial practices depends upon their rationality and coherence. It is often argued that laughter is either a superficial and helpless gesture in the face of power, or, worse, a safety-valve which allows power to operate by providing insignificant spaces of relief which distract from planning 'real' resistance. 'Bakhtin himself could imply that things were not so bad so long as people laughed and swore, mocked and refused to take things seriously' Hirschkop writes for example, 'but . . . laughter and festivity in themselves do not make for fearless people' (1999: 291).

Scott, however, strongly opposes the reading of carnival as a practice which 'harmlessly drains away social tensions that might otherwise become dangerous to the existing social order' (1990: 168). First, Scott argues, it is possible to find ample historical evidence that authorities tried to regulate or suppress carnivalesque practices. 'Why have there been such strenuous attempts to abolish Carnival', Jackson argues similarly in his examination of the Notting Hill carnival in London, 'if it is . . . no more than harmless release of energy?' (1988: 222). Second, it is important to see how carnival creates spaces for alternative imaginations and, in the words of *foreign investment, interferes* with the dominant discourse — disturbs it and makes it less intimidating. This practice of criticism or 'making strange' questions existing power relationships, and, in Scott's words, make the 'normal categories of order and hierarchy' appear '*less than completely inevitable*' (1990: 168; emphasis added). Or, as one member of *foreign investment* describes her experience of the Rio carnival, 'when you have seen the carnival once, you are able to see it throughout the year in everyday life'.

Practices of joking, carnival and refusing to take seriously are not at all incompatible with a larger scale protest, and mass protests such as in Seattle are often accompanied by a carnival atmosphere and artists' challenges of the dominant discourse. For example, the Stop the War campaign's demonstration against the UK visit of President Bush in November 2003, included besides its main mass demonstration an alternative state procession with a mock queen and a mock president, and an invitation to the public to 'attire themselves in colourful raiment in the manner and style of our Royal Person, our Most Loyal Consort the Duke of Edinburgh, members of Our Government'.[9] However, I argue that current calls for coherent resistance and programmatic reform tend to devalue the politics of 'making strange', which, according to Foucault, are indispensable to criticism and transformation. Highlighting the plurality and ambiguity of dissent can contribute to overcoming the 'fear and hopelessness generated by monolithic accounts of the "neoliberal project"', in which only broad-based counter-hegemonic challenges are considered purposeful (Larner 2003: 512). The political practices of dissent discussed here may not form a consistent counter-hegemonic programme, but they do transform people's experiences of monetary instruments and financial discourses in important ways. They challenge the unity, seriousness and reach of contemporary financial practices and open space for alternative imaginations.

Acknowledgements

The author wishes to thank *foreign investment*, Johannes Artus, Heiner Kampf and Michael Kraland. For comments on earlier versions of this chapter, many thanks to Louise Amoore, Martin Coward, Gunther Irmer, Paul Langley, Kees van der Pijl, Erna Rijsdijk, my 'NGO' colleagues, and participants in the Research-in-Progress seminar at the University of Sussex in November 2003.

Notes

* This chapter first appeared in Louise Amoore (ed.), *The Global Resistance Reader*, London: Routledge, 2005. Reproduced with permission.

1. An image of the bill can be found at http://www.thesmokinggun.com/archive/bushbilll.html (accessed 4 October 2013).
2. Interview, *foreign investment*, Newcastle upon Tyne, 15 September 2003.
3. Interview, *foreign investment*, Newcastle upon Tyne, 15 September 2003.
4. Interview, *foreign investment*, Newcastle upon Tyne, 15 September 2003.
5. Michael Kraland, personal correspondence and telephonic interview, Amsterdam, 7 October 2003.
6. See http://www.itulip.com (accessed 4 October 2013).
7. See http://www.itulip.com/productsnew.htm (accessed 4 October 2013).
8. Heiner Kampf, interview, 29 December 2003, Wasungen, Germany.
9. See http://www.stopwar.org.uk/Resources/altstateproc.pdf (accessed 4 October 2013).

References

Note: All websites mentioned here, as well as those in the endnotes, were last accessed in June 2004.

Agnew, J.-C. 1986. *Worlds Apart: The Market and the Theatre in Anglo-American Thought, 1550–1750*. Cambridge: Cambridge University Press.

Amoore, L. and Langley, P. 2004. 'Ambiguities of Global Civil Society', *Review of International Studies*, 30(1): 89–110.

Appadurai, A. 2002. 'Deep Democracy: Urban Governmentality and the Horizon of Polities', *Public Culture*, 14(1): 21–47.

Bakhtin, M. 1968. *Rabelais and His World*, translated by Helene Iswolsky. Bloomington: Indiana University Press.

Barrett, M. (ed.). 2000. *The World Will Never Be the Same Again*, Jubilee 2000 Coalition, December, http://www.jubilee2000uk.org/analysis/reports/world_never_same_again/contents.htm (accessed 4 October 2013).

BBC. 2001. 'Funny Money in Kentucky', 31 January, http://news.bbc.co.uk/1/hi/world/ americas/1147246.stm (accessed 4 October 2013).

Bleiker, R. 2000. *Popular Dissent, Human Agency and Global Politics*. Cambridge: Cambridge University Press.

Cox, R. W. 1999. 'Civil Society at the Turn of the Millennium: Prospects for an Alternative World Order', *Review of International Studies*, 25(1): 3–28.

de Goede, M. 2004. 'Repoliticizing Financial Risk', *Economy and Society*, 33(2): 197–217.

———. 2005. *Virtue, Fortune and Faith: a Genealogy of Finance*. Minneapolis: University of Minnesota Press.

Feng, H., Froud, J., Johal, S., Haslam, C. and Williams, K. 2001. 'A New Business Model? The Capital Market and the New Economy', *Economy & Society*, 30(4): 467–503.

Foucault, M. 1988 [1981]. 'Practicing Criticism', in L. D. Kritzman (ed.), *Michel Foucault: Politics, Philosophy, Culture, Interviews and Other Writings 1977–1984*. New York: Routledge.

Gibson-Graham, J. K. 1996. *The End of Capitalism (As We Knew It)*. Oxford: Blackwell.

Gill, S. 2000. 'Toward a Postmodern Prince? The Battle of Seattle as a Moment in the New Politics of Globalisation', *Millennium*, 29(1): 131–140.

Goggin, J. 2003. 'Images of Nationhood: Currency Art', in Nancy Pedri (ed.), *Travelling Concepts III: Memory, Narrative, Image*. Amsterdam: ASCA Press.

Goux, J.-J. 1999. 'Gash, Check, or Charge?', in M. Osteen and M. Woodmansee (eds), *The New Economic Criticism: Studies at the Intersection of Literature and Economics*. London: Routledge.

Helleiner, E. 2003. *The Making of National Money: Territorial Currencies in National Perspective*. Ithaca: Cornell University Press.

Hirschkop, K. 1999. *Mikhail Bakhtin: An Aesthetic for Democracy*. Oxford University Press.

Jackson, P. 1988. 'Street Life: The Politics of Carnival', *Environment and Planning D: Society and Space*, 6: 213–27.

Kaldor, M. 2000. 'Civilising Globalisation? The Implications of the Battle of Seattle', *Millennium*, 29(1): 105–14.

Kraland, M. 2000a. 'F.Rite Air IPO Wordt Knaller' ('F/Rite Air IPO will be Big Hit'), http://www.iex.nl/Column/852/F-Rite-Air-IPO-wordt-knaller.aspx (accessed 25 September 2013).

———. 2000b. 'Gebakken Lucht Emissie gaat niet Door' ('Hot Air Offering is Cancelled'), http://iex.nl/columns/columns_artikel.asp7colid=853%20 (accessed 4 October 2013).

Larner, W. 2003. 'Neoliberalism?', *Environment and Planning D: Society and Space*, 21(5): 509–12.

Monbiot, G. 2003. 'Seize the Day', *The Guardian*, 17 June, http://www.monbiot.com/archives/2003/06/17/seize-the-day/ (accessed 18 November 2013).

Mwangi, W. 2002. 'The Lion, the Native and the Coffee Plant: Political Imagery and the Ambiguous Art of Currency Design in Colonial Kenya', *Geopolitics*, 7(1): 31–62.

Odysseos, L. 2001. 'Laughing Matters: Peace, Democracy and the Challenge of the Comic Narrative', *Millennium*, 30(3): 709–32.

Pasha, M. K. and Blaney, D. L. 1998. 'Elusive Paradise? The Promise and Peril of Global Civil Society', *Alternatives*, 23: 417–50.

Poovey, M. 1998. *A History of the Modern Fact: Problems of Knowledge in the Sciences of Wealth and Society*. Chicago: University of Chicago Press.

Preda, A. 2001. 'The Rise of the Popular Investor: Financial Knowledge and Investing in England and France, 1840–1880', *The Sociological Quarterly*, 42(2): 205–32.

Scholte, J.-A. 2002. 'Civil Society and the Governance of Global Finance', in J.-A. Scholte and A. Schnabel (eds), *Civil Society and Global Finance*. London: Routledge.

Scott, J. 1990. *Domination and the Arts of Resistance: Hidden Transcripts*. New Haven: Yale University Press.

Shell, M. 1995. *Art & Money*. Chicago: University of Chicago Press.

Smith, Z. 2003. 'Love, Actually', *Guardian Book Review*, 1 November, pp. 2–4.

Stapel, J. K. 1995. 'Money Talks: The First Amendment Implications for Counterfeiting Law', *Indiana Law Journal*, 71(1).

Thrift, N. 2001. 'It's the Romance, not the Finance, that makes the Business worth Pursuing', *Economy and Society*, 30(4): 412–32.

Wenschler, L. 1999. *Boggs: A Comedy of Values*. Chicago: University of Chicago Press.

5

Globalization and New Politics of Micro-Movements

*D. L. Sheth**

Just when the global discourse on democracy has become unidimensional, purveying the neo-liberal model of market democracy as the only universally desirable model, and when the Indian state has linked itself to the vertical hierarchy of global economic and political power, significant countervailing processes have emerged in the form of political and social movements at the grass roots making new, provincial and national-level alliances aimed at countering the state's policies of globalization. These movements, led by small groups of social activists, have been active in different parts of India for over three decades working on disparate issues, albeit all concerning struggles of the economically marginalized and socially excluded, poorer populations. In the decade of the 1990s, many of them have come together and have joined larger, worldwide alliances and forums protesting against hegemonic policies of the institutions and organizations representing global economic and political power.

In this process of opposition to globalization, the micro-movements have begun to raise a new discourse on democracy and invent political practices, expanding the arena of politics beyond the representational institutions of elections and political parties. Thus, although the micro-movements have been fighting politically on several issues concerning the poor much before they joined the debate on globalization, it is the challenge of globalization that has brought many of them together on common political platforms at the provincial and national levels, making issues of participatory democracy a part of their ongoing struggles. It is in this emergent context of globalization that this chapter analyzes the discourse and politics of micro-movements, and their role in reinventing participatory democracy as a form of social action and political practice, creating new spaces and infusing deeper meaning to democracy in the globalizing world.

I
Movements and Globalization

The micro-movements in India represent a varied and complex phenomenon. They are variously referred to as 'grass roots movements', social movements, non-party political formations, social-action groups and movement-groups. In this chapter I shall use these terms interchangeably but the reference is specifically to a particular genre of social movements which became visible and acquired political salience in the mid-1970s and have since been active on a variety of issues which, in their own perception, are — directly or indirectly — related to what they see as their long-term goal of democratizing development and transforming society (R. Kothari 1984; Sethi 1984; Sheth 1984). These movement organizations differentiate themselves self-consciously and sharply from the welfare, philanthropic and such other non-political NGOs. Although there is no systematic survey, compilations made from different sources by researchers and guesstimates provided by observers in the field suggest a figure in the range of 20–30 thousand such movement groups in the country (Kapoor 2000).

In order to understand the terms in which the movement groups conceive and articulate the idea of participatory democracy, it is important to know the context in which they emerged and the challenges they confronted in the initial phase of their formation. A large number of them existed as fragments of the earlier political and social movements, which had their origins in the freedom movement, but were subdued and dispersed soon after Independence when the liberal, modernist English-educated ruling elite began to dominate public discourse in India. These were the groups which had their lineage in the Gandhian, socialist, communist and social reform movements but, by and large, had stuck out as groups of party-independent social and political activists (Sheth and Sethi 1991). They worked in small, stagnant spaces available to them at the periphery of the electoral party politics. But within three decades of independence, new social and political spaces opened up for them as well as for several new groups of social activists.

This became possible, ironically, with the decline of institutional politics, which began in the late 1960s, giving rise to several mass-based movements of protests (R. Kothari 1988b). The issues of protests varied from price-rise to corruption. The protest movements, however, acquired a big momentum in mid-1970s, the largest and politically most high-intensity movement among them being the one led by Jayaprakash Narayan (popularly known as the JP movement). Seen in this context, what we recognize today as movement-groups emerged and were consolidated in spaces made available to them by the decline of mainstream institutions of representative democracy: the legislatures, elections, political parties and trade unions (R. Kothari 1988; Sheth 1983). Although the decline had begun in the late 1960s, it became visible when the Emergency was imposed (1975–77) by Indira Gandhi (R. Kothari 1989; Sheth 1991).

An important, if unanticipated, consequence of the decline of institutional politics was the revitalization of old social movements, with some of them aiming their politics directly against the Emergency regime. The anti-Emergency movements gave rise, especially in the period between the mid-1970s and 1980s, to thousands of new *micro*-movements in the country. These movements were led by young men and women, quite a few of whom left their professional careers to join them. They took up issues and constituencies abandoned by political parties and trade unions, and those ill-served by the bureaucracy. The organizational form they evolved for themselves was not of a political party or a pressure group. It was that of a civil-associational group, leading political struggles on issues articulated to them by the people themselves. The key concept they worked with was democratizing development through empowerment of the people (Sethi 1984).

Discourse of Globalization

In the early 1990s, the grass roots movements confronted an entirely new set of terms justifying the hegemony of the newly established post-Cold War global order. Earlier, till the end of the Cold War, a significant section of grass roots movements in India were active in protesting against the exclusionary, elite-oriented development model that was conceived and sought to be made uniformly and universally applicable the world over, by the post-Second World War Bretton Woods institutions and their sponsor countries.

These protests were, however, articulated largely in the context of the discourse developed by new social movements in the West where the nuclear and environmental threats produced by the Cold War were more poignantly felt. It was through this process that the idea and the campaign for 'alternative development' grew in the West. Although this idea had been propagated and practised in India for long by Gandhian activists, after Independence it was marginalized within the development discourse dominated by India's modernist ruling elite.

The whole discourse on development suddenly changed, globally and in India, when the notion of alternative development was analytically formulated and propagated by the various global groups, clubs and commissions. Some concepts developed by these proponents of alternative development became buzzwords for activists of new social movements: appropriate technology, small is beautiful (à la Schumacher), pedagogy of the oppressed (à la Paulo Freire), eco-friendly lifestyles, limits to growth (à la the Club of Rome) were only a few among them. This discourse of the new social movements in the West found a great deal of resonance among the social activists in India — particularly for the apolitical, Westernized ones, for whom it had almost an emancipatory effect. It gave cultural meaning to their activism and even helped them re-discover their own alternativist M. K. Gandhi.

The idea of alternative development found new votaries even in the consumerist core of Western societies during the Cold War, when the threat of nuclear holocaust loomed large and access to the world's fossil-oil resources was threatened by what was then described as the 'oil crisis'. Concerns were expressed on world policy forums about 'third world poverty'. Strange though it may seem today, deep anxieties were felt and expressed about the growing consumption habits of the middle classes in these countries. For, it was feared that combined with the hunger and poverty of their masses, they may lead to state policies resulting in rapid depletion of the world's natural resources. The conventional argument for development was now made with several caveats, sourced from the theory of alternative development. Thus, sustainability became a key word and consumerism a 'challenge' to cope with. Saving energy and finding alternative energy sources became an important consideration for policy-makers of development.

All this changed as the Cold War ended, affecting a big rupture in the (global) politics of discourse. And this, when the idea of alternative development was just about acquiring wider acceptability and had begun to inform policy processes at the national and global levels. A new discourse descended on the scene engulfing the political spaces, which the new social movements in the West and the grass roots movements in India had created for themselves through working for decades on such issues as peace, and pro-poor, eco-friendly development. The new discourse made its entry rather dramatically as a triumphalist grand-narrative that, among other things, subsumed within it the old idea of development (Wallgren 1998). Its immediate, if temporary, effect was to make protests of the grass roots movements against the hegemonic Cold War model of development and their assertions for alternative development sound shrill and cantankerous, if not vacuous.

This was the discourse of globalization. Conceived and led by the victors of the Cold War, it claimed to establish a new global order which would put an end to the old one that had kept the world 'divided' — economically, culturally and politically. In its place it not just promised, but communicated a virtual experience (as if that world was upon us!) of the world becoming *one* economy, (possibly) *one* culture and (eventually) *one* polity! Such a world could do, globally, without the messy institutions of representational democracy, even as such institutions were to be made mandatory internally for every individual country. It assured that this new global order would be managed by a set of global institutions (served by experts and freed from the cumbersome procedures of representational accountability), which, being set up and controlled by the world's few 'self-responsible' and 'advanced' democracies, would guarantee peace and order to the whole world. Moreover, since the monopoly of violence (including its technology) will be withdrawn from a large number of individual and often 'irresponsible' nation-states (whose natural location is in the south) and be placed collectively in the hands of a few nation-states, which also are 'responsible' and 'civilized' democracies (whose natural location is of course in the north), it not only will eliminate international wars, but alleviate poverty wherever it exists. These outlandish ideological claims of globalization made and propagated globally by the world's most powerful (G-8) countries have been lapped up by large sections of the Indian middle class and the media, as if they represented a policy package offered by some really existing and democratically legitimate World Government.

Counter Discourse of Movements

The grass roots movements took quite some time to recover from the ideological onslaught of globalism and devise their own terms of discourse to counter it. This was mainly because by the end of the Cold War and two decades after the Emergency, the movement-groups were by and large fragmented into an almost isomorphic existence of each group fighting its own little battle independently. Quite a few had lost the élan of social transformation, having acquired a fairly stable and comfortable financial base. Much larger quantities of funds were now made available to them by the international donor agencies which had their own agenda for influencing the politics of discourse in peripheral countries. Most movement-groups had thus become routinized in their activities and functioned as NGO bureaucracies. In short, in the early 1990s, the mood among grass roots movements in India was marked by widespread pessimism among the observers and participants of the movements (R. Kothari 1993). There were indeed some groups, largely of Gandhian, Left and social-democratic lineage, who stuck out and kept fighting their battles for rights and socio-economic reconstruction at the grass roots, thus tenaciously retaining their character as movements. They however did not function at their earlier high levels of energy, and remained starved of funds

All this changed, almost suddenly in the mid-1990s when protests against globalization led by the few movement-groups, which had kept the tradition of struggles alive during the period of drift, acquired momentum, as different sections of the poor in India began to acutely feel globalization's adverse impact. It got a big fillip as many more groups responding to the pressures at the grass roots, returned from their NGO existence to the fold of movements. This produced a high degree of convergence among different types of groups and movements on a wide range of issues concerning globalization. It revitalized the entire spectrum of grass roots movements in the country, giving rise to a new discourse *and* politics aimed at countering the forces of hegemonic globalization (S. Kothari 2001; Sheth 1999) What follows is an account of terms in which the movements view and resist globalization.[1]

First, activists of grass roots movements see globalization as an incarnation of the old idea of Development, but representing politically more explicitly, the institutions of global hegemonic power and creating new forms of exclusion socially. Globalization thus has intensified and expanded the destructive forces of Development — forces which disrupt communities, cultures and livelihoods of the poor without offering them any viable and dignified alternative. Similarly, globalization, like the Development establishment during the Cold War, works for the constituent elements of its power structure — the techno-scientific, bureaucratic, military, and managerial and business elites and a small consumerist class.

Second, a section of social activists, and those who were relatively apolitical but active in alternative development movements earlier, have become acutely aware of the role that politics of discourse plays globally and nationally, in influencing policy choices of governments and international organizations. Consequently, some of them now are participating actively in shaping the terms of discourse globally on such issues as biodiversity, global warming and construction of big dams, regulations concerning international trade and intellectual property rights, and so on. In this process, they have become active in a variety of global 'conventions', forums and campaigns opposing the policies of the global power structure as well as in building more durable trans-national alliances with similar movements in other countries, both in the south and the north. In performing this 'global role' they often explicitly articulate their long-term objective in terms of building and sustaining institutional processes for global solidarity. Put differently, their aim is to create global politics of popular (civil society) movements with a view to building an alternative institutional structure of global governance, based on democratic principles of political equality, social justice, cultural diversity and non-violence, and ecological principles of sustainability and maintaining biodiversity (Sheth et al. 2002). Leading this discourse globally, a group of Indian activists interpret global solidarity in terms of the ancient Indian principle of *vasudhaiva kutumbakam* (Earth as one family) and link it to Gandhi's vision of *swaraj* (self-governance) and *swadeshi* (politics of establishing peoples' own control over their environment — economic, social and cultural) (Pratap 2001). It is in this context that the movements differentiate between the two types of politics they engage in: politics of establishing global solidarity and of opposing contemporary globalization, a distinction that has been conceptually aptly captured by Boaventura de-Souza Santos as the hegemonic vs counter hegemonic globalization (Santos 1997).

Third, another type of movements, representing largely the Left and social democratic strands referred to earlier, see globalization as intensifying further the already existing economic and social inequalities in the country (Sainath 2000). Thus while the votaries of globalization celebrate the growth of the middle class, the social activists see this phenomenon quite differently. In their view the programmes of economic reforms being implemented as a part of globalization package, have consolidated and enriched the old middle class. The 'growth' of this class, in their view, largely represents the rise in the purchasing power of the small middle class that emerged during the colonial rule and expanded during the initial four decades after Independence, covering largely the upper and middle strata of the traditional social structure. The structural adjustment programmes (SAP), implemented in the name of economic reforms — the recipe dispensed by the global financial institutions across the world — far from improving living standards of the poor, have pushed them further down the social and economic ladder, and below the poverty line (Kumar 2000). Indeed some fragments of the traditional lower social strata have entered the 'middle class', but this has been due to the long existing social policies of the state — like affirmative action. In fact, with the state shrinking in the process of globalization, there has been a reversal of this process.

The few avenues of upward mobility that the policies of the Indian state had opened up for the disadvantageously located populations in the traditional social structure are now narrowing. The market is increasingly becoming the only avenue for upward mobility, and that too is monopolized by the upper strata of caste society, using their traditional status resources. Thus economic globalization offers ever rising standards of living to those entering the market with some entitlements usually available to members of upper castes, given their resources: land, wealth, social privilege and education. For large segments of the population outside the charmed circle of the market, and disadvantageously located in the traditional structure, it means malnutrition, semi-starvation, disease and destitution. This relationship of the traditional social structure and globalization is emphasized by the movements but is, strangely, ignored in the academic debates on globalization.

The movement activists thus find it astounding that colonial-type exploitation of primary producers (the vast populations of tribals, artisans, small and marginal farmers and landless labour) by a small urban-industrial elite, and their cognate groups of upper caste rural elite persists, even thrives, in the so-called open economy of the market. In brief, in India the market-economy, instead of making a dent on the iniquitous social structure is being absorbed by it.

Fourth, the movements reject the claim of the Indian state that in the process of globalization, it has been playing a positive role for the poor, giving a 'human face' to economic reforms. Far from enabling the poor to enter and find places in the market, the state undermines their rights to hold on to whatever sources of livelihood that are still available to them. In the view of leaders of some urban movements for citizen rights, the Indian state, in fact, systematically and blatantly discriminates between the rich and the poor in the implementation of economic reforms (Kishwar 2001a). The result is a vast population affected adversely by the market-led model of economic globalization is today unable to make a forceful enough demand in mainstream politics for their survival, let alone 'development'. As the market moves from the fringes of the polity to its centre, democratically conceived political authority is giving way to new notions of economic and political 'order' that are being derived from principles of corporate organization, which by their very nature are not in accord with the democratic principle of representative accountability.

Fifth, the combined impact of the retreat of the state and the globalizing economy is that the poorest among the poor are neither able to become full wage-earners in the economy nor even full-fledged citizens in the polity. For them there is no transitional pathway in sight that can lead them into the market. Nor can they return to the old security of the subjugated, which they arguably had in the traditional social order. They have even lost the claims on the state which the bureaucratic-socialist state at least theoretically conceded. In short, the social-systemic nature of their exclusion continues under globalization as it did under development. State policies which, until recently, aimed at removing the structural barriers facing the poor and bringing them into the mainstream of political economy are now being discarded as 'market-unfriendly'.

Finally, the new ideology of globalization has, in the view of the movements, made issues of poverty and social deprivation in the peripheral countries of the world ever more unintelligible in the global discourse. Even more, it has blunted the transformative edge of the new social movements, which were once (when they really were new) in the forefront of the alternative development movement in the West as well as globally. In effect, the agencies of hegemonic globalization have been able to produce new terms of justification for the old development project, i.e., of retaining the political and economic hegemony of the few rich and militarily powerful countries globally and of a small metropolitan elite within the country. The result is, today, unlike during the Cold War, development is seen and measured in terms of the extent to which a country can 'integrate' (read subjugate) its economy to the world economic (capitalist) system.

Global Discourse of Protests

A significant shift has also occurred in the way the movements in India relate to the global discourse of protests. The increasing focus on issues of 'governance' in the current global discourse has in their view, reduced the importance of issues pertaining to social and political transformation. This has resulted in the agencies of hegemonic globalization seeking, simultaneously, to depoliticize development and undermine democratic movements by co-opting, financially and politically, some protest movements in the developing countries and in the global arena. In the process such issues as environment, gender, human rights and even democracy are being redefined in terms radically different from those that were developed by the grass roots movements in the earlier paradigm of alternative development. For example, the issue of environment is no longer seen as one involving a political process (and movements) for reorganizing the economy and social cultural life locally and globally on the basis of primary ecological principles. Instead, ecological issues are being recast in constantly shifting terms of 'tolerable limits' and 'admissible costs' of environmental damage that is expected to occur increasingly in higher proportions with escalating rates of economic growth — which also are expected and considered desirable. If any 'politics' is involved in this redefinition, it is about transferring environmental costs from one sector of the economy to the other or, even worse, from one region of the world to the other.

The issue of human rights is being viewed in terms of economic and foreign policy considerations of the rich and powerful countries. These considerations pertain not only to establishing their oligopolistic rule over the world, but also to guaranteeing 'smooth' functioning of the multinational corporations in the peripheral countries. This is sought to be achieved by compelling governments of the peripheral countries to yield to conditions and terms the MNCs dictate and think are necessary for such functioning. In the process the multinationals have emerged as powerful global actors, often more powerful and wealthy than many nation-states, which often undermine fundamental human rights (rights to livelihood, habitat and culture) of the poor in peripheral countries, but remain unaccountable to any agency of global governance or a nation-state.

Even some 'international' human rights groups today seem to act as political pressure groups on behalf of the hegemonic global forces, seeking to prevent the peripheral countries from making certain policy choices in areas such as land-use, labour legislation, exports and so on. Although this is done in the name of universalizing human rights, selectivity of issues and the targeting of particular countries often betray their particularistic nationalist (Western) bias. In this new hegemonic discourse the thinking on human rights has been dissociated from concerns like removing poverty, fulfilling basic human needs a social justice. Poverty is increasingly seen as the poor people's own failure in creating wealth, not as an issue of rights of the poor. It is no longer seen as a moral issue. In other words, the global discourse on human rights has ceased to be a discourse regarding social and political transformations; it has, instead, become a discourse about possible conditions that the powerful, 'developed' countries can impose over other countries, ostensibly for bringing about a global-legal regime of rights.

In this discourse on rights it is conveniently assumed that the institutions of global civil society endowing global citizenship (political equality) to all, and the mechanisms of global governance ensuring accountability of transnational organizations and the rule of law in international behaviour, have already evolved and are *in situ*! Such an assumption has made it easy for the global hegemonic powers to target some poor, peripheral countries 'not playing ball' with them for human rights violations, even as they ignore similar violations by governments of the countries pliable to their hegemonic designs. It is a measure of their dominance over the global culture of protests that despite practising such double standards, the global hegemonic powers are able to claim 'commitment' to universalization of human rights and, at the same time keeping transnational corporations outside the pale of the global human rights regime.

In the discourse on democracy, the idea of global governance is gaining ground but, paradoxically, democracy still continues to be viewed as the framework suitable for internal governance of nation-states and not for global governance. Hence it is not difficult for an organization like the WTO to function without reference to any principle of transparency or representational accountability, and also autonomously of the United Nations institutions, even when it sits in judgment on issues that fall in the purview of international law and representative bodies such as the ILO. The institutions of global governance are thus supposed to be self-responsible, not accountable outside their own ambit. They are 'accountable' only to their sponsors who are often the few militarily and economically powerful nation-states.

In the global feminist discourse, sensitivity about the social structural, economic and cultural complexities faced by women in poor countries in securing their rights has vastly receded; in its place the legalist and metropolitan concerns about women's rights in a consumerist society have acquired prominence. Thus, grass roots activists have come to believe that hegemonic globalization is bent upon monopolizing the global discourse of protests, with a view to legitimizing the hegemonic global order and undermining the processes of social and political transformations.

In this globally homogenized culture of protests some movement-groups in India find it increasingly difficult to join international campaigns, even though they may share many of their concerns. To them, such campaigns often seek to undermine the country's national sovereignty and, in their global articulation of issues, show insensitivity to the historical and cultural contexts in which the issues are embedded. As a result, these groups often even refrain from articulating their opposition to the Indian state in terms and forms which, in their view, may delegitimize the role of the state in society. This is done not so much for 'nationalist' considerations as for the fear that it would undermine the by-now established democratic political authority of the state in protecting the secular and democratic institutions in the country. In short, movements-activists in India view globalization as a new, post-Cold War ideology justifying the rule of a hegemonic structure of global power seeking to establish monopoly of a few powerful countries over resources of the whole world. As such, they find globalization to be inimical to basic democratic and ecological values: liberty, equality, diversity, and sustainability. To them, its impact on poorer countries has been to produce new and more dehumanized forms of exclusion and inequality — worse than those created by the Cold War development model, or even by the colonial rule. They are particularly concerned about its adverse impact on democracy in India. For, when the poorer classes have found long-term stake in democracy and have begun to acquire their due share in governance, the power of the state (elected governments) itself is being denuded and undermined by the global power structure in collaboration with the country's metropolitan elites. In other words, they see globalization as undermining and delegitimizing institutions of democratic governance. They see it as a force which seeks to undo India's democratic revolution.

II
New Politics of Movements

Based on such an assessment of globalization's adverse impact both for development and democracy, grass roots movements conceive their politics in the direction of achieving two interrelated goals: (*a*) re-politicizing development and (*b*) reinventing participatory democracy.

Re-Politicizing Development

The main effort of the movements today is to keep the debate on development alive, but to recast it in terms which can effectively counter global and national structures of power. They are thus formulating old issues of development in new political terms, although their objective remains the same as before, namely, those at the bottom of the pile find their rightful place as producers in the economy and citizens in the polity. Accordingly, they now view development as a political struggle for peoples' participation in defining development goals and devising means to achieve them. Their view of development is thus a non-hegemonic, pluralistic process, in articulating which they use inductively arrived insights and criteria evolved through their own struggles. In this process they increasingly relate the globally debated issues such as feminism, ecology and human rights to the economic, social and cultural specificities of India in which these issues are embedded. Consequently, their politics is about making development a bottom-upward process, directly relevant to and an edifying experience for the poor and the oppressed. Thus, rather than altogether 'opting out' of development they now seek to change the power relations on which the conventional model of development is premised. In the process some new elements, essentially political in nature, have entered in the grass roots movements' thinking and practice of development.

First, the old post-colonial critique of development which invoked pre-modern nostalgia has ceased to appeal to a large section of these movements. Although that kind of critique still remains a hobby-horse of some esoteric activist groups and academic clubs, it finds little resonance in the changed aspirations of India's poor. Thus, at one level movement groups see the power elements of the old development model being encoded in the hegemonic structure of globalization which they oppose. But at the level of national politics they see the idea of development as representing political and economic rights of the people who have been denied access to it because of their disadvantageous locations in the power structure. Hence they problematize development, seeking to create a politics for changing power relations in society. This change in perspective was effectively articulated by a well known social activist Aruna Roy when she left a development NGO in mid-1980s to found a movement-group. According to her the need of the time was to 'redefine the paradigm of development — to see the whole process of development from a different perspective'. And such a change in perspective would, she held, enable social activists to see development for what it really is, i.e., a political process. In her words: 'Development is politics and there can be no development without political will … In fact all acts of social and economic living are determined by the nature of politics' (A. Roy 1996a).

Second, the change in perspective was also a response to the change in the post-Cold War global politics of development. Movement-groups in India now have a better understanding of the global politics of development. With the global development establishment having openly and officially given up its old promise of universalizing development for all, they are now able to see the real face of global hegemonic power. They are, therefore, not surprised that it has dismantled the Cold War structures of aid and assistance, and in their place a new global economic regime of trade and fiscal control has been set up. The movements see this change as representing a new political agenda on the part of the global power structure which aims at dispersal of state control over the economies of the peripheral countries on the one hand, and centralization of global political and military power in the hands of the world's already rich and powerful countries on the other. They see this as forming the basis for global hegemony today, through which these countries seek to maintain international economic and political stability under the continuing, rather intensifying, conditions of inequality among and within nations.

This awareness has led some movement-groups to form transnational alliances aimed at democratizing the global power structure. For example, quite a few movement-groups in India have been actively associated with such counter hegemonic global initiatives as the Convention on Biodiversity, Agenda 21, World Commission on Dams, Alliance for Comprehensive Democracy and so on. These initiatives are not just confined to the transcendental global space. They are concretely embodied in their activities at the national and local levels in the form of disseminating awareness and activating organizations at the grass roots level to identify and oppose specific policies, programmes and legislations meant to expand hegemonic global power.[2]

Third, all types of grass roots groups today, including even some conventional development NGOs, articulate basic issues of development in the framework of rights. For example, they no longer view poverty purely as an economic problem. They see it as a function of social-structural locations of the poor, because of which they are excluded from development (which is guarded by the legal, political and economic immunities it provides to its insiders) and imprisoned in poverty (the world constituted of vulnerabilities and exposures to exploitation for its politically unorganized and economically marginalized inhabitants). They, however, do not perceive the division between the two worlds in unidimensional terms of polarization between two economic classes. Their mobilizational strategies, therefore, focus on the new social-political formations which combine the categories of class, caste, ethnicity and gender.

Let me illustrate this point briefly with reference to the human rights, the ecology and the women's movements. The issue of human rights as viewed by the activists of several human rights groups is not limited to the conventional legal notion of civil liberties; it extends to situations in which individuals and groups are denied satisfaction of their basic needs. It is in this context that they articulate the issue of poverty in terms of rights and entitlements (e.g., right to work) the poor must have as citizens and as human beings. The politics of micro-movements, therefore, lies not merely in fighting particular infringements of legal rights of citizens, but in creating and expanding new political and civic spaces for them by converting the survival and development needs of the poor and the deprived into struggles for their economic, political and cultural rights and these not only of individuals qua individuals but of groups and communities surviving on the margins of the civil society. In the process, these movement activists link rights of access to and benefits from the development process with the issues of ethnic identity and human dignity, and view the satisfaction of material needs as a pursuit not detached from the spiritual and cultural aspects of human existence. This is why, several social-action groups whose self-image is not of being human-rights groups, almost routinely take up issues of rights and cooperate with larger human rights movements.

Similarly, the ecology movements at the grass roots do not view ecology as merely a cost factor in development, as some development specialists do. Nor are they interested in specifying tolerable levels of ecological destruction necessary for achieving higher levels of economic development as do the policies of hegemonic globalization. Instead, they view ecology as a basic principle of human existence, which, if reactivated, can yield higher level principles for reorganizing the economy in a humane way and refocus development in terms of well being, in which, to use Gandhiji s well known phrase, 'everyone shall have enough to satisfy one's need, but not greed'.

The activists of the women's movements have lately been defining their problem not merely in terms of achieving equal benefits and access for women, in the present system. They self-consciously take up such issues mainly for finding entry points to the submerged world of Indian womanhood; but their long-term goal, as they put it, is to change the working of the gender principle itself in the economy and society, such that both society and economy become more just and humane. They find the ecological world view of the movements more aligned with the feminine principle. The fusion of the ecological and gender principles, they argue, is conducive for a more humane economic and political organization of the society than that of development which, in their view is founded on the principle of male-domination over all aspects of human life and nature (Shiva 1988). Their project, often working in tandem with the human rights and ecology movements, is thus to change the forms of organization and consciousness in society.

Guided by this broad perspective, movements are often able to forge links with each other in fighting for issues at the grass roots. It is not accidental that ecology movements like the Chipko movement have large participation of women, and that in the Bodhgaya movement for the rights of the landless in Bihar, women played significant leadership roles. Women are in the forefront of the movements fighting for the rights of the population displaced by development projects especially in Madhya Pradesh and Maharashtra. Similarly, human rights organizations often team up with women's organizations on issues of dowry, sati, rape, and equal wages. Similarly, activists in women's groups played an active role in mobilizing and assisting the victims of the Bhopal chemical disaster. At no time in independent India, in the movements led by the parties and trade unions, were there ever such a high degree and such a sustained level of participation by women as we witness today in the non-party political movements at the grass roots.[3]

Fourth, the movements now see more clearly that the roots of rural poverty lie in the pattern of urban growth in India. This has, among other thing, led to greater interaction and building of new organizational linkages between the city-based and village-based social action groups. Further, the movements now realize the inconsequentiality of the established wisdom of 'inputs' serving as a major factor in rural development. This in their view only represents a partial and lopsided understanding of the problem of rural development. For, making 'inputs' available to poor farmers is more a political, than an economic problem. The experience so far is that it has not helped a large majority of the poor who lack economic and organizational capacity to receive and use inputs such as credit, seeds, fertilizers, irrigation and so on. These inputs are simply swallowed up by the upper stratum of the rural society. So, the focus of their activity is now on creating capabilities of self-development among the rural poor, even as they fight for their rights to create and secure resources for collective development.

Thus, by redefining issues of development in political terms, the groups working separately on different issues such as gender, ecology, human rights or in the areas of health and education are now conceiving their activities in more generic terms — as a form of social and political action aimed at countering hegemonic power structures at all levels — locally, nationally and globally. An important consequence of this change in perspective was that the grass roots movements, which were in a state of fragmentation and low morale at the end of 1980s, began to regroup and come on common platforms, on the issue of globalization. In the mid-1990s this led to launching of several new nationwide campaigns and to the formation of organizationally more durable coalitions and alliances. Among many such initiatives the most effective and widespread in recent years, has been the campaign for right to information — a series of local-level struggles for securing correct wages for labourers working in public construction works for drought relief, culminating in a successful nationwide campaign for right to information. The older, ongoing movement of the 1980s the Narmada Bachao Andolan, got a new boost and gave birth to a broad-based alliance of a number of social movements and organizations active at different levels and in different parts of the country. This alliance, known as National Alliance for People's Movements (NAPM) has been launching, supporting and coordinating several campaigns on a more or less regular basis, protesting against programmes and projects of the government and the MNCs, representing the policies of hegemonic globalization. There have been many more such initiatives, but more recent ones among them include: A Campaign for Peoples' Control over Natural Resources comprising several organizations active in rural and tribal areas covering about 13 Indian states; the movement called There Is An Alternative, led by, among others, two previous prime ministers of India; The Living Democracy Movement for linking local democracy decision-making to maintaining biodiversity; the movement for nuclear disarmament called Coalition for Nuclear Disarmament and Peace, and so on. Although some of these movements will be described in some detail in the next section, the point of just mentioning these here is to show how the challenge of globalization has politically revitalized the scene of social movements in India which by the end of 1980s was losing both, momentum and direction; more interestingly, how it became possible for these movements to sustain their politics at a higher level of intensity, in the process, recovering the hope of initiating a long-term politics of non-cooperation and withdrawal of legitimation to the dominant power structures.

To sum up, the politics of different groups and movements, which began to converge in mid-1990s, have acquired a common direction and a fairly durable organizational base. The convergence has been attained on the point of resisting the ongoing efforts of the bureaucratic, technocratic and the metropolitan elites to support policies of globalization and depoliticize development. For, in their view, it is only through politicisation of the poor that they can counter the negative impact of globalization and make development a just and equitable process, and a collectively edifying experience. Thus, by establishing both conceptually and in practice linkages between issues of development and democracy, the grass roots movements have begun to articulate their politics in terms of participatory democracy.

Participatory Democracy and Political Theory

In theoretical discussions and in the practice of representational politics participatory democracy has been treated, respectively, as a parapolitical idea and a peripheral political activity — a desirable but not an essential characteristic of a modern democracy. It is in the politics of grass roots movements, where the scope of democracy is being actively searched and expanded through their everyday political struggles, that participatory democracy is conceived as not just desirable but a necessary organizational form and political practice. Under conditions of globalization, where the national level institutions of representation are being subordinated to hegemonic global power with the structures of political and economic decision-making becoming more remote — even alienated — from people, the movements' continuing politics of participatory democracy has acquired a new relevance. In contemporary democratic theory the notion of political participation is articulated in terms of political obligations and legal-constitutional rights of citizens with respect to electing representative governments and ensuring their democratic functioning (Almond and Verba 1963; Milbrath 1965). By conceiving participation in passive terms of limiting citizen's role and activities to the institutional arena of elections, parties and pressure-groups, the theory secures (or at least seeks to provide justifications for securing) the decision-making procedures of representative governments from the high-intensity politics of mass-mobilization and direct-action, which the occasionally surfacing popular movements generate in a representative democracy.

This indeed has succeeded to a large extent in lending institutional stability and political legitimacy to liberal representative democracy, making it appear as if it is the only natural form that democracy can have. But it has, at the same time, bogged down the theory's political imagination to pragmatic concerns of the old, 'actually existing' democracies of the West. In the process, it has pre-empted options of the new and growing democracies to evolve and experiment with institutional alternatives for deepening democracy and choosing forms appropriate to their own respective cultural and historical contexts. Even more, by treating persistently and for long, the theory liberal representative democracy as the ultimate form of democracy has encouraged the view that in it, human kind has achieved the highest state of political development beyond and outside which no democratic possibility exists This even emboldened a North American political thinker to see the arrival and universalization of liberal democracy as heralding the end of history! (Fukuyama 1992). This high-intensity discourse sustained throughout the Cold War has, ironically, produced an array of theoretical arguments which has succeeded in keeping representative democracy at the level of what Boaventura de-Souza Santos aptly describes as low-intensity democracy — which probably also suits the contemporary politics of hegemonic globalization (Santos 1999). This, however, has resulted in a major theoretical casualty, i.e., of pushing — if not altogether discarding — the concept of participatory democracy on the margins of democratic theory.

Keeping democracy a low-intensity national-level operation may be conducive to integration of the world (capitalist) economy, for, it helps national governments of the peripheral countries to disperse and dispel popular democratic movements opposing implementation of structural adjustments and other policies handed down to them by the global power structure. But it is precisely for this reason that peripheral countries of the world undergoing globalization need to create a strong infrastructure of democracy at the grass roots, without which their democracies cannot survive at the nation-state level; worse, it may even endanger the very survival of their poor citizens.

Two moves made by the theorists of representative democracy have made it possible, on the one side, to incorporate the concept of participation within the theory's structural-functional paradigm (i.e., participation conceived as a particular form of political behaviour of citizens through which they elect governments and are expected to keep their functioning on a democratic track by working through their representatives), and, on the other, to treat participatory democracy either as an archaic form of governance or an impractical ideal which if actually practised — or even experimented with — is fraught with dangerous consequences for democracy itself.

The first argument is elaborated through historicizing democracy in linear, evolutionary terms. It traces the history of democracy from its origin in the Athenian city state where it functioned as a direct, participatory democracy through successive forms it assumed, till it acquired a complexly evolved form of representative democracy — making it possible to function at a much larger scale as of a nation-state (sometimes the state of a continental size). This transmutation has in its view equipped representative-liberal democracy to function even at a global scale and carry out a plethora of programmes and policies pertaining to every aspect of lives of its citizens (Dahl 1989: 1–24).

The point of this exercise, it seems, is to show that the beliefs and practices historically associated with the participatory democracy of a city-state have no relevance today for a democracy located in the nation-state and even less for tomorrow when it is likely to encompass the whole globe as its territorial domain. Participatory democracy, the theory concedes, is indeed a noble idea and some of its elements ought to be functionally incorporated in representative democracy. But it is a regression to think of citizens directly controlling and participating in governmental decision-making and may even turn out to be a recipe for disaster in today's world. In the derivative theoretical discourse of Indian democracy, this fixing of participatory democracy to the dead and gone past of the West has delegitimized any historical-theoretical exploration premised on its existence in India's past. Hence the idea of democracy as symbolized in the concept of the village republic is treated by Indian political theorists as an atavistic idea, not deserving any serious theoretical discussion. The other argument — unlike the previous one which views democracy's history in structural-functional terms — is made in normative-analytical terms. It seems to be based on the fear of romantic appeal (utopian images) that the idea of participatory democracy evokes. In the view of those advancing this argument, propagating the ideal of participatory democracy often promotes simple, populist ideas about democracy. They further argue that the proponents of participatory democracy fail to recognize the fact that modern governments have to routinely depend on specialists and professional experts for their decision-making; the issues involved are so complex and technical in nature that they are beyond the grasp even of elected representatives, let alone ordinary citizens. Concepts like direct or participatory democracy only serve as a distraction to theorization of democracy for the globalizing world (Schmitter 1999). A section of Indian elites who believe that meritocracy provides a better form of democracy and good governance, has always sought political support for their position in this argument. They vociferously argue that for preserving institutional norms of representative democracy it is necessary to strictly limit, procedurally and structurally, the powers of elected representatives through the legal-rational institutions of bureaucracy, and the judiciary. In their view giving legitimacy to the idea of participatory democracy would only further expose representative institutions to majoritarian and populist pressures, often making for bad and irrational decisions which usually are not in public interest. It was the dominance of this discourse in India during the initial decades of Independence that allowed the consolidation of the hegemonic rule, albeit democratically consented, of a small social-political minority consisting of urban and English-educated members of the upper castes. They occupied a large number of positions in different sectors and institutions of the state, especially in higher bureaucracy and judiciary, for over 40 years after Independence. What had become an established, common sense view of governing India, however, began to be challenged by the end of 1970s when the movements of subaltern classes gained strength both in electoral politics and in civil society (Sheth 1995).

Movements' Politics of Participatory Democracy

The idea of participatory democracy was central to Gandhi's political thinking and practice, and had inspired many activists of the freedom movement. He articulated this idea through the concepts of swaraj (self-governance) and swadeshi (community's control over resources) and by invoking the imagery of the 'village republic' (gram swaraj) as representing India's democratic tradition.[4] These formulations were however stoutly refuted and virtually banished from mainstream political discourse after Independence, as representing Gandhi's impractical idealism. The idea of participatory democracy has, however, not only been kept alive but developed conceptually and in practice by a section of grass roots activists who liberally draw on Gandhi's economic and political thinking — although many of them may not want to wear the Gandhian badge (Bakshi 1998). In a different political and ideological context M. N. Roy had critiqued representative form of democracy and pleaded for participative democracy. Based on his vision of participative democracy Roy had prepared a detailed proposal for Constitution of Free India (M. N. Roy 1981). These proposals, which did not receive any serious response in the then prevailing nationalist politics, have now been revived and reformulated by some activist groups in the changed context of globalization (Tarkunde 2003).

The first comprehensive and politically effective proposal on participatory democracy for independent India, however, came from Jayaprakash Narayan (JP). A popular socialist leader of Independence movement JP joined the Gandhian movement about five years after Independence. He raised the political profile of the movement high when in 1954 he made a public pronouncement of dedicating his whole life to the movement; in his words, to 'the Gandhian way'. The issue of deepening democracy was central to his agenda for the movement, without which, he believed, only the elite rule will perpetuate in the name of democracy.[5] This concern found a lasting expression in his 1959 treatise on non-party democracy (Narayan 1959). He critiqued the idea of representation by political parties and argued for a more participative and comprehensive form of democracy constituting a broad democratic base from where the power will flow upward to units using power allocated to them by the units below, on conditions of accountability and transparency. The amount and kind of power to be allocated to a higher unit will be as per the requirement of the unit. JP's thesis however made little impact then beyond the Gandhian circles. It in fact drew sharp criticism from the liberal democratic theorists as well as the party politicians who saw it as a naïve exercise of an idealist, unaware of its dangerous consequences for democracy itself (R. Kothari 1960). The document was virtually 'withdrawn' from public discourse, but within two years JP came up with a politically more potent and a comprehensive statement on the issue of participatory democracy (Narayan 1961). Here JP rebutted arguments of his critics and elaborated his basic thesis by theoretically and historically establishing the need for a comprehensive democracy, where both economic and political power is primarily held and exercised directly by the people from the base of the polity. It did not take very long for his vision of democracy to find a powerful political expression. He launched a massive movement in early 1970s with the aim of, in his own coinage, restoring peoples' power ('lokshakti') in democracy (Narayan 1975). This idea of peoples' power fired the imagination of many young women and men, which besides upstaging the government in Delhi gave rise to a new genre of micro-movements, celebrated and characterized by theorists as the 'non-party political process' (R. Kothari 1984). This genre of movement-groups that emerged from what became known as the 'JP movement' has since been working at the grass roots. They articulate participatory democracy in terms of empowerment of people through everyday struggles for their rights as well as through harnessing their collective efforts to developing local resources for collective well-being.

The most remarkable in this genre was the movement launched by Chhatra-Yuva Sangarsh Vahini in 1978, known as the Bodh Gaya movement. It has since served as a source of inspiration nationally for many movement groups. This movement succeeded in seizing about 10,000 acres of land from the religious establishment in Bodhgaya, a district in Bihar, through non-violent direct action. The land was legally redistributed among families of tillers who were attached to the land for generations. In the course of redistribution, legal entitlements to land were given equally to women and men. More important than its outcome in the form of land redistribution was the process of change through which the movement's larger objectives and values of political and social transformation were kept alive, communicated and partially institutionalized, affecting lives of about 3,000 participant households in the area. In fact the movement-group ensured that the dalits (ex-untouchables) for whose land-rights the movement was launched remained in the forefront and among them the women performed crucial leadership roles. The movement created a new hope among social-action groups all over the country about the efficacy of using non-violent militancy as a means for social and economic transformation.[6]

Another, and equally significant movement of the same genre in recent years, has been the one led by Tarun Bharat Sangh. It is known to the outside world through its Magsaysay award winning leader, Rajendra Singh. He joined and has revitalized the organization through his work since 1985 in the villages of Rajasthan. He and members of his group started work with a deep conviction that the people have the knowledge and the capacity to develop and manage their affairs collectively for their own well-being (that is how he saw JP's message of 'power to the people'), provided they stopped looking to the government for help and become motivated to work on their own. In Singh's own words:

> [O]ur fight (is) against the state for communities to have a say in their development. Administrative system ... tries to foist its own vision of development on communities, without bothering to find out what people need. In fact, it is a myth that development is for people, it is actually anti-people ... Schooled in the ideals of Jayaprakash Narayan and Acharya Vinoba Bhave working for social change was an obvious choice (for us) (Singh 2001).

Beginning their work in mid-1980s this group of social activists was able to establish, in the course of a decade and a half, a self-governing system of land and water management in about 700 villages in the perpetually drought affected and poverty-ridden villages of Rajasthan. This was achieved through reviving recessive knowledge and skills of the people themselves of building water harvesting structures known locally as Johads. In this process the villagers not only went ahead and built a network of check-dams and small reservoirs without government help but took decisions, bypassing the government, on land use in the area, built boundary walls around common lands and afforested a huge barren landmass. This became possible due to social confidence the people could recover with the water becoming available to them by their own efforts. The old forms of economic interdependence and social cooperation were now recovered and imbued with new economic and democratic-political meanings. In Singh's eyes, this is a small, perhaps a short-lived achievement. He sees a long political battle ahead for achieving real democracy for the people. In his words:

> Unfortunately, the state in India does not appreciate communities trying to help themselves. If people start participating in development and questioning the money that ostensibly is being spent on them, it makes difficult for those who run the system. For a bureaucracy schooled in the colonial tradition of ruling rather than working with people, grass roots democracy is an alien concept. So instead of development being a collaborative effort between people and the state, it is actually people versus the state (Singh 2001).

But the government saw all this quite differently: an encroachment on its territory and usurpation of its functions. The administration slapped hundreds of legal cases on the movement-group and the villagers and threatened them with demolition of the dams as they were built without the government's permission and the guidance of experts ('civil engineers'). Here is where the grass roots group's politics of mass mobilization and joining larger alliances helped; it became possible for the group along with the villagers, to withstand the pressure and ultimately get the government to endorse the mode of self-governance they had evolved through political struggles on the ground. Again, Rajendra Singh sees this as a temporary reprieve obtained by winning of a battle, not a war. In his words: 'Unless the communities are empowered and encouraged to develop stakes in development, winning the war is going to be difficult' (ibid.).[7]

In the process of countering hegemonic globalization, the movements have added another dimension to their politics. This is about making law an important site of social and political action/struggles. In the course of implementing the structural adjustment programmes and other globalization-related policies, the state has been actively assisting the Indian and multinational corporations to acquire land and other resources of the villages at a nominal cost. This involves withdrawing constitutional guarantees given to tribals regarding alienation of their land and, in effect, extending such guarantees to MNCs as making land, water and forest-resources available to them cheaply, but at a great cost to the livelihood of the people and ecology of the area. Enactment or implementation of such legislations and government orders are now challenged by the movement-groups not just in the courts of law, but in the larger arena of civil society. The proceedings of public interest litigations which earlier had remained by and large confined to the courtrooms as contentions between the state and the social-legal activists, have now become matters of direct concern and involvement for the people themselves, constituting everyday politics of the movement groups. In the process, new participatory forums have been evolved such as documenting effects of specific government policies and legislation on the people through participatory surveys and studies carried out jointly by social activists (including some professionals among them) and the people themselves, and disseminating results to the wider public, including the media. The most effective and innovative mode of consciousness raising and of political mobilization developed in this process, which has now become a common practice for movement groups all over the country, is organizing big walkathons (*padyatras*). The padyatras are usually organized by activists representing organizations from different parts of the country but sharing a common perspective on and concern for a particular issue they together wish to highlight for mobilizing public opinion. They walk long distances along with the people drawn from different locales but facing a similar problem — for eg., a threat posed to their livelihood by the project of the government or MNC — in a specific area. In the course of the walk they take halts in villages — interact with people, show films, stage plays — highlighting the issues.

One among many such cases is the movement against bauxite mining in tribal areas of Vishakhapatnam in Andhra Pradesh. In 1991 a walkathon, known as the 'manya prante chaitanya yatra', a consciousness raising walk of the area facing ecological destruction was organized by a couple of movement groups, SAMTA and SAKTI, active in the area. Over 50 other social action groups joined the march and prepared a report on ecological destruction they saw and experienced during the march. The report described how the region had come under severe threat to its ecology and to livelihood of people inhabiting it and how if the damage was not controlled could cause ecological disaster for the entire peninsula of south India. The report also spoke of the displacement of 50,000 tribals, the massive deforestation and the problem of flash floods and silting that resulted (report by P. Sivaram Krishna of SAKTI [Mimeo]; see also report in *Newstime*, 13 March 1991).

This chaitanya yatra has since served as a basis for a decade long and still continuing movement for legal and social action in the state of Andhra Pradesh. During the last five years it has widely expanded, covering many other similar issues and movement-groups working on them from different parts of the country. What is of interest here is the kind of politics the movement has developed for expanding its activities and sustaining itself for so long. At one level, through taking the issue of threat to peoples' livelihood to the law courts it has created a nationwide alliance of similar movements, thus garnering a wider support base for its activities. Working through the alliance it has been able to project its work in the national media and contribute to building solidarity of movement-groups. At another more crucial level the movement, through its mobilizational and consciousness raising marches and other myriad activities, has been able to motivate people of the area to build their own community-based organizations, which now assert self-governance as a right, and the preferred way to protect and develop the means of their livelihood and culture.

The participative methodology of preparing and disseminating reports which involved self-reporting by members of the affected communities as well as technical and financial inputs from well known NGOs, movement leaders and reputed activist-professionals, succeeded in drawing nationwide attention regarding the usurpation of tribal lands by corporations, ostensibly by legal means, which deprived the people of their livelihoods, identity and culture.[8]

It was in the background of sustained struggles which the groups in the area carried on for about a decade that it became possible for one of them, i.e., SAMTA, to go to the Supreme Court of India with a plea to close the calcite mines in the area as it threatened to uproot the local population and endangered the ecology of the area. Since the tribals were protected by the Fifth Schedule of the Constitution against alienation of their lands and the mine threatened to destroy their livelihoods, even more, violated their fundamental right to live given by the Indian Constitution to all citizens, SAMTA pleaded that the mine should be closed. Largely accepting the SAMTA plea the Supreme Court of India gave a 400 page judgment in 1997, outlining the steps which needed to be taken to make the tribals partners in the development of scheduled areas (i.e., constitutionally protected areas populated by tribals).

The court ruled that all private and public sector organizations functioning in these areas should give not less than 20 per cent of jobs to local people and an equal amount of seats to their children in educational institutions. The court also stipulated that each industrial unit in the area part with 20 per cent of its profit and make it available for the kind of development that would be in the interest of the local people. In essence the court recognized the local people as legal stakeholders in the development of the area they live in. It made the people's participation in development necessary, and their claim to a share in the benefits of development legitimate. This landmark judgment, known as the SAMTA judgment, has since become a rallying point around which many struggles are now waged jointly by action groups in the country: first, to secure implementation of the court's mandatory rulings as well as its recommendatory provisions. Second, to test and expand legal and juridical meanings of the judgment for wider application; third, to use it politically for creating a bulwark of resistance to prevent implementation of the government policy which, as a part of globalization package and under pressure from multinationals, seeks to withdraw guarantees given by the Constitution to the people under its Fifth Schedule.

In the course of the six years since the Supreme Court's judgment in this, a number of marches, demonstrations and conventions have been held in different parts of the country, on a more or less regular basis by social movement-groups. One remarkable example of how the SAMTA judgment energized the micro-movements, struggling for long but not making much headway in securing ecological rights of the local (tribal) communities is the case of the adivasi movement in the Rayagada district of Orissa. The movement aided and assisted by the National Committee for Protection of Natural Resources (NCPNR), itself a network of over 40 social action groups, succeeded in highlighting the plight of the Rayagada tribals and the injustice done to them by forcibly acquiring their lands for bauxite mining. The movement effectively used the SAMTA judgment in making the government officials aware of their obligation to implement the Supreme Court judgment in Orissa (Hiremath 2001).

Different from the mentioned campaign for preventing the government from enacting certain kinds of legislations, there is a movement which seeks to compel the government to implement its own rules and regulations honestly and efficiently. Its politics centres on holding public hearings and peoples' courts with a view to creating political and social sanctions for the local government administration to compel it to observe and make public the rules and regulations by which it is governed in implementation of development programmes. It began as a struggle launched by a mass-based organization in a village in Rajasthan founded by Aruna Roy who gave up her job in the Indian Administrative Services (IAS) 'to work with the people'. The organization, named Mazdoor Kisan Shakti Sangathan (MKSS), addressed the problem most acutely felt by the people themselves, i.e., government officials cheating labourers working on government construction sites, by not paying them minimum wages fixed by the government.[9] Besides being underpaid, the people in the area did not get enough work through the year, often because sanctioned development programmes usually remained on paper, with the allocated money being pocketed by government officials and elected leaders. Since all this was done with the knowledge of the 'higher-ups' no amount of petitioning helped; only direct democratic action by the people was seen as a possible remedy. In December 1994–95 several public hearings or Jan Sunvai were held by MKSS where the workers were encouraged to speak out their problems with the bureaucracy — especially narrating specific details of underpayment of wages and unimplemented development schemes — in the presence of local journalists, and people of surrounding villages from different walks of life. It took several public hearings to persuade some among the accused parties — the contractors, engineers and local elected leaders — to accept the MKSS invitation asking them to avail of the opportunity of their self-defence by responding to peoples' charges of corruption. All this had little impact on the administration and for people outside the local area until a marathon 40-day sit-in (dharna), was organized in the nearby town of Beawar in 1996, followed by another series of public hearings, demonstrations and processions. This compelled the Rajasthan government to amend the Panchayati Raj Act, entitling citizens to get certified copies of bills and vouchers of payments made and the muster-rolls showing names of labourers employed (for, payments were often made by forged bills and shown against fictitious names of people who never worked on the site). This grew into a state level campaign, demanding that the Rajasthan government pass a comprehensive legislation granting citizens and organizations the right to information. This culminated in organizing a nation-wide campaign — National Campaign for People's Right to Information — which prepared a model of legislation for right to information. By extensively canvassing a model bill, the campaign succeeded with about half a dozen state assemblies passing similar legislations. Eventually, the parliament too was forced to pass such a bill, though in a vastly diluted and truncated form. Expectedly, even after about eight months of its passage, it has not been publicly notified for implementation! But that is a different story.

In short, the innovative politics of the movement-group MKSS — as well as of many other such organizations not reported here — working explicitly on the principle of making democracy participatory and responsive, has initiated a larger and long-term political process by which people can effectively participate in making laws by compelling legislators at the local, state and national level to formulate legislations the people want — in some cases even making the legislatures adopt drafts of laws prepared by the grass roots movements based on the information and insights gained through their own struggles and through wider consultations on different civil society forums.

There are numerous other cases of the movement-groups articulating different elements of participatory democracy in the course of their struggles for democratizing development (S. Kothari 2000b). For lack of space, only a brief mention could be made of a few. For example there are city-based movement-groups like the Self-Employed Women's Association (SEWA) in Ahmedabad, with a long and formidable record of work among self-employed women for their economic and political empowerment and social emancipation (Rose 1992). There are two other recently founded organizations in Delhi: Manushi Forum for Citizen Rights and the Jan Parivahan Panchayat of Lokayan. These organizations have been running campaigns for protecting economic rights and expanding freedoms of self-employed urban poor — such as street hawkers and cycle-rickshaw pullers (Kishwar 2001b and 2001c). As part of the campaign, film shows, photographic exhibitions and marches are organized in the different localities of the city. The media campaigns, on the whole, demonstrate how the implementation of economic reforms blatantly discriminate between the rich and the poor, and how the rules are often used to prevent people to exercise their right to make a living (Kiswar 2001a; Lokayan 2002). Public hearings are held revealing the harassment of hawkers and rickshaw pullers by government officials, which focus not so much on implementation of rules as on collection of corruption money. Similar movement-groups fighting for the rights of the urban poor have been active in Mumbai, Bangalore, Hyderabad, Calcutta, and other cities, whose work is equally, if not more important, but cannot be described here for want of space. The short point is: a new civil society politics — different from conventional trade union politics — has emerged in the cities, focusing on the rights of the urban poor in making livelihood choices and use of urban spaces.

Similar new movements addressing issues of livelihood and use of common spaces have emerged in the rural and tribal areas. They aim at empowering the gram sabhas by making them self-governed and participative decision-making bodies managing affairs of their own villages (S. Kothari 2000a). One such movement, for example, explicitly conceives of participatory democracy as an 'antidote to globalization'. Its politics is about giving organizational shape to Gandhi's ideas of swaraj and swadeshi at the grass roots level. Led by an activist trained in the JP movement, Mohan Hirabai Hiralal, the movement has motivated people to establish their own governance, to begin with, of forests in the area. Today, the villagers themselves maintain the forest-ecology and make judicious use of forest produce (Vivek Deshpande, 21 May 2000). The self-governance movement is now being expanded to many more villages, covering other areas of collective life. The movement's credo is: we are the government in our village and there shall be *our* government in the region, the nation, and the world. Interestingly, this movement-group has also theoretically worked out a 'blue print' of organizational structures required for a participatory democracy from the village to the global level, specifying the long-term objectives and values by which they should be informed (Hiralal 2001).

Conclusion

The distinctive feature of movements-politics is, thus, to articulate a new discourse on democracy through a sustained political practice. This is done at three levels: (*a*) at the grass roots level through building peoples' own power and capabilities, which inevitably involve political struggles for establishing rights as well as a degree of local autonomy for people to manage their own affairs collectively; (*b*) at the provincial and national level through launching nationwide campaigns and building alliances and coalitions for mobilizing protests on larger issues (against 'anti-people projects and policies') and creating organizational networks of mutual support and of solidarity among movements; (*c*) at the global level, by a small section of movements-activists who in recent years have begun to actively participate in several transnational alliances and movements for creating a politics of counter-hegemonic globalization. In all this, the long-term goal of the movements is to bring the immediate environment (social, economic, cultural and ecological) the people live in, within their own reach and control.

Such politics of movements, however, often brings them into confrontation with the state, the bureaucracy, the law and order machinery, the local power structures and now increasingly with the multinationals penetrating the rural and tribal spaces in India. The micro-movements sometimes also come in conflict with political parties and established trade unions. The activists of movements, however, view such confrontations as an aspect of the larger, long-term struggle for political and social transformation, and not as means of competing with political parties in the arena of representative politics, for acquisition of the state power. They thus view their everyday struggles as a process of expanding political spaces trans-locally through raising people's consciousness and building their own organizations. In the process, in the areas they have been active; they contribute to creating a political culture of participative democracy.

The movement activists have developed their own critique of the prevalent macro-structures of political representation as well as a view of local politics. Their critique is not theoretically derived; it has emerged from the experience of day-to-day political struggles on the ground.[10] In their view the representative institutions have imprisoned the process of democratization in the society. The way out from such impasse is the spread of their kind of politics — the politics of micro-movements. Movements, they believe, by involving people deeply in politics will in the long run, change the terms of justification for the state for holding and using power. This probably explains their epistemic preference in articulating their politics in terms of 'reconstruction of state', rather than of 'acquisition of state power'.

Although the movements usually work in local areas they invariably define local issues in trans-local terms. Theirs is thus a new kind of local politics which, unlike the conventional politics of local governments, is not linked vertically to the macro structures of power and ideology, either of a nation-state or of the global order; nor is this politics parochially local. It expands horizontally through several micro-movements of people living in different geographical areas and socio-cultural milieus, but experiencing the common situation of disempowerment caused by mal-development and contemporary forms of governance which are imperiously distant, yet close enough to feel their coercive edge. Thus viewed, the long-term politics of movements is about withdrawal of legitimation to the hegemonic and exclusionary structures of political power and horizontalizing the vertical structures of social hierarchy, through strengthening the parallel politics of local, participatory democracy. In this process, the micro-movements address, on the one hand, the problem of making institutions of governance at all levels more accountable, transparent and participative and, on the other, create new political spaces outside the state structure, in which the people themselves are enabled to make decisions collectively on issues directly concerning their lives. Though, I have no penchant for coining new terms, I think it will be more appropriate to characterize this new politics of movements as 'societies'.

All this, however, does not mean that grass roots actors and organizations define the politics of movements in direct opposition to the institutional framework of Indian democracy. In fact they view institutional democracy as a necessary, though not sufficient condition for pursuing their parallel politics of movements through which they seek to raise social consciousness of people and democratize the hegemonic structures of power in society. In that sense, their politics is about working around and transcending the prevalent institutional structures of liberal democracy — rather than confronting them directly with a view to capturing state power.

In a nutshell, the movements conceive of participatory democracy as a parallel politics of social action, creating and maintaining new spaces for decision-making (i.e., for self-governance) by people on matters affecting their lives directly. As a form of practice, participatory democracy for them is thus a long-term political and social process aimed at creating a new system of multiple and overlapping governances, functioning through more direct participation and control of concerned populations (i.e., of those comprising these governances). It is envisaged that through such politics the almost total monopoly of power held today by the contemporary (totalist) state would be dispersed into different self-governing entities but, at the same time, the macro-governance of the state, albeit confined to fewer nationally crucial sectors, would be carried through democratically elected representative bodies, at one level overseeing the system of micro-governances and at another, being responsive and accountable to them.

Notes

* This chapter was earlier published in *Economic and Political Weekly*, 39(1): 45–58, 2004. For an elaborate discussion in participatory democracy, see Sheth (2007).

1. The following account is based on my close and continuous association and interaction with activists of several movement groups throughout the country, since 1980. I also have extensively used the materials they regularly produce and disseminate in the form of booklets, pamphlets, leaflets and newsletters, which do not easily yield to the academic style of citations. As such, it incorporates parts of my earlier writings on grass roots movements, cited here. The activists and movements appearing in this paper by their names suggest my greater, often accidental, familiarity with their work, inasmuch as the absences suggest my ignorance — and the lack of space — but in no case any lack of their salience in the field.
2. For example, witness activities of a network of grass roots organizations founded by the leading activist of transnational ecological movements, Vandana Shiva; the network is known as *Jaiv Panchayats* — The Living Democracy Movement (Shiva 2000).
3. It is significant to note in this context that major popular movements in India today such as campaign for right to information, campaign for saving the river Narmada (Narmada Bachao Andolan), movement for rights of self-employed women and of street-hawkers and rickshaw pullers in cities, campaign for maintaining biodiversity and against intellectual property rights are all led by women.
4. For concise and pointed exposition of these concepts, see M.K. Gandhi (1968a; 1968b; 1968c; 1968d; 1968e) in Shriman Narayan (ed.): *The Selected Works of Mahatma Gandhi*; Volume Four, Chapter 16, 'Swadeshi' (pp. 256–60), Volume Five, Chapter 15,'Non-Cooperation' (pp. 203–8), Chapter 16, 'Civil Disobedience', (pp. 209–16), Chapter 39, 'Swadeshi', (pp. 336–39) and Chapter 42, 'Village Communities' (pp. 344–47), Navajivan Publishing House: Ahmedabad.

5. For a perceptive, cogent and authentic account of JP's life and work, see 'Introduction' to his selected writings edited by Bimal Prasad (1980).
6. For detailed history and political account of the movement, see Prabhat (1999).
7. All quotes are from the leader of the movement, Rajendra Singh (2001); for a comprehensive account of the contribution made by this movement, see *Manushi*, 2001, no. 123.
8. Surveys and studies carried through participatory action research have, by now, become a common practice for the movement-groups. There are special groups of activist-academics, for eg., Alternative Survey Group, regularly carrying out studies and publishing their findings. Such studies are devised, self-consciously, to counter the politics of positivist knowledge which privilege experts and exclude people from decision-making on matter of vital interest to them (Sheth 1999).
9. The MKSS nearly ideally fits the concept of 'micro-movement' explicated in this paper. The campaign it initiated for right to information has become a nationwide movement. It has built a large network of movement-groups, human rights organizations, media-leaders, intellectuals and professionals. Unfortunately, I cannot do justice to some innovative political concepts and practices developed by this and other such movements in the space available here. For a detailed account of the MKSS movement and the vision of its founder see the following: Bakshi (1998); A. Roy (1996a and 1996b); Roy and De (1999); B. Roy (1999); Dogra (2000).
10. In the course of last five years the issue of participatory democracy has received a more serious and focused attention of the leaders of micro-movements. Several pamphlets, booklets, newsletters and articles have been prepared and disseminated by them for wider discussion and, possibly, for future campaigns. The basic principles and concepts were, as we saw earlier, enunciated by Gandhi and Jayaprakash Narayan. Some activist-thinkers in recent years have incorporated these in their politics and have renewed the debate through their own writings. For example see: A. Roy (1996) and Hiralal (2001); articles in the special issue of *Samayik Varta: Loktantra Samiksha* (July–August 2000) especially by Patnayak, Yadav, Bhatttacharya and Pratap; Kumar (2001); Pratap (2001); Tarkunde (2003). My presentation here of the movements' conceptualization of Participatory Democracy is largely based on the abovementioned materials.

References

Almond, Gabriel and Verba Sidney. 1963. *Civic Culture*. Princeton: Princeton University Press.

Bakshi, Rajni. 1998. *Bapu Kuti: Journeys in Rediscovery of Gandhi*. Delhi: Penguin Books India.

Bhattacharya, Dipankar. 2000. 'Janata ka Zameeni Sangharsh aur Loktantra', *Samayik Varta*, 23(10–11): 18–19.

Dahl, Robert. 1989. *Democracy and its Critics*. Hyderabad: Orient Longman.

Dogra, Madhu and Bharat Dogra. 2000. *MKSS: A Profile of a People's Organization*, published by Bharat Dogra, Delhi.

Fukuyama, Francis. 1992. *The End of History and the Last Man*. London: Penguin.

Gandhi, M. K. 1968a. 'Swadeshi', in Shriman Narayan (ed.), *Selected Works of Mahatma Gandhi*, vol. 4, pp. 256–60. Ahmedabad: Navajivan Publishing House.

———. 1968b. 'Non-cooperation', in Shriman Narayan (ed.), *Selected Works of Mahatma Gandhi*, vol. 5, pp. 203–8. Ahmedabad: Navajivan Publishing House.

———. 1968c. 'Civil Disobedience', in Shriman Narayan (ed.), *Selected Works of Mahatma Gandhi*, vol. 5, pp. 209–16. Ahmedabad: Navajivan Publishing House.

———. 1968d. 'Swadeshi', in Shriman Narayan (ed.), *Selected Works of Mahatma Gandhi*, vol. 5, pp. 336–39. Ahmedabad: Navajivan Publishing House.

———. 1968e. 'Village Communities', in Shriman Narayan (ed.), *Selected Works of Mahatma Gandhi*, vol. 5, pp. 344–47. Ahmedabad: Navajivan Publishing House.

Hiremath, S. R., et al. 2001. 'Report of the Study Team on Adivasi Movement in Rayagada District of Orissa against Forcible Tribal Land Acquisition for Bauxite Mining (in violation of the Supreme Court order in the SAMTA Judgment)', *Samay Parivartana Samudaya*, Dharwad, Karnataka.

Kapoor, Rakesh. 2002. 'Civil Society in India: A Background Paper', prepared for the Centre for the Study of Developing Societies (CSDS) project on Civil Society Building in India. Delhi: CSDS.

Kishwar, Madhu. 2001a. 'Laws, Liberty and Livelihood', *Manushi*, 122: 8–15.

———. 2001b. 'Villages in Rajasthan Overcome Sarkari Dependence', *Manushi*, 123: pp. 4–16.

———. 2001c. 'Bribes, Beatings and Blackmail: Loksunvayi of Delhi's Street Vendors', *Manushi*, 124.

Kothari, Rajni. 1960. 'Jayaprakash Narayan's Thesis: Report on a Discussion', *The Economic Weekly*, 12(15).

———. 1984. 'Non-Party Political Process', *Economic and Political Weekly*, 19(5): 216–24.

Kothari, Rajni. 1988a. 'Decline of the Moderate State', *State Against Democracy: In Search of Humane Governance*, pp. 15–36. Delhi: Ajanta Publications.

Kothari, Rajni. 1988b. 'Decline of Parties and Rise of Grass Roots Movements', *State Against Democracy: In Search of Humane Governance*, pp. 33–54. Delhi: Ajanta Publications.

———. 1989. 'End of an Era', *Politics and the People: In Search of Humane India*, pp. 235–50. Delhi: Ajanta Publications.

———. 1993. 'The Yawning Vacuum: A World without Alternatives', *Alternatives*, 18(2): 119–39.

Kothari, Smitu. 2000a. 'To Be Governed or Self-Govern', *Folio*, 18: 18–21.

———. 2000b. 'A Million Mutinies Now: Lesser-Known Environmental Movements in India', *Humanscape*, October: 5–9.

———. 2001. 'Globalization, Global Alliances and the Narmada Movement', in Kathryn Sikkink, S. Khagram, J. Riker (eds), *Restructuring World Politics: Transnational Social Movements, Networks and Norms*. Minneapolis: University of Minnesota Press.

Kumar, Arun. 2000. *Globalization: A Consensus of Only 3 Per Cent Indians*. Delhi: CSDS (Mimeo).

———. 2001. *Anchoring Indian State and Polity to Vernacular Wisdom: A Small Step towards Swaraj*. Delhi: CSDS (Mimeo).

Lokayan. 2002. 'Report on Cycle Rickshaws in the National Capital Region', prepared by Rajendra Ravi and Jan Parivahan. Delhi: Lokayan.

Milbrath, Lister W. 1965. *Political Participation*. Chicago: Rand McNally.

Narayan, Jayaprakash. 1959. *A Plea for Reconstruction of the Indian Polity*. Varanasi: Akhil Bharat Sarva Seva Sangh.

———. 1961. *Swaraj for the People*. Varanasi: Akhil Bharat Sarva Seva Sangh.

———. 1975. 'Total Revolution: Why and How?', in Bimal Prasad (ed.), *A Revolutionary's Quest: Selected Writings of Jayaprakash Narayan*. Delhi: Oxford University Press.

Patnayak, Kishan. 2000. 'Vishwa Main Loktantra ka Bhavishya', *Samayik Varta*, 23(10–11): 11–17.

Pendse, Sandeep. 1981. 'The Datta Samant Phenomenon', *Economic and Political Weekly*, 16–17: 1–8.

Prabhat. 1999. *Zamin Kiski, Jote Uski: Bodhgaya Bhumi Andolan*. Patna: Kisan Vikas Trust.

Prasad, Bimal. 1980. 'Introduction', in *A Revolutionary's Quest: Selected Writings of Jayaprakash Narayan*, pp. ix–lxviii. Delhi: Oxford University Press.

Pratap, Vijay. 2000. 'Yah Vimarsh Kis Liye', *Samayaik Varta*, 23(11): 3–7.

Pratap, Vijay. 2001. *Vasudhaiva Kutumbakam: A New Alliance for Democracy in the Era of Globalization*. Delhi: CSDS (Mimeo).
Pratap, Vijay and Ritu Priya. 2002. 'Making Institutions Compatible with Southern Movement Aspirations for a Democratic Order: A Minimalist Perspective', in Leena Rikkila and Katarina Sehm Patomaki (eds), *From Global Market Place to Political Spaces*, pp. 87–125. Helsinki: Hakapaino.
Rose, Kalima. 1992. *Where Women Are Leaders: The SEWA Movement in India*. London: Zed Books.
Roy, Aruna. 1996a. 'From Bureaucracy to People's Movement', *Lokayan Bulletin*, 13(1): 51.
———. 1996b. 'Survival and Right to Information: Third Gulam Rasool Memorial Lecture', Forum for Free Expression, Hyderabad.
———. 1999. 'Survival and Right to Information: Third Gulam Rasool Memorial Lecture' (abridged version), *Lokayan Bulletin*, 16(1): 1–13.
Roy, Aruna and Nikhil Dey. 1999. 'Footnotes to a Dharna', *Lokayan Bulletin*, 16(1): 45–51.
Roy, Bunker.1999. 'The Politics of Waste and Corruption', *Lokayan Bulletin*, 16(1): 19–40.
Roy, M. N. 1960. *Politics, Power and Parties*. Dehradun: Indian Renaissance Institute.
Sainath, P. 2000. 'The Age of Inequality', in Romila Thaper (ed.), *India: Another Millennium*, pp. 152–68. Delhi: Penguin India.
Santos, Boaventura de Sousa. 1997. 'Toward a Multicultural Conception of Human Rights', *Zeitschrift fur Rechtssoziologie*, 18(1): 1–15.
———. 1999. 'Reinventing Democracy', *Oficina do* CES, 136, Coimbra.
Schmitter, Philippe C. 1999. 'The Future of Democracy: Could It Be a Matter of Scale?', *Social Research*, 66(3): 933–58.
Sethi, Harsh. 1984. 'Groups in a New Politics of Transformation', *Economic and Political Weekly*, 19(7): 305–16.
Sheth, D. L. 1983. 'Grass-Roots Stirrings and the Future of Politics', *Alternatives*, 9(1): 1–24.
———. 1984. 'Grass Roots Initiatives in India', *Economic and Political Weekly*, 19(6).
———. 2007. 'Micro-Movements in India: Toward a New Politics of Participatory Democracy', in Boaventura de Sousa Santos (ed.), *Democratizing Democracy: Beyond the Liberal Democratic Canon*, pp. 3–37. London: Verso.
Sheth, D. L. and Harsh Sethi. 1991a. 'The NGO Sector in India: Historical Context and Current Discourse', *Voluntas*, 2(2): 49–68.
———. 1991b. 'Crisis of Representation', *Seminar*, 385.

Sheth, D. L. and Harsh Sethi. 1995. 'The Great Language Debate: Politics of Metropolitan versus Vernacular India', in Upendra Baxi and Bhikhu Parekh (eds), pp. 187–215. Delhi: Sage Publications.
———. 1999a. 'Globalization and the Grass Roots Movements', *Seminar*, 473: 77–82.
———. 1999b. *Knowledge Power and Action: Chal-lenges Facing the Grass Roots Movements for Alternative Development: I. P. Desai Memorial Lecture*. Surat: Centre for Social Studies.
Shiva, Vandana.1988. *Staying Alive: Women, Ecology and Survival in India*. New Delhi: Kali for Women.
———. 2000. 'Jaiva Panchayat: A Movement for Living Democracy', *Navadaniya* (pamphlet), Delhi.
Singh, Rajendra. 2001. 'I Was Called a Dacoit, Terrorist and Fraud', *Hindustan Times*, 12 August.
Tarkunde, V. M. 2003. 'Partyless Politics and People's (Humanist) State: A Picture for Public Discussion', *The Radical Humanist*, 66(10): 1–4.
Wallgren, Thomas. 1998. 'Political Semantics of Globalization', *Development: SID Journal*, 41(2): 30–32.
Yadav, Yogendra. 2000. 'Bharat ko Loktantraka ka ek Naya Shastra Gadhana Hoga', *Samayik Varta*, 23(10–11): 27–32.

6

Neoliberalism and Primitive Accumulation in India

The Need to Go Beyond Capital

*Pratyush Chandra and Deepankar Basu**

In 2008, the events that took place in Singur — a town which is less than 40 km away from Kolkata (Calcutta), where the West Bengal government struggled to acquire and sell 1000 acres of agricultural land to Tata Motors — indicate the extent to which capitalist-parliamentarianism can regiment a counter-hegemonic force once it agrees to play by the rules. At the least, it clearly shows that the Communist government, which boasts of being the longest-running democratically elected Marxist government in the world, is hopelessly caught in the neoliberal project. And Singur is not an isolated event. In the state of West Bengal alone, the process of state-led land grab and the resultant opposition is already gaining momentum in at least three different locations: (*a*) Kharagpur, West Medinipur district, where vast tracts of multi-crop farmland is being taken over for yet another Tata vehicle factory; (*b*) in Nandigram, East Medinipur district, where a chemical industries hub is proposed to be set up by the Salim group on a 10,000-acre area; and (*c*) in North Bengal where a Videocon Special Economic Zone (SEZ) is planned to come up in the near future.

This story is not limited to West Bengal. Throughout India, resources are being acquired for SEZs and numerous other industrial schemes meant to facilitate corporate capital expansion. Since laws permitting these acquisitions were passed some years ago, state governments have notified 267 SEZs, which will require more than a half million hectares of land. Of this, the state has already acquired 137,000 hectare for 67 SEZs while another 80 have 'in principle' been approved (Jha 2006). The Government has converted the erstwhile Export Processing Zones located at Kandla and Surat (Gujarat), Cochin (Kerala), Santa Cruz (Mumbai-Maharashtra), Falta (West Bengal), Madras (Tamil Nadu), Visakhapatnam (Andhra Pradesh), and Noida (Uttar Pradesh) into SEZs. In addition, three new SEZs that had been approved for establishment at Indore (Madhya Pradesh), Manikanchan (Salt Lake, Kolkata) and Jaipur have since commenced operations.

In this backdrop, the West Bengal government's adamant attitude towards land acquisition, despite the popular unrest, shows that the Indian state and its agencies, irrespective of their ideological masks, are working relentlessly to provide the private sector with an 'internationally competitive' and 'hassle-free environment'. In this chapter, we wish to conceptualize this political economic process, identifying its different facets and understanding their interlinkages. It is our contention that using the recently re-interpreted Marxist concept of 'primitive accumulation' can provide crucial insights in this regard. We wish to demonstrate that current developments in India can be fruitfully understood by employing the notion of primitive accumulation, understood as a constitutive primitive of capitalism, the process which continuously creates and consolidates the capital-relation. Adopting this new perspective might also help in redefining the agenda of struggles and counter-hegemonic politics in the neoliberal context.

Primitive Accumulation: Two Interpretations

As is well known, Marx had brought up the concept of primitive accumulation to try to understand the historical origins of capitalism. It is generally accepted by economic historians that in pre-capitalist modes of production the primary producers (majority of whom were peasants) had ownership of the means of production, most crucial among them being land. If we agree that capitalism is distinguished from these other modes of production by the relationship of a class of property-less labourers (who have nothing to sell but their labour power) and a class of propertied capitalists (the owners of the means of production) mediated through the market,[1] then the following question naturally arises: how did we arrive at the class of property-less labourers from that of producers who had the ownership (or at least the right of usage) of the means of production? It is this historical question that Marx sought to answer with the concept of 'primitive accumulation'.

In a sense, the answer is already contained in the question. Primitive accumulation is the process by which the producer is divorced from her/his means of production. Since, moreover, land is the primary means of production in pre-capitalist societies, the main focus of primitive accumulation was to separate peasants from the land. While the gradual penetration of market relations had a role to play in this, outright use of force was far more important, and in a sense the key. Only by evicting peasants from their lands and disrupting their livelihood could the development of markets in free labour and land be ensured; and only this could provide the firm basis for the emergence and consolidation of the capital-relation:

> The capital-relation presupposes a complete separation between the workers and the ownership of the conditions for the realization of their labor. As soon as capitalist production stands on its own feet, it not only maintains this separation, but reproduces it on a constantly extending scale. The process, therefore, which creates the capital-relation, can be nothing other than the process which divorces the worker from the ownership of the conditions of his own labor; it is a process which operates two transformations, whereby the social means of subsistence and production are turned into capital, and the immediate producers are turned into wage-laborers. So-called primitive accumulation, therefore, is nothing else than the historical process of divorcing the producer from the means of production. It appears as 'primitive' because it forms the pre-history of capital, and of the mode of production corresponding to capital (Marx 1976: 874–75).

It is worth recalling that Marx studied the 'enclosure movement' in Britain within this overall perspective. One crucial aspect of primitive accumulation should be noted immediately: it effects a redistribution and transfer of claims to already existing assets and resources, rather than creating any new assets. In this sense, it is an accumulation of intangible rights and not that of tangible assets or goods. This aspect of primitive accumulation is important for our purposes because the current frenzy of state-assisted acquisition of land and other resources in India is precisely a process whereby the rights to access and usage of already existing resources are being redistributed and transferred.

The last decade has witnessed a resurgence of debate around attempts to re-interpret the concept of primitive accumulation.[2] This debate has indicated that there are two distinct but related interpretations of primitive accumulation, one that stresses the temporal aspect and the other that emphasises the constitutive or originary aspect. For the first, more traditional, interpretation the 'primitiveness' of primitive accumulation is understood in a purely temporal sense. It is seen as the historical phase that created the preconditions for the development of capitalism by forcing the separation of workers and means of production. The second interpretation notes that there is both a temporal and a continuity argument in Marx's account of primitive accumulation. For this interpretation, therefore, the primitiveness of primitive accumulation does not arise simply from its location in historical time, relevant only as the initial stage of capitalism, rather it is the constitutive primitive of the capitalist system, a process that is essential for perpetuating its fundamental class structure — the separation between producers and means of production.

If primitive accumulation is constitutive, then it must arise as a continuous process within capitalism viewed as a global system. Expanded reproduction of the system requires reproduction of the capital-relation at every moment; separation of workers and means of production must be maintained continuously. In its day-to-day functioning, a mature capitalist economy enforces this separation through the market, i.e., by economic means; but at the boundaries (both internal and external), where capitalism encounters other modes of production, property and social relations attuned to those modes and also to the earlier stages of capitalism, other ways of subsistence, primitive accumulation comes into play. More often than not, direct use of force is necessary to effect the separation at the boundaries. And since capitalism, as a global system continuously encounters other modes of production along with the simultaneity of diverse stages of capitalism in various localities, the constitutive role of primitive accumulation is always in demand. One can probably go so far as to assert that capital accumulation is the extension of primitive accumulation, enforced through the market. In fact, in volume 3 of *Capital,* Marx himself calls the concentration and centralization of capital, which occur during the course of market-induced capital accumulation, as 'simply the divorce of the conditions of labour from the producers [which occurs through primitive accumulation] raised to a higher power' (Marx 1981: 354). But this does not mean that the two are identical. In fact, for the development of our overall argument it is important to grasp especially two differences:

(*a*) '[W]hile accumulation relies primarily on "the silent compulsion of economic relations [which] sets the seal on the domination of the capitalist over the worker", in the case of primitive accumulation the separation is imposed primarily through "[d]irect extra-economic force" (Marx 1976: 899–900), such as the state (ibid.: 900), particular sections of social classes (ibid.: 879), and so on. We can therefore say that primitive accumulation for Marx is a social process instigated by some social actor (the state, particular social classes, etc.) aimed at the people who have some form of direct access to the means of production. This social process often takes the form of a strategy that aims to separate them from the means of production' (De Angelis 2001).

(*b*) 'As opposed to accumulation proper, what "may be called primitive accumulation ... is the historical basis, instead of the historical result, of specifically capitalist production" (Marx 1867: 775). While sharing the same principle — separation — the two concepts point at two different conditions of existence. The latter implies the *ex novo*[3] production of the separation, while the former implies the reproduction — on a greater scale — of the same separation' (De Angelis 2001).

Keeping these differences are important because one comes to the rescue of the other when market processes falter. Since capital accumulation operates through the market, the services of primitive accumulation are required almost by definition when the market is in crisis. During crucial phases of capitalist crisis, primitive accumulation emerges to help transcend barriers to accumulation in two ways: (*a*) by facilitating the transition from the critically fated regime to a new regime of accumulation, and (*b*) by continuously negotiating the spatial expansion (both internal and external) of capitalism. During periods of transition and expansion, 'new enclosures' are required for putting the normal course of capitalist reproduction back on track — securing these enclosures through force and other 'direct extra-economic means' is the function of primitive accumulation. This re-definition allows us to grasp the function of the state and its continuous politico-legal activism at every stage of capitalism.

The present neoliberal phase can probably be understood fruitfully from this perspective. Despite the talk of separating the political from the economic, which is a staple rhetoric of the current phase, it is the state as the instrument of politico-legal repression that facilitates neoliberal expansion. First, the state intervenes with all its might to secure control over resources — both natural and human ('new enclosures') — and second, to ensure the non-transgression of the political into the economic, which essentially signifies discounting the politics of labour and the dispossessed from affecting the political economy. David Harvey notes that '[t]he main substantive achievement of neoliberalization ... has been to redistribute, rather than to generate, wealth and income'; the main mechanisms for achieving this is referred to by Harvey as 'accumulation by dispossession', by which he means,

> the continuation and proliferation of accumulation practices which Marx had treated of as 'primitive' or 'original' during the rise of capitalism. These include the commodification and privatization of land and the forceful expulsion of peasant populations ... ; conversion of various forms of property rights (common, collective, state, etc.) into exclusive private property rights ... ; suppression of rights to the commons; commodification of labour power and the suppression of alternative (indigenous) forms of production and consumption; colonial, neo-colonial, and imperial processes of appropriation of assets (including natural resources); monetization of exchange and taxation, particularly of land; the slave trade (which continues particularly in the sex industry); and usury, the national debt and, most devastating of all, the use of the credit system as a radical means of accumulation by dispossession. The state, with its monopoly of violence and definitions of legality, plays a crucial role in both backing and promoting these processes (Harvey 2005: 159).

Harvey identifies four main features of 'accumulation by dispossession': privatization, commodification, financialization, and the management-manipulation of assets, each feeding on the other, supported by the other and gaining strength from the other. The neoliberal resurgence since the mid-1970s can be understood as capital's counter-revolutionary response to the crisis that enwrapped 'embedded liberalism' internationally in the late 1960s, with 'signs of a serious crisis of capital accumulation . . . everywhere apparent. Unemployment and inflation were both surging everywhere, ushering in a global phase of 'stagflation' that lasted throughout much of the 1970s' (Harvey 2005: 12).

The Politics of Primitive Accumulation in India

What is going on in India today can be understood by employing the concept of primitive accumulation (as understood in the second interpretation) in almost all of the mentioned senses: separating primary producers from land, privatization of the 'public', conversion of common property resources into marketable commodities, destroying non-market ways of living, and so on. To our mind, each of the instances of 'displacement' or state-led 'land grab' are willy-nilly feeding into the overall process of primitive accumulation in India by divorcing primary producers from the land or restricting direct access to other common property resources such as forest, lakes, river, etc. A question crops up immediately. Being a labour-surplus economy, does India need to generate additional labourers, which is an obvious result of primitive accumulation, before absorbing what is already available? Certainly not, if we think from the viewpoint of labour. But the answer changes if we see the whole process from the perspective of capital. Fresh entrants into the already burgeoning ranks of the proletariat will increase the relative surplus population — floating, latent and stagnant — depressing real wages and thereby increasing the rates of profits on each unit of invested capital. Moreover, one of the major features of the neoliberal regime of accumulation has been the incessant 'informalization' of the labour process, and further growth of the relative surplus population makes late-capitalist countries such as India finely attuned to this. As Jan Breman notes:

> Mobilization of casual labour, hired and fired according to the needs of the moment, and transported for the duration of the job to destinations far distant from the home village, is characteristic of the capitalist regime presently dominating in South Asia (1996: 23).

Separation of producers from their means of production and subsistence, especially land and other natural resources, also creates markets for these resources; and thus comes into being the various agencies that thrive through hucksterage in these markets. These intermediaries play the crucial role of facilitating and normalizing the process of primitive accumulation. Examples abound: Trinamool Congress (TMC) goons, grassroots-level Communist Party of India (Marxist) (CPI [M]) leadership, local middle-classes such as school teachers, lawyers and other similar forces in the Singur case state-traders, local elites supported Salwa Judum in Chhattisgarh

The major target of land acquisition in India today is in areas where either peasant movements have achieved some partial success in dealing with capitalist exploitation and expropriation, or areas largely inhabited by the indigenous population whose expropriation could not be increasingly intensified because of the welfarist tenor of the pre-liberalization regime. West Bengal is the prime example of the former, where the Left Front-rule congealed due to its constituents' involvement in the popular movements. Now, the movements' institutionalization and incorporation of the leadership into the state apparatus is facilitating the present-day resurgence of primitive accumulation. Examples of the second kind of area could be parts of Chhattisgarh, Odisha, Andhra Pradesh, or Madhya Pradesh, which the corporate sector is eyeing for mining activities and setting up steel plants.

As an instructive example, if nothing else, let us see how displacement in Singur would have affected the various class forces on the ground. While the state apparatuses were trying to secure resources for corporate capital, sections of the local elite, including the well-off farmers led by the mainstream non-left political parties — such as the Congress and the TMC — had joined the movement against land acquisition essentially to obtain various kinds of concessions, a higher price for giving up the land to the state and perhaps also for increasing the land price for their future real estate speculation around the upcoming industrial belt. For example,

> a TMC leader and ex-pradhan of one of the gram panchayats was initially with the movement, but finally gave away his land. Many of the landed gentry, some of them absentee, who own bigger portions of land, depend on 'kishans' (i.e., hired labours, bargadars, etc.) for cultivation of their lands. They principally depend on business or service and have come forward to part with their land in lieu of cash (Banerjee 2006: 4719).

In case the government talks to the protesters and gives larger concessions, it is these sections that will benefit the most.

The people who were really the backbone of the movement in Singur were the landless working class and poor peasantry. According to a report,

> many agricultural workers and marginal peasants will lose their land and livelihoods. Though the State Government has decided to compensate the landowners, no policy has been taken for the landless agricultural workers, unrecorded bargadars and other rural households who are indirectly dependent for their livelihood on land and agricultural activities (Paschim Banga Khet Majoor Samity 2006).[4]

The region is also inhabited by the poor who

> frequent the nearby town, being employed in factories, shops and small businesses. Some of the youth have migrated to cities like Mumbai, Delhi and Bangalore, working there principally as goldsmiths or construction workers. There were several cases of reverse migration when people came back to their village after the closing down of the industries where they were working or finding it more profitable to work on the land than to work in petty industries or businesses, drawing a paltry sum in lieu of hard labour (Banerjee 2006: 4719).

For this population, as also for the landless workers and marginal peasants, the Singur struggles were existential. As an example of the second kind of land acquisition, we can turn our attention to Chhattisgarh. A report on recent developments in Chhattisgarh notes that, in India,

> [t]ribal lands are the most sought after resources now. Whether it is in Orissa or Chhattisgarh or Andhra Pradesh, if there is a patch of tribal land there is an attempt to acquire it. It is no geographical coincidence that tribal lands are forested, rich with mineral resources (80 per cent of India's minerals and 70 per cent of forests are within tribal areas) and also the site of a sizeable slice of industrial growth. The tribal districts of Chhattisgarh, Orissa, Jharkhand, Karnataka and Maharashtra are the destination of us $85 billion of promised investments, mostly in steel and iron plants, and mining projects. Ironically, these lucrative resources are of no benefit to the local people: an estimate of 10 Naxal-affected states shows that they contribute 51.6 per cent of India's GDP and have 58 per cent of the population. As with Chhattisgarh, all these

> states have a strong Naxal presence and are witness to movements against land acquisition. The state governments say these protests are Naxal-inspired. Local people say, however, that all they are trying to do is protect their land, forests and livelihood (*Down to Earth* 2006).

Here the state's mode of facilitating primitive accumulation is by raising mercenaries, the Salwa Judum. This extra-legal use of force is supported by the traditional exploiters of the indigenous population — traders, usurers, civil servants, and tribal neo-elites — who have functioned as intermediaries in the regime of commerce-based surplus extraction. On the one hand, absence of any recognized land rights of tribal communities has allowed the state to use principles of *terra nullius* and eminent domain to expropriate them. On the other, these communities have continued to exist in defiance of all these legalities. However, with the recent intensification of efforts to secure resources for corporate profiteering, along with the continued presence of primitive extractive modes of exploitation, these communities have been left with no real choice but to arm themselves for securing their unrecognized rights. Hence,

> Most tribal people living in forests are officially 'encroachers'. They live under the constant threat of being alienated from their land and livelihood. While the government completely failed to reach out to them, the Naxals succeeded in connecting to sections of the people. They spread to the state's 11 districts (200 districts in the country). Unable to contain them, government supported the creation of a civilian militia — Salwa Judum (*Down to Earth* 2006).

Besides these widely discussed cases of recent land acquisition and displacement, there have been numerous conflicts around the rights over water resources over the years. In almost all such cases, the state has come forth as being hell-bent upon the construction of big dams and other hydroelectric projects despite all evidence of their net negative marginal costs. For more than two decades Narmada Bachao Andolan has been a prominent force constantly exposing the anti-people, anti-environment character of these projects. Even in the Himalayan region of Uttarakhand (site of the legendary Chipko Andolan), riverbeds and surrounding lands have been 'enclosed' for private capital to be used for power generation and lucrative tourism projects. In fact, recent politics in this region cannot be fully understood without understanding the conflicts around these enclosures. Closer to urban India has been the neoliberal systematization of commercial and financial centres, the 'clearing' of slums, in cities such as Delhi and Mumbai, which have naturally been the hotbed of politics of and against 'new enclosures'.

Understanding all these diverse processes in the framework of primitive accumulation has several strategic implications. Perhaps, most urgently, this can provide a unified framework to locate the numerous struggles going on in the country right from the 'new' social movements, such as landless workers movements, Narmada Bachao Andolan and other local mobilizations of 'development-victims', to anti-privatization movements of public sector workers, all the way to the revolutionary movements led by the Maoists. This unified framework can then possibly facilitate dialogue among these organizations, something that is more than essential at this juncture if the movement of labour against capital is to be strengthened.

A Future beyond Capital

Using this framework will also mean re-evaluating many of the theoretical positions that are currently being used. For example, it will be necessary to rethink the classical communist position that characterizes the Indian state as semi-feudal and semi-colonial, and thereby sees the struggle of the peasantry as being directed primarily against feudal oppression. It is possible that the inherent limitations of this ideological framework disallow revolutionaries and other radicals to formulate effective strategies against the whole system, a system that preserves various vestigial forms to facilitate accumulation but is not defined by them. Thus, movements struggling against different forms of these vestiges are easily localized, regionalized, marginalized, dispersed, and even utilized in the intra-ruling class competition and conflicts. The state of the official Indian left is illustrative in this regard. It, too, stresses on the presence of 'vestiges' and the insufficiency of development, but then turns around and justifies its accommodation in the neoliberal capitalist project as a fight against these vestiges!

Despite the apparent popularity of the new movements of Latin America among the official left in India, their attachment to a schematic notion of national capitalist development retains all its strength. The devastating consequence, of course, is the deferral of the revolutionary moment till that development is attained; in reality, this amounts to postponing the revolutionary moment beyond the horizon of all concrete possibilities. Surely, this is not simply an ideological problem coming from a faulty understanding of the dynamics of capitalism or socialism. It is a consequence of the official left leadership's accommodation in the capitalist-parliamentary framework, an accommodation that moreover forces them to participate in the competitive race for representation. In the pursuit of presenting itself as the legitimate representative of the 'plurality of opinions', which parliamentary politics poses against the notion of class struggle, the left reproduces this plurality within itself, along with its built-in hierarchy. With partial successes in this exercise, representative of the opinions that count — that is the hegemonic class interests — solidify themselves within the party structures. And it is this congealment within the Left Front in West Bengal that leads the 'communists' to vocalize neoliberal myths of neutral industrial development, dubbing every protest against its policies as anti-developmental, backward and manipulative. Parallels with the neoliberal demonization of the transgression of the political into the economic can hardly be missed. Echoing well-heeled mandarins in Delhi, the Left Front government regularly uses the classic threat of capital flight to regiment all protesting voices.

Without comprehending the function of vestiges of earlier modes of production within capitalism or the role of earlier stages of the capitalist mode of production in sustaining capital accumulation, any fundamental challenge to the hegemonic forces in a late capitalist society like India cannot be formulated. It can hardly be denied that,

> we suffer not only from the development of capitalist production, but also the incompleteness of that development. Alongside the modern evils, we are oppressed by a whole series of inherited evils, arising from the passive survival of archaic and outmoded modes of production, with their accompanying train of anachronistic social and political relations. We suffer not only from the living, but from the dead. *Le mort saisit le vif* [The dead man clutches onto the living]! (Marx 1976: 91).

We will have to recognize the fact that during the stage of imperialism, and more so in the present postcolonial situation, 'a high level of capitalist development no longer require[s] the elimination of the traditional class of "small producers" and other pre-capitalist "remnants"' (Uno 1980: 125). Even in a country like Japan, 'in which capitalist society developed only at the so-called finance-capitalist stage of world capitalism, a high level of capitalist development has not been incompatible ... with the survival of the traditional class of "small producers"' (ibid.).

Indian capitalism, like Japanese, came into being in the stage of imperialism, when finance capital and inter-imperialist rivalries were already subjugating the whole world. Moreover, development under direct colonialism foisted some unique features on to the general characteristics of 'late capitalism'. During the colonial period, 'self'-expansion of Indian capital beyond the physical horizons of India was implausible because this would have required an Indian state committed to these interests. Colonialism ruled this out almost axiomatically. However, there were other channels available. The simultaneous existence of various socio-economic formations at diverse levels of Indian society allowed some possibility of 'internal' colonialism and 'enclosures', thus, providing the basis for capitalist expansion. Even after Independence, Indian capital relies heavily on the 'diversity' (or unevenness) of Indian economy and society for primitive accumulation and expansion. Additionally, 'semi-feudal' conditions at various locations within the country provide a vast reserve army of labour. The important characteristic of this insecure and docile population is that they can be pulled out of their original locations and thrown into the growing labour market without disturbing the essential fabric of the society. In other words, pre-capitalist forms of exploitation provide vast and near-permanent pools of cheap labour, which competes with the urban proletariat, thereby bringing the latter under political and economic control. Moreover, this seems to resolve the 'agrarian problem' of Indian capitalism, by 'externalising' rural and underdeveloped India from the 'core' industrial islands.[5] Concentrating capitalist agricultural development in particular locations of India (for example in West and North-west India), Indian capitalism could afford to under-develop other locations so that they could serve as 'external markets' and as reserves of 'footloose labour'.

Because unevenness is the essential feature of capitalist development, any mode of regulation, including neoliberal globalization, has to negotiate with diverse stages of societal development. Hence local reactions against this new wave of capitalist consolidation and accumulation are bound to be diverse. The revolutionary vision consists in coordinating these diverse forces for building a formidable challenge to capitalism. Even the struggles against vestigial forms, if they have to be decisive, need to be recognized as contesting capitalist relations that sustain them and are articulated through them. In the Indian context, they are all struggles against a stuttering capitalism, against the inherent brutalities of primitive accumulation. We will have to realize that the movements are not about 'saving' tribals/indigenous populations or their way of lives; it is a movement of labour against capital. Tribals, poor peasants, marginal peasants, landless labourers, informal sector workers, all these sub-classes are fighting against the tyranny of capital, against being fed — with their labour and resources — into the capitalist machinery. Obviously, in this fight against capital, we cannot cling on to any nostalgia for a pristine past; rather our vision must be directed towards the future that is built on the transcendence of capital, a socialist future rooted in a participatory economy and polity. Only then can the vast majority, suffering at the margins of capitalism and toiling under vestigial relations, can make a concerted, decisive effort to end the tyranny of capital.

Notes

* This chapter is a revised version of the article 'Neoliberalism and Primitive Accumulation in India: The Need to Go beyond Capital', *Radical Notes*, 7 February 2007, http://radicalnotes.com/2007/02/07/neoliberalism-and-primitive-accumulation-in-india/ (accessed 20 December 2013). Reproduced with permission.

1. Marx refers to this as the capital-relation.
2. See the contributions in *The Commoner*, no. 2., September 2001, http://www.commoner.org.uk/index.php?p=5 (accessed 13 September 2013).
3. *Ex novo* is used in the sense of 'original' or 'from scratch'.
4. This text is from a leaflet which was issued by Paschim Banga Khet Majoor Samity in the year 2006.
5. Japanese Marxist Kozo Uno stressed that capitalism is incapable of solving the agrarian question. 'We can say that it became clear on a world scale that the ability to solve the agrarian question would entail the ability to construct a new society to replace capitalism, and we may regard the League of Nations as having been one such attempt.

The solution to this problem, of course, means no more than the external expression of the internal contradictions of capitalism, and cannot occur unless the issue of class relations is solved. In this sense, the failure of the League of Nations was only to be expected' (quoted in Barshay 2004: 128).

References

Banerjee, Parthasarthi. 2006. 'Land Acquisition and Peasant Resistance at Singur', *Economic and Political Weekly*, 18–24 November, 41(46): 4718–20.

Barshay, Andrew E. 2004. *The Social Sciences in Modern Japan: The Marxian and Modernist Traditions*. California: University of California Press.

Breman, Jan. 1996. *Footloose Labour: Working in India's Informal Economy*. Cambridge: Cambridge University Press.

De Angelis, Massimo. 2001. 'Marx and Primitive Accumulation: The Continuous Character of Capital's "Enclosures"', *The Commoner*, no. 2, September, www.commoner.org.uk/02deangelis.pdf (accessed 12 October 2006).

Down to Earth. 2006. 'Anti-Naxal Operations a Cover for Exploiting Tribal People', 15(11), October 18, http://www.downtoearth.org.in/node/8561 (accessed 20 November 2006).

Harvey, David. 2005. *A Brief History of Neoliberalism*. Oxford: Oxford University Press.

Jha, Prem Shankar. 2006. 'Compensation not enough', *Daily News & Analysis*, 2 October, http://www.dnaindia.com/report.asp?NewsID=1056324&CatID=19 (accessed 10 November 2006).

Marx, Karl. 1976 [1867]. *Capital*, vol. 1. London: Penguin Books.

———. 1981 [1894]. *Capital*, vol. 3. London: Penguin Books.

Paschim Banga Khet Majoor Samity. 2006. 'Terror Cannot Suppress Them: People's Resistance to Forced Land Acquisition in Singur', 6 December, Kolkata.

Uno, Kozo. 1980 [1964]. *Principles of Political Economy*. Sussex: Harvester Press.

7

What is 'New' in the New Social Movements?

Rethinking Some Old Categories

Maitrayee Chaudhuri

The 1990s saw the introduction of new economic policies by the Indian government to integrate the economy into global capitalism. In 2011 India emerged as a not so inconsequential global player in global capitalism. The 1990s also witnessed the collapse of the existing socialist states. In 1989, Francis Fukuyama and his supporters, a resident scholar at the RAND Corporation, Washington, DC, argued that Western liberal democracy and capitalism had won an irreversible victory over all their ideological competitors, most importantly over socialism. I state these bare but defining facts to emphasize the privileged position and interests of global capital and, therefore, of an increasingly transnational capitalist *class*. Indian capitalists themselves have been increasingly investing globally and form part of this transnational class.[1] Class matters even if working class movements appear to have been overtaken by a host of other social movements based on caste, gender, ethnicity, sexuality, and environment. Class matters because division of labour and division of property remain indivisible in contemporary capitalism. It is in this context that I argue that any analysis of social movements, even that of the New Social Movements (NSMs), which appear to break away from a class-centric perspective, has to therefore engage with class.

This chapter attempts to look at NSMs, both as an *empirical phenomena* and a *conceptual claim*. Old Social Movements (OSMs) were seen as primarily class-based with reorganization of power as a central goal, which usually functioned within the frame of political parties. NSMs in contrast were not about changing distribution of power in society but often about quality-of-life issues — such as a clean environment, personal choices such as alternate sexualities, expressions of cultural identities — and were non-party based. Central to the distinction was the retreat of 'class'-based movements empirically and a decline of class analysis theoretically. I would like to argue that 'class' remains a fruitful analytical category today and can be productively used to understand the 'new' social movements whether caste- or gender-based or those led by an aggressive new middle-class 'civil society'.[2] In other words, class analysis (a conceptual matter) should not be conflated with empirical presence or absence of class-based movements.

I seek to build this argument by drawing from the Dalit and women's movements, the new visibility of the Indian middle-class in the public sphere and the new kind of 'civil society'-led social movements often rendered hyper-visible through both the old and new media. My analysis would therefore include: (*a*) the *historical contexts* within which the NSMs emerged in the West; (*b*) a look into two social movements — the Dalit and women's movement — to examine whether they can be accurately defined as NSMs; (*c*) an exploration of the *visibility of the Indian middle-class* in contemporary India and a simultaneous refashioning of the 'public' by a powerful media to understand new models of 'social movements' led by this middle-class; (*d*) a look, albeit cursory, at the dominant conceptual frameworks used in the study of social movements in Indian sociology to understand why NSMs as a conceptual claim found such ready acceptance. I further seek to link this with extant pedagogic practices in India that made the schematic, feature-wise contrasts between NSMs and OSMs particularly amenable for incorporation in the existing syllabi, ideally suited for memorizing, reproduction in examinations and scoring of marks — the end goal of education.[3] In an attempt to address these four tasks I hope to draw attention to the obvious but much neglected aspects — that concepts emerge in specific historical contexts, ideology and theory are closely linked, and every theory has a propensity to focus attention on some aspects of society and render others invisible. In my treatment of NSMs I seek to show how both 'class' and 'capital' disappeared, not empirically but conceptually, much like 'gender' at one time. Further, in an attempt to make them visible, both an empirical and theoretical effort has to be made. This chapter seeks to do this.

I
Contexts and Concepts

NSMs emerged at a distinct historical point of time in the West. A wave of social movements arose in Western Europe and the United States of America (USA) in the 1960s and 1970s, quite different from those of an earlier period. Post-World War II had seen a host of intense anti-colonial movements, often with a fare presence of working class and peasantry. The Indian national movement is a good example of this. Prior to the rise of a host of nationalist movements in the non-Western region, the West witnessed a wide range of socialist movements. While one strand moved towards formation of state socialism (Soviet Union, East Europe and China), the other moved towards a social democratic consensus (much of Western Europe) with a state committed to social welfare and protection of basic needs of its citizens — health, education and shelter. In all cases, whether the social movements were anti-colonial, socialist or social democratic, they were *party-led* and driven by wider goals of *universal social justice* and *equity* — characteristics of OSMs. The state then was itself constitutive of social movements, no matter how different their subsequent trajectories could be.

The movements in Western Europe and USA in the 1960s and 1970s arose during the war in Vietnam where forces led by USA were involved in a bloody conflict in the former French colony against Communists. In Europe, Paris was the nucleus of a vibrant students' movement that joined workers' parties in a series of strikes protesting against the war. In USA, Martin Luther King led a civil rights movement and Malcolm X the Black Power movement. The anti-war movement was joined by tens of thousands of students who were being compulsorily drafted by the government to go and fight in Vietnam. The women's movement and the environmental movement also gained strength during this time of social ferment. Significantly, the West at this point was marked by unprecedented growth and prosperity, a context where class inequalities did not stare at one's face as it does in our parts of the world.

Further, it was difficult to classify the members of these NSMs as belonging to any one class or even nation. Issues such as environment and gender, race and sexualities were raised in a fashion and scale not seen before. It was now argued that class-based movements had perforce subjugated all other identities. Each identity had an equal right to articulate its presence and class could not subsume the other identities that people had. This was also a time when an increasingly multi-cultural West sought to celebrate distinct identities and argue that identities were not fixed, immutable but fluid and multiple. Theoretically the rise of cultural studies and postmodern ideas theorized this plurality and fluidity. At another end, the late 1980s and early 1990s saw the incredibly swift and apparently sudden collapse of USSR and other socialist states. Class analysis appeared redundant and retreated from the academia, for obvious empirical, theoretical and ideological reasons. OSMs were thus replaced by NSMs, movements more suited to the new times.

One has already alluded to the fact that the category of NSMs with the related assumption of the decline of OSMs was readily accepted within Indian social science. However, talking of contexts and concept, the pertinent question here is whether India did witness the rise of NSMs comparable to the West. In other words, did the ready acceptance of this classification of social movements have empirical and theoretical justification?

Indeed India has experienced a whole array of social movements involving women, peasants, dalits, adivasis, and others. Can these movements be understood as 'NSMs'? The fact of the matter is that concerns about class inequality and unequal distribution of resources continue to be important elements in these movements. Farmers' movements have mobilized for better prices for their produce, peasants for better wages and right to employment, tribals for access to forest and land rights. Dalit labour has acted collectively to ensure that they are not exploited by upper-caste landowners and money-lenders. The women's movement has worked on issues of gender discrimination in diverse spheres, such as the workplace and within the family, and foregrounded the multiple oppressions of the working class and the dalit women. Questions of inequality have remained very central to the NSMs, though of course neither were they just about economic inequalities, nor were they organized along class lines alone. A quick reference to the Chipko movement would elucidate the point better. At one level we could define the movement as ecological and therefore an NSM, context-specific, issue-based, and outside political party control. A closer look would suggest that what was at stake was the question of subsistence — the villagers' right to get firewood, fodder and other daily necessities from the forest. The economy of subsistence was pitted against that of profit. It was also a movement of women and right to resources. Questions of class and differential relationship to property and resources were central even as it entailed ecological, gender and caste issues. What to me appears more distinctive to the NSMs is the major shift from 'others' speaking on their behalf to self-representation, whether it is of the Dalits[4] or 'adivasis',[5] women or gays.[6] One recognizes the historical significance of this shift. At the same time, I argue, it is productive to deploy class analytics to understand NSMs and identity politics itself.

What is meant by class analytics? Broadly I draw from Marxist understandings of society as constitutive of material and social relations of production. Social movements too would likewise emanate from the tensions and dynamics of these relations. What is perhaps a shared view between Weber and Marx would be that individual's life chances are constrained by their location within their society. What distinguishes Marxist class analytics is a very specific understanding of social relations of production, in this case capitalist, that not just determines class locations but form the very motor of production and reproduction of a given class society. Capitalism sans division of owners and non-owners of means of production does not exist. What does exist is the differential form and nature of this relationship. Thus, if Fordism is best suited for capital to function at one time, flexible labour could be best at another. Indeed the current neoliberal era itself can be better appreciated from this perspective.

This return to Marxist theory may appear strange given that it has been widely acclaimed as failed, particularly within Indian sociology within which it was anyway very weak. I instead argue that the very victory of capitalism that heralded the 1990s means that a theory of capitalism, delineated at length in the many works of Marx, would be productive *even as* workers of the world may not unite to end capitalism. What remains illuminating are some basic insights into the making and working of social formations that help us to understand contemporary class relations, contestations between them and the state, and most significantly the defining role of capitalism in all of this. In other words, it may help us understand why 'Dalit capitalism' and 'professional feminism' discussed later in this chapter are one face of 'social movements' in contemporary India.

II
The Old and the New in the Women's Movement

A central contention of the NSM thesis has been the rise of issue-based, often identity-based array of diverse movements instead of the older class-based movements articulated outside the political party mode of mobilization. In India too in the late 1970s the rise of the autonomous women's organizations made an expressed break from what were seen as party-affiliated women's organizations where women's issues were rendered secondary. Significantly, the decades that followed saw a broad consensus between party-led women's organizations and autonomous women's groups. Left party-led women's groups took up issues such as sexuality and violence, while questions of development, livelihood and equity were accepted as important by autonomous groups. More recently, in a post-liberalized India, developmental issues and questions of inequity have once again acquired renewed salience within both the women's and Dalit movements. It is important to underscore the fact that the incredible prosperity that post-World War West witnessed, buttressed by a strong state welfare agenda, conducive to NSMs often 'lifestyle' demands was not replicated in India. However, in post-liberalized India we do see lifestyle feminism making its presence felt, as we shall see later in this chapter.

Shifts in Gender and Developmental Frameworks

In the neoliberal framework the informal sector is at the heart of the market economy and represents its prime model. Since women are seen to predominate in this sector, it is their creativity and potential that needs special attention (see Kalpagam 1994). A significant development in this period is the appropriation of feminist findings by the developmental sector and international institutions to further models of development, which run counter to feminist premises. Mary John, in an analysis of one such World Bank report, observes how it focuses on 'the incredible range of tasks poor women perform, their often greater contribution to household income despite lower wage earnings, their ability to make scarce resources stretch further under deteriorating conditions' (John 2004: 247). These were documented and debated in the past, but now the feminist findings have been reworked. 'Through a crucial shift in signification, these findings are no longer arguments about *exploitation* so as much as proofs of *efficiency*' (ibid.). Not surprisingly, therefore, a great deal of development gender discourse is now exclusively addressed within the microcredit framework, premised upon the idea that women are efficient managers and can be trusted to repay. The strength and resilience of the poor woman that feminist scholarship had highlighted was reinterpreted by international institutions such as the World Bank as a justification of withdrawing state support. The argument was that since poor women are not passive victims but potentially generators of wealth, the correct prescription was not state subsidies but market credit (ibid.).

Commenting on this appropriation of feminism by neoliberal discourse, Nancy Fraser argues that what was truly new about the second-wave women's movement was the way it wove together, in a critique of andro-centric state-organized capitalism, three analytically distinct dimensions of gender injustice: economic, cultural and political. Subjecting state-organized capitalism to wide-ranging multifaceted scrutiny, in which these three perspectives intermingled freely, feminists generated a critique that was simultaneously ramified and systematic. In the ensuing decades, however, the three dimensions of injustice became separated, both from one another and from the analysis of capitalism. With the fragmentation of the feminist critique came the selective incorporation and partial recuperation of some of its strands. Split off from one another and from the societal assessment that had integrated them, second-wave hopes were conscripted in the service of a project that was deeply at odds with the larger, holistic vision of a just society. 'In a fine instance of the cunning of history, utopian desires found a second life as feelings currents that legitimated the transition to a new form of capitalism: post-Fordist, transnational, neoliberal' (Fraser 2009: 99).

The Women's Reservation Bill: Class, Caste or Gender?

The fate of the Women's Reservation Bill (WRB) seeking 33 per cent reservation for women in parliament still remains uncertain more than 15 years after its birth, with a display of persistent and fierce resistance to its passing. The Bill has evoked a wide set of varying responses, ranging from the crude anti-women remarks that the presence of women would invoke catcalls and whistles[7] to a more politically correct invocation of the downtrodden women which this Bill would purportedly marginalize. Fears are being expressed that the Reservation Bill would generate possible shifts in the nature of political influence of different social groups. The argument is that ever since the rise of middle castes in contemporary India, subsequent to the Green Revolution and land reforms, the traditional, pre-dominantly upper-caste ruling class has been feeling decidedly uncomfortable, shaken by the prospect of an almost certain loss of cultural and political hegemony. In the WRB they see a possible way back to capture political and cultural dominance. The assumption is that the Bill would erode the base of these new sections, particularly so because the rotational system proposed in the Bill would disturb their hold on the constituencies. *What one witnesses therefore is ruling class negotiations and contestations among its different fractions, even as the site of contestation is caste and gender, buttressing my basic contention that class still matters and class analytics allow us to explore the deep structures of society.* The events referred to later in this section illustrate this.

The Congress heading the current coalition government that came to power in 2009, was initially disinclined to conduct a caste census, demanded by the parties representing the Other Backward Classes (OBCs). However in an attempt to woo the support of these political parties on quite different but critical matters, namely the passing of the Finance Bill and the contentious Nuclear Liability Bill[8] in a parliament where the ruling coalition was not sure of majority support, it revised its view on caste census.[9] That the same group has been spearheading the anti-WRB has obvious implications for the fate of the Bill. This propensity of gender issues to become sites where larger political battles are fought has been a constant of sorts in the history of modern India. Significantly, the demand for caste census by social justice movements was to map socio-economic indicators. What however came to be was enumeration, counting of numbers with a sole intent of the struggle for hegemony. It is therefore no surprise to see that the WRB has been opposed tooth and nail, sometimes directly,[10] sometimes by ridicule,[11] sometimes disingenuously using politically correct social justice language,[12] and sometimes as a strategic tool to manipulate people (Teltumbde 2010: 15).

Honour Killing: Caste and Gender? Struggle for Class Hegemony?

In a 21st-century India where women's presence in public life is widely visible, the fierceness of some of the 19th century and early 20th century resistances return to haunt us as we bear witness to a growing number of honour killings, executed at the behest of the Khap Panchayat, or traditional village councils, to punish defiant young adults for marrying outside society's norms. As seen time and again, community/caste boundary maintenance is about following community rules of marriage. A violation of one rule necessarily amounts to a violation of the other. However, the matter of honour killing is also an assertion of social hegemony over the public domain. The message sent out by the Khap Panchayat is that not only do they control the community, but their ownership of both land and capital ensures their place within the ruling class, which control political parties and thereby also the state. It is this relationship that class analytics is most suited to unravel. Recent years have seen a growing challenge of the entrenched social group within the village by both 'lower caste' and women's social movements.[13] Honour killings are a brutal resistance to change but articulated in a rhetoric of tradition against modernity, customs against state law, indigenous against the Western. The defenders of honour killing have rightly identified that there is a gap between the state law (product of long years of social movements — nationalist and women's) and the social law (in this case, congealed practices of dominant classes/castes). In the absence of a commensurate law, the 'society' has to exercise sanction, murderously if needed, to deter erring members (Bhardwaj 2010).

The Dalit Movement: Of the Old and the New, of the National and the Global

The rise of the Dalit movement in the last decades has been momentous to say the least. The strength and visibility of the movement has been such that the left political parties themselves have been introspecting their purported failure to take caste into consideration in their exclusive focus on class. At one level, therefore, quite clearly, this indeed is a retreat from class-based movements and a loud assertion of identity claims. The claim for recognition was sharper than that for redistribution. I would however also like to maintain my assertion that *if we have an empiricist understanding of caste or class we would fail to recognize that in a class society, it is imperative that class relations and contestations would operate even if played out in the language of caste or gender, ethnicity or culture*. Certain developments within the Dalit movement interestingly throw light on the manner a movement for social justice can get transformed and appear conducive with the neoliberal model of globalization. And how claims for recognition could also be transformed to those for greater say within the state and nation while shifting the terrain of the movement to a global level, drawing both the mobilizing power of the diaspora as well as using the instruments provided by international institutions.

The Durban Conference itself was a high point that raised the issue of Dalit discrimination at the United Nations level. More recently, the British government has recognized caste to be a practising form of discrimination within the United Kingdom. I would like to look at some of these developments, namely: the perceived need and theoretical claim of a Dalit bourgeoisie for growth; the possibilities of the neoliberal regime for development and therefore the position articulated on globalization; the persistent focus on reservation; and finally, the internationalization of the movement itself apart from the active role of the international institutions.

Why a Dalit Bourgeoisie is Considered Important

Recently, a newspaper report covered the meet of the Dalit entrepreneurs and the Finance Ministry as part of the pre-Budget confabulations.[14] This was not a one-off event but a part of a well-thought-out programmatic way forward by the Dalit movement. The first tangible beginnings for this felt-need were expressed at the Bhopal meet, held on 12–13 January 2002, where a decision was taken to earmark 22.5 per cent of the government's procurement from Dalit manufacturers and traders. Chandra Bhan, the noted Dalit intellectual, rued that while Dalits constituted a very large percentage of India's population, no millionaire or billionaire could be counted among them. He argued that wealth creation among Dalits was critical for the growth of the community, and the state could ensure this by committing itself to purchasing a set portion of its requirements from Dalit entrepreneurs. The government could, for instance, buy a Compaq PC from a Dalit trader at the same MRP rates as elsewhere in the market without losing any money, as governments all over the world buy billions of goods from the open market. The margin money will would then go to the Dalits who were historically excluded from such processes.

Focus on the Doable

The argument spelt out by those such as Chandra Bhan has some obvious implications. One is that the extant path of global capitalism is taken for granted as the only way forward. It has thus been argued:

> [F]rom the outset, the new *dalit* movement focused on the 'doable' — on policies which did not run counter to the neoliberal development agenda as it unfolded in the 1990s, on the policies which could be argued from within the neoliberal discourse. Dalit activists dug deep into liberal US academic discourse and policy tradition, and based their core arguments on the applicability of this to the Indian context. The compatibility with the (neo)liberal thinking was a necessary ingredient in the strategy. There was ample 'policy space' for a (re-)formulation of caste discrimination within the international human rights discourse. The detailed lesson-learning by the new *dalit* movement, of liberal ways of combating discrimination of minorities, took the reformulation logic a step further, by influencing the policy focus of the movement (Lescher 2008: 257).

This practical approach is a product of the broader ideological moment where, in a very real sense, there simply appears to be no alternative. This orientation however has very obvious implications. Engaging with the international mainstream policy agenda meant that certain policy alternatives, rather than another, were given lower priority. The Dalit empowerment agenda could not gain the same impetus from engaging with the international development community. Empowerment of a social group does not figure in neoliberal individualist policy-making, where 'power' is seen in relation to individual capabilities, not to group-level social oppression, and where solutions are based on enabling such individual capabilities. Emphasizing 'employment' (and that too for a minority of the Dalits) over empowerment may be as much an unintended consequence of the internationalization strategy, as a choice based on the self-interest of the Dalit elites.

Connected to this persuasive view of doing the doable, I wish to touch upon the idea of utopia more generally, and the need for a critical analysis within social sciences more particularly. In other words, I return very briefly to the sociology of knowledge question, the matter of contexts and concepts with which we began. For an engagement with theoretical questions alone would equip us to explore whether there is indeed a justification to proceed with the handy feature enumeration mode of analysis of the old and new social movements; and whether class as an analytical category offers any possibility of productive enquiry to see the deeper structures of capital, class and state at work.

Social movements have often held some form of a better future, a utopia if you like. However social movements in the current context have to be understood as operating with an anti-utopia project, a dominant state of belief. By the end of the 20th century, utopia had come to be reviled as illusory, dangerous and against human nature (Couton 2009: 93–94). This chapter's attempts to question given frameworks of understanding new and old social movements should be read in this light.

The International Advocacy Network and the Dalit Movement

It has been argued that the focus of the new Dalit movement on affirmative action also relates to the fact that the new movement formed part of a transnational advocacy network. There are several aspects to this. First, given the strong involvement of the Ford Foundation and Human Rights Watch in the formative years of the new movement, it appears that the Indian-based new Dalit movement was not in the driving seat in the relationship with the international advocacy network. Rather, there seems to have been a more symbiotic relationship between the national Indian elements and the non-Indian organizations involved in the network (Lersche 2008: 257–58).

Within the confines of liberal thinking, the Dalit movement successfully extended the existing policy space, in India and internationally. Without the Dalit movement campaigning, international mainstream development organizations would not have expressed positive views on 'Dalit' Corporate Social Responsibility, nor partaken in and co-funded Dalit international policy conferences. Without campaigning, the argument that the US experience regarding private sector affirmative action was relevant for India would not have won the day in the country. More generally, the question that remains is how an advocacy-based 'shortcut', without the active involvement of the Dalit grassroots, would be able to achieve the quite major social changes that are required in order to change the power relations underlying the social discriminations of Dalits. Or is this a story about hegemonic contestations and Dalit capitalism?

That caste and gender are my preferred sites for arguing my position on class and struggles for hegemony in state and society is linked to my view that we need to seriously look afresh at the received wisdom about old and new social movements. One of the central tenets of the NSMs is purportedly the retreat of the universal cause on the one hand, and metanarratives as explanatory schemes on the other. What we witness worldwide is however an ascendency of global power, global decision-making, global institutions, transnational corporations, and even a global developmental sector. One has sought to show how both the women's and the Dalit movements are inextricably engaged with not just the state but international institutions. An understanding of the transformed nature of capital, functioning increasingly, at a global level, provides insights into changes in the nature of social movements Perhaps the buzz word 'glocal' captures the point. I shall return to this in my conclusion for the genesis and growth of the term 'glocal' allows us to interrogate the received wisdom of NSMs. For now, I would like to turn to the third part of my illustrative instances, namely the centrality of the middle-class in contemporary Indian public discourse, and its role in the media to argue my case that we need to examine the given ideas of the features of the NSMs at greater length.

III

The Centrality of the Middle-class: Implications for Class Analytics

The introductory section of this chapter has already set the post-liberalized Indian context within which I am looking at the phenomenon of NSMs. This manner of entering this exposition on NSMs offers us a vantage point to understand how the world and how

India has changed. This invocation of the 'world' and of 'India' at once is deliberate. For I argue that many of the recent changes that have undermined the strength of 'old social movements', such as class-based movements of workers and peasants, are consequences of state policy shifts in developmental models globally, in particular the growing hegemony of neoliberalism. Yet not all sources of change can be directed to global developments. There is an Indian story here. The intended and unintended consequences of many decades of a developmental state and the new economic policies that formally can be dated to 1991 are both many and deep. The social structure that defines India is certainly transformed even as it contains many of the old and persistent forms of inequalities. *There is a class contestation, even as it may appear to be that of a caste or ethnic or tribal one. The class contestations are those between ruling blocs from primarily an old-established, usually twice-born caste groups and those of an assertive ascending ruling class bloc from the backward and marginalized caste groups*. This essentially ruling section contest for hegemony, backed by their respective middle-class constituencies, renders other conflicts and tensions invisible to public media except for the episodic and violent ruptures. The earlier exposition on the WRB and honour killing explicates these tensions. Working class movements may have declined but labour strife and peasant unrest are very much present.[15] Does the empirical retreat of class-based movements and ascendency of identity-based movements (NSMs) imply that class analytics cease to be fruitful in understanding contemporary India? I would argue that class analytics would help analyze both the emergence and visibility of middle-class politics, which we witness today and which may appear to go against a 'prophecy' of ascendant working class struggle.

I argue that this celebration of the middle-class is perhaps justified, as the beneficiary sections of the economic reforms are indeed largely middle-class, numerically large and rapidly increasing, even if in terms of percentages it is small. This centrality of the middle-class in India's public life has its own very specific historical past, which needs reiteration. A colonially mediated modernity had led to the emergence of a Western-educated middle-class imbued with modern, liberal, bourgeois ideological visions but with no family resemblance to the Western bourgeoisie in structural terms.

> On the one hand they were products of an English education introduced by the colonial masters and therefore victim to a Eurocentric view of

modern society, on the other, they were victim to the feeling of historical denial which the original stock of middle class that could most profit by contacts with the West slowly got on its bones (cited in Chaudhuri 2011: 12).

The story did not change substantially in independent India. The bourgeoisie never achieved hegemonic status and working class formation was weak and fragmented. *Instead the middle-class had a major role to play in managing the ruling bloc, which included the bourgeoisie and landed interests*. It has been further pointed out that at the macro level the new middle-class has been 'forged at the intersection of a liberalization and a political context marked by organized political challenges from below' (Fernandes and Heller 2009: 147).

I have argued elsewhere that, in the context of Indian media, the construction of a new Indian middle-class with new world visions was a central task undertaken by the media. In the early years of liberalization, advertisements were a key agent to change public discourse even as it created the new Indian man and woman (Chaudhuri 2001). Ten years later, the news, everyday details, editorials, features, everything together has transformed the meaning of 'public' (Chaudhuri 2010b). Since the media has had a very special role to play in this new transformed India, I shall return to its analysis at greater length, the key role it has played to project a new middle-class vision of global India and its position and role in the democratic process.

This trumpeting of the new middle-class needs to be taken seriously. It cannot be dismissed as propaganda that have little to do with reality. And if we take propaganda as half-truth then the 'half' has to be taken note of seriously. I contend: (*a*) that the middle-class in this current context has a critical ideological role to play. My discussion on the media in the last part of the chapter will discuss this; (*b*) *India Incorporation*'s projection of the successful Indian middle-class announces India's arrival as an economic power, as an amorphous body fêted for its consuming power. And significantly marks for itself far more direct say in the Indian state; (*c*) for the *Indian state* it means flouting its global power and visibility; (*d*) for the *middle-class* themselves this is a loud assertion of their success upon which rests *a concomitant claim for greater political visibility and power within the state and society*. This focus on the state may appear a bit dated given that dominant rhetoric of globalization suggests a retreat of the state and greater say of international institutions. I argue that if one were to focus on a movement, such as the women's movement or the Dalit movement, one would notice that the matter is more about transformed nature of class power of the state and the manner that this power gets played out through often strategic alliances between the state and international institutions. It is not an either-or choice. One shall see this in the global Dalit movement's lobby of their case through international institutions, which often are posited as against the Indian state; for instance, the Durban conference and the Dalit movement's assertion to get caste discrimination recognized as racial discrimination in the United Nations. At the same time the Dalit movement would work with the state whether to hear the voice of Dalit entrepreneurs or ensure reservation in both employment and education. *If we see the state as relational and constitutive of changing class dynamics and the assertion of the elite from marginalized groups, whether Dalit or backward, we would see class at work even as the rhetoric remains that of identity and the claim that of cultural recognition.* Here I do not wish to enter into the civil society movement against corruption with an unlikely leader in Anna Hazare that India witnessed in 2011. But its middle-class support and character is self-evident.

This loud assertion of success by the middle-class, and a claim for greater political power, I argue, is done in two related but apparently dissimilar fashions: (*a*) if we take the case of caste and gender on one hand, a story unfolds which pits one section of the middle-class against the other, often evident in social movements for and against reservation. The debate over the WRB plays out middle-class contestation for hegemonic control even as no one wishes to leave the rhetoric of social justice just as yet; (*b*) if one takes the rise of illiberal social and political assertions of the middle-class on the other hand, we tangibly notice a veritable backlash within the women's movement and the wider representation of women's issues. I have argued earlier and at length about the manner in which 'feminism' is represented in the media. There is a loud and categorical assertion of the individuated woman whose claim to success is precisely her ability and competence, and not because she had anything remotely to do with collective movements such as the women's movements which anyway give a bad image to the story of India's middle-class success. This individual model of achievement also becomes a part of developmental models for poor achieving women, which is a section of this larger story of ideological transformation; (*c*) the acceptance that the *issue of reservation* has in public space needs further explanation Both the proponents and opponents have deep angst and anger which they deem appropriate to vent in public domain and address to the state. In part I explain this with reference to the clout that the middle-class, of whichever shade, (notwithstanding the persisting control over the media by the 'twice-born' middle-class) has come to occupy in public space. To some extent, I link this to the rise of identity politics, which privilege claims for 'recognition' rather than those for 'redistribution'. For as Nancy Fraser puts it,

> after all, this capitalism would much prefer to confront claims for recognition over claims for redistribution, as it builds a new regime of accumulation on the cornerstone of women's waged labour, and seeks to liberate markets from social regulation in order to operate all the more freely on a global scale (2009: 112).

If this is so, can we really go along with the idea that the rise of gender or caste-based social movements indicates a retreat of class? *What is probably a more accurate description is that while class remains, class contestations play out not as class-based social movements but identity movements of various kinds.*

V
Media and Social Movements

I proceed with Charles Tilly's view that social movements are historically specific, and that national states played an essential part in the creation of the modern national social movement. Further, and this is important for my broader argument, nation states 'play an essential part in the creation of the modern national social movement' (Tilly 1979: 19). The mentioned exposition on women's and Dalit movements suggests that negotiation with the state remains a key site and mode of social movements, but at the same time international institutions and global strategies become increasingly significant. Tilly further argues that mapping and explaining the changes in the collective action repertoire is an important task. Today mass media have reshaped our perceptions and tactics (ibid.).

The role media has had in representing social movements, and more importantly in shaping broader understandings of the meaning of democracy in neoliberal times, cannot be overemphasized. My study of changes within the Indian media since the 1990s has shown how centrally it has played a role in the transformation of India from its earlier economic and political vision to one where neoliberal ideas work as both the operational economic framework as well as an ideological vision. My argument was that a 'concerted ideological campaign thus has to be carried out to establish the legitimacy of the new economic regime, to which advertising contributes' (Chaudhuri 2001: 375).

> The two important social processes within which any meaningful reading of popular media and feminism can be attempted today are the women's movement and the process of economic liberalization initiated in India. The two have very different geneses and very different trajectories. But as is the wont of history, there are times when disparate social processes meet and new social forms take shape. While the Indian state heralded the policy of liberalization and opening up the Indian market in the 1980s, the tangible impact on the media, on the lifestyle of a new middle class, on urban life in general made its presence felt only in the 1990s. Increasingly visible now are the more upmarket magazines' projection of a post-liberalized post-feminism, where the individual corporate woman is the icon (Chaudhuri 2000: 264).

I had contrasted this assertion of the individuated woman to an earlier period where issues of class, caste, tribe, poverty, and social justice formed an intrinsic part of feminist struggles in India, both in colonial and independent India. I had noted that autonomous women's groups which emerged in the 1970s contested the centrality of class in the formulation of women's organizations affiliated to the left. Their point was that this tended to obfuscate the specificity of the women's question. Both groups have moved a long way since then. 'While left groups have played a visible role in the women's movement, autonomous groups have increasingly taken up questions of economic deprivation and matters of class' (ibid.: 269). Quite clearly the rise of the women's movement did not displace class issues in the manner that models of NSMs would suggest. To return to our central contention about the role of media I draw examples primarily from the women's movement and its representation in the media, with which I am most familiar. A look at the transformation of the Woman's Day is instructive.

International Women's Day has been traditionally celebrated by women's organizations and other political unions that aligned themselves quite unambiguously with democratic and progressive forces. We now have a riot of ads with the specific day's messages appearing on 8 March every year. Ponds has an advertisement titled 'The Millennium Miracle: A Curtain Raiser' with an image of a woman's mask, an hourglass and some paintbrushes. The text reads:

> As we are poised for a flight into the year 2000, what does it portend for women? A closer look at the trend-setting explosions on the careers, fashion, fitness and beauty minefields ... She's what make the world go round. Yesterday. Today. In the new millennium. And for eternity (Chaudhuri 2000: 270).

Advertisements, representative of high-powered beauty shows, were marketed through the 1990s as matters of choice, upward mobility, success and agency. Feminism is projected as a matter of choice. A deliberate break was made with the women's movement, yet the language used for the construction of the new woman was often appropriated from the women's movement. And this works, as all co-options do, as simultaneously a form of sharing in the spoils and a displacement (Sunder Rajan 1993: 132).

The broader argument I make is that an advertisement-driven media actually altered a broad consensus within the public discourse and the middle-class about the importance of social movements and a perception that they were morally worthy.

> I would like to claim that India's colonial history of struggles, whether by reformers, nationalists, peasants, workers or women, were seen as part of the larger anti-imperialist struggle and perceived as inherently moral and worthy. Therefore, unlike the West, in India a formal consensus existed about the legitimacy of oppositional movements and organizations. Concern for the dispossessed formed part of the rhetorics of nationalism and entered the consciousness of independent India's middle class. Liberalization ushered in the new Indian who disassociates himself or herself from movements unless it is a question of celebrity endorsements of causes. The strength of dominant ideologies is their 'naturalness'. Where advertisements defining how we ought to live appear natural and celebrate choices, a campaign by a woman's organization to oppose this would appear as a violation of choice and a killjoy attack (Chaudhuri 2000: 274).

Studies on media representation of social movements would show the shifting priority of the media and reveal to what extent a new construction of the nation, in a kind of mirror reflection of the post-liberalization middle-class, has gained ground and legitimacy. The implications for collective social movements of peasants and tribals, workers and craftsmen is that they get rendered not just invisible, but marginal to the new mainstream consensus where politics is seen as disruptive, and economics the steering wheel of change.

One has to locate this change in the transformed nature of the state. Three decades ago, the structure of state power in India was usually described in terms of a coalition of dominant class interests — capitalists and the rich farmers as the two dominant classes, competing and aligning with one another within a political space, aided by a powerful bureaucracy and supervised by state, *relatively* though not entirely autonomous of dominant classes. The changes introduced since the 1990s have transformed this framework of class dominance. Recent events have shown how both the state and the media are increasingly dependent on the corporate sector. Where would the space for autonomy for the state or for the media stand in such a case? In a recent piece I have argued that:

> This often strident appropriation of the nation and the Indian 'public' by a middle class ideologically aligned with the project of liberalization is most evident in the media today. I argue that this is done in two ways: by an overt ideological defence of an unbridled market and an attack on the very idea of an interventionist and welfare state; and by the everyday quotidian features and news that inscribe corporate speech, create a new imaginary of a global Indian and a global Indian middle class (Chaudhuri 2010b: 62).

VI
Returning to the Conceptual Question

I return in the tail end of this chapter to two dominant conceptual frames that have often been deployed to study social movements in India. My choice of only two, namely, structural functionalism and postmodernism, may appear arbitrary. I justify this preference on the grounds that while the former has been the most dominant theory deployed in Indian sociology/social anthropology, the latter has been hugely influential in the West and in significant quarters in contemporary Indian academia.[16] That however is not my sole reason to invoke postmodernism. I do so for it captures, in a way, the spirit of global capitalism, the idea of NSMs, the retreat of class analytics, and critique of foundational epistemology. Both approaches do not address either the issue of production relations, class or the specific dynamics of capitalism. This chapter has foregrounded the privileged position and interests of global capital which has had its own impact on the direction and form of NSMs.

Structural functionalism looked at social movements as systemic responses to felt needs and response to some kind of malintegration. I have referred to few scholars here, who were dominant from the 1930s until the 1960s in the USA.[17] For J. Davis (1930), a social movement emerges to meet a 'new-felt need', while for H. Blumer (1951) they arise out of 'undefined or unstructured situations', which cause stresses in the system. Linton (1943) looks at social movements as attempts to compensate for the frustrations of the society's members, while Banks (1964) point out that social movements are functions of dissatisfaction with the existing social order. Conceptualizing society as a system necessarily implied that one did not enter either questions of production relations or interest groups and conflicts. The idea of needs was a generalized one emergent from the society as a system. While scholars have critiqued structural functionalism and been careful to emphasize 'the *property of the situation* in which they originate and crystallize' (Oommen 2004: 196; emphasis added), studies on social movements have operated primarily by identifying certain elements of social movements — namely, goals, organization, ideology, and leadership of social movements, rather than the historical specific context within which social movements emerge. Studies within Indian sociology on the dynamics of production relations, class and ideology, which led to the rise of a social movement are few. (Dhanagre 1988). A. R. Desai's work on the social background of nationalism is an exception. In a context already marked by a paucity of class analysis, it is not surprising that NSMs as a conceptual claim found such ready acceptance (Desai 2005).

For postmodern analysis, I would like to draw from Arjun Appadurai's take on NSMs. He writes:

> [S]uch movements are, in their aspirations, democratic both in form and telos. And increasingly *they are constructing the global not through*

> *the general language of universal problems*, rights, or norms but by tackling one issue, one alliance, one victory at a time. The great progressive movements of the past few centuries, notably the working class movements which have characterized the nineteenth and twentieth centuries with universalist principles of solidarity, identity and interest, for aims and against opponents, also conceived in universalist and generic terms. The new transnational activisms, always worked have more room for building solidarity from smaller convergences of interest, and though they may also invoke big categories, such as "the urban poor," to build their politics, they build their actual solidarities in a more ad hoc, inductive, and context-sensitive manner. *They are thus developing a new dynamics in which global networking is put at the service of local imaginings of power* (Appadurai 2008: 305; emphasis mine).

Sharply in variance with Appadurai's contention that 'global networkings is put at the service of local imaginings of power', my chapter has shown how strands within the women's movement and Dalit movement have often been at the service of global networkings.

An argument that has informed this chapter has been that the decline of class as a critical category of political mobilization cannot be seen as the end of relevance of class as an analytical category, for the simple reason that we live in a class society. The intent of this chapter, however, has been not just to 'see' class dynamics in NSMs but also to emphasize the importance of understanding the nature of production and reproduction relations that define class and class society at any specific historical juncture. This includes both the production of material and ideological relations. In the present context, this means engaging with the present regime of capitalism and the complex institutional and ideological structures that it spawns. Such an approach alone would help us address the role of the state, the role of international institutions and understand how social movements have changed. The state from such a perspective is not an entity over and above the divisions of society but constitutive of them. This I argue is not very different from the dynamics that inform the functioning of international institutions, which we saw has had an increasingly significant role to play.

Apart from constantly 'revolutionizing the instruments of production, and thereby the relations of production, and with them the whole relations of society'(Marx and Engels 1848), capitalism has an incredible ability to *assimilate critique*. The women's and

Dalit movements have borne witness to this. I would like to wind up this chapter by bringing back a concept, in some disuse today, namely 'utopia'. Social movements, especially old social movements, have often held some form of a better future — a utopia if it may be called. While anti-utopia is the dominant state of belief with a focus on the 'doable' — a point alluded to in this chapter. Frederic Jameson associates utopian literature (and I contend social analysis) not with the capacity to imagine a more progressive future society, but rather with the failure to escape the constraints of the present in order to do so:

> Its function lies not in helping us to imagine a better future but rather in demonstrating our utter incapacity to imagine such a future- our imprisonment in a non-utopian without historicity or futurity — so as to reveal the ideological closure of the system in which we are somehow trapped and confined (cited in Couton 2009: 97–98).

Notes

1. I have argued elsewhere how this has had far reaching implications for nationalism and feminism. See Chaudhuri (2010a).
2. Two examples would be the media-led campaign to punish the murderer of Jessica Lal and the recent campaign against corruption and for the formation of a Lok Pal to check corruption and ensure accountability at the highest level.
3. A random example of the way NSMs would be taught is a list of features, such as those given as follows with no reference to contexts:
    - critical of modernism and progress
    - focused attacks on bureaucracy — they emphasized interpersonal solidarity (not class solidarity)
    - wanted to reclaim autonomous spaces (rather than seeking material advantage)
    - structures were open, fluid organic (unlike the often highly disciplined labour movement)
    - were often non-ideological, encouraging inclusive participation
    - put more emphasis on social or cultural aspects than on the economic
4. The shift to the term 'Dalit' illustrates the point best. Three decades ago Gandhiji's coinage of the term 'Harijan' was widely prevalent. Today it would be seen as both derogatory and humiliating.
5. There has been considerable debate on the terms 'adivasi', 'tribal', and 'indigenous' itself. (See Xaxa 2010).

6. India has witnessed a strong and very visible gay movement. The Supreme Court decriminalized homosexuality in 2009.
7. Mulayam Singh Yadav's statement came at a Samajwadi Party event that was organized to mark the birth centenary of Ram Manohar Lohia. Yadav had said that women members of parliament (MPs) belonging to families of businessmen and bureaucrats if elected to the Parliament would be whistled at by young boys around (http://dance.www.withshadows.com, March 24th 2010, accessed 3 April 2010).
8. The media carried captions that read 'Women's Bill traded for UPA's Survival: Yadavs call the Shots'.
9. Under pressure from the backward-class lobby cutting across political parties, the Congress-led UPA government gave in to the demand for caste-based Census for 2010 late on Friday, 7 May 2010.
10. Lalu Yadav representing the OBC voice ridiculed the BJP and Congress for their support to the Bill, saying that they are living in an illusion that they would get women's votes if the Bill is passed. *'It's a male-dominated society and women will do what their men would say'* was the shocking statement from Lalu on International Women's Day (8 March 2010; emphasis mine).
11. 'Congress members are telling me, "please save us as we are being made to sign on our death certificates by supporting this legislation"', he said while speaking briefly on the Bill. In a speech full of sarcasm, he even dubbed the Bill as an onion that will bring tears to the eyes of the members once they peel it (rediffnews 11 March 2010, accessed 19 April 2010).
12. Addressing a gathering of Muslim Community in Patna, Yadav said, '[t]he government will have to throw me out of the Lok Sabha by deploying marshals or military then only the bill will be passed. I am not against the Bill'. 'But Muslim women, poor women, backward women and women who are wage labourers, they are also daughters of India and must be brought to Parliament', he added (ANI 14 March 2010).
13. Jagmati Sangwan, State President of the All-India Democratic Women's Association (AIDWA) has a force of over 1,000 women activists. When the powerful panchayat in Karora village of Jind district was adamant on the social boycott of the family of Manoj after the infamous honour killing in which he and his wife Babli were murdered for marrying 'despite belonging to the same gotra', Sangwan was the first to support their families (Siwach 2010).
14. 'Dalit Millionaires Hold Biz Meet', 3 January 2011, *India Realtime*, http://blogs.wsj.com/indiarealtime/2011/01/03 (accessed 30 June 2011).
15. The post-Independence ideal of a secure, protected labour force in India has been supplemented by the more typical phenomena of

capital's pursuit of cheap, flexible informal workers without state protection; the percentage of workers in the formal sector has dropped by 2 per cent since 1990. India's agrarian sector offers evidence of crisis and armed conflict. In April 2006, India's Prime Minister Manmohan Singh addressed the chief ministers of six states affected by violent agrarian insurgency: 'It would not be an exaggeration to say that the problem of Naxalism is the single biggest internal security challenge ever faced by our country' (Singh's comments in GOI 2006).

16. Recent writings and presentations would confirm this. See ICSSR Trend Report (Chaudhuri and Jaichandra, 2013) *Theory and Methods in Indian Sociology*.
17. This may appear redundant but not if one looks at curricula and textbooks deployed widely in Indian colleges and universities even today. This takes us back to the question of links between ideology, theory and pedagogy that I referred to at the start of this chapter.

References

Published Sources

Appadurai, A. 2008. 'Grassroot Globalization', in Ruggiero V. and N. Montagna (ed.), *Social Movements: A Reader*, pp. 303–6. London: Routledge.

Banks, J. A. and O. Banks, 1964. 'Feminism and Social Change: A Case of Social Movement', in G. K. Zollschan and W. Hirsch (eds), *Explorations in Social Change*, pp. 244–57. London: Routledge and Kegan Paul.

Blumer, H. 1951. 'Social Movements', in A. M. Lee (ed.), *New Outlines of the Principles of Society*. New York: Barnes and Noble.

Chaudhuri, M. 2000. 'Feminism in Print Media', *The Indian Journal of Gender Studies*, 7(2): 263–88.

———. 2001. 'Gender and Advertisements: The Rhetorics of Liberalization', *Women's Studies International Forum*, 24(3/4): 373–85.

———. 2010a. 'Nationalism is not what it used to be: Can Feminism be any Different', *Nivedini—Journal of Gender Studies*, vol. 16, November/December.

———. 2010b. 'Indian Media and its Transformed Public', *Contributions to Indian Sociology*, 4(1&2): 57–78.

———. 2011. *The Indian Women's Movement: Reform and Revival*. New Delhi: Palm Leaf.

Chaudhuri M. and J. Jaichandra. 2013. 'Theory and Methods in Indian Sociology', in Yogendra Singh (ed.), *ICSSR Trend Report on Theory and Methods in Indian Sociology*, vol. 1, chapter 2. New Delhi: Oxford University Press.

Couton, P. and J. J. Lopez. 2009. 'Movement as Utopia', *History of the Human Sciences*, 22(4): 93–121.

Davis, J. 1930. *Contemporary Social Movements*. New York: D. Appleton Century Company.

Desai A. R. 2005. *The Social Background of Indian Nationalism*. Mumbai: Popular Prakashan.

Dhanagre, D. N. 1988. 'Subaltern Consciousness and Populism', *Social Scientist*, 16(11): 18–35.

Fernandes, Leela and P. Heller. 2009. 'Hegemonic Aspirations: New Middle Class and India's Democracy in Comparative Perspective', in R. J. Herring and Rina Agarwala (eds), *Whatever Happened to Class: Reflections from South Asia*, pp. 147–65. London and New York: Routledge.

Fraser, Nancy. 2009. 'Feminism, Capitalism and the Cunning of History, *New Left Review*, no. 56, March–April, pp. 97–117.

John, Mary. 2004. 'Gender and Development in India, 1970–90s: Some Reflections on the Constitutive Role of Contexts', in M. Chaudhuri (ed.), *Feminism in India*, pp. 246–58. New Delhi: Women Unlimited.

Kalpagam, U. 1994. *Labour and Gender: Survival in Urban India*. New Delhi: Sage Publications.

Lescher, Jens. 2008. 'Transnational Advocacy Networks and Affirmative Action for *Dalits* in India', *Development and Change*, 39(2): 239–61.

Linton, Ralph. 1943. 'Nativistic Movements', *American* Anthropologist, 45(2): 654–60.

Oommen T. K. 2004. *Nations, Civil Society and Social Movements: Essays in Political Sociology*. New Delhi: Sage Publications.

Sunder Rajan, Rajeswari. 1993. *Real and Imagined Women: Gender, Culture and Postcolonialism*. London: Routledge.

Tilly, Charles. 1979. 'Social Movements and National Politics', CRSO Working Paper no. 197, Center for Research on Social Organisation, University of Michigan, Michigan.

Xaxa, V. 2010. 'Tribes as Indigenous People of India', in M. Chaudhuri (ed.), *Sociology in India: Intellectual and Institutional Practices*. Jaipur: Rawat Publications.

Websites

Bhardwaj, A. 2010. 'Khap gets Rap: 5 Sentenced to Death for Honour Killing', March, available at http://www.dnaindia.com/india/report_khap-gets-rap-5-sentenced-to-death-for-honour-killing_1365366 (accessed 3 April 2010).

'Dalit Millionaires Hold Biz Meet', 2011, *India Realtime*, 3 January, available at http://blogs.wsj.com/indiarealtime/2011/01/03 (accessed 30 June 2011).

GoI (Government of India). 2006. 'Prime Minister Manmohan Singh's Address', 13 April, available at http://pib.nic.in/newsite/erelease.aspx?relid=56577 (accessed 30 January 2011).

Marx, Karl, and F. Engels. 1848. *Manifesto of the Communist Party*, available at http://www.anu.edu.au.polsci/marx/calssic/manifesto.html (accessed 21 July 2011).

Siwach, S. 2010. 'This Woman Wages a lone Battle against Khaps', available at *Times News Network*, 15 May, http://articles.timesofindia.indiatimes.com/2010-05-15/india/28293473_1_khap-panchayats-ganga-raj-karora (accessed 19 April 2010).

Teltumbde, A. 2010. 'One more Reservation', *Countercurrents*, available at http/:www.countercurrents.org/telumbde (accessed 8 April 2011).

8

Anti-Statism and Difference Feminism in International Social Movements

*Jane Mansbridge**

In her article, 'Feminism and the Challenges of the "Post-Cold War" World', Jane Jaquette sounds an alarm. She exposes the dangers of ignoring the state and the dangers of 'difference feminism'. She also shows how these are linked. Although I will underscore the merits of anti-state activity and difference feminism, I agree that a feminist strategy that neglected or deplored state action would be weak indeed. So would a strategy that relied on women's differences from men.

First, the merits of Jaquette's argument.

One strand in feminist theory and practice greatly suspects the state. This suspicion can escalate into outright rejection, with potentially grave consequences for women.

The philosophical case for the state is relatively simple. Collective action can improve human lives. Efficient collective action requires coercion. Instruments of collective action involving coercion can, paradoxically, increase human freedom. We are freer to do many things if we can bind ourselves with legally enforceable contracts. Rather than enforcing these contracts privately, it is more efficient and potentially more just to give a monopoly of legitimate violence to one entity, so long as that entity can reasonably claim to be more just than the alternatives. Humans have long struggled to devise relatively legitimate forms of coercion. The history of democracy is part of that struggle, although that history has nowhere produced national-level institutions that are highly legitimate. Despite their incapacity to be fully legitimate ever, however, we still need both states and international institutions to help solve collective action problems and to give scope to the human capacity for justice.

Regarding women, the practical case for the state must be grounded in contemporary realities. In some states, such as Sweden, women do better, compared to men, than in the most egalitarian of known pre-state entities, such as the !Kung. Moreover, although the dangers of state power for women are great, it is not practical to contemplate returning to pre-state entities. Human beings seem to want the goods produced by more extensive forms of cooperation, including those that require legitimate coercion. Given that states will not disappear in the near future, what stance should we take towards them? My answer is: wary usage. State power will be used against women, just as other forms of power are used against women, unless we intervene. One response is to establish barriers, such as constitutional or internationally enforceable rights, to certain kinds of invasions by state power. Another is to make states more likely to act in the interests of women.

In the United States both theory and institutional practice carry suspicion of the state farther than in most countries, with some malign consequences. Ours has been a 'liberalism of fear' more than an Enlightenment liberalism that envisions a common good. Americans are wary of state power, encouraged in that wariness by powerful capitalist interests. Jaquette rightly warns against this. State power can serve both as a brake on the negative externalities of capitalism and as a positive force for material redistribution. Particularly when patriarchal power takes violent forms in the private sphere, state power can help women struggle against that violence as well as other non-state evils.

The question, then, is how far to carry wariness of state power and of theories of state universalism and impartiality. I believe we must both use state power and place bounds on it. Because the state as a tool is dangerous and flawed, we need to use it with caution.

Jaquette faults contemporary feminist anti-state theorists not for wanting to abolish the state but for spending their energies on wariness rather than on how to use it for redistribution. How important one thinks this problem is depends on how one judges the current balance within feminist theory. Many feminist theorists — e.g., Susan Okin, Nancy Fraser, Iris Young — call for redistributive reforms requiring state power. Perhaps in Latin

America, from which Jaquette takes her lead, theorists of the North are represented by anti-state theory. In that case, one must ask why these are the theorists Latin American feminists choose to read. Anti-state discourse may have informed radical practice in Latin America not because anti-state theory is dominant in the North but because activists in Latin America find that anti-state discourse meets their organizing needs. Anti-state discourse may reflect the reality of individuals working on the margins of states that are either relatively corrupt or, even more obviously than most, enforce the interests of dominant classes.

Jaquette also rightly warns of the dangers of valorizing action in civil society to the neglect of state action. However, we need evidence that the more women participate in NGOs the less they participate in the state. Without such evidence it seems equally plausible that the more women participate in NGOs the more they will acquire the skills and contacts required for involvement in state politics. Some individuals also will not be able to deal with the hierarchy, coercion and male dominance embedded in all states. They will need to work in social movements. Political activism usually sustains a division of labour, with the individuals who can best deal with established institutions doing just that and those who are most repelled by those institutions charting another course. The directions they take sometimes conflict with one another.

Women and feminists trying to achieve places in the state, whether as democrats or politicians, face major barriers but also major attractions. I do not know how much we should worry that they will not be attracted to these jobs because of radical anti-state discourse. In the United States this does not seem to be a huge problem. In some countries, women who could be agents of feminist change turn down jobs in the state because those jobs are boring and unsatisfying. When these women speak of their frustrations, radical anti-state discourse appears to play a small or non-existent role.

In short, Jaquette is right that an established anti-state discourse within radical movements makes productive interaction with states less likely, but I am not sure that such discourse is created by feminist theory.

Jaquette also points to distortions produced by difference feminism. It is true that any stress on women's differences reinforces the tendency of dominant groups such as white or middle-class women to interpret 'women's' experiences primarily in light of their own experiences. In recent years, women of colour have produced the greatest advances in feminist theory, forcing white feminists to look more closely at their hegemonically defined concepts of commonality; this work has given all feminists the tools to understand better differences within their groups and subgroups.

In addition, in most areas of presumed personality difference between men and women, the differences are extremely small. The currently definitive meta-analysis of studies on Carol Gilligan's hypothesis shows that — at least in the United States, in the highly educated populations where she argues that differences should appear — only very small differences can be found. Most studies do not show women taking a different approach to justice or behaving more cooperatively than men. Studies designed to elicit behavioural gender differences often generate practically none.

In-groups, we now know, exaggerate similarities within their group and their differences from other groups. The human brain makes these predictable cognitive and emotional mistakes in in-group/out-group differentiation. Recognizing this tendency, we should constantly struggle to take into account the fact that our social and first-order cognitive estimates of such differences are usually exaggerated. In the case of gender, all societies also engage in 'gratuitous gendering' — giving gendered meanings to nouns and patterns of action that do not functionally require that identification. These processes increase our perceptions of gender difference even more.

Today we have little idea what differences might or might not emerge between men and women in a non-oppressive society. It seems mistaken, therefore, to insist on difference rather than focusing on the effects of dominance.

Finally, as Jaquette warns, promising different political results, based on the premise that women are different from men, is dangerous. We are almost certain not to deliver on that promise, at least in the short run. The backlash after the US suffrage movement was undoubtedly caused in part by disillusion at the lack of change when women won the vote.

And yet, small differences that do appear between men and women can take on major symbolic significance, precisely because of our human tendency to exaggerate group differences. Although using that significance is dangerous, not only because it exaggerates reality but also because it underlines the very stereotypes that have been used to keep women in their place, the existence of danger does not mean that we should reject this tool — any more than forswearing the tool of state action. Just remember: when using a dangerous tool, take active precautions against its potential harms.

Difference arguments for electing women are not just arguments from 'utility', as Jaquette reports Marian Sawer's point. For example, the fact that women are perceived as more honest than men can advance an attack on corruption by associating its female leaders with honesty. Using positive stereotypes of women in this way need not be degrading. Successful uses may even result in males adopting certain features of female symbolism to signify their own adherence to better standards.

In another example, among professional populations in the United States, women are somewhat more likely than men to adopt participatory, egalitarian styles of leadership. The difference probably derives from women's relative powerlessness, which teaches skills of persuasion rather than command. In the US women's movement of the late 1960s and 1970s, women used the gender differences they perceived in listening, interpreting body language and participatory style to create significant departures from the prevailing styles of left politics in organizations dominated by men. The message, 'We do things differently' is exhilarating. It prompts greater effort in trying to forge a new model, because the effort is associated not only with a different culture that can replace the old one but also with a different self and associated selves.

Turning from practical politics to political theory, concepts are also often gender-coded. Freedom and self-interest, for example, are often coded as male, community and altruism as female. It is not surprising, then, that when feminist theorists entered the field of theory, some explicitly supported certain values previously denigrated as female. Although the arguments made for these values might not be female, their proponents often were. Moreover, having been raised in a subculture that had been allocated cultural responsibility for these values, women had often thought about them more thoroughly than men. Women had also usually experienced the denigration of these values first-hand.

In short, Jaquette is right that stressing women's differences from men is fraught with danger. But values and practices that many cultures associate with women are often good in themselves, denigrated because of their association with women. Asserting the value of these ideals and practices from a stance *as women* often makes emotional, cognitive and political sense. Importantly, Jaquette identifies a link between anti-state discourse and difference feminism. A number of anti-state theorists who are also strongly anti-essentialist would deny this identification. But in social movements themselves, the identification makes sense. The state is male; hence difference feminists should be anti-state. The state is instrumental, self-interested and hierarchical; women are communal, nurturing and participatory. To the degree that these associations are simply accepted as unchangeable truths, they compound the most problematic anti-state mistake.

I agree wholeheartedly with Jaquette's fears in seeing no visible trend toward a renewed interest in the politics of economic justice, at least in the United States. In contrast to the creativity in the struggle against globalization, there has been an absence of 'street-level' activism against, for example, the revolutionary shift in tax burdens in the United States. More positively, the anti-sweatshop movement has had some good effects in raising consumer consciousness and bringing younger activists in touch with international labour movement organizing. As for the causes of the shift away from the politics of economic justice, I agree with Jaquette that it is related to the post-Cold War era and the temporary triumph of capitalism. I am not so sure that it has much to do either with activists' anti-state discourse or with difference feminism.

This commentary has concentrated on the caveats to Jaquette's thesis. I conclude by again stressing my fundamental agreement with her argument. Feminists have a 'stake in a capable state'. It would be catastrophic to be so carried away by the theoretical virtues of civil society or by anti-state discourse as to deaden oneself to the practical need to work with the state to improve the lives of women.

Because ideas have influence, it is worth stressing Jaquette's point that 'norms adopted internationally depend on states to implement them'; and only states can change the rules for women and other disadvantaged groups. The welfare state is a huge improvement over the arbitrary power of men in private families. Women's groups must therefore work closely with governments or remain on the fringe. Feminists will not only have to 'learn to live with the state'. They should learn to work with the state. For those who do not already know this, Jaquette's chapter is required reading.

Note

* This chapter was earlier published in *International Feminist Journal of Politics*, 5(3): 355–60, 2003. Reproduced with permission of the publisher (Taylor & Francis Ltd, http://www.tandf.co.uk/journals). I thank Ann Tickner for helping edit these comments after a misunderstanding had led me to write a far longer piece.

References

Jaquette, Jane. 2003. 'Feminism and the Challenges of the "Post-Cold War" World', *International Feminist Journal of Politics*, 5(3): 331–54.

Fraser, Nancy and Axel Honneth. 2003. *Redistribution or Recognition?: A Political-Philosophical Exchange*. London: Verso.

Gilligan, Carol. 1982. *In a Different Voice: Psychological Theory and Women's Development*. Cambridge, MA: Harvard University Press.

Mansbridge, Jane. 1993. 'Feminism and Democratic Community', in John W. Chapman and Ian Shapiro (eds), *Democratic Community: NOMOS XXXV*, pp. 342–77. New York: New York University Press.

Okin, Susan Moller. 1989. *Justice, Gender and the Family*. New York: Basic Books.

Sawer, Marian. 2000. 'Parliamentary Representation of Women: From Discourses of Justice to Strategies of Accountability', *International Political Science Review*, 21(4): 361–80.

Young, Iris Marion. 1990. *Justice and the Politics of Difference*. Princeton: Princeton University Press.

———. 2000. *Inclusion and Democracy*. Oxford: Oxford University Press.

9

Deep Currents Rising

Some Notes on the Global Challenge to Capitalism

Harry Cleaver

Despite neo-conservative illusions of a hegemonic Pax Americana, the persistent efforts of supranational state institutions such as the IMF and the WTO to impose neoliberal policies throughout the world and the US government's efforts to use its post-9/11 'war on terrorism' to leverage the power of capital against all opponents, the basic institutional structures of modern capitalist society continue to be challenged on all levels by diverse currents of grassroots struggle. In their increasingly common rejection of business priorities these struggles recall Marxist notions of class warfare. Yet the common opposition to capitalism is not accompanied by the old notion of a unified alternative project of socialism. On the contrary, such a vision is steadily being displaced by a proliferation of distinct projects and a common understanding that there is no need for universal rules. In response to these struggles, the threatened global order is responding in various ways, sometimes by military and paramilitary force, sometimes by co-optation aimed at reintegrating the antagonistic forces. The problem for us is finding ever new ways to defeat these responses and continue to build new worlds. To find those new ways, we need to understand the character of the currents of struggle now in motion. Among such diverse currents conceptual approaches have naturally differed. In the sections that follow I evaluate a few of those concepts and offer some new ones.

Global Challenge and Theoretical Innovations

There can no longer be any doubt that proliferating interconnections among diverse, geographically dispersed, grassroots social struggles — e.g., those of waged workers (often precariously waged), indigenous peoples, human rights advocates, ethnic and cultural minorities, environmentalists, women, students, immigrants — are resulting in a deepening and broadening threat to the contemporary capitalist social order. On the one hand, it is the very proliferation, intensity and interlinkages of struggles attacking one or another dimension of capitalist domination that is so striking — virtually all types of existing social relationships of control are being challenged. On the other hand, one of the most important and widely recognized dimensions of increased collaboration is its global or transnational character. Those involved in local and national struggles who have fought local and national battles, are quite consciously seeking and finding ways to connect up with those struggling elsewhere and to make their efforts complementary and visible. This has taken at least three main forms: first, increasingly effective transnational mobilization in support of particular struggles in specific locations, e.g., support for the Zapatista rebellion; second, global convergences of thousands of protestors besieging various supranational state institutions and their meetings, e.g., those of the World Trade Organization, the International Monetary Fund and World Bank and the G8; and third, coordinated, simultaneous actions in diverse locations with a common purpose, e.g., the 18 June 1999 'global ambush of capitalism.'

One dimension of this multi-pronged, increasingly global attack on capitalist hegemony has been the effort to grasp theoretically what is new about this situation. This project has occupied both those involved in or sympathetic to the attacks and those threatened by them and desperate for counter-strategies. New metaphors and concepts about social conflict are born with insights flowing from the recognition of new situations that don't seem to fit existing theories. One kind of new situation involves hitherto unknown or unrecognized phenomena; another occurs when some known, but previously secondary phenomena have taken on a new importance and have become progressively more central in the challenging of existing institutional structures and mechanisms of control. The genesis of new theoretical approaches then results from efforts to imaginatively resolve apparent contradictions between existing theory and these new perceptions and insights in order to inform strategy and tactics for dealing with the new situations. In recent years there has been a veritable scramble to grasp the nature of the dizzying array of new disjunctures, connections, contradictions and complementarities that make up the current proliferation of interconnected challenges to global capital.

Transnational Networks and Social Netwars

Perhaps the most common new theoretical approach has been to interpret the pattern of interconnections among proliferating struggles in terms of 'networks'. Among those challenging capitalist domination neither what is now called 'networking' nor the concept of networks are entirely new. The entire history of challenges to capital has been replete with the efforts of its opponents to break out of their isolation and form mutually beneficial linkages with others in similar situations. This is true of early resistance to its primitive accumulation and true of the rise and development of trades unions, political parties and other organizational forms against its ongoing efforts to accumulate people as workers and labour power. As a general rule the wider and deeper the linkages, the more successful struggles have been, the greater the isolation, the more likely defeat.

As for thinking about such linkages in terms of 'networks', some roots of today's common use of the concept by activists can be found in Italy in the 1960s where the Marxist sociologist Romano Alquati in his studies of workers' conflicts with the Italian auto giant FIAT meshed the Marxist analysis of class composition with that of networks, at the factory, national and international levels.[1]

Other sociologists and then political scientists took the concept of networks over from mathematical graph theory to analyze a wide variety of social relationships. These have included individual behavior, small group interactions, organizational behaviour and social movements — most recently transnational movements.[2] Of these, the last two would seem to have the most salience here. Organizational theorists and observers have traced the emergence within businesses and to some degree the state sector, of network forms of organization that appear distinct from more traditional hierarchies and market systems.[3] Recent applications of network analysis to transnational social struggles have drawn on past sociological studies of local networks, on organizational studies and on empirical work on particular network-based campaigns to knit together a synthetic view of 'those relevant actors working internationally on an issue, who are bound together by shared values, a common discourse and dense exchanges of information and services'.[4]

Similar work has been done by national security analysts, who have examined the implications of the emergence of network forms of organization for the United States Department of Defense. One early study was that of Pentagon analyst Charles Swett who focused in on the role of the Internet.[5] The most perceptive and influential work has been done by RAND's David Ronfeldt and his co-authors. Drawing on studies of the changing organization of business and the state, such as that of Walter Powell, they have taken over the juxtaposition of networks to markets and hierarchies and argued that a wide variety of contemporary social conflicts have been evolving networked organizations capable of unleashing 'transnational social netwars'. On the one hand, they were among the first to identify such structures in terrorist organizations, e.g., Al Qaeda — a recognition that has since become increasingly commonplace. On the other hand, they also pointed to emerging transnational networks of 'information age activism' based on associations among non-governmental organizations (NGOs) concerned with modern and postmodern issues such as the environment, human rights, immigration, indigenous peoples and freedom in cyberspace.[6]

The Zapatista Rebellion

In much of this recent work, a primary reference point for the study of transnational networks has been the rebellion waged by Zapatista communities in Chiapas, Mexico since the beginning of 1994 and the activities of its supporters around the world. That rebellion — organized by a culturally and linguistically diverse array of collaborating, indigenous communities — was the latest in a long history of struggles by such people to defend themselves from recurrent efforts to separate them from their land and their means of production.[7] Those efforts date back to the Spanish Conquest but have never been entirely successful.[8] In some periods, such as the Mexican Revolution that began in 1910, such enclosure has been partially reversed and reforms have restored some previously stolen lands. More recently, neoliberal government policies have increasingly threatened surviving communities by closing legal options for reversing enclosure while facilitating its extension.[9] These deepening threats helped set the Zapatista rebellion in motion.

The first activist analysis of the communicational dimension of that rebellion noted that the 'most striking thing about the sequence of events set in motion on January 1, 1994 has been the speed with which news of the struggle circulated and the rapidity of the mobilization of support which resulted' (Cleaver 1994: 133–45).[10] It went on to note how modern computer communications, through the Internet and the Association for Progressive Communications networks, made it possible for the Zapatistas to get their message out despite governmental spin control and censorship. Mailing lists and conferences also facilitated discussions and debate among concerned observers that led to the organization of protest and support activities in over 40 countries around the world. The Zapatista rebellion, the analysis concluded, was not only built on local indigenous networks but through much wider networks was able to catalyze the weaving of a global 'electronic fabric of struggle'.

Subsequent studies at the US Defense Department and at RAND also focused on the networked character of the rebellion and of its supporters as well as the role of computer communications in the mobilization of that support (Arquilla and Ronfeldt 1996: 73; Ronfeldt and Martínez 1997: 371; Ronfeldt et al. 1998). The lesson they drew was the need for the US government to develop its own 'networks' — both military and civil — to counter those of their opponents. In 1998, as a part of their study of the development of transnational human rights networks, Keck and Sikkink reported on how:

> [T]he [Mexican] government could no longer control information as it had in 1968 ... The press and domestic and international NGOs monitored the conflict closely, and electronic mail became one of the main mechanisms through which the EZLN communicated with the world (1998: 115).

More recently network analysis has been applied empirically in some detail to understand the international struggles connected to the Zapatistas. From hyperlink analysis designed to identify the structures of Zapatista support networks, to more extensive efforts both to discover the nature of, and relationships within the transnational Zapatista support network and to explore the connections with, and impact on, other networks of counter-globalization, we find a variety of sympathetic efforts being elaborated to understand this ever-growing set of experiences.[11]

From Static Networks to the Dynamics of Struggle: Swarming

One problem with the application of the concept of 'network' to social struggles has been the tendency to think about 'networks' in static terms. Even when the noun 'network' is turned into a verb — 'networking' — it just means 'building networks' or 'operating through a network' with no specification of the dynamics involved. Recognizing patterns of connectivity is not enough; the key thing is how they work dynamically. Capitalist strategists need to know how networks function to threaten them so that they can develop countermeasures — to block, crush or absorb the threats. Those building opposition to capitalist domination need to understand how networks are established, strengthened and can be used for mobilization and attack, but they also need to understand how and to what degree networks constitute viable approaches to the organization of post-capitalist social relations.

Following up their earlier advice of devising state networks to counter oppositional networks, David Ronfeldt and his primary co-author John Arquilla have also argued for the adaptation by such state networks of one method they have identified as being used by such opponents: 'swarming', defined as 'a deliberately structured, coordinated, strategic way to strike from all directions, by means of a sustainable pulsing of force'. Some examples that they cite are from historical military experience but others are from anti-capitalist social struggle, e.g., Mikhail Bakunin's proposal of 'general strikes' and the rapid mobilization of support networks in response to Mexican government's moves against the Zapatistas. The concept is also, obviously, evocative of the periodic convergence of thousands from diverse struggles who have gathered to besiege various capitalist institutions. In their essay devoted to this subject, Ronfeldt and Arquilla juxtapose swarming to other types of military tactics, e.g., melee, manoeuvre and massing, and propose 'battleswarming' as a successor to current US military doctrines such as LandAir Battle (Arquilla and Ronfeldt 2000: vii).

The concept of 'swarming' has subsequently been appropriated by some activists for their own purposes. One example, hactivists — whose coordinated 'ping' attacks on targeted websites were one example of swarming for Ronfeldt and Arquilla — quickly adopted their adversaries' conceptualization for their own purposes; 'digital Zapatismo' became 'InfoSwarm Systems'.[12]

The responses to such actions on the part of those involved in various social struggles have often been highly critical. One criticism has been that the hacktivists have chosen bad targets and have done so because they are neither connected to, nor did they consult with, the particular struggle their actions were aimed at supporting. A second criticism has been that the use of such tactics could open movements to the charge of violating their own rules of free speech and set them up for being attacked in the same way.[13] A third objection has revolved around the difficulty in demonstrating that such actions are not the rogue actions of a few individuals but do indeed involve thousands of people and are thus politically significant. Although the ping engines can generate information about the numbers and addresses of those who logged into a site and used it, there remain the questions of circulating that information, making it believable and gaining legitimacy for such actions.[14]

When this tactic was used by US activists to attack Mexican government and financial websites, there was protest from within Mexico by activists who had not been consulted and who felt placed at risk by these actions. When it was used within the US to attack newspapers about coverage of the Mumia case, it was severely attacked by lawyers defending Mumia as counterproductive. As a result of such criticisms, no social movement that I know of has generalized the use of this tactic.[15]

Another adaptation of 'swarming' explores the dynamics of real-time mobilization during protests and demonstrations on the streets. An essay written by the activist group 'Why War?' recognizes and adapts the work of Ronfeldt and Arquilla to their own purposes:

> Swarming, for the purposes of protesting, can be thought of as the technique of quickly massing a large number of individuals from all directions onto a single position in order to attain a specific goal. There are roughly four different phases in a successful swarm: locate the target, converge, attack, disperse. For these four phases to work correctly they

> must be synchronized between a diversity of seemingly disconnected individuals. Therefore, there must be a layer of instantaneous communication between these individuals.[16]

The essay also offers detailed analysis about how swarming can be facilitated by protestors using portable communication devices such as cell-phones and text-messaging. This adaptation of flash mobs analyzes possible police counter-measures and discusses some concrete cases.[17]

The Dynamics of Struggle: Rhizomes

As an alternative to 'networks' and 'networking', the theoretical work of Michel Foucault, Gilles Deleuze and Félix Guattari offered a quite different set of metaphorical and conceptual approaches for analyzing the dynamics of struggle. Leaving behind some traditional orthodox Marxist frameworks, such as structuralism, dialectics and a preoccupation with the overall war between capitalists and workers, they elaborated a number of new concepts to explore and illuminate the micro-politics of individual psychology, class power and interconnected social conflicts. For my purposes here, the most salient of their ideas — because the most widely taken up by others — are the ones associated with the metaphor of the *rhizome*: a subterranean system of horizontal roots and above ground stems (Deleuze and Guattari 1987: 3–25). They juxtaposed this to more familiar form of trees. Obviously, both trees and rhizomes grow, they propagate dynamically; the difference lies in the pattern of growth. Trees grow vertically with their branches radiating from the central trunk; rhizomes propagate horizontally elaborating tuberous root systems in all directions — from which new sprouts arise. (These botanical examples provide the core of their metaphor in *Thousand Plateaus*, although they also called rats and their burrows rhizomes.) Through the metaphor of the rhizome they explored the characteristics they argued could be found in horizontally linked human interactions: connectivity, heterogeneity, multiplicity, and rupture.

Closely related to the metaphor of rhizome are two other concepts they elaborated: deterritorialization and nomadism. Like 'rhizome' both obviously evoke not only space (as does 'network') but movement through space. Whereas capital has tended to impose specific 'territorializations' — fixing people in particular positions where they can be controlled as workers, the struggles of those people, elaborated rhizomatically, tend to rupture that fixing by finding or creating new spaces for autonomous activity. Thus deterritorialization is an autonomous prison-break and nomadism is another way of thinking about such autonomous movement.[18] Just as traditional nomads, e.g., the Roma of Europe or the herders of the Sahel, have escaped the control of centralized Powers, whether kings, emperors, or national governments, so do modern workers sometimes escape specific institutions and mechanisms of capitalist control, e.g., school drop-outs, precarious workers, trans-sexuals and immigrants.

This dynamic metaphor and these concepts of the kinds of dynamism involved have been taken up by those involved in such struggles and used for thinking about and organizing their own activity, both locally and internationally.[19] Rhizomatic self-organization and 'rhizomatic' thought have quite explicitly challenged older conceptions of organization, e.g., the welfare state or Leninist party, and the associated kinds of thinking that accompanied and justified those kinds of social organization. Acolytes of those older kinds of thinking, not surprisingly have condemned these newer approaches.[20]

If we compare and contrast Deleuze and Guattari's concepts of the dynamics of rhizomes with Ronfeldt and Arquilla's concepts of the dynamics of networks we can see how the latter reflect and pertain mainly to moments of attack, while those of the former provide much more insight into the dynamics of political recomposition that not only make attack possible but possibly establish organizational points of departure for alternatives to capitalism. These differences undoubtedly flow from the different locations of the authors amidst contemporary social struggles. Whereas Deleuze and Guattari's concepts were enunciated by men who were trying to think from within opposition to capitalist ways of organizing the world, Rondfeldt and Arquilla's work for the Pentagon has situated them most firmly within the defense of the current order.

The Dynamics of Struggle: Currents

Every metaphor, like every analogy, has its limits. Even with the analysis of swarming we can see how the concept of networks used by both the theoreticians of 'netwar' and some of their opponents grasps only part of the reality of those loosely connected, yet restless, actors and sets of actors who share a common, creative opposition to contemporary capitalism and sometimes seek to go beyond it. What is missing is the sense of ceaseless, fluid motion among those antagonistic actors who make up that opposition in which 'organizing' may not take the form of 'organizations' but rather of an ebb and flow of contact at myriad points that only sometimes results in massed or simultaneous attack.

On the other hand, Deleuze and Guattari's fecund metaphor of 'rhizome' does evoke ceaseless growth in various directions, albeit a slow and subterranean kind. But despite its horizontal propagation and connectiveness, the plant rhizome is a fixed form (and the restlessness of rats is obviously quite limited.) The iris rhizome in flowerbeds or the cattail rhizome in ponds do propagate themselves in all directions and send up shoots from old and new nodes, year after year. But the shoots with their leaf structures, flowers or heavy heads of pollen, are always the same. So here too restlessness exists only at the margins as a given structure reproduces itself. Indeed, the truth is that many of Deleuze and Guattari's most creative insights escape their own metaphor. The deterritorialization of the plant rhizome is obviously very limited, as are the metamorphoses of which the rhizome is capable. The insight into nomadism definitely evokes a degree of mobility far beyond its possibilities. These important concepts are quite separable from the metaphor of the rhizome.

An alternative metaphor for thinking about the ceaseless movement that forms the political life and historical trajectory of those resisting and sometimes escaping the institutions of capitalism, is that of water, of the hydrosphere, especially of ever restless ocean currents. Currents are masses in motion, not just masses of homogeneous water but of whole ecologies of differentiated water molecules and the myriad forms of life that thrive and perish amidst them — floating or swimming with the flow or struggling across or against it. Everything is in motion, nothing is stable, deterritorialization is virtually constant, there is no 'safe haven', no 'secure foundation' other than familiarity with the ever rushing, ever changing flow.[21] Yet nomadic whales sing and dolphins play as they traverse thousands of miles of ocean.

In some places these flowing ecologies move faster, in others more slowly, in some places they are warmer, in others colder, in some places they run deep, in others on the surface. The most visible currents — those that run on the surface of the ocean — are warmer, while the deeper currents are colder. Ocean waters also differ in both salinity and in the array of life that populates them. But precisely because they are in constant motion all these things change. Sometimes deeper and colder nutrient-rich water rises in an upwelling that brings it to the surface where its molecular components warm up and grow more agitated. On the other hand, when ocean water enters polar regions it gets colder, becomes saltier, denser and either freezes or sinks. When water does freeze, it crystallizes into rigidity, but mostly it melts again, undoing one molecular form to return to a process of dynamic self-organizing that refuses crystallization yet whose currents, of varying directions and power, can be observed and tracked. When currents connect in the ocean they sometimes interact to form giant eddies: 'gyres' or circular movements that pile up water in 'mounds' whose surfaces rise above that of the nearby ocean. Or, more dramatically still, crosscurrents may interact to form killer 'rogue waves', mini-tsunami's capable of destroying and sinking huge ships.[22]

Finally, the movement of ocean currents are affected not only by the makeup (temperature, salinity, density, nutrient load) of different masses of water but by the topology of the ocean's floor, gravity and also, especially for surface currents, by sun, wind and the coriolis force.[23] In other words, currents move according to the nature of the water that composes them, but that movement is shaped by surrounding forces.

All of these characteristics are evocative of the behaviour of those forces in opposition to capitalism. Like ocean currents, social struggles have both their internal dynamics — shaped by the class composition and imaginations of the people involved — and they are shaped by the forces that surround them: capitalist institutions that constrain them or other struggles that may counter or reinforce them. They are fluid, often changing and only momentarily forming those solidified moments we call 'organizations' — sometimes small, like patches of ice, sometimes quite large, like icebergs. However, such moments are constantly eroded by the shifting currents surrounding them so that they are repeatedly melted back into the flow itself. There is, of course, a certain kind of power in rigidity —

frozen seas block ships and an iceberg sank the Titanic — but recognizing the inevitably transitory character of organizations necessarily must broaden our attention to the flows out of which they have crystallized and to which they must sooner or later return.

Some currents of opposition are quite visible, on the surface as it were, sometimes steady, sometimes turbulent. When they connect reinforcing each other the social equivalent of rogue waves and gyres are the swirling turbulence of public struggle: short term upheavals such as massive protests, e.g., the Battle of Seattle against the World Trade Organization, or the heady, intense days of the Zapatista intercontinental encounters, or more protracted, widespread upheavals such as insurgencies.

But, it is worth remembering that oppositional movements on the surface of society are like the surface currents of the oceans — they only involve a small percentage of the total mass.[24] Most currents of opposition run deep, below surface appearances, but like deep waters that are rich in salt and nutrients they can be rich in social connections, anger and creativity.[25] When such deep currents surface in surprising, massive upwellings of social struggle they can nourish wider conflict and change the world. Such were the world-shaking eruptions in the 20th century of the Mexican, Russian, Chinese, Cuban, and Hungarian Revolutions; such too were sudden appearances of Solidarity in Poland in 1980, the Zapatistas in 1994 and, perhaps, the Oaxaca City Commune of 2006.[26] In every case the biggest mystery and the hardest thing to explain have been what was going on in those invisible, deep, but rich currents of struggle that made possible and led to their sudden, explosive and world changing upwelling. Thus the importance of the various kinds of study that have sought to understand these largely invisible forces, e.g., analyses of everyday life, of the 'weapons of the weak', of class composition, of certain aspects of popular culture.[27]

It has always been easier to identify the outside forces shaping social struggles — the social equivalents of seafloor topology, gravity, wind and solar energy — than their internal dynamics. Just as undersea landslides and earthquakes can cause abrupt changes in seafloor topology and trigger tsunamis, so social analysts often look for events that trigger social upheavals, e.g., the Mexican government attack on communal lands and the imposition of NAFTA that convinced the Zapatistas that they had to act quickly or see their lands privatized and their communities dispersed. Marxists, in particular, have often devoted far more time to analyzing the 'laws of motion' of capitalist development and its consequences for workers than they have the internal, self-organization of the working class.[28] They have more readily seen and understood how capitalist imposed patterns of development, exploitation and institutional structures have confined and shaped the development of social struggles than they have grasped the internal relationships of those struggles. When those relationships have frozen into overt organizations, e.g., political parties, labour unions, NGOs, guerrilla groups, they have become the focus of intense research. Unfortunately, the molecular dynamics of the flows that have gestated self-organization but have only occasionally resulted in visible organizations have remained, all too often, largely out of sight and unanalyzed.

Many have also tended to think in terms of a one-sided causality between changes in capitalist institutions, policies and actions and working-class reactions rather than seeing how the self-activity of workers may bring about those changes. Within the framework of my oceanographic metaphor, for example, capitalist policy changes, e.g., attacks on peasant land holdings, may be seen as the result of persistent resistance to enclosure and success at reversing it — just as undersea landslides may be triggered by the erosion caused by turbulent ocean currents. Or, just as hurricanes are intensified by warming ocean water, so too is capitalist desperation and murderous flailing about often the result of their loss of control due to suddenly visible, rapidly circulating struggles.

Such invisible, deep currents — the inevitable consequence of alienation and exploitation throughout the history of capitalism — have been a source of endless frustration to those who would harness the power of those flows, whether the institutions of Western capitalism or the Leninist party. Power would harness power, but power lies in the flow itself, in the broad, deep and partly invisible currents that traverse society. Imagine the challenge to these would-be dictators or managers, standing in the middle of a world of swirling, powerful social currents, trying to manage the flows. It is easy to see how the frustration of early capitalists who had very little grasp of the flowing, living ecologies they sought to dominate would often drive them to desperate, violent efforts. It is also easy to see how later capitalist policy-makers, although more experienced, have often been at a loss as to any other way to handle those ecologies and have resorted, over and over again, to force — thus the cruel brutality of much of capitalist history.

Harnessing Flows

But, over time, the more perceptive of capitalist policy-makers have fostered and financed the development of an array of 'social sciences' whose primary purpose has been to identify and analyze the social currents that have given rise to overt attacks on business' domination of society. In many Western countries, such as the United States, anthropologists, sociologists, political scientists, psychologists, and economists have all been drawn, by ideology or financial reward, into the study of such threats, either potential or actual, with a view towards providing policy-makers with both understanding of the struggles that threaten and strategies for coping.[29]

As a result, in its more genial moments capital, like engineers who have designed devices to harness the power of ocean waves, currents, tides and even salinity gradients, has understood enough to design institutions to harness antagonistic social flows without trying to simply dam or crush them. One example of such harnessing can be found in the Keynesian period when workers' struggles were used to stimulate capitalist investment, productivity growth and accumulation. By shaping worker-formed unions into institutions that would not only negotiate but impose contracts on workers, capital was able to, at least to a degree, convert struggles over wages and working conditions into motor forces of its own development.[30]

Much earlier Marx captured such harnessing in his adaptation of Quesnay's metaphor of circulation to sketch the 'circuits of capital'.[31] While those circuits — whether of money, commodity or productive capital — represent flows of capital, at the heart of the flows is the living labour of workers. The various moments of the circuits and their interconnections constitute the general framework through which capital organizes or manages life as living labour. The metaphor returned, in a small way, in mainstream macroeconomics' portrayal of the circular character of economic relationships and its sharp distinction between flows and stocks. In both cases social relationships are conceptualized as flows, but they are harnessed flows, like rivers or ocean tides diverted into hydroelectric plants to drive turbines.

Such harnessing and the constraints it imposes, quite unsurprisingly, are endlessly resisted by the restlessness of a humanity that has so many, many different ideas about interesting forms of self-organization. From shop-floor to street, rice paddies to mountain forests, people have organized and reorganized to escape this harnessing. As a result, some contemporary Marxists have not only recognized the autonomous power involved in this resisting and these efforts to escape but have analyzed how such struggles 'circulate' from sector to sector of the working class, rupturing capitalist circulation in the process — thus taking over and using the metaphor of 'circulation' for their own purposes.[32]

In line with this metaphor we can think about the conflicts described earlier not so much in terms of wars between set pieces (chess, go, military confrontations) or wars between classes for Power (Leninist revolution versus the capitalist state), but rather in terms of the vast imagination and capability of self-organization of a multiplicity of struggles straining against capitalist rules that bind, limit and distort.[33] There is a kind of class war here that involves more and more resistance to the unity of global capitalism. But the resistance flows not from an increasingly unified class seeking a new unified hegemony, but rather from myriad currents seeking the freedom of the open seas where they can re-craft their own movement and their interactions with each other free of a single set of constraining capitalist rules.

Given the diversity of approaches to thinking about the emergence around the world and connections across borders of such a wide variety of social struggles that have increasingly challenged capitalism, there have also been a variety of approaches to the characterization of the subjectivities involved in those struggles.

Civil Society?

Ever since East European dissidents resurrected the concept of 'civil society' as a way of talking about social initiatives that escaped the control of Soviet-style states, the use of the term has proliferated across the political spectrum. From Left to Right, from opponents of capitalism to its defenders, the concept has been deployed, as it has in the past, in a variety of ways. 'International civil society', 'transnational civil society' and 'global civil society' have all been evoked to characterize the kind of widespread challenges to contemporary capitalist policy I have been discussing. But when we examine what people mean by these terms we find the same varied meanings as when the concept of 'civil society' has been applied to local social structures in the past.[34]

Many have tended to reduce the meaning of 'civil society' to formal NGOs.[35] This reduction has been more or less severe, largely depending on the interests of those using the words. For many state agencies, either national or supranational, the term NGO is used so broadly as to include the private business sector. For others the term refers only to non-governmental and non-business organizations. In this case, however, there is often a failure to distinguish between NGOs that are obviously integral parts of capitalism such as the Rockefeller and Ford Foundations from grassroots organizations opposed to it. Conceptualizing 'civil society' only in the form of NGOs is a reductionism not surprising in a society where political Power is usually vested in formal institutions. It is not, however, satisfactory. Oppositional NGOs should be seen as only particular organizational crystallizations of much more general and fluid social struggles. Indeed, partly in reaction to the growth and behaviour of some transnational NGOs, various critiques have emerged along with a quite conscious search for alternative ways of organizing. One such critique has been of an observed tendency for NGOs to become bureaucratic and self-preserving institutions, increasingly operating above and independently from their supporters. This critique parallels similar ones that have been directed at traditional labour unions and political parties by the Zapatistas who have been unusually successful in articulating these critiques in ways that have resonated widely among those who have become disenchanted with such organizations.

A second critique has been that such NGOs have cut deals with the state and with business in ways that have betrayed the purposes for which the organizations were formed. One example has been the willingness of some big environmental organizations to collaborate with the World Bank or the World Trade Organization — thus lending legitimacy to those institutions whose policies have generally been ecologically destructive. Here again, parallels can be drawn with the behaviour of 'business' unions and political parties.

These critiques have effectively recast the notion of 'civil society' in a narrower sense. 'Civil society' has become, for the Zapatistas and many others, a term applied *only* to those moments and struggles within society that resist subordination to capitalist institutions and, in many cases, fight for alternative ways of organizing society.

Unfortunately, both historically and in the contemporary world the concept of 'civil society' has been given so many different meanings as to render its meaning opaque. When you have to go into a long discourse to explain the particular meaning of your use of a term — as opposed to the way many others use the term — it is usually a good time to seek a different vocabulary. Although what interests me here is most closely approximated by the last definition of 'civil society' given earlier, I prefer to eschew the use of the term altogether to avoid misunderstanding.[36]

Social Movements?

Conceptualizing widespread but interconnected challenges to existing institutions in terms of 'social movements', rather than just unusual 'collective behaviours', grew out of the experience of the 'civil rights', 'black power', 'counter-cultural', student, women's and other 'movements' of late 1950s and 1960s. Those of us engaged in struggle thought of ourselves as being part of a 'movement' and so did those many who analyzed us from within or from without, whether sympathetically or critically. The very term 'movement' not only evoked struggle for change, but also the absence of any centre, of any hierarchical organizational structures that could command the widespread, frequent protests and related actions. Cohesion in movements has often been thought to derive from common goals and shared collective identities (Melluci 1995, 1996).

The identification of separate organizing by separate movements, e.g., black power groups organizing separately from civil rights groups, women organizing themselves autonomously from men, led many to speak of 'new' social movements — as distinct from the traditional labour movement — and sometimes to skeptical characterizations of these movements as being balkanized, essentially reformist efforts that ultimately posted no real threat to 'the system' as a whole, however much this or that aspect of it was being contested. Whether enthusiastic or skeptical, the number of academic researchers, especially in sociology, focused on 'new social movements' multiplied rapidly and churned out a huge body of work, first articles and then collections of those articles. Books with titles such as *Social Movements and Culture* or *Cultural Politics and Social Movements* began to appear in the mid-1990s (Melucci 1995, 1996; Darnovsky et al. 1995). Political scientists and historians joined in and a variety of approaches have been offered to explain patterns of movement development and behaviour. Among the most influential have been those of 'political process' and 'resource mobilization' where the former emphasizes changes in the larger political situation that opens up or closes down opportunities for movement formation and action and the latter focuses on how movement activity is shaped by all the resources available, including political, economic and communicational ones.[37]

As recognition has grown of how struggles for particular changes have been flowing together into collaborations whose impact is already larger than the sum of the individual influences, many have come to speak of a 'movement of movements' and optimistically, for the first time in quite a while, to declare that 'another world is possible' or 'other worlds are possible' (George 2004; Harvie et al. 2005; Mertes 2004).

As one might expect both the commonplace use of the term 'movement' to characterize these struggles as well as the academic 'social movement' literature on them have been critiqued in various ways. One example is, the paper by the Leeds May Day Group sees this characterization as too restrictive because it highlights the actions of activists while ignoring much more widespread actions on the part of 'people who do not consider themselves "activists" or "political" but who nevertheless have to struggle against oppression and exploitation in their everyday lives — people who, just like us, are struggling for new ways of living' (Leeds May Day Group 2001).

More generally, because these 'new' social movements have been identified as falling outside the labour movement, they have also been identified as falling outside the Marxian concept of class struggle. While this has permitted such 'post-Marxist' approaches to successfully create an accepted space for their work within an overwhelmingly anti-Marxist academic establishment, it has done so only by defining 'class struggle' very narrowly and marginalizing it as one kind of conflict among others. As with the broader space of 'post-modern' studies — which has executed a similar strategy — the overly simplified characterization and abandonment of Marxist thought has often led to an identity politics blind to, and thus vulnerable to, the threat of a common enemy.

Working Class?

Although the 'post-Marxist' and 'post-modernist' characterizations of Marxian thought has rung true among those who have identified Marxism with its orthodox varieties — e.g., Leninist, Maoist, Trotskyist — it has rung quite false among those familiar with less orthodox and more adaptive varieties of Marxist thought. Whereas orthodox Marxists have tended to react to the struggles of those outside the waged industrial proletariat — and there have been such throughout the history of capitalism — by demanding that they get a waged job, join the working class and *its* struggles, other Marxists, long ago, saw the political and theoretical flaws in such a response. On the one hand, critical theorists of the Frankfurt School and those who followed them, recognized and analyzed how capitalist mechanisms of domination had been extended to the sphere of culture and everyday life — even if they were not always able to either recognize or analyze the struggles against those mechanisms. On the other hand, first Marxist feminists and then others began to recognize how 'the' working class has always included the unwaged as well as the waged and how varied struggles have been among both. As a result, for many Marxists the concepts of working class and working class struggle have been so widened beyond its orthodox association with waged factory labour as to encompass all of those struggles that have threatened the rules and institutions of capitalist domination throughout society and frequently sought to go beyond them. Beyond Marx's 'collective worker' at the point of production, they saw a collective worker acting in both spheres of the 'social factory': production and reproduction.[38] One name for this collective worker was bestowed by Italian Marxists Romano Alquati and Antonio Negri: the 'social' or 'socialized' worker (Alquati, Negri and Sormano 1976; Negri 1979, 1988).

Such a broadened concept of working class has made possible Marxist analyses of the wide variety of social struggles around the world that have challenged capitalism in ever more interconnected ways. Such analyses have employed Marxist analytical and political categories, e.g., value, exploitation, alienation, class struggle, but have elaborated and adapted them in ways that take account of the breath and variety of the struggles among both waged and unwaged. Among the first examples of such analyses were those of class conflicts of the Fordist or Keynesian period in which the factory model had been extended to, and hence contested, throughout society. In other words, both deskilled industrial workers and others outside industry — but whose lives were shaped in ways designed to feed into (schools), or support (nuclear families), or manage the reserve army of (the welfare state, foreign aid, neocolonialism) industry — were organized as effectively as Keynesian planners could manage as one great social factory. The result, of course, was the inevitable, equally thorough appearance of class struggle against such shaping and all of its miserably constrained conditions of life.

The point of departure for analyzing the complexities of such a multi-dimensional working class and its struggles was, naturally, Marx's own analysis of the way capital imposed a division of labour in production and the way it pitted some groups of workers against others, e.g., Irish against English or the unemployed and unwaged (the reserve army) against those with jobs and wages. But whereas Marx's focus was on the methods of capitalist control and exploitation, the need of those in struggle against such control demanded an inversion of perspective, from top-down to bottom-up. Just as Marx had studied everything he could find on division of labour, including theoretical essays by economists and engineers and factory inspector reports, so a new generation of Marxists in the post-World War II era undertook to study, sometimes in similar sources, sometimes at actual points of production (and later at the points of reproduction) the contemporary shape of class relationships.[39]

The result was the elaboration of a 'workerist' analysis of 'class composition' that looked at the division of labour explicitly in terms of the power relations between capital and workers and among the latter with a view to providing theoretical concepts for grasping changes in those relations brought on through workers' struggle. Thus workers' efforts to tip the scales of power in their favour were conceptualized as processes of 'political recomposition' while capitalist attempts to thwart or reverse such efforts were seen to involve the imposition of new divisions in processes of class 'decomposition'. Similarly, attempts to theorize the ability of workers to take the initiative in the class war and to craft alternative non-capitalist relations among themselves led from the concept of workers' autonomy to that of self-valorization — an appropriation and inversion of a term Marx used to describe capitalist expanded reproduction.[40] Methodologically, these ideas implied taking workers struggles, in all their variety and interrelationships, as points of departure for understanding both particular organizational crystallizations, e.g., unions, political parties, NGOs, and capitalist strategies and tactics.

Applied to the international level such an analysis tended first, to recognize how supranational institutions such as the International Monetary Fund, the World Bank and the General Agreement on Trade and Tariffs were not merely vehicles of post-World War II US imperial hegemony but were intended to manage a global Keynesian hierarchy of development and underdevelopment and therefore, second, to bypass traditional orthodox theories of imperialism to focus on the commonalties and interconnections among particular struggles. Thus, for example, while some viewed the anti-Vietnam war or anti-apartheid mobilizations in the US as examples of anti-imperialist solidarity, others came to see them as interconnected moments of class struggle challenging a global capitalist order. Similarly, this approach led to an analysis of the crises of Keynesianism in the late 1960s and 1970s as political crises of that global order brought on by an international cycle of those interconnected class struggles.[41] In turn, 'economic' crises since the 1980s must be understood in part as the product of capitalist counterattacks and in part as the result of continuing working class resistance. In other words, from this Marxist perspective the global drama of the last 30 years or so has not only been — in the words of Subcomandante Marcos — a 'Fourth World War', but a class war between capitalists trying to wield neoliberal policies to regain control around the world and a diverse working class resisting those policies and fighting to build new worlds (Marcos 1999).

Multitude?

The kind of analysis of class struggle sketched earlier was taken by some Marxists, mostly working in France and Italy, and crossed with concepts from some 'post-modernist' thinkers such as Michel Foucault, Gilles Deleuze and Felix Guattari. The primary products of this melding that deal with conflict at the global level and are known in the English speaking world are the later works of Antonio Negri and especially his two books with Michael Hardt, *Empire* (Hardt and Negri 2000) and *Multitude* (Hardt and Negri 2004). These works are the outcome of over 20 years of collective efforts to understand precisely the nature of the processes of 'political recomposition' that brought on the crisis of Keynesianism and shaped capitalist efforts at 'decomposition' in the years since. From a wide-ranging series of studies of diverse struggles, mostly in Europe, whose results have been published in several European journals, including *Futur Antérieur* and *Multitudes* in France and *Derive Approdi* in Italy, these writers elaborated a theory of the nature of contemporary class relationships that reformulated the concept of working class into that of 'multitude' and that of capitalist sovereignty into 'empire'.

The concept of Empire designates a new organization of command, beyond imperialist competition between national blocs of capital backed by nation states, in which, through both national governments and supranational state institutions capital has begun to act as a more unified whole at a global level. A ferocious debate has followed this thesis — one that is strongly reminiscent of that which followed Karl Kautksy's proposed theory of ultra-imperialism just before World War I — as it was attacked by those who argued (*a*) national rivalries are still very much alive, (*b*) the US government still dominates all 'supranational' state institutions and (*c*) American imperialism is obviously rampant in the invasions of Afghanistan and Iraq and in neoconservative plans for a new Pax Americana.[42]

The concept of multitude for Negri and Hardt designates the new collective subject that overthrew Keynesianism and imposed a new organization on capitalism. Their concept of that new subject is clearly a variation on that of the collective worker in the social factory theorized more than a decade earlier. Historically, multitude designates a metamorphosis of what Alquati and Negri earlier had called the 'socialized worker'. The difference between the world of the social factory and the 'socialized worker' and that of Empire and multitude, would seem to lie in their perception that worker successes in rupturing and fleeing the social factory and capital's successes in adapting to those ruptures and checking that flight have resulted in a more thorough domination of every aspect of life. Their theorization of this supposedly new, thorough domination is based on two related concepts: biopower — a concept taken over from the work of Michel Foucault — and immaterial labour – a concept adapted from Jean-François Lyotard.

In a manner similar to the work of Deleuze and Guattari, Michel Foucault's research on capitalist domination shifted focus from macro-class forces to the micro-politics of control. His study of Bentham's proposal for the management of prisons via panopticon arrangements led to his investigations into how such control was spread throughout society, the bodies and brains of those living within it (see Deleuze 1986 and Foucault 1977, 1978). In the process he revealed hitherto invisible arrangements of power through which individual lives were subtly managed through induced forms of internalized control. In Hardt and Negri such bio-political arrangements are presented as thorough and complete; all of life, within formal work places, but also in the home and in the community have become places of work for capital. 'Power is thus expressed as a control that extends throughout the depths of the consciousnesses and bodies of the population — and at the same time across the entirety of social relations' (Hardt and Negri 2000: 24). As a result, they argue, Marx's labour theory of value is no longer relevant because if it is no longer possible to differentiate between work and non-work, between work time and non-work time, then there is no way to measure 'labour', and hence Marx's value.[43]

But what is the nature of this work to which all of life is reduced? While they recognize that older forms of work still abound — such as manual labour in fields or factories — they argue that the most important capitalist adaptation to the emergence of the multitude's subjectivity has been capital's ability to capture, organize and subordinate the increasingly important mental labour of generating information and managing communication flows and the affective labour through which personal and social relations are constructed and managed. Hardt, Negri and Maurizio Lazzarato call these kinds of work 'immaterial labor' (Lazzarato and Negri 1991; Lazzarato 1996).

While this sounds like a more thorough variation on the vision of critical theorists who saw total capitalist domination as having spread not only through the sphere of production but through that of culture, Hardt and Negri insist that the 'multitude' thus subsumed by capital is nevertheless a subject capable of revolt. The source of the power of the multitude to revolt, they argue, lies in its 'constitutive power' — a formulation taken over from their, and Deleuze's, reading of Spinoza where they identify the power to create or constitute (*potentia, puissance, potenza, potencia*) being distinguished from the Power (*potestas, pouvoir, potere, poder*) to command (Negri 1991, 1992, 2003). The actual generation of information, communication and affect is, like more traditional forms of labour, the activity of the multitude. Thus, the bio-political Power of Empire is exercised against the bio-political constituent power of the multitude, but that bio-power — which can only be harnessed but not eliminated — not only breaks free from time to time, here or there, but has the potential to free itself from Power completely. Moreover, 'freeing itself' means power destroying all of the mechanisms through which Power has constrained and harnessed it and achieving complete self-determination. And if Empire is world wide, so, necessarily is the multitude on which it is based.

How much of this analysis of multitude is really new? How much does it really differ from the earlier Marxist analyses of class struggle from which it drew? Let's examine some of the key concepts. First, what of (constituent) power vs. Power? While the two linked terms of this dichotomy may have originated in Spinoza, is it really that different from Marx's own dichotomy of living-labour and dead-labour? In Hardt and Negri's analysis it is power that is constitutive and Power that merely controls and manages. In Marx's analysis the living labour of the working class is the real life force within capitalist society and capital's ability to survive and expand depends entirely on its ability to control, subordinate and exploit that force. That subordination, in turn, had to be exercised, from the beginning, throughout society, starting with the expulsion of people from previous social relations (primitive accumulation) and then finding ways to continue to control the dislodged in factories, fields and communities. Although the array of skills and creative forces of living labour have evolved over time, including the communicative abilities essential to cooperation and collective work, these things have always been present. Applying Spinoza's term constituent power to living labor merely emphasizes its creative and productive character that was already highlighted by Marx. Hardt and Negri's location of the revolutionary potential of the multitude in its constituent power thus appears as a mere reformulation of Marx and many autonomist Marxists' grounding of the revolutionary potential of the working class in its own self-activity (only temporarily harnessed by capital as labour power).

Second, what of 'immaterial labour', of kinds of work that can be characterized as productive of information, communication and affect? To begin with, the adjective 'immaterial' here is clearly designed to differentiate this kind of mental work from manual labour that produces durable physical commodities; indeed the adjective is simply taken over from the idea of 'immaterial goods' such as services and communication. However, there is really nothing immaterial about the various kinds of work that produces services, information and communication, so the adjective is confusing. Although the perspective is reversed (Hardt and Negri see immaterial labour as absolutely central to contemporary work) this distinction between material and immaterial labour reminds one of the Soviet distinction between real work that produced real physical commodities and other kinds of activity, not worth counting as value production, that produced services. The 'immaterial' work of information production, processing and communication clearly involve considerable mental labour which is every bit as material as manual labour.

The same is true of 'affective labour' — a term that highlights the emotional dimension of mental labour (as opposed to its rational component). Whether affective labour is understood as producing services (e.g., health care, entertainment) or social networks and community through direct, or indirect, human contact, it is every bit as material as any other kind of work. Nor is this kind of work new. To begin with Marx recognized, though analyzed far less than he might, the necessary work of producing and reproducing human life as labour power.[44] Hardt and Negri even admit that 'affective labour' has been around for a long time, acknowledging how 'Feminist analyses in particular have long recognized the social value of caring labor, kin work, nurturing, and maternal activities'.[45] A recent, excellent example of such recognition and analysis by a Marxist feminist is the book *Caliban and the Witch* by Silvia Federici who has shown how, from the very first, capital sought to control not only production but the labour of reproduction (Federici, 2004). What they do claim is new is 'the extent to which this affective immaterial labour is now directly productive of capital and the extent to which it has become generalized through wide sectors of the economy' (Hardt n.d.). If 'directly productive of capital' refers to the direct production of profitable commodities, then this corresponds to the growth of the service sector and certainly it has grown as a proportion of capitalist industry. If it means directly productive of capital understood as class relation then it has been true from the beginning. As to becoming generalized, clearly the work of reproduction has always been necessary in every sector even if its modalities have changed over time.

Third, what of the contention that capital has succeeded in so extending its bio-political control throughout all of life to the point where it is no longer possible to distinguish work from non-work or to measure either? Clearly the imposition of capitalism has always involved the imposition of the work of producing the commodity labour power as well as the work of producing other, profitable, commodities. The question is: what was the basis for distinguishing these different kinds of work in the past and has that basis disappeared? Hardt and Negri argue that because communicative or affective activities in the sphere of reproduction have come to play a larger and larger role in the sphere of waged work, the distinction has been breaking down. However, in Marx's analysis any and all activities that produce labour power, i.e., the willingness and ability to work, have fed into what goes on in the sphere of production! What actually distinguished work in these two spheres was that, one had to be paid for and one did not; thus the acute capitalist preoccupation with measuring the time of work. Those who performed unwaged work had to be supported, of course, or the reproduction of labour power would falter and collapse, thus the family wage, charity and eventually welfare and unemployment insurance. Quite clearly this distinction between work that is directly paid for and work which is not still exists.

The classic 'working day' discussed by Marx in chapter 10, volume I of *Capital* is the waged working day, but it was by no means the entire working day. The rate of surplus value, or the rate of exploitation measured only the ratio of the work time that capital had to pay for over and beyond that required to reproduce labour power (in the aggregate, that required to produce goods and services consumed by workers) and ignored the work time in the sphere of reproduction. At the same time, neither was the entire time of waged workers actually spent working for capital, nor was the time spent by others, e.g., spouses or children, entirely filled with the work of reproducing labour power. Within the factory, Marx discussed the 'pores' of non-work in the working day and the endless efforts of capitalists to eliminate them to avoid paying for non-work.[46] Although he never analyzed them, the same kind of 'pores' of non-work have always existed in the home, school, community, and so on.[47] The 'pores' in his discussion were temporal ones — time momentarily freed from capitalist imposed work — but they must also be spatial ones as well; time spent not working has to take place somewhere, whether directly on the shop floor, at the water fountain, in a restroom or in specially appropriated spaces away from the workplace.

As the ability of workers to hammer down the time of waged work grew, the capitalist preoccupation with time outside that sphere grew apace, thus countless efforts to shape 'leisure time' and 'culture', i.e., to turn society into a social factory, to make sure that as much unwaged time as possible has been used to produce and reproduce labour power rather than being used for non- or anti-capitalist activities. Thus, too, multiplying efforts to measure how time is actually spent in various spheres of reproduction, e.g., homes, schools and communities.[48] Those efforts demonstrate a capitalist awareness of the importance of a continuing difference between work and non-work that disappears in the writings of Hardt and Negri.[49] This disappearance, although consistent with their emphasis on the thoroughness of capitalist bio-political control, is odd considering their contention that the multitude has the power to rupture that control through the exercise of its own bio-power. Does rupture actually occur? If so, then capitalist bio-political control is not omnipresent but full of 'pores' blown open by struggle and what we need are detailed analyses of the methods of rupture and of the actual exercise of the multitude's bio-power to constitute new kinds of social relationships autonomously of capital. Many of the studies of actual struggles whose results have appeared in the journals mentioned earlier do provide useful information on such issues but, unfortunately, little of it makes its way into Hardt and Negri's books.

Conclusion

The array of concepts discussed earlier has included sketches of several different approaches: (*a*) to thinking about the interconnectedness of struggles in terms of networks, of the dynamics of struggles in terms of swarming, rhizomes or currents, and (*b*) to characterizing the subjectivities in motion in terms of civil society, social movements, the working class or multitude. What do I make of these? Let me answer briefly in terms of two criteria: first, their usefulness in understanding the spreading, interconnected struggles that are challenging capitalism around the world, and second, their usefulness in terms of helping us figure out how to do better.

The concepts of de-centered networks and rhizomes do provide attractive metaphors for the patterns of interconnectedness that can be identified in a wide variety of grassroots struggles. But while the people and organizations in networks or rhizomes may sometimes converge or swarm to focus protest or disruption against some moment of capitalist domination, understanding how such networks or rhizomes have developed to the point where such behaviour is possible leaves something to be desired. Similarly, it's one thing to point, as I have done here, to the fluidity of self-organization through the metaphor of currents of struggle, and quite another to identify exactly how such currents form, how they gather or lose strength, how they interact and how and why organizations sometimes crystallize into being or melt back again into the flow. The concept of civil society, in all of its permutations, is of no help here. The work of social movement theorists is helpful in identifying permissive or restrictive parameters of such growth but less so in revealing its internal dynamics. Those analyses of everyday life, of the weapons of the weak, and of certain aspects of popular culture mentioned earlier help us understand something of the social dynamics that gestate networks or rhizomes but generally have been unable to specify the actual processes of quickening that brings these to life. Again, some Marxist analyses of the general patterns of the capitalist organization of social life, like some of the restrictions on self-organization identified by students of social movements, are helpful in understanding constraints on self-activity but not on understanding the dynamics of self-activity itself.

On the other hand, both the Marxist theory of political recomposition and the theory of multitude — which I see as a mutation or hybrid of class composition theory — provide concepts that focus our attention precisely on the character of self-activity involved in the genesis of networks, rhizomes or currents of struggle. Both theories, of the autonomous power of the working class (in production and reproduction) or the bio-power of the multitude throughout society, are formulated in ways intended to provide an understanding of how struggles shape and reshape themselves.

What is all too scarce, however, in the elaborations of all these theories are concrete analyses of *how* networks, rhizomes, currents or organizations have been formed, of their growth and of their effectiveness, strengths and weaknesses. In other words, far too much of the work done so far has focused on understanding the general character of these struggles and far too little on examining exactly how they have emerged, grown — and sometimes withered — in such ways as to permit drawing useful lessons from them about how to improve our abilities to bring about the changes we seek. The work that has been already done analyzing these struggles can, I think, be mined for material that can help us draw such lessons. But there is also a need to reorient our efforts away from crafting general theories and toward figuring out, on the one hand, what has worked, to what degree, why and how, and on the other hand, what has failed, to what degree, why and how.

For example, at the beginning of this chapter I mentioned three main forms through which global connections among diverse struggles have been organized and surged upward into public view. One of those has been the physical convergences of thousands of protestors. Now, the massive convergence against the G8 that took place in Genoa in July 2001 arguably involved the greatest number of participants since such mobilizations first began. How exactly was that degree of mobilization achieved? Some of the approaches discussed earlier provide general suggestions about where to look to answer that question, but we need concrete answers. This is especially true because, as has been widely remarked, since Genoa there has been an apparent lessening in the participation and intensity of such mobilizations against capital's global policy-makers. Protests have continued right up through the September 2006 meetings of the IMF and the World Bank in Singapore, but on a much smaller scale. What has happened? Some have attributed this to the events of 11 September 2001 and the subsequent actions of the Bush administration: the invasion and brutal occupation of two other countries and repression at home, e.g., blatant violations of civil rights, refusal to protect workers' rights, attacks on environmental activists, and the not-so-secret CIA kidnappings and torture, all justified by the rhetoric of a 'war on terrorism'. But such an appeal to a change in the political climate does not explain how any of this has changed the behaviour of the forms of self-organization and mobilization that gave rise to such protests prior to this new capitalist offensive.

It seems more likely that the judgments of participants and sympathetic observers, based directly on the experiences of the mobilizations, that what has been gained through these actions has been limited enough to warrant redirecting one's efforts into finding or elaborating alternative forms of struggle. Certainly the sharing of experience, multiplication of contacts and increased collaboration that has occurred at each of these events has been almost universally judged positive, even exhilarating. Eventually, a few of the positive demands made by protestors at these convergences have borne fruit, e.g., debt reduction, but clearly most have not been achieved despite the enormous resources, personal and collective, expended in these efforts. But has there been such a consensus over the results (if not the factors taken into account) of such cost-benefit calculations as to explain the reduced participation in such efforts? One approach to testing this hypothesis involves examining the ex-post discussions and evaluations of the experience at Genoa (and other such convergences). The few evaluations that I have read suggest that this is indeed the case, but real verification would require more extensive investigation than I have undertaken.

Two examples, on a smaller scale, of how and why shifts in the direction of struggle have taken place can be found in the reorientations of Zapatista struggle that occurred in the wake of their extremely well organized and extremely public, 3000 mile long March for Indigenous Dignity in 2001. The March took the form of a sizable caravan to Mexico City to demand from the Mexican congress the enactment into law of the San Andrés Accords on indigenous autonomy agreed to in 1996 but never implemented. This was understood by those in the Zapatista communities as a reformist demand but desired as a step that would facilitate further struggle. The caravan was a huge undertaking involving not only the movement of Zapatistas and the many supporters who accompanied them but also the organization of dozens of stops and encounters with thousands of people involved in local struggles along the way, and in Mexico City when they arrived — organizing undertaken not by the Zapatistas alone but by dozens of local groups. Despite these day-after-day displays of widespread public support the Mexican congress refused to pass a law or constitutional amendment that would implement the Accords. The Zapatistas returned to their communities in Chiapas.

The first shift in Zapatista struggle that occurred in the wake of these events was a turning inward and abandonment of any dialogue or negotiation with any wing of the Mexican government. From their point of view the March had been both a stunning success and an abject failure. The success lay in the mobilization of thousands of other people that demonstrated not only their continuing power of convocation and support for their demands but also extremely widespread opposition to Mexican government policies. The failure lay in the effort to leverage that support and opposition into sufficient pressure on Mexican politicians to achieve the long sought legalization of indigenous autonomy. The professional politicians in all three major parties, including the so-called leftist PRD, ignored the voices rising from the streets of Mexico and refused to recognize indigenous autonomy. In the discussions that ensued within the communities agreement was reached to abandon the struggle for the legalization of their autonomy and to proceed (*a*) with concrete projects that would strengthen their actual autonomy, i.e., their ability to organize themselves autonomously from Mexican capital's plans for their assimilation and cultural genocide and (*b*) to protect themselves from future attacks.[50] Among the more striking of those projects was the organization of regional governments they call *caracoles* or 'Good Government Councils' to coordinate activities among their various autonomous communities.[51]

The second shift in Zapatista struggle came after four years of the kind of internal work mentioned in the previous section. In the summer of 2005, they issued a 'Red Alert', closed their communities to the outside world and engaged in intensive internal debate over strategies of struggle. The result was the issuance in June of the 'Sixth Declaration of the Lacandona' that recounted what the Zapatistas had been doing, analyzed and condemned capitalism in general and neoliberal Mexican capitalism in particular and announced plans for a new outward-oriented offensive. The reasons given for this new offensive are clear: the war with capital is global, what can be accomplished in isolation is too limited (even for struggles as well organized internally as that of the Zapatistas), so people must organize themselves across space and differences to win the war. As a step toward such organization, they proposed:

a series of dialogues with others in struggle throughout Mexico. They also called for a series of meetings in August and September to discuss what others in struggle thought about this proposal for dialogue and if they approved, contributions as to how it could be achieved. Their idea for organizing such dialogues directly involved what they dubbed (during a year of presidential elections) an 'Other Campaign' in which a handful of Zapatistas, led by their spokesperson Subcomandante Marcos would travel to community after community, wherever the people involved in local struggles would invite them to come, to listen, to learn from and to share experience. The meetings were held, organization began and the Other Campaign was launched in January 2006.

While an analysis of Zapatista communiqués clarify the reasons for these two shifts in strategies of struggle, it is also true that because the Zapatista communities have been besieged by police, military and paramilitary harassment and violence ever since 1994 the internal discussions that led to these shifts were closed to outsiders. As a result, those of us on the outside know more about the decisions made than we do about the processes through which they came to be made. This brief account, moreover, provides few details on exactly how these strategies were, and are being, implemented. Nevertheless, it seems to me that the kinds of evaluations of experience, discussion of lessons to be learned and possible new strategies based on those lessons that can be found in the Zapatista communiqués provide an approximation of the kind of concrete analysis that we need to complement the more theoretical conceptualizations sketched in most of this essay. At the same time, those theoretical approaches lead us to ask questions about these struggles whose answers are not found in those communiqués and therefore prompt us to further investigation.

In short, and to truly conclude, whatever inspiration and insights we may draw from general theories of the growing interconnectedness and global character of our challenges to world-wide capitalist domination, what we really need in order to advance our struggles is more concrete investigation of how we have achieved what we have, what limits we have encountered, what others have achieved and how, what limits they have encountered and what we can learn from each other through a multiplicity of dialogues about where we are and what to do next.

Notes

1. See Alquati (1975). Although this work has never been translated, a synopsis of its ideas on networks has circulated widely and influenced many.
2. A useful overview of the development of network theory, from mathematics to sociology, can be found in the Introduction to Mitchell (1969). An adaptation of this approach to the understanding of social struggles was made in Italy by the Marxist sociologist Romano Alquati in his studies of workers' conflicts with the Italian auto giant FIAT (see Alquati 1975).
3. An influential moment of this literature is Powell's work (1990: 295–336).
4. Of particular relevance here are: Castells (1997); Keck and Sikkink (1998); McCaughey and Ayers (2003); Van de Donk, Loader, Nihon and Rucht (2004); Tarrow (2005); and Bob (2005). See also the earlier work by Thorup (1991: 12–26) and with Ronfeldt (1993). Not surprisingly Thorup went on to work for both the United States Agency for International Development and the National Security Council on building relationships with NGOs.
5. See Charles Swett's piece (1995) titled 'Strategic Assessment The Internet' at http://www.fas.org/cp/swett.html (accessed 4 October 2013).
6. The RAND researchers are by no means alone among policy-makers in being concerned about the growing power of such networks. Reviewing the Keck and Sikkink book on transnational advocacy networks for the elite journal *Foreign Affairs*, Francis Fukuyama warned: 'Like Stalin, one might ask "how many divisions do transnational networks have?" The answer is that they have information, greatly abetted by modern communications technology, and thus the ability to set agendas for nation-states and transnational organizations like the World Bank, Shell Oil Corporation, or Nestle' (Fukuyama 1998: 123).
7. Such separation was analyzed by Marx as an essential moment in the creation of a 'working' class dependent on the labour market for survival under the rubric of 'primitive accumulation' — a variation of Adam Smith's term for the same process: 'original accumulation'.
8. The recurrent capitalist efforts to impose and maintain such separation, sometimes blocked and sometimes reversed by resistance, has resulted in a debate over the transitory or permanent character of primitive accumulation.
9. The prime example of recent years was the gutting of Article 27 of the Mexican Constitution that protected indigenous and peasant *ejidal* (communal) lands, and hence communities, from privatization This was intended to set the stage for the final enclosure of the Mexican countryside and was executed by the Salinas government as a gift to

multinational corporations to help get the North American Free Trade Agreement enacted.

10. This early chapter has been followed by a series of others most of which are available at http://www.eco.utexas.edu/faculty/Cleaver/hmchtmlpapers.html (accessed 4 October 2013).
11. See, for example, Garrido and Halavais (2003) or the broader and more detailed study by Olesen (2005).
12. See Dominguez, et al., at http://www.thing.net/~rdom/ecd/swarm.html (accessed 4 October 2013).
13. The September 1998 counterattack by the Pentagon's Defense Information Systems Agency has demonstrated precisely the kind of dangers feared. See report by computer security writer (Winn Schwartau 1999). For more on the debate see the archives of the Chiapas95 listserv beginning in May 1998 (http://www.eco.utexas.edu/faculty/Cleaver/chiapas95.html, accessed 4 October 2013).
14. See Cleaver (1998) for my intervention into the debate.
15. Such methods have been used from time to time, especially in Italy where 'netstrikes' have been called in support of local struggles and international ones, e.g., against Turkish government and business sites in support of Kurdish Rebels in Turkey whose leader had recently been seized.
16. See 'Swarming and the Future of Protesting', at http://www.why-war.com/features/read.php?id=4#part4 (accessed 4 October 2013).
17. For a brief history of flash mob protests of various kinds see: http://en.wikipedia.org/wiki/Flash_mob (accessed 4 October 2013).
18. As Deleuze and Guattari's analysis makes clear, capital can also intentionally deterritorialize, i.e., uproot people from one location to fix them in another as a method of achieving and managing exploitation or displace its fixed capital with the aim of exploiting people in other locations. The slave trade, the recurrent use of immigrant labour, runaway shops and outsourcing are obvious examples on an international scale.
19. See, for example, Perez (1990) or the webpage of the Rhizome Collective of East Austin, Texas at: http://www.rhizomecollective.org/ (accessed 4 October 2013). One example of the direct application of this kind of thinking to a particular series of struggles is Gattolin and Lefebvre (2004).
20. A good example of such clashes are two articles by Richard Barbrook, who attacks the work of Deleuze and Guattari, and Bifo who defends it. See Barbrook (2001) and Berardi (2001).
21. We can also add, with Werner Bonefeld, that everything is uncertain. See Bonefeld (2005: 265–72).
22. See the analysis by the Department of Mathematics at the University of Bergen, Norway: http://www.math.uio.no/~karstent/waves/index_en.html (accessed 4 October 2013) or, for a dramatic account, the programme on the subject produced by the History Channel.

23. The physical configuration of seafloor topology obviously affects currents, sometimes channeling them, sometimes deflecting them. Earth's gravity affects all water but pulls denser water toward the bottom of the ocean. Lunar gravity causes tides. The sun's rays warm surface waters — more in some areas than others — and indirectly, and to an ever lesser degree the deeper waters beneath them. Wind pushes surface water through friction. Wind blown surface water in turn affects water below it, also through friction; its differential impact according to depth produces the Eckman Transport Spiral that helps form gyres and mounds of water in the ocean. It also contributes to upwellings of deep water where the wind blows offshore and downwellings where it blows onshore. The coriolus effect is a deflection of wind patterns caused by the Earth's rotation.
24. In the case of the oceans the surface currents are only 10 per cent of the total ocean water mass. As a result wind only affects, directly and indirectly, some 20 per cent of the mass.
25. This is akin to Karl Marx's 'old mole' — a proletariat whose subterranean struggles periodically erupt onto the surface of society bringing revolution — or Sergio Bologna's 'tribe of moles' in Italy of the 1970s or his more recent metaphor of invisible 'termites' eating away wooden beams from within in ways that are free of mediation and can bring about the ultimate collapse of a whole structure. See Bologna (1979: 67–91; 1980), and 'An Interview with Toni Negri' (Cocco and Lazzarato 2001). Hardt and Negri (more or less following Deleuze, who more or less follows Foucault, on the crisis of the 'society of discipline' leading to the 'society of control') have argued that the 'old mole' is being replaced by a 'snake' because all of today's struggles take place on the surface of 'superficial, imperial landscapes'. While it is true enough that all the 'environments of enclosure', and hence of discipline, have been thrown into crisis by struggle, it is not at all obvious that all struggles are clearly visible 'on the surface'. Unfortunately, we rarely see or understand the underlying turbulence that gives rise to those clearly visible struggles that we can not help but recognize. See Hardt and Negri (2002); Deleuze (1990).
26. At this writing the popular occupation of Oaxaca City has now shut down the governments of both city and state and substituted its own self-organization for longer than the Paris Commune of 1871.
27. Well-known among such studies are those of Michel Foucault, Pierre Bordieu, Michel de Certeau, James Scott, Romano Alquati, and John Fiske. Included here must also be the work of those historians who have unearthed the hitherto buried histories of everyday struggle out of which impossible-to-ignore insurrectionary uprisings have emerged, e.g., Christopher Hill, Edward Thompson, Peter Linebaugh, Marcus Rediker, Silvia Federici and contributors to 'subaltern studies'.

28. This way of thinking has involved a clear-cut dichotomy between capital and the working class such that the dynamics of the former, including its crises, could be theorized independently of the activity of the latter. Fortunately, in recent years this approach has been progressively superseded by an understanding of capital as class relationship that allows us to see how the struggles of workers have shaped, and sometimes ruptured 'capitalist' development bringing crisis, threatening its very existence and elaborating possible alternatives.
29. The failure of Soviet-style regimes to use social scientists in this way — as opposed to using them for mere ideological justification of policies — was one reason for the ignorant and ultimately self-defeating brutality of the state's response to all forms of struggle. The brutality drove the currents of resistance deep below the surface where, out of sight and out of the state's mind, they circulated, interacted and gradually gained the strength to surface and overthrow the regime.
30. The classic texts that most clearly articulated this analysis were: Tronti (1966) and Negri (1987). A much elaborated analysis along these lines is de Angelis (2000).
31. Quenay's 'circulation' was essentially a biological metaphor adapted from Harvey's analysis of the flow of blood in the human body.
32. Such analysis of the 'circulation of struggles' was a factor in my coming to rethink the Zapatista and counter-globalization 'networks' in terms of currents.
33. In one line of contemporary Marxist thought this imagination and capability is conceptualized in terms of 'a general intellect' (a concept plucked from 'the fragment on machines' in Marx's 1857 *Grundrisse*) and is manifest not only in the increasingly central role of mental labour, but in its tendencies to autonomy. See, for example, Vierno (1996, 2004).
34. There are a number of books outlining and analyzing the history of the concept of 'civil society' and that history is much too long to recapitulate in his essay. See, for example, Ehrenberg (1999).
35. See for example Frederick (1993).
36. For a different critique of the common evocation of 'civil society' as the prime agent of anti-globalization movements see Bonefeld (2006: 39–59).
37. For a sketch of the variety of approaches see McAdam et. al. (1996).
38. For one very brief sketch of the international development of such non-orthodox Marxisms see the Introduction to Cleaver (2000) available at: http://www.eco.utexas.edu/facstaff/Cleaver/357krcp.html (accessed 4 October 2013). But also see the much more detailed account of the emergence of such recognition among Italian Marxists in Steve Wright (2002) as well as such detailed historical explorations of the long history of the role of the unwaged in working class struggle

in studies such as: Linebaugh (2003); Linebaugh and Rediker (2000); Federici (2004).

39. Among those who went into the factories to discover what was the actual state of the class composition of their times were the members of the Johnson-Forest Tendency in the United States, those of *Socialisme ou Barbarie* in France and associates of *Quaderni Rossi* in Italy (especially Romano Alquati). These interlinked efforts are described briefly in the Introduction to Harry Cleaver, *Reading Capital Politically* (2000). For a more detailed discussion of Alquati and his work see Chapter 2 of Wright (2002).
40. On self-valorization, see Negri (1992); Cleaver (1992).
41. A now classic example of this kind of analysis is laid out in the two issues of the American journal *Zerowork* (1975 and 1977).
42. Kautsky's classic essay is available at: http://www.marxists.org/archive/kautsky/1914/09/ultra-imp.htm (accessed 4 October 2013). One collection of articles critical of the 'empire' thesis is Balakrishnan (2003).
43. Negri's attack on the 'law of value' pre-dates *Empire* and goes back at least to his 1971 article on the 'Crisis of the Planner State: Communism and Revolutionary Organization', available in English in Negri (1989).
44. See, for example, his analysis of simple reproduction in Chapter 23 of Volume I of *Capital.*
45. A seminal text in the history of such recognition is Dalla Costa (1971).
46. This discussion is in the discussion of the intensification of labour in Chapter 15 of Volume I of *Capital.* As has been often pointed out, it was partly against such pores — as well as in order to intensify work itself — that Frederick Taylor and Henry Ford reorganized work with stopwatch and assembly line.
47. Marx also failed to examine the flip side of capitalist 'nibbling and cribbling' to lengthen the working day pointed out in Chapter 10 of Volume I of *Capital.* Pitted against such efforts, workers have also found innumerable ways to shorten their work time, not only at the beginning and at the end (showing up late, leaving early, taking long lunches) of a working day but in the middle, by carving out precisely those 'pores' that have so preoccupied their bosses. They have done the same within the working week through fake sick leave and other forms of absenteeism.
48. See the recent paper by de Angelis and Harvie (2006). For another discussion of the 'measuring' of various kinds of unwaged schoolwork see Cleaver (2006).
49. For a different, but useful, critique of Hardt and Negri's thesis of immeasurability, see Caffentzis (2005).

50. This protection took the form, primarily, of clearly separating the EZLN from community self-governance. The story of their worries about possible attack and the preparatory steps they took has now been told in Marcos (2006).
51. A fairly detailed description of these caracoles, why they were formed, how they operate, their successes and failures can be found in two series of communiqués issued by the Zapatistas in 2003 and 2004.

References

Alquati, Romana. 1975. *Sulla FIAT*. Milano: Feltrineli. http://libcom.org/library/network-of-struggles-italy-romano-alquati (accessed 4 October 2013).

Alquati, R., N. Negri and A. Sormano. 1976. *Università di ceto medio e proletariato Intellectual*. Torino: Stampatori.

Arquilla, John and David Ronfeldt. 1996. *The Advent of Netwar*. Santa Monica: RAND.

Arquilla, John and David Ronfeldt. 2000. *Swarming & the Future of Conflict*. Santa Monica: RAND, National Defense Research Institute.

Balakrishnan, Gopal. 2003. *Debating Empire*. New York: Verso Press.

Barbrook, Richard. 2001. 'Le cyber-commnisme, ou le dépassement du capitalisme dans le cyberspace', *Multitudes* 5, Mai.

Berardi, Bifo Franco. 2001. 'Techo-nomadisme et pensée rhizomatique', *Multitudes* 5, Mai.

Bob, Clifford. 2005. *The Marketing of Rebellion: Insurgents, Media and International Activism*. New York: Cambridge University Press.

Bonefeld, Werner. 2005. 'Notes on Movement and Uncertainty', in D. Harvie, K. Milburn, B. Trott and D. Watts (eds), *Shut Them Down! The G8, Gleneagles 2005 and the Movement of Movements*. New York: Autonomedia.

———. 2006. 'Anti-globalization and the Critique of Socialism', *Critique*, 34(1): April.

Bologna, Sergio. 1977. *Primo Maggio*, No. 8, Spring.

———. 1979. 'The Tribe of Moles: Class Composition and the Party System in Italy', in *Working Class Autonomy and the Crisis*. London: Red Notes and CSE.

———. 1980. 'The Tribe of Moles: Class Composition and the Party System in Italy', *Semiotext(e)*, 3(3).

Caffentzis, George. 2005. 'Immeasurable Value? An Essay on Marx's Legacy', *The Commoner*, No. 10, Spring–Summer 2005, available at: http://www.commoner.org.uk/10caffentzis.pdf (accessed 4 October 2013).

Castells, Manuel. 1997. *The Informational Society: Economy, Society and Culture* (vol. 2, *The Power of Identity*). London: Blackwell.

Cleaver, Harry. 1992. 'The Inversion of Class Perspective in Marxist Theory, from Valorization to Self-Valorization', in W. Bonefeld, R. Gunn and K. Psychopedis (eds), *Open Marxism*, vol. 2, London: Pluto Press.

———. 1994. 'The Chiapas Uprising and the Future of Class Struggle in The New World Order', *Riff-Raff: Attraverso la produzione sociale* (Padova, Italy), marzo pp. 133–45, available at http://www.eco.utexas.edu/faculty/Cleaver/hmchtmlpapers.html (accessed 4 October 2013).

———. 1998. 'A Contribution to the Discussion of ECD', 1 May. (http://www.eco.utexas.edu/faculty/Cleaver/chiapas95.html, accessed 4 October 2013).

———. 2000. *Reading Capital Politically*, London: AK Press and Anti Theses. Also available at http://www.eco.utexas.edu/facstaff/Cleaver/357krcp.html (accessed 4 October 2013).

———. 2006. 'Schoolwork and the Struggle Against It', available at http://www.eco.utexas.edu/facstaff/Cleaver/OnSchoolwork200606.pdf (accessed 4 October 2013).

Cocco, Giuseppe and Maurizio Lazzarato. 2001. 'An Interview with Toni Negri' (translated from the French journal by Thomas Seay and Hydrarchist), *Multitudes*, no. 7, December. Also available at http://www.nettime.org/Lists-Archives/nettime-bold-0202/msg00006.html (accessed 4 October 2013).

Communiqués issued by the Zapatistas in 2003 and 2004, available at http://www.eco.utexas.edu/facstaff/Cleaver/aguascalientes.html and http://www.eco.utexas.edu/facstaff/Cleaver/leerunvideo.html (accessed 4 October 2013).

Costa, Mariarosa Dalla. 1971. *Women and the Subversion of the Community*. 29 December, available at http://www.eco.utexas.edu/facstaff/Cleaver/357kDallaCostaSubversion.html and http://www.eco.utexas.edu/facstaff/Cleaver/357kDallaCostaSubversionTable.pdf (accessed 4 October 2013).

Cunninghame, Patrick. 1995. 'An/other Anti-capitalism in Mexico: the Sixth Declaration of the EZLN and the 'Other Campaign', available at http://www.eco.utexas.edu/facstaff/Cleaver/TheOtherCampaign.html and http://www.eco.utexas.edu/~archive/chiapas95/ (accessed 4 October 2013).

D'Anjou, Leo. 1989. *Social Movements and Cultural Change: The First Abolition Campaign Revisited*. New York: Aldine.

Darnovsky, Marcy et al. (eds). 1995. *Cultural Politics and Social Movements*. Chicago: Temple University Press.

de Angelis, Massimo. 2000. *Keynesianism, Social Conflict and Political Economy*. London: Palgrave Macmillan.

de Angelis, Massimo and Harvie, David. 2006. 'Cognitive Capitalism and the Rat Race: How Capital measures ideas and affects in UK Higher Education', available at http://www.geocities.com/immateriallabour/angelisharviepaper2006.html (accessed 4 October 2013).

Deleuze, Gilles. 1986. *Foucault*. Paris: Minuit.

Deleuze, Gilles and Félix Guattari. 1987. *A Thousand Plateaus: Capitalism & Schizophrenia*. Minneapolis: University of Minnesota Press.

Deleuze, Gilles. 1990. 'Postscript on the Society of Control', available at http://www.eurozine.com/articles/2002-02-13-hardtnegri-en.html and http://www.nadir.org/nadir/archiv/netzkritik/societyofcontrol.html (accessed 4 October 2013).

Dominguez, Ricardo; Stefan Wray; Brett Beestal and Osea. 'SWARM: An ECD Project for ARS Electronica Festival '98', available at http://www.thing.net/~rdom/ecd/swarm.html (accessed 4 October 2013).

Ehrenberg, John. 1996. *Civil Society: The Critical History of an Idea*. New York: New York University Press.

Fantasia, Rick. 1989. *Cultures of Solidarity: Consciousness, Action and Contemporary Workers*. Berkeley: University of California Press.

Federici, Silvia. 2004. *Caliban and the Witch: Women, the Body and Primitive Accumulation*. New York: Autonomedia.

Foucault, Michel. 1977. *Discipline and Punish: The Birth of the Prison*. New York: Pantheon Books.

———. 1978. *The History of Sexuality*, volume I. New York: Pantheon.

Frederick, Howard. 1993. 'Computer Networks and the Emergence of Global Civil Society', in Linda M. Harasim (ed.), *Global Networks: Computers and International Communication*. Cambridge: MIT Press.

Fukuyama, Francis. 1998. 'Review of Activists Beyond Borders: Advocacy Networks in International Politics', *Foreign Affairs*, July–August, 77(4): 123.

Garrido, Maria and Alexander Halavais. 2003. 'Mapping Networks of Support for the Zapatista Movement: Applying Social-Networks Analysis to Study Contemporary Social Movements', in Martha McCaughey and Michael D. Ayers (eds), *Cyberactivism: Online Activism in Theory and Practice*. New York: Routledge.

Gattolin, Andre and Thierry Lefebvre. 2004. 'Stopub: analyse provisoire d'un rhizome activiste', *Multitudes 16*, Printemps.

George, Susan. 2004. *Another World is Possible IF....* New York: Verso.

Hardt, Michael. n.d. 'Affective Labor', available at http://makeworlds.org/node/60 (accessed 4 October 2013).

Hardt, Michael and Antonio Negri. 2000. *Empire*. Cambridge: Harvard University Press.

———. 2002. 'Marx's Mole is Dead!', *Eurozine*, 13 February. Also available at http://www.eurozine.com/articles/2002-02-13-hardtnegri-en.html

and http://www.nadir.org/nadir/archiv/netzkritik/societyofcontrol.html (accessed 4 October 2013).

———. 2004. *Multitude: War and Democracy in the Age of Empire*. New York: Penguin Press.

Harvie, David, Keir Milburn, Ben Trott and David Watts (eds). 2005. *Shut Them Down! The G8, Gleneagles 2005 and the Movement of Movements*. Leeds: Dissent! and Brooklyn, NY: Autonomedia.

Keck, Margaret E. and Kathryn Sikkink. 1998. *Activists beyond Borders: Advocacy Networks in International Politics*. Ithaca: Cornell University Press.

Lazzarato, Maurizio. 1996. 'Immaterial Labour', in Paolo Virno and Michael Hardt (eds), *Radical Thought in Italy*, Minneapolis: University of Minnesota Press. Also available at http://www.generation-online.org/c/fcimmateriallabour3.htm (accessed 4 October 2013).

Lazzarato, Maurizio and Toni Negri. 1991. 'Travail immatériel et subjectivité', *Futur Antérieur*, 6: Été.

Leeds May Day Group. December 2001. Anti-capitalist Movements, available at http://freelyassociating.org/anti-capitalist-movements/ (accessed 10 January 2009).

Linebaugh, Peter. 2003. *The London Hanged*. London: Verso Press.

Linebaugh, Peter and Marcus Rediker. 2000. *The Many-headed Hydra: Sailors, Slaves, Commoners, and the Hidden History of the Revolutionary Atlantic*. Boston: Beacon Press.

Marcos, Subcomandante. 1999. 'The Fourth World War', 20 November 1999. Available at http://www.inmotionmagazine.com/auto/fourth.html (accessed 4 October 2013).

———. 2006. 'The Zapatistas and the Other: The Pedestrians of History', (September). See http://enlacezapatista.ezln.org.mx/la-otra-campana/ (accessed 4 October 2013).

McAdam, Doug, et al. (eds). 1996. *Comparative Perspectives on Social Movements: Political Opportunities, Mobilizing Structures and Cultural Framings*. Cambridge: Cambridge University Press.

McCaughey, Martha and Michael D. Ayers. 2003. *Cyberactivism: Online Activism in Theory and Practice*. New York: Routledge.

Melluci, Alberto. 1995. 'The Process of Collective Identity', in Hank Johnston and Bert Klandermans (eds), *Social Movements and Culture*. Minneapolis: University of Minnesota Press.

———. 1996. *Challenging Codes: Collective Action in the Information Age*. Cambridge: Cambridge University Press.

Melucci, Alberto and Marcy Darnovsky, et al. (eds). 1995. *Cultural Politics and Social Movements*. Chicago: Temple University Press.

Mertes, Tom (ed.). 2004. *A Movement of Movements: Is Another World Possible?* New York: Verso.

Mitchell, Clyde J. 1969. *Social Networks in Urban Situations: Analyses of Personal Relationships in Central African Towns*. Manchester: Manchester University Press.

Negri, A. 1979. *Dall'operaio massa all'operaio sociale*. Milan: Multhipla Edizioni.

———. 1987. 'John M. Keynes and the Capitalist Theory of the State in 1929', in Toni Negri, *Revolution Retrieved: Selected Writings on Marx, Keynes, Capitalist Crisis and New Social Subjects, 1967-83*. London: Red Notes.

Negri, A. 1988. 'Archeology and Project: The Mass Worker and the Social Worker', in *Revolution Retrieved: Selected Writings of Toni Negri*. London: Red Notes.

———. 1989. *Revolution Retrieved: Selected Writings on Marx, Keynes, Capitalist Crisis & New Social Subjects*, 1967–1983. London: Red Notes.

———. 1991. *The Savage Anomaly: The Power of Spinoza's Metaphysics and Politics*. Minneapolis: University of Minnesota Press.

———. 1992. *Il potere costituente*. Milan: Sugerco.

———. 1992. *Marx beyond Marx: Lessons on the Grundrisse*. New York: Autonomedia.

———. 1994. *Insurgencies: Constituent Power and the Modern State*. Minneapolis: University of Minnesota Press.

———. 2003. 'Constitutent Republic', in W. Bonefeld (ed.), *Revolutionary Writing: Common Sense Essays in Post-Political Politics*. New York: Autonomedia.

Olesen, Thomas. 2005. *International Zapatismo: The Construction of Solidarity in the Age of Globalization*. New York: Zed.

Paolo Vierno. 1996. 'Notes on the General Intellect', in S. Makdisi, C. Casarino and R. E. Karl (eds), *Marxism Beyond Marxism*. New York: Routledge.

———. 2004. *A Grammar of the Multitude: For an Analysis of Contemporary Forms of Life*. New York: Semiotext(e).

Perez, Rolando. 1990. *On An(archy) and Schizoanalysis*. Brooklyn: Autonomedia, also available at http://www.rhizomecollective.org/ (accessed 4 October 2013).

Powell, Walter W. 1990. 'Neither Market nor Hierarchy: Network Forms of Organization', *Research in Organizational Behavior*, 12: 295–336.

Ronfeldt, David and Armando Martínez. 1997. 'A Comment on the Zapatista 'Netwar', in John Arquilla and David Ronfeldt (eds), *In Athena's Camp: Preparing for Conflict in the Information Age*. Santa Monica: RAND.

Ronfeldt, David, John Arquilla, Graham Fuller, and Melissa Fuller. 1998. *The Zapatista 'Social Netwar' in Mexico*. RAND Publication MR-994-A.

Schwartau, Winn. 1999. 'Cyber-civil Disobedience', *Network World*, 11 January, available at http://www.eco.utexas.edu/faculty/Cleaver/chiapas95.html (accessed 4 October 2013).
Tarrow, Sidney. 2005. *The New Transnational Activism*. New York: Cambridge University Press.
The Sixth Declaration. Available at http://www.eco.utexas.edu/facstaff/Cleaver/SixthDeclaration.html (accessed 4 October 2013).
Thorup, Cathryn. 1991. 'The Politics of Free Trade and the Dynamics of Cross-border Coalitions in U.S.-Mexican Relations', *Columbia Journal Of World Business*, 26(11): 12–26.
Thorup, Cathryn and David Ronfeldt. 1993. *North America[cut:n]* in *The Era of Citizen Networks: State, Society, and Security*. Santa Monica: RAND.
Tronti, Mario. 1966. *Operai e capitale*. Torino: Einaudi.
Van De Donk, Wim, Brian D. Loader, Paul G. Nihon and Dierter Rucht. 2004. *Cyberprotest: New Media, Citizens and Social Movements*. New York: Routledge.
Wright, Steve. 2002. *Storming Heaven: Class Composition and Struggle in Italian Autonomist Marxism*. London: Pluto Press.

10

Social Movements, Autonomy and Hope

Notes on the Zapatistas' Revolution

*Ana Cecilia Dinerstein**

Introduction: On Collective Autonomy and Hope

> In our dreams we have seen another world, an honest world, a world decidedly more fair than the one in which we now live ... this world was not something that came to us from our ancestors. It came from ahead, from the next step we were going to take (Sub commander Marcos in Ponce de Leon 2001: 18).

> Too much still persists all around us, and ultimately we still are not (Ernst Bloch, *The Spirit of Utopia*, 1918/2000: 267)

The purpose of this chapter is to explore autonomous practices by the Zapatista movement and offer a more general conceptualization of such practices by social movements as a *form of organizing hope*. The practice of autonomy (i.e., self-determination, self-government, independence from unions and political parties) has come a long way in Latin America (predominantly among indigenous communities), but recently has been invigorated by social movements as the means for social transformation. Countless mobilizations and autonomous undertakings by those so-called 'socially excluded' have emerged and developed concurrently with a great sense of resistance to power, by those living in conditions of unemployment, poverty and repression. New movements led by rural workers, peasants, indigenous groups and the unemployed recovered radical politics through the symbolic reaffirmation of collective values, such as dignity, democracy and social justice against dystopian neoliberal globalization, state power and the power of transnational corporations. Against ideas that Latin America was depoliticized and governed by technocratic democracies (Silva 1999), these movements reintroduced *hope* in democratic politics (Dinerstein and Deneulin 2012). If there is anything for what neoliberalism will be remembered for is its capacity to discursively reduce almost everything to the realm of 'possibility'. Inversely, if there is anything vital to many of the social movements that emerged out of neoliberal globalization is the attempt to create collectively another reality in the belief that the world is essentially 'unfinished' and, without the possibility of an alternative, any reality is incomplete.

In this chapter, I discuss the Zapatista's autonomy with the intention to explore how autonomous practices create symbolic and/or territorial spaces for what I call the *organization of hope*. I suggest that autonomy creates a *territory of hope* where the utopian impulse is articulated, made concrete, put/move forward, realized, experienced and, as I will argue later, also disappointed. The term *hope* is frequently used to describe 'romantic', 'utopian' and somehow 'unrealistic' projects. In the Zapatistas case has been used to describe their wish to change the world. By engaging with Bloch's *principle of hope* (1986), I deal with hope as the *real* and material process of anticipating of the future, which, in the Zapatista case this means the pursuit of human dignity by means of the practice of indigenous autonomy. I treat hope as a political category, which must not be understood as a 'wish' or a 'remote utopia', but as what Bloch calls the 'Not-Yet-Become' (ibid.) that lives within reality. As a 'lived utopia' (Mattiace 2003: 187) autonomy — I suggest — is a form of mediating the *Novum*.

Secondly, by focusing on the relationship between the Zapatistas and the state, I point to the 'irresolvable' tension that underpins autonomous practices, that is the tension between autonomy as a tool for resistance (as mentioned earlier) and autonomy as a tool for integration by the state (Böhm et al. 2010) via policy and World Bank programmes, which encourage 'participation from below' (see Evans 2008) but in fact they are effective governmental tools directed to 'discipline the poor' (Cornwall and Brock 2005: 7).

Finally, I translate the tension between rebellion and integration into the language of hope as the movement between 'real possibility' and 'disappointment'. On the one hand, I suggest that the realization of the hope that inhabits the autonomous project is 'really possible'. As Bloch explains, this means that autonomy is not 'scientifically to be expected' but its conditions exist but they are not yet fully assembled. On the other hand, hope is 'perpetually exposed to the radical danger of disappointment' (Richter 2006: 51). What really matters is how autonomy opens a space for the anticipation of the future and the changes that are produced in such pursuit of human realization.

In what follows, I briefly introduce the Zapatista movement and explore the process leading to the formation of their new governing bodies. Then, after briefly explaining their main features, I address the contentious politics between the Zapatistas and the Mexican state, in particular the Zapatistas' practice of autonomy *de facto*, and how it influenced the government strategic shift from direct repression to the implementation of new state counter insurgent policy-making, aiming at incorporating the Zapatistas' autonomy into new forms of governance in Chiapas. Then, I decipher the tension underpinning the Zapatistas' autonomous organising as the tension between real possibility and disappointment that underpins the process of organisation of hope and briefly discuss the implications of both the Zapatistas' project and an understanding of autonomy as a form of *organizing hope*.

The Zapatistas' Revolution

On 1 January 1994, the insurrectionary group of indigenous Mexicans, the Zapatista National Liberation Army (*Ejército Zapatista de Liberación Nacional*, EZLN), surprised the world when it occupied several counties of the Chiapas Region of Mexico at the sound of the scream 'enough is enough!' (*Ya Basta*) The Chiapas region (with almost four million inhabitants) is both an economic strategic area with abundant natural resources (biodiversity, oil, water, and hydroelectric energy) and one of the poorest states in Mexico (see Ceceña and Barreda 1998; Pickard 2004). The incorporation of Mexico to the NAFTA treaty obliged the Mexican state to undertake a constitutional amendment — under the presidency of Salinas de Gortari, which opened up indigenous lands (*ejidos*) for large agro-business. On 1 January 1994, the first day of NAFTA, the Chiapas' peasants represented by the EZLN exclaimed *Ya Basta!*, they declared the war to the Mexican government, called neoliberal globalization 'a war against humanity' (Subcomandante Marcos 1997), i.e., 'a war to conquest the entire world, a world war' (Subcomandante Marcos and the Zapatistas 2006: 99) and, with their faces covered by ski masks 'to make themselves visible', they expressed no intention to seize power.

The EZLN was formed as a conventional guerrilla *foco* in 1983 by a small number of activists influenced by Maoist and Guevarist ideologies, liberation theology and indigenous communal tradition. During the years of preparation in the jungle, the incipient movement evolved into an insurgent movement of a new type which contested revolutionary traditions concerned with class, exploitation and power with a new discourse centred on human *dignity* as the fundamental value and goal of their revolution. Adler Hellman suggests that 'unlike the classic guerrilla *foco* that hopes to attract a following after revolutionary activity has been launched, the Zapatistas were firmly supported by thousands of adherents in villages throughout their zones of operation' (2000: 165).

The overall meaning that the Zapatistas give to their action directed to 'change the world' through 'simple demands' of justice, dignity and democracy (Ponce de León 2001) is quite different from those revolutionary proposals of the traditional left. The Zapatistas' uniqueness is that they 'want to change the world without taking power' (Holloway 2002b). The attainment of self-determination, solidarity and self-realisation are incompatible with the logic of state power and money.

The Zapatistas are also famous for their electronic methods of communications (Cleaver 1998), their capacity to convey an emotional intelligent discourse simultaneously based on respect for diversity and resistance against power, and their 'intergalactic' encounters for humanity against globalization (e.g., Chiapas 1996 and Madrid 1997) have contributed to transform the Zapatistas into an emblem of resistance for those seeking dignity and democracy against neoliberal globalization worldwide.

In what follows I look at the Zapatistas' relationship in and against the Mexican state during the period of negotiation 1995–1996 and the political dynamics around the San Andres Accords, which led to the Zapatistas' disappointment and further reformulation of their organizational autonomous strategy.

Free Municipality vs Autonomous Community: The San Andres Accords and the Zapatistas' Disappointment

Until 2003 the Clandestine Indigenous Revolutionary Committee (*Comité Clandestino Indígena Revolucionario*, CCIR) operated in five regions of Chiapas, called Aguascalientes. In 1995, after the ceasefire, negotiations between Zapatistas and the Mexican government mediated by the Commission for Agreement and Pacification (*Comisión para la Concordia y la Pacificación*, COCOPA) began. In 1996, the San Andres Accords were signed between the Zapatistas and the Mexican government, wherein the latter promised to produce a constitutional reform that would lead to the recognition of the indigenous people's right to autonomy and the guarantee of self-government and collective production. The COCOPA provided protection to the rebels, ensured a peaceful process of negotiation and opened a path for the potential creation of a *plurinacional* state (González Casanova 2001).

But the San Andres Accords were *not* put into practice under President Ernesto Zedillo who opted for a repressive policy instead. The massacre of Acteal — where 45 people died (including many children) — not only contradicted the government's willingness to negotiate, demonstrated during the San Andres negotiations, but also marked a breaking point in the use of repression by the state (Ceceña 2001; also Subcomandante Marcos and the Zapatistas 2006).

The arrival of president Fox to power in December 2000 brought new hope among the Zapatistas as this indicated a political change with the end of 71 years of rule of the Institutional Revolutionary Party (PRI). The Zapatistas demanded the new government, the removal of seven military bases in Chiapas, the release of all Zapatistas political prisoners and the implementation of the San Andres Accords (Replogle 2005).

Since these demands were not fulfilled, the Zapatistas mobilized in what it became to be known as the 'March for Indigenous Dignity', which began on 24 February 2001 and lasted for 37 days during which the demonstration passed through 12 Mexican states, gathering people in 77 public acts and ended in Zocalo, the Mexico DF city centre (Ceceña 2001: 10; OSAL 2001).

The constitutional reform of 2001 was finally put into practice by the Mexican government but it soon became apparent that what was being legally validated was *not* what the Zapatistas had signed for and expected, i.e., the respect for autonomous communities. While the law accredited the right to self-government to indigenous communities, it also stated that 'the bases of the territorial organization, and of the political and administrative organization of the state [was] the *free municipality*' (idem. ant.). The law also specified what kind of indigenous authorities were legally recognized by law and how they should be elected — by free and secret ballot (idem. ant.). In short, the legislation proposed a form of local democracy (see Burguete Cal y Mayor 2004) that encouraged 'decentralization', 'empowerment' and 'participation from below' as in the World Bank Development programmes. For governmental projects of decentralized governance, local 'autonomy' becomes 'the organizational means by which governments channel resources down to local level and citizens channel demands up' (Lazar 2006: 187). In Subcomandante Marcos' words: 'The communities will not be capable of deciding within their own territories, nor will be able to design their own plans that have to do with ethnodevelopment in which communities get to decide' (Subcomandante Marcos 2003, cited in Otero 2004: 229).

Deeply disappointed, the Zapatistas embraced their dream of autonomy and rejected the constitutional reform of 2001 and after sometime of reflection and the use of 'silence as a strategy' (Muñoz Ramirez 2008: 292), the EZLN began, in 2003, a process of demilitarization of the movement towards the strengthening of its civil component, i.e., the autonomous communities.

Hope Beyond the State: The Snails and the Good Government Juntas

The Zapatistas' disillusionment initiated a process of reflection and discussion about the development of autonomy among the communities, which culminated in the creation of their autonomous self-government political bodies. In August 2003, the EZLN publicly announced the death of the *Aguascalientes* and the creation of the Snails and GGJ. The Zapatistas Rebel Autonomous Counties (*Municipalidades Autónomas Rebeldes Zapatistas,* MAREZ) that constitute the Zapatista realm were reorganized in five bodies called Snails (*Caracoles*), each of which has a Good Government Juntas (GGJ). By 2007 these self-organized and governed political spaces covered almost 40 per cent of the Chiapas state, i.e., 30,000 km^2, involving 1.100 communities of 300/400 inhabitants each (Ouviña 2007). The Snails are territorial spaces for the operation of the GGJ, the Vigilant Commission of the GGJ, the school, the hospital and the administration of the Zapatistas cooperatives. The Snails are the visible face of the movement and the expression of communitarian organization:

> The *Caracoles* are the doors of entry into and exist from communities; as windows so we can see into ourselves and so that we may see the outside; as horns that will broadcast our word far and wide and will allow us to hear another words from afar (EZLN cited in SIPAZ 2003: 1)

The implementation of the principle of 'command while obeying' requires a process of consultation that constantly moves forward and backwards. The Snail and its spiral shell represent this. The Zapatistas revolution

> spirals outward and backward, away from some of the colossal mistakes of capitalism's savage alienation, industrialism's regimentation, and toward old ways and small things; it also spirals inward via new words and new thoughts ... They travel both ways on their spiral (Solnit 2008).

In the Zapatistas *Caracoles*, decision-making occurs at three distinguishable levels. At the local level, each of the many community of every town elects its authorities, i.e., the communal agent (*Agente Communal*) as well as representatives to the Autonomous Juntas (*Consejos Autónomos*), the decision-making body. All posts are voluntary. At municipal level, delegates of each villa meet in assemblies, which can last for three days, to reach consensus about decision involving design and execution of community projects. Representatives to the Good Government Juntas and the permanent representatives to the five Snails are elected. Finally, the state (*estadual*) level comprises five Snails: Oventic, Roberto Barrios, Morelia, La Realidad, and La Garrucha. The Snails are also cultural spaces, gathering schools, assembly rooms, sport and rest zones, health centres, and cooperatives.

The GGJs work within the Snails. Two representatives per each autonomous council participate in the regional GGJ. Each GGJ administrates justice, mediates conflicts between autonomous councils and government councils, issues identity cards, discusses goals related to welfare provision, promotion and supervision of community projects and programmes in the health, education, work, agrarian areas; denounces violations to human rights, guarantees bi-cultural education. For example, the GGJ of the Oventic Snail has 23 members who hold monthly and *ad hoc* meetings. Within the GGJ there are no division of powers and all representatives remain in their posts for a brief period of time to avoid bureaucratization and the formation of technocrats and to practise horizontal democracy (Almeyra and Thibaut 2006). Cortez Ruiz highlights that 'the Assembly is the space of common identity' and decision-making about daily issues (2004: 79). The GGJ suggests a course of action, which is discussed by the communities. It is also the voice of the Snail before the national and international civil society as well as deals with hosts, visitors, administrates resources, reception of issues from the autonomous councils.

Important is to mention that since the formation of the GGJ, the EZLN has retreated from its hitherto prominent political role in the construction of the Zapatista autonomy. According to Subcomandante Marcos and the Zapatistas

> we also saw that the EZLN, with its political-military component, was involving itself in decisions, which belonged to the democratic authorities, "civilians" as they say. The problem here is that the political-military component of the EZLN is not democratic, because it is an army. And we saw that the military being above, and the democratic authority below, was not good (2006: 79).

Since the creation of the Snails and the GGJ

> the EZLN leadership has no longer involved itself in giving orders in the villages' civil matters, but it accompanies and helped the authorities democratically elected by the people. It has also kept watch that the people, and national and international civil society, are kept well-informed concerning the aid that is received and how it is used. Now we are passing the work of safeguarding good government to the Zapatista support bases, with temporary rotating positions, so everyone learns and carries out this work. We believe that people that doesn't watch over its

> leaders is condemned to be enslaved . . . [the EZLN] also handed over to the Good Government Juntas and the autonomous municipalities the aid and contacts which we had attained throughout Mexico and the world during these years of war and resistance (ibid.: 83)

It is to the contentious politics and the tension between rebellion and integration that underpin the Zapatistas' practice of autonomy that I now turn.

Steering the Tension between Rebellion and Integration

Autonomy *De Facto*

In Chiapas, the Zapatistas practice autonomy *de facto*. Autonomy *de facto* means the creation of 'new jurisdictions and parallel governments in rebellion' (Burguete Cal y Mayor 2003: 1991; Mattiace 2003; Mora 2007). Thus, they rejected any kind of autonomy that could be integrated into institutional designs, and which embraces 'empowerment' and 'participation'. They vindicate instead an autonomy based on 'habits and customs' as a form of *resistance* (Aubry 2003: 220). Caly Mayor (2003: 206) mentions 8 non-linear phases that followed the declaration of autonomy: geographical and jurisdictional demarcation, creation of a normative framework, mobilization and rebellious acts to reject state power, the physical and institutional organization of the autonomous self-governmental bodies and a politics of alliances.

The self-government bodies replace or displace the state in addressing significant public concerns (e.g., justice, environmental protection, health, education, land distribution, work cooperatives).

The GGJ administer justice to the communities. Justice is understood as the respect for the decision made by all those who belong to the community. Education is also central to the Zapatistas' autonomous enterprise. In 2005, nearly 40 per cent (38.8 per cent) of the indigenous population has no access to education. The formation of cadres (promoters) and the creation of secondary and primary autonomous rebel schools was a response to the neglect by the 'bad government'. In addition to making Castilian (Spanish) and Tzotzil accessible to the indigenous population, particularly women autonomous rebel education facilitates that young people acquire knowledge and also acknowledge their background, history, and customs.

Education serves the purposes of conscientization of the political goals of Zapatismo. The main problems are (*a*) is how to fund the system, which is highly dependent on international solidarity (*b*) lack of official recognition of Zapatista education and subsequent discrimination.

Each Snail has also an organized health system in coordination with the other four. In Oventic, the *La Guadalupana* clinic (1990) facilitates access to health and preventive medicine. Paradoxically, despite 54 per cent of hydroelectric energy coming from Grijalva River, Chiapas communities have no electricity or sewage systems. In 2000, poverty affected 76 per cent of the population (Pickard 2004). In rural areas, 85 per cent of the EAP lives in extreme poverty and 71 per cent of the population live in unhealthy and poorly constructed housing. Malnourishment is the third highest in the country, affecting 71.6 per cent of the population. Death from curable diseases, such as diarrhoea, among children amount to 34.8 per 1,000 children. Health promoters work with patients as well as with the communities, improving hygiene and raising awareness about disease prevention. The Zapatistas' health system aims to recover and socialize ancient medical practices, herbs and massages. There are three main problems: training (need for volunteers, dependence on charity), financial (medicines, technology) and cultural (difficulties to promote reproductive health, family planning).

Finally, it is worth mentioning the Agrarian Revolutionary Law, which legislate the redistribution of the land and the creation of production cooperatives (corn and coffee), aimed at recovering a form of community production that put the collective interest before individual needs. The law limits property of the land to up to 100 hectares of bad land and up to 50 hectares of good land. Since August 2005, the Zapatistas' communities have formed cooperatives for the production, commercialization and fair trade of their products (e.g., coffee), which are advertised through internet. The internal market and domestic consumption are priorities and the organization of these cooperatives implies learning process through which the communities recognize their capacity to produce and sell their products autonomously avoiding intermediaries (*coyotes*). Not only does the community obtain a fair price for their products but also looks after the environment, contributes to regional development and generates resources to be used in other community projects.

Counter Insurgent Policy: Democratic Planning and Development

So far, I have addressed how the Zapatistas' autonomous practices articulate and organize hope, which for the indigenous communities of Chiapas means the possibility of governing themselves. In this section, I explore the various responses from the Chiapas and the national states to the Zapatistas' uprising and their further exercise of radical democracy and autonomy *de facto*. From start, such responses aimed at dismantling the movement using inconsistent repression and negotiation techniques (Adler Hellman 2000), that involved military and paramilitary forces, and state policy-making (national, *estadual* and international). Between 1994 and 2000 the army had a strong presence in Chiapas both in the streets and within governmental institutions (Castro and Hidalgo 1999). Paradoxically, after the San Andres peace treaty supervised by COCOPA, between 1996 and 1997, violence perpetuated by the state increased in Chiapas, coinciding with the exponential growth of the support for the Zapatistas movement. During 2000–2006, under President Fox, there was some retreatment of military bases, camps, control posts, migrations, and police controls in Chiapas. The demilitarization of the movement and the change of strategy that put democracy and autonomy at the centre of the Zapatistas' political debates, particularly since 2006 — after the Zapatistas' Sixth Declaration of the Lacandon Jungle was made public, made governmental strategies shift from disarming the EZLN to disarming the communitarian power of the Zapatistas autonomous communities. In the 'Sixth Declaration', the Zapatistas assessed their revolution thus far and discussed 'what we want to do' and 'how we were 'going to do it', that is their plan to expand, through the 'other campaign' (that anticipates the 2006 presidential campaign) to 'link non partisan anticapitalist national liberation struggles around the country' (Mora 2007: 64; Subcomandante Marcos and the Zapatistas 2006). The 'Other Campaign' became the tool for both the creation of a space among and for those who struggle 'against neoliberalism and for humanity' like the Zapatistas (Subcomandante Marcos and the Zapatistas 2006: 131), (without the Zapatistas' hegemony), and the dispute of the popular support to the PRD.

The Chiapas state moved onto more flexible approach, with a more subtle police and paramilitary control of the communities legitimated as the fight against narcotraffic. Direct military action was replaced by a low intensity war, where direct repression was replaced by intention to influence public opinion by manipulating information, alliances with political forces and civil society sectors to network (Hidalgo Domínguez 2006). Paramilitary organizations became NGOs and began to promote the formation of cooperatives and facilitating the access to the deed to the indigenous land, thus taken on board a key issue for the Zapatistas communities, i.e., the land, and competing with the 'illegal' land distribution undertaken by the EZLN via the revolutionary agrarian reform (Dinerstein, Ghiotto and Pascual 2013). For example, in order to dispute the Zapatistas' support, the OPDDIC (*Organización Para la Defensa de los Derechos Indígenas y Campesinos*), former Anti-Zapatista Indigenous Revolutionary Movement, organizes productive projects among the chiapanecos, which are subsidised by political parties (CIEPAC August 2008).

Although the low intensity war, repression and military surveillance of the Chiapas region remain in place, a series of (counter-insurgent) policies were launched and implemented between 2006 and 2008. The governmental goals are threefold: to reorganize and channel citizens' demands; to geographically reorganize the population of Chiapas; and to launch public policy directed to introduce and provide services to the Chiapas territory.

Organizing Civil Society

The creation of the Chiapas Solidarity Institute (ICS) in 2007 aimed at organizing '"civil society" through the state "democratic planning". With regional and municipal delegates and a large budget, the ICS members see themselves as "an army which supports society"' (ICS Interview, August 2008). The explicit idea behind the creation of the ICS is to open institutional channels for participation to solve the crisis of democratic representation in Chiapas. Indigenous communities are being organized in neighbourhood assemblies, which are to deliver and identify needs, demands and priorities, which are passed on to a series of committees for regional development.

The Zapatistas interpreted this 'democratic planning' as an attempt to institutionalize governance in Chiapas. The strategy of re-municipalization of the Chiapas territory (clearly 'anti-Zapatista') is abandoned on behalf of a new approach based on the recognition of the indigenous as 'citizens' and to help them to articulate their demands democratically. The Institute had a significant role in supporting the neighbourhoods and facilitating participation. The Institute mediates between the Chiapanecos and the state and thus competes directly with the Zapatistas self-government.

The Geographical Reorganization of the Population

In 2007, the programme Sustainable Rural Cities was launched to fight against 'exclusion via dispersion'. In Chiapas, 15,000 out of 24,000 localities have less than 100 inhabitants distributed in 8,000 households, generally enjoying few or no basic services. The programme will relocate and reorganize the population in eight new cities to maximize service provision. To the Zapatistas, the plan matches the Word Bank Programme Puebla-Panamá (PPP). Following Alvarez Béjar as a regional development strategy

> [the] PPP intends to amalgamate a dense tangle of interests related to oil, gas and petrochemical, biodiversity, mines, construction and transport (railways and motorways), airports and telecommunications, which aspire to clean the legal and political obstacles to the exploitation of resources in the Southeast of Mexico up to Panamá interests, some of them involving indigenous lands (Béjar 2001: 127, author's translation).

The programme of Sustainable Rural Cities entailed in this respect a geographical reorganization where the reallocation of the population will strategically vacate land for commercial, tourist and natural resources exploitation by private investors (CIEPAC August 2008).

Social Policy and Development

During this period, the Chiapas government increased the portion of the budget dedicated to implement development policy that responds to community needs. There have been efforts to address indigenous poverty in Chiapas.

As already mentioned autonomous practices by non-governmental public actors at local levels have seen an encroachment from official policy as international bodies and national governments aim to integrate resistance, such as World Bank funded Community Driven Development (CDD) programme supports 'participatory decision-making, local capacity building, and community control of resources'.[1] This official approach facilitates that social movements' 'autonomy' can achieve legal recognition by the state, for example for the purpose of contributing to local development and/or receiving institutional financial and technical support (Dinerstein 2010). Within this framework, the Mexican government carried out the San Andres Accords of 1996 and the constitutional reform of 2001 unilaterally, alternative development strategies seeking to incorporate the Zapatistas autonomy have been incorporated into policy.

The 'domestication of dissident claims' (Cornwall and Brock 2005) by means of the state's 'co-responsibility' with the affected population (Mora 2007: 67, 68) are key to the neoliberal governance. For example, through cash transfers to women, the plan Oportunidades (formerly *Progreso*) aims to 'transform the poor from passive recipients to active empowered modern subjects with the freedom to make choices about their lives': '[The most important impact of the program] is the change in habits and in the attitude of the participating women' (Regional *Oportunidades*; delegate cited by Mora 2007: 68).

The Zapatistas' Critique: Anticipating the Future

Democracy and Citizenship or Governing Ourselves?

Esteva has highlighted that the Zapatistas' practice of radical democracy, i.e., 'democracy in its most essential form', distances itself from formal or representative democracy in that 'it does not allude to a kind of government but to a government end . . . with the word democracy people are not alluding to present democracies . . but to people's power' (1999: 155). In radical democracy, the idea of individuals who delegate power is rejected on behalf of women and men governing themselves. Indigenous movements in general have challenged the abstraction underpinning liberal democracy by calling into question homogeneous citizenship and demanding the recognition of 'diverse citizenry', homogeneous modes of representation and also homogeneous forms of political authority (Yashar 2005: 285–87). The Zapatistas contest notions such as 'active citizenship' and 'participative governance' that underpin social programmes.

The practice of autonomy *de facto* has lead to a conflict between 'legal' and 'legitimate' for both the Mexican state and the Zapatistas. To the government, a legitimate form of government needs to be legally recognized. For the Zapatistas, who leave outside the liberal law, the constitutional legality is illegitimate. Not without problems, the Zapatistas aim to construct a new legitimacy based on their own understanding of the law, which is *incompatible* with the Mexican state's understanding of legal and legitimate (Aubry 2003; Colectivo Situaciones 2005). The following dialogue illustrates this point:

> "Aren't the *autónomos* illegal? We asked Rodrigo, out of curiosity
>
> "Pues, si!" he answered. Yes, they're illegal. But they're legitimate" (Earle and Simonelli 2000: 160).

Civil Society: Governance or Self-Empowerment?

The fundamental difference between the liberal concept of 'autonomous civil society' and the Zapatistas' autonomy is that whereas the former can fit well into institutional designs that celebrate 'empowerment', 'participation from below' and 'autonomy', i.e., 'pseudo autonomy' (Esteva 2003), the latter does not. The Zapatistas reject state power and therefore the *complementarity* between civil society and the state. Civil society would not counterweigh (or substitute) the power of the state but makes it superfluous (Esteva 1999). To those taking up mainstream notions of civil society for a conceptualization of democracy, civil society has the crucial role of both restricting state power and of legitimizing the state through various forms of consent as well as dissent. They warn us about the dangers of too much autonomy of civil society, as an alienated civil society from the state, and this can create a major tension in democratic development, and of the need for limits on autonomy (Diamond 1994, cited in Dinerstein 2009).

Those sympathetic to *Zapatismo* consider the autonomy of civil society as an attractive goal, but point at its pitfalls (Stahler-Sholk 2007) and 'complexities' (Hellman 2000). For example, how much the Zapatistas' 'administrative decentralisation' would 'alter existing political hierarchies or the role of the state as broker for global capital?' (Stahler-Sholk 2007: 48). If autonomy is conceived as mere disengagement 'would it leave autonomous communities cut off from resources and unprotected from the forces of the global market?' (idem. ant.). Similarly, in her critical analysis of Zapatismo, Hellman (2000) points to the political importance of the Chiapanecan situation and the 'complexities' of the Zapatistas' project such as the problems of land tenure, the role of religion the relative support for autonomy, the use of internet, how information is produced and distributed, among others. As for civil society, Hellman intends to prove that when Subcomandante Marcos refers to civil society and the struggle for autonomy he might not be representing the idea of many other political actors who think differently. Her interviewees argue that despite its international support, many in Chiapas lack enthusiasm for autonomy and prefer a 'serious redistributive policy'.

Without denying either the existence of serious problems and pitfalls for the collective construction of autonomy by the Zapatista movement, or the importance of maintaining a critical view rather than romanticize the movement, I think that what is missing in these analyzes is the Zapatistas' *hope*, that is, their profound critique of civil society. Such critique *denaturalizes and reconceptualizes* the taken-for-granted separation between civil society and the state and attribute it a different meaning than 'decentralization' or 'participation' (Dinerstein 2009). Liberal theories of civil society rely on the separation — complementarity between civil society and the state. What 'we' usually understand by 'civil society' is Eurocentric rather than universal, as it is based on the separation of spheres, which leads to a particular form of democratization and a specific role for 'civil society' actors (Baker 1998). Such separation is at the centre of modern European social thinking (Lively and Reeve 1997) and makes civil society such a 'powerful concept' (Colas 2002: 26).

The Zapatistas' autonomy posits civil society as the *sphere of self-empowerment*: collective action is directed to build counter-power, and therefore make the power of the state superfluous

(Esteva 1999). In the Zapatistas' definition of civil society, binary splits dissolve and the 'very essence of society [becomes] political' (Slater 1994: 29). In short an autonomous civil society ceases to be only the site where the legitimization of hegemonic social relations occurs to become a political and symbolic space where the contention between hegemonic and counter hegemonic practices takes place.

(Alternative) Development or Alternatives to Development?

Earle and Simonelli suggest that Zapatismo is an 'experiment in alternative logic' of development (2005: 20). Like many other movements in the global South, they have been experimenting with and anticipating alternative forms of social and productive organization, confronting not only capitalist production relations and challenging the (alternative) development discourse. The Zapatistas' experiment belongs to the post-development discourse (Escobar 1992a, 1992b, 2010; Esteva 1985; Santos and Rodriguez Garavito 2006) that claims that human flourishing cannot be achieved by improving the 'management' [or alternative managerialism] and 'distribution' of wealth, but rather by articulating alternatives to development (Dinerstein and Deneulin 2012) that emerged out of the civilizational crisis of modernity (Lander 2010). To the Zapatistas development and alternative to development are both part of the 'Westernisation of the world' (Latouche 1993: 161).

The Zapatistas imagine alternatives *to* development for which the role of social movements seems crucial, particularly in creating 'alternative visions of democracy, economy and society' (Escobar 1992: 22). Clearly, the search for autonomy as anti-development is contradictory and is embedded in political economic and sociocultural contexts that, somehow, determine such pursuit (Böhm et al. 2010). My point is that the search for alternatives *to* development is a political struggle, which has been frequently (and wrongly) seen as a romantic 'return to the [indigenous] past', it is rather a form of *anticipating the future*: the Zapatistas' critique of development articulates the 'dialectical tendency-latency, open to the *Novum*, of material process no pre-ordered' (Bloch 1995: 1373). In short, it embraces 'hope'. Lear has correctly argued that 'what makes hope radical', is not the plan to be fulfilled, but the fact that

> it is directed towards a future goodness that transcends the current ability to understand what it is. Radical hope anticipates a good for which those who have the hope as yet lack the appropriate concepts with which to understand it (2006: 103).

Translating the Tension: Autonomy, Between Real Possibility and Disappointment

Autonomous practices are counter hegemonic in that they widen the universe of what is politically thinkable, thus showing that narratives and discourses are politically reversible (Cornwall and Brock 2005). As Bloch suggests, the not-yet-become is a material component of every reality. Autonomy creates the *possibility* (contradictory and contested) of creating a new world. To the Zapatistas: 'autonomy is the heart and soul of our resistance. It is a new way of doing politics. It is part of the construction of democracy justice and dignity' (Member of the Zapatista Autonomous Municipality 17 de Noviembre, cited by Mora 2007: 64). The process of building autonomy makes room for the development of what Bloch calls the *utopian function of hope*. Autonomy facilitates the experience of an anticipatory consciousness in that it relies on the 'not-yet-become', thus it escapes institutionalization, integration and regulation.

The Zapatistas 'want to change the world but not by taking power, not to conquer the world, but to make it anew' (Holloway 2002b). Indeed, to change the world would be, according to the Zapatistas, very difficult. The task, they controversially argue, is to create new worlds. Does this mean, as suggested by Cohen and Arato (1997), that the Zapatistas is a 'self-limiting revolution', which shows a 'self-understanding that abandons revolutionary dreams in favour of radical reform that is not necessarily and primarily oriented to the state'? Rather the opposite. Their revolution is expansive and is driven by the dream of attaining self-realization to create collectively in solidarity with the purpose of *recovering the future* against capitalism and colonialty. The Zapatistas contentious project seems to indicate a move that Laclau and Mouffe discuss well before the

Zapatistas' uprising: the move from a 'strategy of opposition' to a 'strategy of construction of a new order' (1999: 189). Thus, the Zapatistas' revolution constitutes *one of the* 'nodal points from which a process of different and positive reconstruction of the social fabric could be instituted' (idem. ant.).

I pointed at the dilemma of the autonomy: rebellion and integration. The 'local', Dirlik suggests is the site for both 'promise and predicament' (1996: 32). As the Zapatistas 'walk', their local autonomy opens up, on the one hand 'the frontiers for resistance and change towards radical practices, and equal society and self-organisation. On the other, there is always a danger of hegemonic regimes to take up the all for autonomy and incorporate it into their own project' (Böhm et al. 2010: 28). Since total subordination to the state or absolute autonomy from the state are both impossible, it is rather the contested relationship between movements and the state what facilitates the production of counter hegemonic practices. Autonomy is then an '(im)possible project' (idem. ant.).

Translated into the grammar of hope, the (im)possibility of autonomy is better informed by the movement between 'real possibility' and 'disappointment'. On the one hand, autonomy is 'really possible' in that it is capable of developing the utopian function of hope within it, capable of *organizing hope*. In other words, autonomy — as already argued — is a practice interweaved with the movement of hope that can superbly facilitate the 'organization' of the not-yet-become. The distinction between 'really possible' and 'objectively possible' made by Bloch in *The principle of hope* is relevant here:

> [W]e must of course distinguished between the merely cognitively or objectively Possible and the real-Possible ... Objectively possible is everything whose entry, on the basis of a mere partial-cognition of its existing conditions, is scientifically to be expected, or at least cannot be discounted. Whereas really possible is everything whose conditions in the sphere of the object itself are not yet fully assembled; whether because they are still maturing, or above all because new conditions — though mediated by existing ones — arise for the entry of a the real. Mobile, changing, changeable Being, presenting itself as dialectical-material, has this unclosed capability of becoming, this Not-yet-Consciousness both in its ground and in its horizon (1995: 196–97).

To Bloch, real possibility

> does not reside in any ready-made ontology of the being of That-Which-Is up to now, but in the ontology, which must constantly be grounded anew, of the being of That-Which-Is-Not-Yet, which discovers future even in the past and in the whole of nature. Its new space thus emphasizes itself in the old space in the most momentous manner: real possibility is the categorical In-Front-of-Itself of material movement considered as a process: it is the specific regional character of reality itself, on the Front of its occurrence. How else could we explain the future-laden properties of matter? There is no true realism without the true dimension of this openness' (ibid.: 237–38).

Autonomous practices defy 'objective reality' and therefore, challenge the power that constructs hegemonic reality. Following Mouffe, 'social objectivity is constituted through acts of power. This means that any social objectivity is ultimately political and that it shows the traces of exclusion which governs its constitution' (2000: 147).

On the other hand, hope must be disappointable precisely because it 'opens in a forward direction, in a future-oriented direction . . . is committed to change rather than repetition and what is more, it incorporates the element of chance, without which there can be nothing new' (Bloch 1961, cited in Richter 2006: 51):

> hope holds the condition of defeat precariously within itself: it is not confidence. It stands too close to the indeterminacy of the historical process, of the world-process that, indeed, has not yet been defeated, but likewise, has not yet won' . . . 'And 'hope does not surrender when setbacks occur' (Bloch 1961, cited in Richter 2006: 51, 52).

Conclusion

My argument has been that autonomy is a *form of organizing hope* and that autonomous practices can creates symbolic and territorial spaces for such an organisation. These are territories of hope. To Bloch, concrete utopia requires mediation:

> Concrete utopia has in process-reality a corresponding element: that of the mediated *Novum*. Only this process-reality, and not a fact-basedness torn out of it which is reified and made absolute, can therefore pass judgement on utopian dreams or relegate them to mere illusions (1959/1995: 197).

Autonomy is one of the possible *organizational mediations of hope*. The process of 'organization of hope' consists of a series of actions directed to realize the anticipatory consciousness that lives in the not-yet-become. The not-yet-become is indefinable, as it represents the 'lack' or the 'unrealized' (Dinerstein 2002).

The organization of hope results from an ongoing movement between real possibility and disappointment. The Zapatistas' revolution is inspirational and, as Marcos has suggested, 'an intuition'. Walking in the direction of the *Novum* the Zapatistas' revolution made evident to articulate collective dreams is 'really possible' but such — anticipatory — dreams can be disappointed at any point. Two examples are the San Andres Accords and the unsuccessful 'Other Campaign'. The organization of hope by social movements can differ enormously but there are at least two echoes of the Zapatista experience that might be of assistance. The first (practical) is the capacity to navigate the tension between resistance (hope) and integration (disappointment) by acknowledging that such tension works in the realization of hope, but also that hope must be disappointable. The second echo refers to their talent of 'looking awry' (Žižek 2000), i.e., to think outside the box by embracing hope. This exposes our urgent need to both engage with the movement's own theorizing (Cox and Nielsen 2007; Holloway 2002b) and acknowledge our indecision in embracing hope. To Bloch (and the Zapatistas),

> [i]t is a question of learning hope. Its work does not renounce, it is in love with success rather than failure. Hope, superior than fear, is neither passive like the latter, nor locked into nothingness. The emotion of hope goes out of itself, makes people broad instead of confining them, cannot know nearly enough of what it is that makes them inwardly aimed, of what may be allied to them outwardly. The work of this emotion requires people who throw themselves actively into what is becoming to which they themselves belong (Bloch 1995: 3).

Acknowledgements

This chapter draws on findings from the research project 'Social movements and Autonomous Organizing in Latin America' (comparative project from 'The Movement of the Unemployed in

Argentina') funded by the Economic and Social Research Council (ESRC), Non-Governmental Public Action (NGPA) programme, Centre for Civil Society, London School of Economics (LSE), UK (RES-155-25-0007). I would like to thank the ESRC and the NGPA programme for their support. I am indebted to all interviewees, participants in focus groups and those who facilitated access to valuable information, material and documentation used in this chapter, and research team members Luciana Ghiotto and Rodrigo Pascual for data collection, research reports and insightful ideas. I am also grateful to Ravi Kumar for his patience and his encouragement to publish this chapter. For their insightful comments on earlier versions of this chapter, I appreciate the help of colleagues and students who attended my presentations at the CINEFOGO Conference, Centre for Civil Society, LSE, at the final ESRC Non-Governmental Public Action Conference, LSE, at the Centre for Development Studies Seminar Series, University of Bath, and at the 3rd Latin American and European Meeting on Organisation Studies (LAEMOS), Buenos Aires, between 2008 and 2010. All the usual disclaimers apply.

Notes

* For a more elaborate and developed argument about social movements, autonomy and hope in Latin America, see Dinerstein (forthcoming).

1. Available at http://go.worldbank.org/24K8IHVVS0 (accessed 1 October 2013).

References

Almeyra, G. and E. Thibaut. 2006. *Zapatistas: Un Nuevo Mundo en Construcción*. Buenos Aires: Maipue.

Alvarez Béjar, A. 2001. 'El plan Puebla Panamá: ¿desarrollo regional o enclave transnacional?', *Observatorio Social de América Latina*, 4: 127–33.

Aubry, A. 2003. 'Autonomy in the San Andres Accords: Expression and Fulfilment of a new Federal Pact', in J. Rus, R. Hernandez Castillo and S. Mattiace (eds), *Mayan Lives, Mayan Utopias: The Indigenous Peoples of Chiapas and the Zapatista Rebellion*, pp. 219–42. Oxford: Rowman & Littlefield.

Baker, G. 1998. 'From Structuralism to Voluntarism: The Latin American Left and the Discourse on Civil Society and Democracy', *Contemporary Politics*, 4(4): 391–411.

Bloch, E. 1986 [1959]. *The Principle of Hope*, three volumes. Cambridge: The MIT Press.

Böhm, S., A. C. Dinerstein and A. Spicer. 2010. '(Im)possibilities of Autonomy: Social Movements in and Beyond the State, Capital and Development', *Social Movement Studies*, 9(1): 17–32.

Castro, G. and O. Hidalgo. 1999. 'La Estrategia de Guerra en Chiapas', Project Counselling Service, *CIEPAC*, San Cristobal de las Casas.

Ceceña A. E. 2001. 'La Marcha de la Dignidad Indígena', *Observatorio Social de América Latina*, 4: 9–14.

Ceceña A. E and A. Barreda. 1998. 'Chiapas and the Global Restructuring of Capital', in J. Holloway and E. Pelaez (eds), *Zapatista! Reinventing Revolution in Mexico*, pp. 39–63. London: Pluto Press.

Cleaver, H. 1998. *The Zapatistas and the Electronic Fabric of Struggle*. London: Pluto Press.

Cohen, J. and A. Arato. 1997. *Civil Society and Political Theory*. Cambridge: MIT Press.

Colás, A. 2002. *International Civil Society*. Cambridge: Polity Press.

Colectivo Situaciones. 2005. *Bienvenidos a la Selva: Diálogos a Partir de la Sexta Delaración del EZLN*. Buenos Aires: Tinta Limón.

Cornwall, A. and K. Brock. 2005. 'Beyond Buzzwords: "Poverty Reduction", "Participation" and "Empowerment" in Development Policy', *Overarching Concerns Programme*, paper 10, UNRISD.

Cox, L. and A. Nilsen. 2007. 'Social Movements and the "Movement of Movements": Studying Resistance to Neoliberal Globalisation', *Sociology Compas*, 1(2): 424–42.

Cortez Ruiz, C. 2004. 'Social Strategies and Public policies in an Indigenous Zone in Chiapas, Mexico', *Institute of Development Studies Bulletin*, 35(2): 76–83.

Cuninghame, P. and C. Ballesteros Corona. 1998. 'A Rainbow at Midnight: Zapatistas and Autonomy', *Capital & Class*, 66: 12–22.

Díaz Polanco, H. 2001. 'La Autonomía Indígena y la Refroma Constitucional en México', *Observatorio Social de América Latina*, 4, CLACSO: 15–22.

Dinerstein, A. 2002. 'Regaining Materiality: Unemployment and the Invisible Subjectivity of Labour', in A. Dinerstein and M. Neary (eds), *The Labour Debate: An Investigation into the Theory and Reality of Capitalist Work*, pp. 203–25. Aldershot: Ashgate.

Dinerstein, A. 2009. 'The Snail and the Good Government: A Critique of "Civil Society" by the Zapatista Movement', *NGPA Working Paper*,

36, Centre for Civil Society, LSE, available at http://www.lse.ac.uk/collections/NGPA/publications/ngpa_wp36.htm (accessed 1 October 2013).

———. 2010. 'Autonomy in Latin America: Between Rebellion and Integration: Echoes from the Piqueteros Experience', *Community Development Journal*, 45(3): 356–66.

———. Forthcoming. *Autonomous Movements in Latin America: The Art of Organising Hope in the 21st Century*. New York: Palgrave Macmillan.

Dinerstein, A. and S. Deneulin. 2012. 'Hope Movements: Naming Mobilisation in a Post Development World', *Development & Change*, 2(43): 585–602.

Dinerstein, A., L. Ghiotto and R. Pascual. 2013. 'Municipio libre o comunidad autónoma rebelde? Construyendo el 'nosotros revolucionario' Zapatistas, México', in A. Dinerstein et al., *Movimientos Sociales y autonomía colectiva: La política de la esperanza en América Latina*, pp. 117–45. Buenos Aires: Capital Intelectual.

Dirlik, A. 1996. 'The Global in the Local', in R. Wilson and W. Dissanayake (eds), *Global/Local: Cultural Production and the Transnational Imaginary*, pp. 21–45. Durham: Duke University Press.

Earle, D. and J. Simonelli. 2005. *Uprising of Hope: Sharing the Zapatista Journey to Alternative Development*. Walnut Creek: AltaMira Press.

Escobar, A. 1992a. Imagining a Post-development Era? Critical Thought, Development and Social Movements', *Social Text*, 31(32): 20–56.

———. 1992b. 'Reflections on "Development": Grassroots Approaches and Alternative Politics in the Third World', *Futures*, June, 411: 36.

———. 2010. 'Una Minga Para el Postdesarrollo', *ALAINET*, 445: 26–31, available at http://alainet.org/publica/445.phtml (accessed 26 November 2010).

Esteva, G. 1999. 'The Zapatistas and People's Power', *Capital & Class*, 68: 153–82.

———. 2003. 'The Meaning and Scope of the Struggle for Autonomy', in J. Rus, R. Hernandez Castillo, and S. Mattiace (eds), *Mayan Lives, Mayan Utopias: The Indigenous Peoples of Chiapas and the Zapatista Rebellion*, pp. 243–70. Oxford: Rowman & Littlefield.

———. 2010. 'Mas Allá Del Desarrollo: La Buena Vida', *ALAINET*, 445, available at http://alainet.org/publica/445.phtml (accessed 26 November 2010).

Evans, B. 2008. 'The Zapatista Insurgency: Bringing the Political back into Conflict Analysis', *New Political Science*, 30(4): 497–520.

González Casanova, P. 2001. 'Los Zapatistas del siglo XXI', *Observatorio Social de América Latina*, 4: 5–14.

Hellman, J. Adler. 2000. 'Real and Virtual Chiapas: Magic Realism and the Left', *Socialist Register*, 36: 161–86.

Hidalgo Domínguez, O. 2006. 'Tras los Pasos de Una Guerra Inconclusa (Doce Años de Militarización en Chiapas)', *CIEPAC*, San Cristobal de las Casas.

Holloway, J. 2002a. '*Zapatismo* and Social Sciences', *Capital & Class*, 78: 153–60.

———. 2002b. *Change the World Without Taking Power*. London: Pluto.

Laclau, E. and C. Mouffe. 1999. *Hegemony & Socialist Strategy: Towards a Radical Democratic Politics*. London: Verso.

Lander, E. 2010. 'Estamos Viviendo una Profunda Crisis Civilizatoria', *ALAINET*, 452, available at http://alainet.org/publica/452.phtml (accessed 26 November 2010).

Latouche, S. 1993. *In the Wake of the Affluent Society: An Exploration of Post-development*. London: Zed Books.

Lear, J. 2006. *Radical Hope: Ethics in the Face of Cultural Devastation*. Cambridge: Harvard University Press.

Lively, J. and A. Reeve. 1997. 'The Emergence of the Idea of Civil Society', in R. Fine and S. Rai (eds), *Civil Society: Democratic perspectives*, pp. 63–75. London: Frank Cass.

Mattiace, S. 2003. 'Mayan Utopias: Rethinking the State', in J. Rus, R. Hernandez Castillo, and S. Mattiace (eds), *Mayan Lives, Mayan Utopias: The Indigenous Peoples of Chiapas and the Zapatista Rebellion*, pp. 185–90. Oxford: Rowman & Littlefield.

Mayor, Araceli Burguete Cal Y. 2003. 'The *de Facto* Autonomous Process: New Jurisdictions and Parallel Governments in Rebellion', in J. Rus, R. Hernandez Castillo, and S. Mattiace (eds), *Mayan Lives, Mayan Utopias: The Indigenous Peoples of Chiapas and the Zapatista Rebellion*, pp. 191–218. Oxford: Rowman & Littlefield.

———. 2004. 'Chiapas: Nuevos Municipios para Espantar Municipios Autónomos', in R. Hernández et al. (eds), *El Estado y los indígenas en tiempos del PAN*. México: CIESAS.

Mora, M. 2007. 'Zapatista Anticapitalist Politics and the "Other Campaign": Learning from the Struggle for Indigenous Rights and Autonomy', *Latin American Perspectives*, 153, 34(2): 64–77.

Moulaert, F. and O. Ailenei. 2005. 'Social Economy, Third Sector and Solidarity Relations: A Conceptual Synthesis from History to Present', *Urban Studies*, 42(11): 2037–53.

Muñoz Ramirez, G. 2008. *The Fire and the Word: A History of the Zapatista Movement*. San Francisco: City Lights.

Observatorio Social de América Latina. 2001. 'Documentos del conflicto', *Observatorio Social de América Latina*, 4: 27–36.

Otero, G. 2004a. 'Contesting Neoliberal Globalism from below: The EZLN, Indian Rights and Citizenship', in G. Otero (ed), *Mexico in*

Transitio: Neoliberal Globalism, the State and Civil Society, pp. 221–35. London: Fernwood Publishing & Zed Books.
Ouviña, H. 2007. *Zapatismo: Del EZLN y el SubMarcos a La Otra Campaña*. Buenos Aires: Era Naciente.
Pickard, M. 2004. 'La Contradictoria Economía de México y Chiapas', *Boletín del CIEPAC*, 416, available at http://www.ciepac.org/boletines (accessed 5 January 2011).
Replogle, J. 2005. 'Caravan of Hope, a Zapatista March', *Towards freedom*, available at http://www.towardfreedom.com/americas/138-caravan-of-hope-a-zapatista-march-0501 (accessed 4 January 2011).
Reygadas, L, T. Ramos and G. Montoya. 2009. 'Pandora Box: The Implications of Social Movements on Development: Lessons from the Lacandona Jungle in Chiapas', *Social Movement Studies*, 8(3): 225–41.
Richter, G. 2006. 'Can Hope be Disappointed? Contextualising a Blochian Question', *Symploke*, 14(1–2): 42–54.
Rus, J., S. Mattiace and R. Hernandez Castillo. 2003. 'Introduction', in J. Rus, R. Hernandez Castillo and S. Mattiace (eds), *Mayan Lives, Mayan Utopias: The Indigenous Peoples of Chiapas and the Zapatista Rebellion*, pp. 1–26. Oxford: Rowman & Littlefield.
Santos, B. de S. 2008. *Another Knowledge is Possible*. London: Verso
———. 2010. 'Hablamos del Socialismo del Buen Vivir', *ALAINET*, 452, available at http://alainet.org/publica/452.phtml (accessed 26 November 2010).
Santos, B de S. and C. Rodriguez Garavito. 2006. 'Introduction: Expanding the Economic Canon and Searching for Alternatives to Neoliberal Globalisation', in B de S. Santos (ed.), *Another Production is Possible: Beyond the Capitalist Canon*. London: Verso.
Silva, P. 1999. 'The new Political Order in Latin America: Towards Technocratic Democracies', in R. Gwynne and C. Kay (eds), *Latin America Transformed: Globalisation and Modernity*, pp. 51–65. London: Arnold.
Servicio Internacional para la Paz (SIPAZ). 2003. *Report*, 8(2): April.
Slater, D. 1994. 'Power and Social Movements in the other Occident: Latin America in an International Context', *Latin American Perspectives*, 21(2): 11–37.
Solnit, R. 2008. 'Revolution of the Snails: Encounters with the Zapatistas', 16 January, available at www.commondreams.org/archive/2008/01/16/6407 (accessed 7 November 2011).
Stahler-Sholk, R. 2007. 'Resisting Neoliberal Hegemonization: The Zapatista Autonomy Movement', *Latin American Perspectives*, 34: 48–63.
Subcomandante Marcos and the Zapatistas. 2006. *The Other Campaign/La otra Campaña*, Open Media Series. San Francisco: City Lights.

Subcomandante Marcos. 1997. 'The Seven Loose Pieces of the Global Jigsaw Puzzle', available at http://flag.blackened.net/revolt/mexico/ezln/1997/jigsaw.html (accessed 5 January 2011).

Swords, A. 2007. 'Neo-Zapatista Network Politics: Transforming Democracy and Development', *Latin American Perspectives*, 153, 34(2): 78–93.

Yashar, D. 2005. *Contesting Citizenship in Latin America: The Rise of Indigenous Movements in the Post-neoliberal Challenge*. New York: Cambridge University Press.

Žižek, S. 2000. *Looking Awry*. Cambridge: MIT Press.

11

The Privatization of Public Interest

Theorizing NGO Discourse in a Neoliberal Era

*Sangeeta Kamat**

If the twentieth century represented a 'top-down' approach to social and economic growth, then with the dawn of a new century we have entered a new era of 'bottom up' growth and social improvement. In this new model, national and international non-governmental organizations (NGOs) are the primary catalysts of change rather than experts from large bureaucratic institutions (including the state). NGOs have been identified as the preeminent, if not sole, organizational forms that can implement the global commitment to 'bottom up' development. Indeed, the discourse of 'bottom up' development cannot be dismissed as a rhetorical and superficial gesture on the part of states and international donor agencies. It has truly established itself within the policy process and plans of all official agencies of development that accord a significant and often directive role to NGOs in development projects and programmes (Chambers 1997; Clark 1991; Gardner and Lewis 1996).[1]

NGOs have become a global phenomenon, emerging with amazing alacrity in countries merely on the threshold of establishing democratic states (Henderson 2002; Kuropas 1997). The globalization of NGOs is reflective of the new policy consensus that NGOs are *de facto* agents of democracy rather than products of a thriving democratic culture (Edwards 2000; Holloway 1998; Nye and Donahue 2000). In this chapter, I argue that the agentic role prescribed to NGOs is not an innocent one but one that foretells a reworking of democracy in ways that coalesce with global capitalist interests. My analysis calls attention to current efforts by global policy institutions to regulate the 'third sector' in ways that interlink with neoliberal economic reform and challenges the popular understanding that NGOs equal democratization. I review the policy discourse on NGOs to show that the restructuring of democracy within a global reform context requires the regulation of NGOs at specific sites of their operation.

Current debates on the role of NGOs point to the dangers of NGOs replacing the state as representatives of democracy. Given expanding market economies, and shrinking states, NGOs are stepping in to respond to the needs and demands of the poor and marginalized sections of society (Robinson 1997; Wood 1997). Pointing to this emergent trend, development analysts caution that unlike governments and state bureaucracies, there are no mechanisms by which NGOs can be made accountable to the people they serve, and suggest that a balanced relationship or partnership between states and NGOs can best serve the interests of society. In a similar vein, much of the current discussion on NGOs is caught up in addressing issues of strengthening NGO accountability, autonomy and organizational effectiveness (Fowler 1997, 2000; Korten 1990; Lewis and Wallace 2000).[2] The debate on NGOs remains trapped within an atheoretical framework of state versus civil society, in which Left democrats warn of the erosion of state power, and neoliberals herald the same as a step toward democracy.

In this chapter, I highlight how NGO analysts reify state and civil society as 'totemic motifs' (White 1999: 309) and obfuscate the ways in which NGOs are being integrated into global capitalist relations. I argue that the NGO phenomena must be theorized in relation to the global economic and political process that involves an overall restructuring of public good and private interest. At stake is not the struggle between state and civil society, but a revaluation of private interest and public good. In the first part of the chapter, I briefly visit the post-war phase of development in the Third World in which scholars and policy analysts understood state and civil society differently from to the present context. In this discussion, I clarify the two characteristic positions on state and civil society — the liberal and the social democratic — that diverge on the proper relation between private interest and public good. The end of the Cold War and the triumph of market liberalism signal the vindication of the liberal position on state and civil society (Hulme and Edwards 1997).

In the second part of the chapter, I provide a general introduction to the emergence of NGOs and their uneven relations with state and international agencies.[3] Here, I emphasize how Community-Based NGOs (CBOs) and Advocacy NGOs have carved a unique space for themselves as representing the public interest that presents a problem for global capitalist institutions. I develop this argument in the third and main section of the chapter with a focus on global policy actors such as the UN, the World Bank and WTO and their efforts to accommodate NGOs within current reform processes. I highlight two main strategies by which global policy actors incorporate the role of NGOs in ways that advance the economic agenda of their institutions. The two strategies entail (*a*) *pluralizing* the public sphere, and (*b*) *depoliticizing* the private sphere; the former operative at the global policy (inter-state) level, and the latter at the level of local communities (understood as civil society). Each of these strategies represents a trend towards the privatization of the public sphere. My analysis suggests that any discussion of the limits and potential of NGOs must take account of the emergent international economic order and its neoliberal notion of democracy.

Civil Society in International Development

Civil society has emerged only recently as a distinct political actor within international development discourse, and its ascendancy can be traced to the end of the Cold War and the launch of the global free market. Prior to this phase, development policy and programmes in the Third World followed a largely social democratic model that prescribed a central role to the state in building democratic societies. Civil society in the Third World was seen as largely underdeveloped, and the state was entrusted with the responsibility of promoting the common good, redirecting self-interested political and economic behaviour towards broader public goals of national development and social welfare (Bardhan 1984; Gendzier 1985; Young 1988). In this period, roughly from the 1950s to the 1980s, 'the state' was used in accordance with its social democratic meaning as the embodiment of 'the public interest' or general welfare. Conversely, civil society was used to refer to 'private sectarian interests' that were represented through religious organizations, business associations, trade unions, and so forth.

In a curious flip-flop of what served as a universal conceptual frame for development planning, the state, today, is represented as fragmented by private interests (otherwise referred to as corruption), and hence inept at representing the will of the people, whereas civil society is seen as the honest broker of 'the people's interests'. In advancing this proposition, the role of NGOs is provided as evidence of the new capacities of civil society, mediating the excesses of the state. The dynamic rise of the NGO sector is seen as clear evidence of the evolution of civil society to be able to self-regulate and self-manage its own interests. Thus, in this new discourse, civil society, and NGOs in particular, are seen as fully cognizant rational actors capable of going beyond sectarian interests and acting upon matters of general welfare. In the literature on state–civil society and NGOs, a question rarely asked is, what enables civil society to be rid of its putative elements and commit itself to the common good? The transfer of loyalties of the international development 'community' from state to civil society, which has been rather dramatic to say the least, requires a theoretical explanation.

More importantly, this new conception of civil society does not fit neatly with neoliberal conceptions of state and civil society either. Liberal democratic theory understands civil society as constituted by competing private interests and individual desires that are stabilized by free interactions in the market place. Given the neoliberal economic consensus within development institutions, how is the avowedly public mandate of NGOs situated within a framework that idealizes the pursuit of private interest? The expansion of NGOs is therefore a challenge not only for advocates of the state but also for advocates of liberal individualism and an autonomous private sphere. The question that I seek to address here is, how is the public commitment of NGOs accommodated within the liberal democratic framework? In what ways are the contradictions between NGOs as guardians of public interest and 'free market' policies of neoliberalism mediated by global policy institutions? The fusion of contradictory discourses of public and private within civil society suggests that it is not as much an inversion of state–civil society relations, but a new equation between public and private interests that is being formulated.

A related issue is the articulation between NGOs and the market economy. In equating NGOs with civil society, NGO analysts sidestep the determinative constituents of civil society, namely, private property relations and the capitalist market (Wood 1990).

The NGO debate remains focused on the state, and is largely silent on the issue of NGOs and the capitalist economy. The tendency among NGO analysts is to disengage from the structural reality of civil society, and locate NGOs/civil society as the 'third sector', separate from the market and the state. I argue that this theoretical disengagement can prove illusory in a rapidly expanding capitalist economy. Its utility is limited to allowing NGOs to make a moral claim to democracy and justice that is disconnected from political economic relations of capitalist expansion (Mercer 2002). In the remainder of this chapter, I explore these questions more fully drawing upon contemporary development policy discourse on state–civil society relations, with specific reference to NGOs.

NGOs Negotiating the State

Even a cursory review of the literature on development reveals that NGOs are the new patrons of public interest, posing a serious challenge to the legitimate function of the state. That is, among the range of organized forces and institutions of civil society, NGOs are regarded as representing the interests of the people, to the greatest extent possible. In other words, NGOs have come to replace other well-established political organizations such as trade unions, welfare associations, religious organizations, and trade associations that traditionally represent the interests of various constituencies of society. In relation to these organizations, it is argued that NGOs represent the interests of the broadest swath of people, the poor and the underprivileged of society, who tend to have no structures of representation in public affairs, except perhaps the right to vote during election time.

NGOs are not representative organizations in the strict sense of the term, that is, the personnel managing an NGO are not elected and are most likely to be self-appointed. Nevertheless, they are seen to be genuine representatives of the people's will because the success of their work depends upon the involvement of their specific constituency (whether urban street children, landless agricultural labour, rural women, or indigenous communities) often within a limited geographical region (sometimes a few villages to a few districts). Locally based NGOs are the more typical model of NGOs in the South, and are known as CBOs or Grassroots Organizations (GROs) to distinguish them from other models of NGOs that have emerged within less than a decade.[4] In the next section, I clarify in greater detail the role of CBOs and Advocacy NGOs and the changing context in which they operate.

Community-based NGOs

Justifiably, the legitimacy of CBOs derives from the fact that their work in a local context requires them to develop a membership base — known as the 'target' or 'beneficiary' group in development language — which actively participates in the various social and economic projects managed by the CBO. It requires CBOs to interact with their membership base on a daily basis, to build relations of cooperation and trust with them, to understand their needs and plan projects that respond to these needs.

Consequently, CBOs tend to have close and intimate working relations with men and women of the community and local leaders, some of whom may also work as paid staff for the NGO.[5]

CBOs emerged in the post-war period between 1950s and 1980s in response to the failure of post-colonial states to ensure the basic needs of the poor. For the most part, the leaders of CBOs were socially conscious, middle-class citizens, many of whom had been active in women's movements or radical left movements of the post-independence period. These NGOs promoted a 'development with social justice' approach, and developed political rights awareness campaigns alongside health and economic projects (Garain 1994). Donor NGOs such as OXFAM in England and Swedish International Development Cooperation Agency (SIDA) in Sweden, which have strong liberal traditions, were eager to directly fund CBOs since they were more committed and effective in reaching the poor than were the governments of these countries.

Since then, international development agencies have come to rely upon CBOs a great deal because they are seen as efficient and effective implementers of social and economic programmes such as maternal health care, literacy and small scale income generation projects (Clark 1997). In the development literature, CBOs or GROs have the greatest support from all segments of the international development community for they are seen as the main catalysts for 'bottom up' development, i.e., working with actual 'communities'[6] and implementing development projects at the local level (Bebbington and Farrington 1992; World Bank 1998). These NGOs are seen to be accountable to the people, although their dependence on external funding and compliance with funding agency targets has raised questions about whether their accountability lies with the people or the funding agencies (Hulme and Edwards 1997).

This early history of CBOs that signified the birth of pluralist democratic cultures in many postcolonial countries stands largely compromised today in the current policy environment of free market reform and the dismantling of social democratic states. The imposition of structural adjustment policies in the South with decreased state spending has led to an exponential increase in community development NGOs, leading critics to argue that this phenomenon is analogous to 'franchising the state' (Wood 1997). Financial institutions that, on the one hand, recommend the withdrawal of state support from the social sector allocate aid to community-based NGOs for those very same social services, an indication that the expansion of the NGO sector has been externally induced by foreign policy decisions (Robinson 1997; Wood 1997).[7]

This dual policy of aid institutions undercuts the early history of NGOs as symbolic of a thriving political culture, independent of patronage from state and international institutions.

Advocacy NGOs

Advocacy NGOs are a more recent phenomenon in the Third World and have complicated the norms by which to judge the representative character of NGOs. Advocacy NGOs do not operate locally, that is, they do not represent a particular geographically defined community. Rather they tend to be issue based and the constituency they represent may encompass different regions and countries. Advocacy NGOs organize national and international campaigns for particular kinds of policy or legislative changes, and in this way function more as a lobby group, entirely different from CBOs that seek to organize a mass base. Also, in comparison to CBOs, Advocacy NGOs are better funded, professionally staffed and are housed in metropolitan centres such as Washington, DC or New Delhi.

Advocacy NGOs have gained considerable visibility and influence within international development policy circles, causing concern among states and international lending agencies on how to verify the credibility and legitimacy of NGOs as people's representatives.

While concerns about accountability of NGOs in general, and of Advocacy NGOs in particular, are pertinent, it is important to note that these concerns are being raised by international agencies at a time when Advocacy NGOs have mobilized highly successful international campaigns against trade agreements that challenge the autonomy of Third World govenments.[8] The advocacy campaigns of NGOs have redefined narrow policy issues such as violence against women to include war crimes against women and the economic rights of women in the global economy (Sparr 1994). Given their success in raising public awareness around global policy issues and influencing transnational reforms on a range of important political and economic issues, the question of how to assess their accountability remains fuzzy and unresolved. Although such NGOs do not have a specific membership body, their record shows that they may be equally capable of representing the general public interest, no more and no less than do CBOs.

Ironically, the success of advocacy NGOs has been accompanied by increased scepticism on the part of international policy actors as to whether advocacy NGOs should be considered legitimate participants within global policy forums (Fox and Brown 1998; Paul 1999). The influence that advocacy NGOs wield in international policy forums is seen to undermine the sovereignty of state and international institutions. On occasion, advocacy NGOs have come into direct conflict with their own governments on a particular policy, and has raised questions about who legitimately represents the national interest (Fox and Brown 1998).[9] This is a crucial concern that is at the crux of the state–civil society debate, though, as we shall see, the manner in which the international policy community addresses the issue has less to do with democratic governance and more to do with the interests of transnational capital.

Implications of the New Policy Environment on NGOs

Quite clearly, in the new policy context of privatization and a shrinking state, governments and international agencies depend on CBOs to a significant extent for their technical expertise and knowledge of local communities. It is not unreasonable to surmise that this dependence on the part of states and international agencies has led to greater support for CBOs over Advocacy NGOs. Advocacy

NGOs, on the other hand, compete with state and supra-state agencies to determine public policy at the national and global level. In the following section, I expand this general discussion of the emergent political-economic context of NGO activity to a more detailed analysis of how NGOs are being located within the global reform process. The differences between these NGOs cannot be mediated by a uniform set of regulatory practices, but call for a differentiated response from states and global policy actors. I highlight the specific processes of depoliticization and pluralization, and show how the former relates to the workings of community-based NGOs while the latter functions in relation to Advocacy NGOs. The pluralization of the public sphere operates more visibly at the policy-making level, and therefore impacts Advocacy NGOs most directly. The process of depoliticization operates in relation to local development projects, therefore visibly impacting the political process at the local level. I draw upon recent policy documents of the United Nations and the World Bank, as well as independent research on NGOs to illustrate how these regulatory practices are being embedded within the dynamic process of global reform.

NGOs and the New Policy Context: The Privatization of the Public Sphere

A review of the historical record on NGOs shows that the United Nations and its related bodies such as the UNDP and UNIFEM have been the most open supporters and friendly collaborators of NGOs, both in their development and advocacy roles. The UN officially established the term NGO to describe 'a specific relationship between civil organizations and the intergovernmental process' (UNRISD 1999: 10). During the 1980s and much of the 1990s, the United Nations was highly responsive to NGO demands for participation and created important institutional space for NGOs to participate in international policy forums on population, human rights, the status of women, and the environment. UN Secretary General Boutros Boutros-Ghali's provocative statement in 1995 speaks to the prevailing sentiment within the UN on the role of NGOs:

> Non-governmental organizations are a basic form of popular representation in the present-day world. Their participation in international

> relations is, in a way, a guarantee of the political legitimacy of those international organizations. It is therefore not surprising that in a short space of time we have witnessed the emergence of many new non-governmental organizations (UNRISD 1999: 16).

The radical democratic stance of the United Nations signifies the progressive history of the UN with leadership from countries of the South.[10] This legacy distinguishes the UN from the Bretton Woods institutions and other international aid agencies whose primary mandate is to stimulate economic growth and investments rather than democracy and human rights, and whose leadership has been restricted to Western industrialized countries, primarily the US, France, the UK, and Germany. Another crucial difference that separates the UN from the Bretton Woods institutions is that the former represents member states while the latter represents states as well as multinational corporations and banks. Each is therefore accountable to a different constituency with different interests and priorities that explains their different stance towards NGOs. Notwithstanding the progressive political history of the UN, an equally compelling reason for their support of NGOs is the decline in financial and administrative capacities of the UN to the extent that it is unable to even minimally meet its official mandate. UN officials acknowledge that they simply do not have the resources to fulfill their mandate of providing relief and humanitarian services, and depend upon the assistance of the NGO sector (Anan 2000).[11] Today, NGOs are involved in UN overseas operations that range from conflict management, refugee settlement, post-conflict reconstruction, drought and famine relief, to addressing the AIDS epidemic.

The declining power and influence of the UN is not fortuitous and needs to be understood in relation to global capitalism and the related shifts in world leadership. While in the post-war phase of development, the United Nations was considered the most legitimate institution of global governance, in the present context of global reforms, it competes with a range of new organizations that wield more power in the international policy arena. Within the UN these changes are clearly acknowledged:

> The political authority of the UN is clearly in a period of nemesis. Limping along in the face of crippling financial and moral abuse from

> the United States, an almost financially bankrupt UN sees its status and role in international governance usurped by the new and ascending nexus of multilateral economic institutions (UNRISD 1997: 9).

The new institutions referenced here are the Bretton Woods institutions, namely, the World Bank and IMF that have risen to new levels of power and prominence, and the World Trade Organization (WTO), the new apex body of governments and experts that will determine global policy on trade and investments. Unlike the UN, these new economic institutions are not representative bodies, and are instead dominated by a small group of Northern ministers, academics and consultants.[12] A central mandate of these institutions is to enable 'free market' conditions, in other words, policies that strengthen trade liberalization and the private sector globally. Therefore, a prime objective of the institutions of economic governance is to ensure a 'good investment climate' for transnational corporations, in other words, an efficient bureaucracy and a stable and peaceful society. As we shall see, this new policy consensus of the ruling economic institutions has profound implications for CBOs and advocacy NGOs.

An effective policy for trade liberalization and privatization requires a minimalist state and a dynamic civil society. It follows that in order to stimulate private capital investments and establish transnational market relations, it is necessary to divest from the state as well as minimize state regulation of the private sector. In most countries of the Third World, this policy change involves a massive shift from a state managed and state protected economy to a 'free enterprise' economy with minimal state subsidies.[13] However, the work of the state still needs to be done, particularly in sectors that are not profitable for private investors. NGOs are encouraged to step in here to manage literacy and health programmes, respond to the AIDS crisis and create employment programmes for the poor. In post-communist regions of Central Asia, as well as in China, development analysts make an unambiguous case for the role of NGOs in hastening the formation of an entrepreneurial civil society (Cernea and Kudat 1997; Jude 1998; Moore 2001).

The shift in economic policy involves important cultural changes within the body politic. A fundamental cultural transformation involved in the transition from state-led development to a deregulated market economy is that citizens have to forego their sense of entitlement and have to acquire an entrepreneurial citizen identity that derives from liberal values of independence and autonomy.[14] The new economic institutions are engaged in this process of advancing a new citizen culture, aiding in the development of an active and dynamic civil society in which all citizens, including the poor, are encouraged to be enterprising and seize the opportunities of the global economy. Not surprisingly therefore, the promotion of liberal democracy goes hand in hand with the institution of market economies in the current policy context. However, as I elaborate later, within the framework of neoliberalism, the contradictions between liberalism and democracy are blatantly exposed. Liberalism promotes self-determination for the individual, protecting the individual from state and societal regulation whereas democracy involves state and its people actively constructing public institutions and a public sphere that guarantees the welfare of the majority (Held 1996). Pulled apart in their meanings, we must conclude that an active civil society based on liberalism does not equal a democratic civil society, although the two meanings are often conflated in NGO analysis (Mercer 2002). The disjuncture between the two agendas of neoliberalism and democratization is best revealed by the ways in which CBOs and Advocacy NGOs are positioned within the new policy agenda.

The Pluralization of the Public Sphere

The events of Seattle, Genoa and DC demonstrate that Advocacy NGOs, supported by social movements and trade unions, are in a position to disrupt and stall the formation of the global capitalist market, a task that new economic institutions take as their primary goal. Given that NGOs are here to stay, and are seen as legitimate participants in global policy forums, how is their role accommodated in these forums? The new economic actors draw upon the liberal notion of democracy with its moral claim to pluralism and autonomy (Kumar 1998; Cohen and Arato 1994). The report of the UN Commission on Global Governance (CGG) indicates this emergent construction:

> At the global level, governance has been viewed primarily as intergovernmental relationships, but it must now be understood as also involving non-governmental organizations (NGOs), citizen's movements, multinational corporations, and the global capital market. Interacting

> with these are global mass media of dramatically enlarged influence (1995: 2–3).

In this quote, no distinction is made between profit-seeking corporations and citizen's movements representing vulnerable populations. Each is afforded an equal opportunity to participate in the global governance process. Civil society here is used in accordance with the liberal roots of the term, quite different from the usage popularized by NGO advocates. In a manner of speaking, the new economic institutions are taking back a term that had been appropriated by NGO advocates, but this time restoring to it its original meaning, namely economic and social relations outside the state. Taking this quote as an example, civil society includes the global capital market as well as citizen movements. Further, the lack of distinction between the market, NGOs and citizen's movements implies that the role of each is equally legitimate and important for global governance. As may be apparent, such an all-encompassing definition of civil society seriously limits the power and influence of advocacy NGOs within global governance forums.

Second, the new economic actors are adopting a formal definition for NGOs that does not differentiate between people-oriented NGOs, government NGOs and corporate NGOs. As a result, business and industry associations are now equally a part of 'NGO representation' in international policy forums, making it impossible for progressive NGOs to build a common alliance against corporate interests. The business and industry associations (also referred to as BINGOs) are technically NGOs but represent powerful corporate interests linked to pesticide, pharmaceutical, tobacco companies, and other such interests. Though the participation of BINGOs is challenged by a lobby of Public Interest NGOs (PINGOs), the latter group is clearly at a disadvantage. Not only are business NGOs part of the ideological consensus on trade and economic reform, but they also have greater access to the forums in terms of the financial resources at their disposal. More importantly, international agencies, including the UN, are committed to promoting the role of BINGOs in international policy deliberations. This is made apparent in the Commission's report that lauds the efforts of the Secretary General of the UN in 'repairing its ties with the private sector' by opening up to business NGOs such as the International Chamber of Commerce and embracing the role of private firms in

UN programmes and projects.[15] The World Bank, an important player in the global reform process, advances a similar pluralist approach to the global policy-making:

> [O]ur partnerships must be inclusive — involving bilaterals and multilaterals, the United Nations, the European Union, regional organizations, the World Trade Organization, labor organizations, NGOs, foundations and the private sector. With each of us playing to our respective strengths, we can leverage up the entire development effort (speech by Wolfensohn 1997: 5).

The quotes mentioned clearly indicate that each of the member-participants in these forums are seen as equal stakeholders in the global restructuring process, each representing a legitimate 'interest group' to be included in the 'dialogue' to guarantee a 'democratic' governance process.[16] Advocacy NGOs are located within this pluralist liberal democratic space in which they, like their private counterparts, represent a specialized constituency in the global forum. The notion of a 'common partnership' constitutes a central discursive device through which the multiple and disparate entities of civil society are integrated into a unified whole in which each representational body has different, albeit complementary responsibilities. Issues of conflict and contestation between different civil society groups are at best marginally referenced as tensions and awkwardness that are a normal aspect of new partnerships (Annan 2000). There is little, if any, consideration given to the unequal power relations between different representational bodies or to the fundamentally different interpretations among them about the constitution of public welfare.

The pluralization of the global policy forum by multiple particular interests constitutes a privatization of the public sphere, and delegitimizes any notion of the public interest. Thus, not only is the state decentred as the legitimate representative of the public interest, but equally, the multiple divergent private interests of civil society are accorded legitimacy and prominence. Far from being radically democratic, this conception of civil society harks back to the classical liberal notion of democracy in which common interest is nothing but the sum of private interests (Held 1996).

The pro-poor and anti-capitalist agenda of Advocacy NGOs is effectively marginalized by such a pluralist and non-discriminatory approach to global governance.[17] In response, Advocacy NGOs lobby to improve access to important international forums.[13] However, negotiating better access within a pluralist, liberal democratic framework may do little to challenge the terms of the debate on the goals and objectives of global policy. It is equally necessary to problematize the dissolution of the meanings of public and private that are embedded within the global governance discourse.

The Depoliticization of Local Development

Diversifying global policy forums with many special interest groups is a partial, albeit important, mode by which the public sphere is reclaimed by the private sector. The presence of numerous NGOs at the grassroots that provide services to underprivileged populations, and at the same time mobilize them for their rights also presents a threat to the neoliberal agenda of privatization. Grassroots NGOs (or CBOs) work with marginalized sections of society such as poor women, landless peasants, and urban street children, and serve as intimate witnesses to the devastation wrought by privatization and marketization of the social and economic sectors. In certain countries, grassroots NGOs have allied with Left parties and radical movements to challenge the policies of international institutions (Hammami 1995). In countries of the South, the Leftist origins of CBOs are reflected in their opposition to structural adjustment policies, which may not translate into an organized movement, but it nevertheless poses a problem for economic reform.

Scholarship on community-based NGOs points to a process of professionalization and depoliticization of NGOs at the grassroots (Alvares 1998; Hammami 1995; Kamat 2002; Miraftab 1997; Schilds 1998). Based upon fieldwork in different countries, the studies reach a common conclusion about the shift in the organizational character of NGOs and the nature of their work. For instance, Miraftab traces the evolution of Mexican NGOs 'from organizations that aimed deep social change through raising consciousness, demand making and opposition with the government, to organizations that aim incremental improvement of the poor's living conditions through community self-reliance and formulation of workable solutions' (1997: 362). In each case, the authors show that community based NGOs have moved away from education and empowerment programmes that involve structural analysis of power and inequality and instead adopt a technical managerial solution to social issues of poverty and oppression. Although each study presents a unique narrative of NGO history, the authors conclusively establish the shift from broad-based political education and organization of the poor to providing social and economic inputs based on a technical assessment of capacities and needs of the community. This phenomenon represents a marked shift from the Freirean model of consciousness-raising and popular organizing for social change that was typical of CBOs from the 1960s to the 1980s.

The changes in the focus of NGO activity have had a deep impact on the organizational character of NGOs. As described earlier, the leadership of community-based NGOs typically constituted middle-class Leftists who identified closely with the poor and were committed to social justice work at the grassroots. In many cases, activists were conscious of the need to 'de-professionalize' in order to build relations with the poor (Kamat 2002; Miraftab 1997). The shift to a managerial and functional approach to social change has led to a more professionally oriented approach to an extent that professionally trained staff constitute a significant component of the leadership in CBOs.

The scholarship points to the neoliberal policy context as an important cause of the trend toward professionalization and depoliticization of CBOs. The decline in state entitlements to the poor has led donor agencies to channel greater amounts of aid to grassroots NGOs. The influx of money and pressure to lead where the state is absent has had a significant impact on local NGOs. Donor monitoring and accounting systems require NGOs to implement social and economic projects in an efficient and effective manner. Although other factors may play a role, the authors agree that the new economic regime has led to a culture of professionalization and depoliticization of NGOs.

The World Bank's assessment of the strengths and weaknesses of CBOs makes it clear that CBOs make viable partners for donor agencies only if they diminish their political character and enhance their managerial and technical capabilities:

> NGOs are important to the Bank because of the experience and resources they bring to emergency relief and development activities. The Bank's 1989 Operational Directive 14.70 (OD) describes the perceived strengths and weaknesses of NGOs and CBOs and encourages

> Bank staff to involve those organizations in Bank-supported activities within the framework of the borrower government's policies. The OD identifies NGOs' potential strengths as their ability to reach poor communities and remote areas, promote local participation, operate at low cost, identify local needs, build on local resources and introduce new technologies. The directive refers to NGO weaknesses such as their limited replicability, self-sustainability, and managerial and technical capacity, a narrow context for programming, and politicization (World Bank 1998: 3).

Not only is the activity and identity of NGOs increasingly professionalized and depoliticized but they also have to compete with a growing number of non-membership NGOs that have sprung up to respond to donor enthusiasm for community-based development. 'Operational NGOs', a relatively recent term adopted by the World Bank, describes the character of these NGOs. The term 'operational NGOs' defines NGOs that are 'engaged primarily in design, facilitation and implementation of developmental sub projects' (World Bank 1998).[19] The apolitical and managerial approach to community development draws upon the liberal notion of empowerment wherein the poor are encouraged to be entrepreneurial and find solutions to their livelihood needs. The entrepreneurial notion of empowerment (not unlike the American motto of 'pulling oneself up by one's bootstraps') is altogether different from the understanding of empowerment for social justice that characterized the work of CBOs in the post-war development period. The latter involves political sensitization and organizing the poor for their social and economic rights from the state and economic elites.

The neoliberal notion of empowerment implies a focus on individual capacities and needs of the poor, and consequently minimizing the social and political causes of poverty. The individual is posited as both the problem and the solution to poverty rather than as an issue of the state's redistribution policies or global trade policies. The popularity of microcredit programmes among donor agencies can be understood within this context where the state is no longer responsible for creating employment, and the poor are expected to strengthen their own capacities toward livelihood security. Livelihood security becomes a matter of optimal utilization of the abilities and resources that one possesses. In the absence of critical education and awareness building, alternatives to the dominant economic regime are less likely to emerge, as are new understandings of collective good. *The World Bank Participation Sourcebook* provides insight into the implications of the neoliberal approach to empowerment:

> As the capacity of poor people are strengthened and their voices begin to be heard, they become 'clients' who are capable of demanding and paying for goods and services from government and private sector agencies ... We reach the far end of the continuum when these clients ultimately become the owners and managers of their assets and activities (1995: 7).

The neoliberal notion of empowerment leads unmistakably to the marketization of social identities and relations. The idea of public goods and services is all but non-existent in this version of empowerment and participation. Individualizing the process of empowerment where each has to build his/her capacities to access the marketplace reduces the concept of public welfare to private interest. In this discourse, public welfare is reduced to an aggregate of individual gains, and the social democratic notion that public welfare is something that must prevail over and above private gain ceases to exist. Operating within the neoliberal framework of development, democracy is rendered an unviable and impossible project. My analysis of depoliticization and professionalization of community-based NGOs when located within the broader structural context of neoliberal economics suggests that here too we see the privatization of public good, similar to the privatization of the public sphere in the global policy arena.

Conclusion: The Question of Public Interest

Privatizing the notion of public interest corresponds to the privatization of public industries that is an integral part of the New Policy Agenda currently in force in most countries of the world. The New Policy Agenda is seen to comprise two principle strategies — marketization/privatization of economic and social sectors (such as health and education) and democratization of civil society (Hulme and Edwards 1997). To the extent that privatization concentrates power and resources rather than diffuses it, and democratization implies the diffusion of political power, the paradoxical juxtaposition of these two agendas has, in my view, made it difficult for progressive scholars to critique the New Policy Agenda for its fundamentally undemocratic frame. For the most part, these contradictory propositions remain insufficiently interrogated, and have been explained away as part of the duality or paradox of globalization (Appadurai 1996).

However, an analysis of how the discourse of global governance constitutes civil society as a discrete set of private interests suggests the reinvention of the term 'democracy' in ways that cohere with the imperatives of marketization and privatization. Within the neoliberal framework, democracy is re-defined as the free and full expression of each specific constituency, with little regard for the uneven relations of power that characterize the different interest groups. Further, my analysis suggests that democracy is being redefined in very different ways at the global and local level, articulating to produce a common effect. At the global level, the space is opened up for many different interests to be represented with partnership and co-operation as the directive principles of interaction in global policy forums. Market imperatives of privatization and deregulation are assumed to be more or less non-negotiable, and corporations, Advocacy NGOs and governments are expected to negotiate the interests of their particular constituency to the extent possible.

At the local level, the reverse is at play: instead of a pluralization of forces (stakeholders, in the policy discourse), the scope of NGO activity is restricted to managerial and administrative tasks directed at improving the capacity of the poor to compete in the marketplace. An effect, operative at both levels, is privileging the interests of the particular (individual or specific group) over the well-being of the general. In reclaiming the public space as a negotiation between different private interests, the concept of the public good is impossible to identify, let alone defend. Thus, rather than deepening the gains made on the basis of popular democratic struggles, NGOs are being re-inscribed in the current policy discourse in ways that strengthen liberalism and undermine democracy. Given this trend, it is unlikely that NGOs can be the honest brokers of people's interests. Further, it raises the disquieting question that if neither the state nor NGOs represent the public good, then who does?

Finally, my analysis also shows that constructing the NGO debate as 'state versus civil society' creates a false position that may be analytically misleading. In this chapter, I show how NGOs, conventionally understood to be part of civil society, are part of the remaking of state institutions and state processes, as much as they are part of reconfiguring civil society. The reification of state and civil society as actual sites with marked boundaries obscures their function as signifiers of public and private will, as representing a mode of relating the private interests with public good. In other words, state and civil society serve as 'totemic motifs' in the struggle to define relations between the individual and the collective, between the private and the public. These relations between private and public are being reconstituted through a myriad of social, political and economic institutions. NGOs are one among a range of institutional forms through which these relations are being reconstituted in the global context. The study of NGOs at the local and global level can reveal much about how these relations, and the very meaning of the private and public are being re-articulated at the level of localized political practice as well as at the level of global institutional practice.

Notes

* This chapter was earlier published in *Review of International Political Economy*, 11(1): 155–76, 2004. Reproduced with permission of the publisher (Taylor & Francis Ltd, http://www.tandf.co.uk/journals). An earlier version of this was presented at the American Anthropological Society Meeting, Washington, DC, November 2001, titled 'NGO-graphy: The Critical Anthropology of NGOs and Civil Society'.

1. By the mid-1990s, enthusiasm about NGOs led the American Vice President to commit 40 per cent of Overseas Development Assistance to NGOs (Van Rooy 1998).
2. The World Development Special Issue 'Development Alternatives: The Challenge of NGOs' is one of the first systematic reviews of the NGO phenomenon (Drabek 1987). Much current scholarship reiterates the issues discussed in this special issue.
3. Although, there are unique aspects to the NGO history of each country, there are sufficient common features to this history by virtue of a fairly standard policy approach toward NGOs by international donors and multilateral agencies.
4. Today, the term NGO describes a wide range of organizations including Community-based Organizations (CBOs), International NGOs (INGOs), Government-run NGOs (GONGOs), Donor-organized NGOs (DONGOs), Advocacy NGOs (ANGOs), National NGOs

(NNGOs), Social Movement Organizations (SMOs), and most broadly, Civil Society Organizations (CSOs). Each differs from the other with respect to scale, size, purpose, staffing, funding, and operations. Equally important, they differ in the extent to which they are regarded as legitimate representatives of poor communities in the South. For example, donor and Advocacy NGOs are seen more as support organizations, supporting the activity of NGOs that have a popular base.

5. Although paid staff members in CBOs are often drawn from the community being served by the CBO, the senior managerial staff tends to be urban educated middle class upper caste persons who are 'not of the community'. The two-tiered employee structure in CBOs has led to criticisms against NGOs in India of reproducing an unequal work structure and work culture despite its rhetoric of egalitarianism and participation (Bijoy et al. 1994).
6. 'Communities' are themselves artificially constructed through the very process of NGO and State intervention. In order to meet limited and clearly identified project goals, a development project requires the construction of a unified bounded local community of beneficiaries-participants, excluding how 'the community' is sustained through extra-local relations. See Maia Green (2000) for an excellent exposition of the construction of community via a Tanzanian development project.
7. In this instance, I refer to the World Bank which, along with its sister institution, the IMF has imposed structural adjustment on the social sector of many Third World countries, and is directly funding NGOs for education and health programmes.
8. For example, the Canadian based advocacy NGO, Rural Advancement Fund International along with other NGOs has run successful campaigns against multinational agro-business corporations and the US government for patenting of seeds and human cell tissue. See http://www.rafi.org (accessed 1 October 2013) for details. Advocacy NGOs along with social movements have carried out highly effective public campaigns against the Multilateral Agreement on Investments (MAI) and other such trade policies that reproduce North-South inequities.
9. A highly publicized case of NGO opposition to governments occurred at the 1992 UN Earth Summit at Rio where NGOs proposed alternative environmental treaties for governments to sign. See http://www.igc.apc.org/habitat/treaties/ngoatgf.html (accessed 1 October 2013) for details of the NGO alternative proposals.
10. In the early phase, many administrators and directors of programmes at the UN were intellectuals of anti-colonial struggles in their countries.
11. The UN's budget deficit has worsened in the past decade mainly due to the US refusal to pay its outstanding dues of $1.4 billion. To a large extent, the UN financial crisis has been offset by extensive partnership with NGOs in UN operations.

12. The WTO is only formally a representative body and has 141 member countries (as of May 2001). Although many developing countries have member status in the WTO, the decision-making process is exclusionary and undemocratic. It is headquartered in Geneva, and developing countries cannot afford to maintain staff in Geneva or at the most have one official posted in Geneva to participate in the several dozens of committee meetings held daily at the headquarters. Developed countries on the other hand have several staff members and can also afford to fly in representatives as and when needed. Further, poor countries cannot afford the legal fees involved to contest an unfavourable trade ruling made by the WTO (Clarke 1999, *Independent*, available at http://www.igc.org/globalpolicy/socecon/bwi-wto/wto99-11.htm (accessed 1 October 2013). Decision-making in the World Bank and IMF is explicitly in favour of developed countries, since votes are weighted in terms of the financial investments of a country in these organizations (that is, one dollar, one vote). The five countries that have the largest shares of capital stock (the US, Japan, France, Germany and the UK) have the greatest powers in the two organizations.
13. In reality, heavy state subsidies are given to multinationals that invest in Third World countries. A recent case in India is the subsidies provided to the energy giant Enron (Mehta 2000).
14. To what extent such a cultural transition is realistic given the well-entrenched culture of the state in postcolonial societies is anybody's guess.
15. The follow-up millennium report by the Commission on Global Governance (CCG) is clear that 'the private sector has more to offer besides capital, notably expertise and experience on many functional, financial and managerial questions' (CGG 2000: 7).
16. The Commission on Global Governance similarly emphasizes partnerships between all members of civil society and reproaches NGOs for their 'harsh stance towards the private sector' and encourages them to 'reconsider their attitudes in the light of changing circumstances' (United Nations 2000: 22).
17. The UNRISD confirms that '[g]iven the enormous economic disparities between big business and the global poor, the lack of distinction between groups associated for profit (BINGOs) and those associated for public interest (PINGOs) rankles NGOs struggling to put development issues on the international agenda . . . The women's health organizations from the public interest sector adopted a resolution banning the participation of transnational corporations from their caucus meetings . . . in order to ensure that public interest NGOs were free to meet, reach consensus, set policy, plan and strategize without the presence and influence of organizations formed to protect the financial and business interests of their members'. One NGO stated 'it is unconscionable that people-

centered groups should have to share their one channel to policy makers with profit-making concerns' (UNRISD 1997).

18. The question of access to NGOs has reached a critical point since 1997. Two new regulations at the UN signal the disciplining of NGOs at the global policy level. One is to charge user fees to NGOs for the digitally stored UN documents which will specially impact Southern-based NGOs who are not as well-funded as the Northern-based NGOs. Second, is the new agreement initiated by the US that in the interests of efficiency the UN will not sponsor any more global conferences. The global conferences sponsored by the UN over the last two decades have served as prime sites for NGO advocacy work. Both sets of reforms reflect the UN's adaptation to market-based principles of governance (Paul 1998).
19. The World Bank also identifies the same two categories of NGOs: operational NGOs and advocacy NGOs. The latter are defined as NGOs 'whose primary purpose is to defend or promote a specific cause and who seek to influence the policies and practices of the Bank'. The Bank's activity and guidelines pertain only to operational NGOs which are further classified into three main groups: 'community-based organizations (CBOs) which serve a specific population in a narrow geographic area; national organization s which operate in individual developing countries, and; international organizations which are typically headquartered in developed countries and carry out operations in more than one developing country. Throughout the 1970s and 1980s, most examples of World Bank–NGO collaboration involved international NGOs. In recent years, however, this trend has been reversed. Among projects involving NGO collaboration recorded in FY94, 40 per cent involved CBOs, 70 per cent involved national organizations and 10 per cent involved international organizations' (World Bank).

References

Alvarez, Sonia. 1998. 'Latin American Feminisms "Go Global": Trends of the 1990s and Challenges for the New Millenium', in S. Alvarez, E. Dagnino and A. Escobar (eds), *Cultures of Politics Politics of Culture: Revisioning Latin American Social Movements*. Boulder, CO: Westview Press.

Anan, Kofi. 2000. 'Global Networks, the Most Promising Partnerships of our Globalizing Age', *United Nations Press Release at the Fifty Third Annual DPI/ NGO Conference*, 28 August, available at http://www.un.org (accessed 1 October 2013).

Appadurai, Arjun. 1996. *Modernity at Large: Cultural Dimensions of Globalization*. Minneapolis, MN: University of Minnesota Press.

Bardhan, Pranab. 1984. *The Political Economy of Development in India*. New Delhi: Oxford University Press.

Bebbington, Anthony and James Farrington. 1992. *Private Voluntary Initiatives and Governments, NGOs and Agricultural Development*. London: Overseas Development Institute.

Bijoy C. R., K. Arjun and Raju. 1994. 'Other Side of NGOs — Part III', *Anubhav*, 6: 35–41.

Carroll, Thomas. 1992. *Intermediary NGOs: The Supporting Link in Grassroots Development*. West Hartford, CT: Kumarian Press.

Cernea, Michael and Kudat, Ayse. 1997. *Social Assessments for Better Development: Case Studies in Russia and Central Asia*. Washington, DC: World Bank.

Chambers, Robert. 1997. *Whose Reality Counts? Putting the Last First*. London: Intermediate Technology.

Chege, Sam. 1999. 'Donors Shift More Aid to NGOs', *African Recovery, The UN Department of Public Information*, June 1999, available at http://www.globalpolicy.org/ngos/issues/chege.htm (accessed 1 October 2013).

Clark, John. 1991 *Democraticizing Development: The Role of Voluntary Organizations*. West Hartford, CT: Kumarian Press.

———. 1997. 'The State, Popular Participation and the Voluntary Sector', in D. Hulme and M. Edwards (eds), *NGOs, States and Donors: Too Close for Comfort?*. New York: St. Martin's Press.

Cohen, Jean and Andrew Arato. 1994. *Civil Society and Political Theory*. Cambridge, MA: MIT Press.

Commission on Global Governance. 1995. *Our Global Neighborhood*, available at http://www.cgg.ch/ contents.htm (accessed 1 October 2013).

———. 2000. *The Millennium Year and the Reform Process*, available at http://www.cgg.ch/millenium.htm (accessed 1 October 2013).

Drabek, A. Gordon (ed.). 1987. 'Development Alternatives: The Challenge for NGOs', *World Development*, vol. 15, supplement.

Edwards, Michael. 2000. *Future Positive: International Co-operation in the 21st Century*. Earthscan Publications.

Ferguson, James. 1994. *The Anti-Politics Machine: 'Development', Depoliticization and Bureaucratic Power in Lesotho*. Minneapolis, MN: University of Minnesota Press.

Fowler, Alan. 1997. *Striking a Balance: A Guide to Enhancing Effectiveness of NGOs in International Development*. London: Earthscan Publications.

———. 2000. *The Virtuous Spiral: A Guide to Sustainability for NGOs in International Development*. London: Earthscan Publications.

Fox, Jonathan and David Brown (eds). 1998. *The Struggle for Accountability: The World Bank, NGOs and Grassroots Movements*. Cambridge, MA: MIT Press.

Garain, Swapan. 1994. 'Government-NGO Interface in India: An Overview', *Indian Journal of Social Work*, 55(3): 337–46.

Gardner, Katy and David Lewis. 1996. *Anthropology, Development and the Postmodern Challenge*. London: Pluto Press.

Gendzier, Irene. 1985. *Development Against Democracy*. Boulder, CO: Westview Press.

Green, Maia. 2000. 'Participatory Development and the Appropriation of Agency in Southern Tanzania', *Critique of Anthropology*, 20(1): March.

Hammami, Rema. 1995. 'NGOs: The Professionalization of Polities', *Race and Class*, 37(2): 51–63.

Held, David. 1996. *Models of Democracy*. Stanford, CA: Stanford University Press.

Henderson, S. L. 2002. 'Selling Civil Society: Western Aid and the NGO Sector in Russia', *Comparative Political Studies*, 35(2): 135–67.

Holloway, Richard. 1998. *Supporting Citizen's Initiatives: Bangladesh's NGOs and Society*. London: Intermediate Technology Publishers.

Howell, Jude. 1998. 'An Unholy Trinity: Civil Society, Economic Liberalization and Democratization in Post-Mao China', *Government and Opposition*, 33(1): 56–70.

Hulme, David and Michael Edwards. 1997. 'NGOs, States and Donors: An Overview', in D. Hulme and M. Edwards (eds), *NGOs, States and Donors: Too Close for Comfort?*. New York: St. Martin's Press.

Kamat, Sangeeta. 2002. *Development Hegemony: NGOs and the State in India*. New Delhi: Oxford University Press.

Kumar, Krishnan. 1993. 'Civil Society: An Inquiry into the Usefulness of a Historical term', *British Journal of Sociology*, 44(3): 375.

Kuropas, Myron. 1997. 'Will NGOs Save Ukraine?', *Ukraine Weekly*, 35: 31 August.

Korten, David. 1990. *Getting to the 21st Century: Voluntary Action and the Global Agenda*. West Hartford, CT: Kumarian Press.

———. 1998. *Globalizing Civil Society: Reclaiming our Right to Power*. New York: Seven Stories Press.

Lewis, David and Tina Wallace. 2000. *New Roles and Relevance: Development NGOs and the Challenge of Change*. Hartford, CT: Kumarian Press.

Mercer, C. 2002. 'NGOs, Civil Society and Democratization: A Critical Review of the Literature', *Progress in Development Studies*, 2(1): 5–22.

Mehta, Abhay. 2000. *Power Play: A Study of the Enron Project*. New Delhi: Orient Longman.

Miraftab, Faranak. 1997. 'Flirting with the Enemy: Challenges Faced by NGOs in Development and Empowerment', *Habitat International*, 21(4): 361–75.

Moore, R. 2001. 'China's Fledgling Society: A Force of Democratization?', *World Policy Journal*, 18(1): 56–66.

Ndegwa, Stephen. 1996. *Two Faces of Civil Society: NGOs and Politics in Africa*. Hartford, CT: Kumarian Press.

Nye, Joseph and John Donahue. 2000. *Governance in a Globalizing World*. Washington, DC: Brookings Institution Press.

Paul, James. 1999. 'NGO Access at the UN', *Global Policy Forum*, available at http://www.globalpolicy. org/ngos/analysis/jap-accs.htm (accessed 15 June 2002).

Robinson, Mark. 1997. 'Privatizing the Voluntary Sector: NGOs as Public Service Contractors', in D. Hulme and M. Edwards (eds), *In NGOs, States and Donors: Too Close for Comfort?*. New York: St. Martin's Press.

Schilds, Veronica. 1998. 'New Subjects of Rights? Women's Movements and the Construction of Citizenship in the "New Democracies"', in S. Alvares et al. (eds), *Culture of Politics and Politics of Culture*. Boulder, CO: Westview Press.

Sparr, Patricia (ed.). 1994. *Mortgaging Women's Lives: Feminist Critiques of Structural Adjustment*. Atlantic Highlands, NJ: Zed Books.

Wolfensohn, James. 1997. 'The Challenge of Inclusion', Annual Meeting Address in Hong Kong, China, 23 September, available at http:// www.worldbank.org/html/extdr/am97/jdw_sp/jwsp97e.htm (accessed 1 October 2013).

UNRISD. 1997. 'Globalization and Civil Society: NGO Influence in International Decision-Making', *Discussion Paper No. 83*, April 1997.

Van Rooy, Alison (ed.). 1998. *Civil Society and the Aid Industry*. London, UK: Earthscan Publishers.

White, Sarah. 1999. 'NGOs, Civil Society and the State in Bangladesh: The Politics of Representing the Poor', *Development and Change*, 30: 307–26.

Wood, Geof. 1997. 'States Without Citizens: The Problem of the Franchise State', in D. Hulme and M. Edwards (eds), *NGOs, States and Donors: Too Close the Comfort?*. New York: St. Martin's Press.

World Bank. 1998. *The Bank's Relations with NGOs: Issues and Directions*. Washington, DC: World Bank.

———. 1998. *Key Issues and Themes /NGO Capacity Building of Southern NGOs — The Experience of the World Bank*, available at http://www. worldbank.org (accessed 1 October 2013).

———. *World Bank Participation Sourcebook*. 1995. Washington, DC: World Bank.

Wuthnow, Robert (ed.). 1991. *Between States and Markets: The Voluntary Sector in Comparative Perspective*. Princeton, NJ: Princeton University Press.

12

Other Worlds are (Already) Possible

Self-Organization, Complexity and Post-Capitalist Cultures

*Arturo Escobar**

This chapter is a call for greater awareness of the theoretical frameworks we use to understand the world and what to do about it. It stems from the realization that there is always a tight connection between social reality, the theoretical framework we use to interpret it, and the sense of politics and hope that emerges from such an understanding. This connection is often overlooked. It can be said without much exaggeration that our hope and politics are largely the result of a given framework. It is particularly important that we reflect on this fact in times of profound transformations, such as today. This chapter is less intended as a critique of established frameworks (say, Marxism and liberalism), than as a presentation of the elements of a way of looking at social reality, seemingly on the rise, that can at least provisionally be said to be apt to explain some of the social dynamics we are witnessing today, and to do so in a novel way. The implications for politics should be apparent.

This new way of seeing is emerging from unsuspected quarters, chiefly a set of alternative (but increasingly visible) theories that find their source in mathematics and the natural and physical sciences, and which usually go under the label of 'complexity theory'. One of the most interesting, and controversial, claims of this theory is that the same dynamics and processes might be at play in many domains of material, biological and social life. Fancy categories such as self-organization, non-linearity, strange attractors, and non-hierarchy are used to spell out these processes. In addition, for many, complexity in natural and social life unveils an underlying, and until now largely uncharted, principle: networks. This principle is clearly revealed in the domain of cyberspace; however, it could be increasingly visible in the domain of global movements.[1]

The Argument for a New Way of Looking at Reality

Over the past few hundred years, economic and social lives have tended to be largely organized on the logic of order, centralization and hierarchy building. Pushed by capitalism and its drive to accumulation, this logic has resulted in systems in which the few privilege at the expense of the many. What has remained largely hidden, however, is that this logic is present not only in those social structures that are evidently exploitative, but that similar logics have animated allegedly alternative systems, including socialism and most organizations on the Left. A different logic of social organization (which was always at play, albeit marginalized) has become increasingly visible in the most recent decades. This logic seems most clearly manifested in two domains: digital technologies (cyberspace, as the universe of digital networks, interactions and interfaces); and the sciences of complexity, particularly in biology and other aspects of natural life. In this chapter, I would like to describe what I believe is the appeal of complexity and its potential for explaining, and providing clues for, social movements opposed to neoliberal globalization (NLG). As a prelude, however, I would like to introduce briefly the argument for looking at cyberspace.

Cyberspace: Towards Subaltern Intelligent Communities?

Cyberspace, it can be argued, is based on a model that is very different from that of modern media. In the conventional model, information flows one-way from a world of active emitters to that of passive receivers; there is tight ideological control, so that the media reflects the world as seen by those who rule it. In other words, modern media operates on the basis of a top-down, action-reaction model of information. The model fostered by information, computer and communications technologies (ICTs) contrasts sharply with this dominant model. First, it is based on 'interactivity', which refers to an altogether new framework of interaction (a profoundly relational model in which negotiated views of reality may be built, where all receivers are also potentially emitters, a space of truly dialogical interaction, as in the best examples of net.art). Second, at least in principle, cyberspace can be seen as a decentralized archipelago of relatively autonomous zones, in which communities create their own media and process their own information.

Third, ICTs and cyberspace tend to promote the creation of networked cultures without the homogenized identities assumed by the mass media; they foster routes for the circulation of ideas that are not so subject to centralized controls, and the irruption of sub-cultures that are aware of the need to re-invent social and political orders. As a space for inter-cultural exchange and for the construction of shared artistic and political strategies, cyberspace affords unprecedented opportunities to build shared visions with peoples from all over the world (in this sense, Porto Alegre can be seen partly as a result of this dynamic). At play is a micropolitics for the production of local knowledge made possible by the 'fluid architecture' of cyberspace, emphasizing the 'molecular' (as opposed to molar, or characterized by large, homogeneous conglomerates) nature of cyberspace. This micropolitics consists of practices of mixing, reusing, and recombination of knowledge and information.

In other words, cyberspace may be seen as embodying a new model of life and world-making. Variously called by enthusiasts a knowledge space, a space of collective intelligence, and a 'noosphere' (sphere of collective thought), cyberspace, in these views, constitutes a signifying space of subject–subject interaction (individually and collectively) for the negotiation of visions and meanings. The resulting systems of networked intelligence could be of great cultural, social and political potential. They could make up an inter-networked society of *intelligent communities*, centered on the democratic production of culture and subjectivity. Rather than at the service of capital, this new economy of knowledge would be at the service of an emerging humanity of cooperation, pluralism (singularity) and collective learning. It would be receptive to a multiplicity of life forms and cultures rather than contributing to the flattening of identities effected by capital's steam-rolling media. For cyberspace visionaries, this realization could enable a re-signification of social and biological life and of freedom, a platform for the self-production of social and natural worlds.[2]

Complexity and the Principle of Self-organization

In its utopian conception, cyberspace can thus be seen as enacting a decentralized, non-hierarchical logic of self-organization. Self-organization is also at the heart of complexity in biological and social life. Ants, swarming moulds, cities, and certain markets are among the entities that show what scientists call 'complex adaptive behavior'.[3] These examples evince the existence of bottom-up processes in which simple beginnings lead to complex entities, without there being any master plan or central intelligence planning it. In these cases, agents working at one (local) scale produce behaviour and forms at higher scales (e.g., the great anti-globalization demonstrations of the last few years); simple rules at one level give rise to sophistication and complexity at another level. Scientists have a new word for this discovery, *emergence,* when the actions of multiple agents interacting dynamically and following local rules rather than top-down commands result in some kind of visible macro-behaviour or structure. There is more: these systems are (sometimes, not always) 'adaptive': they learn over time, responding more effectively to the changing environment.

Emergent behaviour — such as in the examples mentioned earlier — usually shows a mix of order and anarchy, self-organizing networks and hierarchies (e.g., myriad encounters in sidewalks vs. rule-governed behaviour, to mention the example of cities). The important issue is to recognize the self-organizing potential of diverse agents or multiplicities. It is important to respect and build on this logic (some new software and interfaces attempt to do just this, by learning to recognize complexity). This entails building on the logic of distributed (neither centralized nor decentralized, but mesh-like), bottom-up intelligence as opposed to unified, top-down forms.

Complexity theory points at a pervasive logic underlying many domains of biological, social and economic life, that of networks and interconnection. Networks constitute the basic architecture of complexity. Networks are 'in' at present in the explanation of many types of processes; from nature to computers, from business to movements, anywhere one looks there seems to appear a web-like universe. Physical and natural scientists are currently busy mapping networks of all kinds, and trying to ascertain network structures, topologies, and mechanisms of operation. Social scientists are beginning to get into the bandwagon of complex networks research. As a pioneer and advocate of this research said in a comprehensive introduction to the subject, 'networks will dominate the new century to a much greater degree that most people are yet ready to acknowledge ... Network thinking is poised to invade all domains of human activity and most fields of human inquiry' (Barabási 2002: 7, 222). Be that as it may, the fact is that network thinking is here to stay, at least for a while, and that it has interesting lessons for rethinking many aspects of left (and all kinds of) politics, from organizational structures to movement dynamics.

Often, networks assemble themselves by following the logic of self-organization. The scientists' most striking claim, however, is that there are some basic laws governing all networks. For instance, networks are highly interconnected, so that huge networks constitute 'small worlds' in the sense that all elements in the network are only a few links away from all others, particularly due to the presence of clusters, hubs and connectors. And of course not everything goes in networks, since some sites and hubs are much more connected than others, so that there are hierarchies of interconnection. Often, an entire network topology is determined by a few large hubs, as in the case of the World Wide Web, where links such as Google, Yahoo or amazon.com have a much greater weight in defining the web's architecture than millions of much smaller nodes. These hubs determine preferential attachments; in the emerging global economy, large corporations have a profound role in shaping the networked economy; something similar happens in global movement networks, in which Zapatista and a few other key nodes (including the WSF) are crucial to the structuring of the overall network. In sum, even if self-organized, networks of this type follow certain rules, which scientists refer to as 'power laws' (Barabási 2002).

The Mexican theorist Manuel de Landa (1997, n.d., 2003) has introduced a useful distinction between two general network types: hierarchies, and flexible, non-hierarchical, decentralized and self-organizing meshworks. This is a key distinction that underlies two alternative philosophies of life. Hierarchies entail a degree of centralized control, ranks, overt planning, homogenization, and particular goals and rules of behaviour; they operate under the tyranny of linear time and tree-like structures. The military, capitalist enterprises and most bureaucratic organizations have largely operated on this basis. Meshworks, on the contrary, are based on decentralized decision-making (such as the 'swarming effect' described earlier), self-organization, and heterogeneity and diversity. Since they are non-hierarchical, they have no overt single goal. They develop through their encounter with their environments, although conserving their basic structure. Other metaphors used to describe these phenomena are tree-like structures or 'strata' (for hierarchies) and 'rhizomes' or 'self-consistent aggregates' for meshworks (from philosophers Deleuze and Guattari 1987). The metaphor of rhizomes suggests networks of heterogeneous elements that grow in unplanned directions, following the real-life situations they encounter. Hierarchies shun heterogeneity and diversity, meshworks welcome it. In short, they represent two very different life philosophies. An open question is whether rhizomatic meshworks escape the power laws that characterize most ('scale-free') regular networks.

It should be made clear that these two principles are found mixed in most real-life examples. They could also give rise to one another (as when social movement meshworks develop hierarchies and centralization). The internet is a case in point: having grown mostly on the model of self-organization, it became increasingly colonized by hierarchical forms (from the military to e-business), which have attempted to turn it into another space of mass consumption of commodities and information. Today, the internet can be said to be a hybrid of meshwork and hierarchy components, with a tendency for the elements of command and control to increase. The reverse could be said about the global economy. Twentieth-century corporate economy was based on a tree-like hierarchical model; today, corporations are seeking to evolve towards a networked form with flexible command structures. This contradicts with the trend towards large conglomerates, so that the capitalist economy continues to be a mixture of decentralized networks and hierarchies. As de Landa put is, 'the new view of markets stresses their decentralization (hence corporations do not belong there), and this can hardly justify globalization which is mostly the result of corporations' (2003: 5). Global movements could get ahead of the game by opting decidedly for the meshwork logic.

To sum up, what I am suggesting is that in cyberspace and complexity we find a viable and at least potentially meaningful model of social life (in terms of, say, less hierarchical and more meshwork-like possibilities). This model is based on self-organization, non-hierarchy and complex adaptive behaviour on the part of agents. This model contrasts sharply with the dominant model of capitalism and modernity, particularly in their incarnation as neoliberal globalization (NLG). This model is closer in spirit to philosophical and political anarchism and anarcho-socialism and may provide cues for internationalist networking. The model of self-organization (SO), finally, constitutes an *entirely different form* for the creation of biological, social and economic life. Without proposing it as the only model and for all efforts world-wide, I suggest that leftist and progressive peoples in many parts of the world should consider this model seriously in their organizing, resistance and creative practices. In the long run, this may amount to reinventing the dynamics of social emancipation itself. The left is thus confronted with a novel sociology and politics of emergence from this perspective.

Some Questions of Strategy

The transformation in question may already be happening, as anti-globalization social movements (AGMs) indicate. These movements may be seen as fostering a sort of emergence in their attempt to counter the deadening, hierarchy-laden systems of NLG. None of the movements making up the AGM can by itself tackle the entire 'system' or the global situation, yet they have shown that they can work together in some fashion. They do not take their cues from any central committee, but act largely in response to local/national concerns, albeit having in mind some global issues.[4] With AGMs, in short, we have a case where local collective action results in global behaviour, at least some times.[5] In other words, while no single movement can 'see the whole' (e.g., for an Italian movement it is hard to see the complexity of a local movement in a Colombian rainforest, and for both hard to see the complexity that their combined action might create, let alone when linked to a greater number of more diverse movements), the fact that there are forms of globally emergent behaviour affects what particular movements think and do. In other words, place-based and other local movements contribute to emergent behaviour, that is, to forms of macro-intelligence and adaptability, even if the 'overall state of the system', or the character of 'the enemy' might be difficult to assess (actually such assessments are always a perilous reduction, even if having some strategic sense of the whole might be important). In these cases, global forms of knowledge and strategy-making cannot be reduced to the individual movements making it up. The 'global movement' may indeed develop its life and adapt over a much longer time span than any individual movement that contributes to it.

In other words, AGMs can be thought about in terms of self-organizing networks (a meshwork) of movements that produce behaviour that goes beyond each individual movement. There have to be means for enabling suitable interactions (through face to face encounters, cyberspace, flexible and innovative organizational structures, etc.). These interfaces would have to foster complex learning that does not happen just locally. This suggests that when thinking about AGMs it is important to think about two dynamics: the day-to-day lives of individual movements; and the historical scale of collective movement over the years. To this we might add the macro-scale of human society over long periods. Movements (and persons) are not very good at keeping these various levels in mind, and at responding to changing patterns over time, for good reasons. It is important to recognize the role of SO behaviour so as to foster it, to the extent that this is possible or desirable.[6]

Of course, not every interface or collection of agents is likely to produce adaptive, emergent behaviour. Many environments suppress such behaviour, hence the need to nourish it. There has to be both connection and organization that promote higher-level learning. Self-organization needs to be steered in specific ways to produce the kinds of collective intelligence that are needed. The greater the interconnectedness, the greater the likelihood of positive feedback. Negative feedback is also important in attempting to steer a system into particular goals, making it into a complex adaptive system. From a theoretical perspective at least, what is needed is a combination of ever-widening positive feedback and some negative feedback — again, SO with some measure of leadership, structure and regulation. Theoretically again, the need for a measure of self-regulation and decentralized control arises when the community/system cannot reach a constructive balance on its own. Movements would need to learn to 'read the signs' and adapt, but also learn to capitalize on the swarming behaviour and positive feedback of SO. To foster interactivity conducive to these ends it is necessary to think about the rules of interaction. In the jargon of ICTs, the system needs to be wired accordingly.[7]

This double dynamic seems already present in principle in the proposal for a Social Movements World Network. Taking advantage of the virtual and real spaces created by the WSF, this proposal aims at creating a minimal basis for a world network of social movements. The proposal stems from the recognition of the need for 'new structures, decision-making processes and new formations to articulate and drive a radical democratic, feminist, internationalist and anti-imperialist agenda'. The network 'would help us develop the conditions so that the diverse social movements of the world can exchange analyses, opinions and information on the present conjuncture and establish some shared priorities and necessary tasks'. The objective is to go beyond episodic encounters among the movements, to construct a deeper political debate, to establish horizontal structures that facilitate exchange and common actions, and to extend the reach of the movements in all the continents. At this level, the proposal resonates with the logic of complexity and self-organization, combined with some elements of structure and regulation just described. As Adamovsky (2003) has rightly warned, however, the danger could start if and when those facilitating the process — themselves working within hierarchical organizations — attempt to create a structure that claims to represent 'the totality' of the social movements, or impose agendas instead of letting each node enter and exit network coalitions in terms of their own interests and needs.

To get back to movements, AGMs could be thought about as building decentralized intelligence partly with the help of, and following the non-colonized logic of, ICTs, particularly cyberspace. Adaptive self-organization is the best alternative available. This 'politics of emergence' shows that there can be collective intelligence and 'real results' (in terms of power) in self-organizing behaviour. If it is true that global capitalism and information society are attempting a restructuring towards the network form, movements could be better off by building on this logic and getting ahead of the game. The movements have the advantage since, unable to really pursue a strategy of collective intelligence, capitalism will progressively loose out to an AGM which, when all is said and done, will have learned to 'think like a swarm' (Johnson 2002). Movements will develop a degree of self-awareness that only distributed intelligence can muster: that of contributing with every action and political act to long term processes of alternative world-making.[8]

In sum, the question before us is: Can AGMs create a sort of collective intelligence that opposes the sociology of absences of NLG? If so, social movements would exhibit complex adaptive and emergent behaviour of their own, and would promote it for society as a whole out of their own local work. The 'behavioural ecology' of AGMs shows that they have indeed developed adaptive behaviour to the changing environment of cyberspace. Leftist visions of the future could then build on the relational, radically self-organizing principle of networking as the one most appropriate to the social movements of today. Perhaps it is on this basis that an international/ist challenge and alternative to NLG can be most effectively advanced.

A final caveat is in order. What does all this have to do with power? Is here a sense of power in complexity? I can only make a few remarks on this crucial question here. For the vision presented earlier to have a chance it has to be accompanied by an ineluctable obligation: 'to the local/locale; to the marginalized; to the public sphere, to a constant critical self examination' (Waterman 2003). This is not easy to accomplish, since the very same ICTs foster a disregard for locality, body and place, plus tremendous forms of inequality; they produce a degree of global de-localization and erasure of place perhaps greater than ever before. Some feminists and environmentalists are very much aware of this fact (Escobar 1999; Harcourt 1999; Virilio 1999). Who are most marginalized and disempowered by these trends? It is often the case that the answer to this question is: women, ethnic minorities, and of course poor people. This means that we need to pay special attention to the political economy of ICTs in the broad sense of the term, that is, to the capitalist, patriarchal and ethnocentric tendencies and structures that today regulate ICTs and Net practices. This analysis should also give us clues about which agents should be — and at times actually are — at the forefront of struggles over ICTs (see, for instance, Maria Suárez's work with the FIRE radio and internet network in Costa Rica 2003).

There is a political ecology of cyber culture that suggests that the 'cultures' developed out of ICTs-supported networking need to be conscious of the double character of the struggle: over the very nature of cyberspace and ICTs, and over the real restructuring of the world affected by ICTs-led transnational capitalism. This means that if the aim is to create subaltern intelligent communities, these need to be ecological and ethical in the broad sense of these terms. There is thus a cultural politics of cyberspace that resists, transforms and presents alternatives to the dominant real and virtual worlds. Consequently, this cyber cultural politics can be most effective if it fulfills two conditions: awareness of the dominant worlds that are being created by the same technologies on which the progressive networks rely; and an ongoing tacking back and forth between cyberpolitics and place-based politics, or political activism in the physical locations where networkers or netweavers sit and live. This is precisely the politics that some of today's movements are attempting to develop in creatively combining local and global strategies for action, local and global goals, local and global interaction.[9]

Notes

* This chapter was earlier published in Jai Sen, Anita Anand, Arturo Escobar, and Peter Waterman (eds), 2004, *World Social Forum: Challenging Empires*, New Delhi: Viveka, pp. 349–58. Available at http://www.choike.org/nuevo_eng/informes/1557.html, and http://www.openspaceforum.net/twiki/tiki-index.php?page=WSFChallengingEmpires2004 (accessed 4 October 2013). Reproduced here with permission of the author and the editors.This chapter is based on a longer piece prepared for the panel on Cyber-space organized by Peter Waterman within the 'Life after Capitalism' (LAC) sessions at the 'Third World Social Forum' in Porto Alegre (htpp://www.zmag.org/lac.htm, accessed 1 October 2013), January 2003. I have preserved the general spirit of the LAC panels, that is, the focus on vision ('What do we want') and strategy ('How do we get it?'). Hence the generally utopian and tentative character of the piece, which is offered here as food for thought, more than an accomplished proposal.

1. Calls for a new way of looking at reality came initially in the mid-1980s, from scientists advocating for a transition from the rationalistic, linear and predictability assumptions of classical science to positions highlighting irreversibility, unpredictability, non-linerarity, becoming, and the like. The most well-known statement in this regard was Prigonine and Stengers's work (1984). At about the same time, Boaventura de Sousa Santos (1992) was calling for a similar paradigmatic transition in the social sciences.

2. Pierre Lévy (e.g., 1997) has most powerfully articulated this thesis in recent years. The liberation theologian Leonardo Boff's recent work (2000) on *religación* — a 'reconnecting' of humans with nature, each other, the earth, the cosmos, god — could also be interpreted in this light (he appeals explicitly to complexity). Discussions of the impact of ICTs on daily life abound, including those examining 'cybercultures' (e.g., Harcourt 1999; Bell and Kennedy 2000; Burbano and Barragán 2002). Kari-Hans Kommonen and the ARKI Research Group at the Media Lab at the Helsinki University of Art and Design are developing a framework to study the impact of growing digitalization on everyday life. For these researchers, the internet is a first step in the development of a far more complex Mediaspace that is emerging as a result of pervasive digitalization. This Mediaspace will be central to crafting and negotiating ideas, structures and practices, hence the need to develop an explicit approach to designing this space as a means to social, cultural and political innovation. See http://www.arki.uiah.fi (accessed 1 October 2013).
3. Common examples include: Thousands of invisible single-celled mould units which occasionally coalesce into a swarm and create a visible large mould; ant colonies that develop over a long time span with no central pacemaker; local markets which, in the past, efficiently linked myriad producers and consumers, allowing prices to set themselves in a way that was understood locally, without great hierarchies or central control; and the way in which cities developed without much central planning on the basis of interfaces between pedestrians, vehicles, goods and services, etc. See the fine introduction on emergence in complex systems by Johnson (2001). A more technical work that attempts to rethink social structure form the perspective of complexity is Kontopoulos (1993); it pays attention to issues of emergence, stability, scale, and heterarchical forms of organization in ways that could be useful for thinking about emergent structures and possibility spaces in AGMs. Above all, I have relied on Manuel de Landa's sustained effort at pushing complexity forward by focusing on social systems.
4. A somewhat similar argument has been made by Osterweil (2002) for Italian movements, Peltonen (2003) for the Finnish environmental movement, and my own studies of the social movement of black communities of the Pacific (2000). Chesters (2003), Escobar (2002) and Peltonen (2002) are among the few applications of complexity to social movements to date.
5. Or is there a global effect *always going on*, besides and beyond the visible global events? Is there a stifling 'Seattle effect' that does not let us see the always ongoing swarming that goes on at the local/regional levels, that in some way is also 'global'?.

6. From the perspective of complexity, the theoretical utopia would be a phase transition as a result of AGM activity, that is, a radical change in state and organization at a critical juncture, perhaps promoted by some sort of non-linear dynamics in the mechanisms of the world economy, ecology, ideology, etc.
7. Some of the concerns with the WSF expressed by critics in this volume can be interpreted in this light. What kinds of interfaces and correctives would be needed to foster the movement networks adumbrated by Adamovsky and George, for instance, or for lessening the invisibilities unveiled by Osterweil?
8. Electronic art, net.art and software design are also fields where great innovation is taking place in the direction of self-organization, multiplicity and non-hierarchy. See the original version of this chapter for some references. See also Critical Art Ensemble (1996); Burbano and Barragán (2002) for recent Latin American experiments. Application of network theory to movements and global issues include Waterman (1992), King (2000) and the dissertations on Zapatista networks by Solano-Leyva (2001) and Olesen (2002). A study of networks from a dominant perspective is Arquilla and Ronfeldt (2001).
9. See, for instance, the Women and the Politics of Place project organized by the Society for International Development, SID (http://www.sidint.org/, accessed 1 October 2013).

References

Adamovsky, Ezequiel. 2003. 'The World Social Forum's New Project: "The Network of the World's Social Movements"', available at http://www.nadir.org/nadir/initiativ/agp/free/wsf/ (accessed 1 October 2013).

Arquilla, John and David Ronfeldt. 2001. *Networks and Netwars*. Santa Monica, CA: Rand Corporation.

Barabási, Albert-László. 2002. *Linked: The New Science of Networks*. Cambridge: Perseus Publishing.

Bell, David and Barbara Kennedy (eds). 2000. *The Cybercultures Reader*. London: Routledge.

Boff, Leonardo. 2000. *El Cuidado Esencial*. Madrid: Editorial Trotta.

Burbano, Andrés and Hernando Barragán (eds). 2002. *Hipercubo/ok/.arte, Ciencia y Tecnología en Contextos Próximos*. Bogotá: Universidad de los Andes/Goethe Institut.

Chesters, Graeme. 2003. 'Shape Shifting: Civil Society, Complexity and Social Movements'. Unpublished manuscript, Centre for Local Policy Studies, Edge Hill University College, Lancashire, UK.

Critical Art Ensemble. 1996. *Electronic Civil Disobedience*. Brooklyn: Autonomedia.

de Landa, Manuel. 1997. *A Thousand Years of Nonlinear History*. New York: Zone Books

———. 2003. '1000 Years of War. CTHEORY Interview with Manuel de Landa', available at http://www.ctheory.net/text_file.asp?pick=383 (accessed 1 October 2013).

———. n.d. 'Meshworks, Hierarchies and Interfaces', available at http://www.t0.or.at/delanda/ (accessed 1 October 2013).

Deleuze, Gilles and Félix Guattari. 1987. *A Thousand Plateaus*. Minneapolis: University of Minnesota Press.

Escobar, Arturo. 1999. 'Gender, Place, and Networks: A Political Ecology of Cyberculture', in Wendy Harcourt (ed.), *Women@Internet: Creating New Cultures in Cyberspace*, pp. 31–54. London: Zed Books.

———. 2000. 'Notes on Networks and Anti-Globalization Social Movements'. Paper presented at AAA Annual Meeting, San Francisco, 15–19 November, available at www.unc.edu/~aescobar/ (accessed 1 October 2013).

Harcourt, Wendy (ed.). 1999. *Women@Internet: Creating New Cultures in Cyberspace*. London: Zed Books.

Johnson, Steven. 2001. *Emergence*. New York: Scribner.

King, Mary. 2000. 'Of Unknown Quantity: NGO Network Organizing and Global Environmental Politics'. Paper presented at the session on 'Actors, Networks, Meanings: Environmental Social Movements and the Anthropology of Activism', AAA Annual Meeting, San Francisco, 15–19 November.

Kontopoulos, Kyryakos. 1993. *The Logics of Social Structure*. Cambridge: Cambridge University Press.

Lévy, Pierre. 1997. *Collective Intelligence: Mankind's Emerging World in Cyberspace*. New York: Plenum Trade.

Leyva Solano, Xochitll. 2002. 'Neo-*Zapatismo*: Networks of Power and War.' PhD dissertation, Department of Anthropology, University of Manchester.

Olesen, Thomas. 2002. 'Long Distance Zapatismo: Globalization and the Construction of Solidarity'. PhD dissertation, Department of Political Science, University of Aarhus.

Osterweil, Michal. 2002. 'Re-thinking Politics and Resistance: Ethnography and the Italian "New Global" Movements'. Paper presented at the AAA Annual Meeting, New Orleans, 20–24 November.

Peltonen, Lasse. 2003. 'Fluids without a Cause? Tracing the Emergence of a Local Green Movement' in Yrjö Haila and Chuck Dyke (eds), *How Does Nature Speak? The Dynamics of the Human Ecological Condition* (unpublished book manuscript, University of Helsinki).

Prigogine, Ilya and Isabel Stengers. 1984. *Order Out of Chaos*. New York: Bantham Books.

Santos, Boaventura de Sousa. 1992. 'A Discourse on the Sciences', *Review*, 15(1): 9–47.
———. 2002. *Towards a New Legal Common Sense*. London: Butterworth.
Suárez, María. 2003. FIRE's Internet Radio Station: An Autochthonous Creation by Feminists in Cyberspace, available at http://www.zmag.org/lacsite.htm (accessed 1 October 2013).
Virilio, Paul. 1999. *Politics of the Very Worst*. New York: Semitext(e).
Waterman, Peter. 1992. 'International Labour Communication by Computer: The Fifth International?', working paper series no. 129, Institute of Social Studies, the Hague.
———. 2003. 'Some Propositions on Cyberspace after Capital-ism'. Paper presented at Cyberspace Panel, Life after Capitalism Pro-gramme, World Social Forum, Porto Alegre, 23–28 January, available at http://www.zmag.org/lacsite.htm (accessed 1 October 2013).

13

New Social Movements

The Role of Legal Opportunity

*Christopher J. Hilson**

Historically, when examining how interest groups seek to achieve their public policy goals, most European Union (EU) political scientists have focused on lobbying of EU political institutions by such groups (eg., Mazey and Richardson 1993; Warleigh 2000). It is only more recently that political scientists have begun fully to explore the way in which EU law-based litigation strategies in national courts have also been used to further important policy objectives (Alter and Vargas 2000; Tesoka 1999). In doing so, they have built on work that lawyers have already done on this (Barnard 1995; Harlow and Rawlings 1992; Rawlings 1993). Finally, it is also only relatively recently that the role of protest as a means of applying policy pressure has been examined in an EU context (Imig and Tarrow 1999; Kriesi 1995; Marks and McAdam 1996; Tarrow 1995; Reising 1998).

One of the weaknesses of the mentioned treatments is that they consider the three different types of policy strategies in relative isolation. The literature on lobbying is singular in focus. And while the literature on litigation strategies considers the interplay between law and politics, it has ignored the role of protest. This is in large measure because it has considered only one policy area — workplace gender discrimination — where protest has historically been absent. Similarly, although the new social movement literature on protest considers the interplay between protest and conventional politics, it tends at best to underplay and, at worst, to ignore the role of law and the courts. From a lawyer's perspective, such an approach is erroneous because recourse to law can be seen as a distinct strategy in its own right — not that lawyers are in a position to claim the high ground. Where they have looked at protest, it has typically involved a doctrinal examination of the laws of public order that constrain it. In other words, the effect of law on protest has been limited to a study of 'top-down' law — law as repression. There has been little socio-legal analysis of how 'bottom-up' litigation affects protest.

The aim of this chapter is therefore to place all three strategies — lobbying, litigation, and protest — within a coherent analytical framework. It will do so by adopting a revised new social movement perspective. Most political science literature on new social movements places great emphasis on political opportunity structure (POS) or political opportunity (PO) in explaining unconventional protest activity (Kitschelt 1986; Kriesi 1995; Tarrow 1994, 1998). To these will be added the idea of legal opportunity (LO).

The chapter will argue that a lack of PO may influence the adoption of litigation as a strategy in place of lobbying, and that the choice of protest as a strategy may be influenced by poor political and legal opportunities. The emphasis on 'influence' here is important. The chapter is not suggesting that choice of strategy is uniquely determined by PO or LO — far from it. There are numerous other factors which may also influence the choice of strategy in any particular case — such as resources, identity, ideas, and values — and these will be examined briefly in a later section. However, the proposition that PO and LO may have an important influence appears to be borne out by the series of longitudinal, single country, cross-movement examples which the chapter goes on to analyze. The four movements involved are the environmental, animal welfare, lesbian and gay, and women's movements, and the country chosen is the UK. Although single-country in nature, the examples are placed firmly in a multi-level, European, political, and legal context. Thus, a lack of political or legal opportunity at the national level may be compensated for by EU-based political or legal opportunities. Where EU laws are capable of outflanking domestic policy in this manner, protest may be prevented. However, where both domestic and EU political and legal opportunities are poor, groups within civil society are more likely to have recourse to protest.

Movements and Strategies

The environmental, animal welfare,[1] lesbian and gay, and women's movements are all examples of what are now commonly described as 'new social movements', in contrast to old social movements such as the labour movement. New social movements consist of numerous social movement organizations (SMOs) and — in the case of the environmental and animal rights movements — some 'disorganizations'.[2] Some of these organizations adopt conventional tactics such as political lobbying and bringing court proceedings, whereas others and the disorganizations utilize a range of unconventional protest tactics, often referred to as 'direct action'.[3] These unconventional tactics typically involve the purposeful disruption of lawful social or economic activity[4] and may be violent (more commonly to property rather than persons) or nonviolent in nature. The unconventional activity itself may be lawful, but — particularly after the introduction of the offence of aggravated trespass in the UK by sections 68–9 of the Criminal Justice and Public Order Act 1994 — it is just as likely to be unlawful in nature.

Alternative Explanations for Strategy Use

Although it is being claimed here that PO and LO are important factors influencing strategy choice, they are clearly not the only such factors. Alternative theories, which have sought to explain the existence of new social movement activity, stress instead the role of inter alia, resources, identity, ideas, and values. While all of these have been explicitly developed in order to explain protest, many are equally suited to explaining the use or non-use of political lobbying and litigation as strategies.

First, there are 'resource mobilization' (RM) theories, which — in contrast to POS/PO theories, which focus on external factors — focus on the internal resources available to SMOs (Kitschelt 1986). While classical theories of the 1960s and early 1970s emphasized the role of discontent or grievances in explaining the emergence of social movements, RM theorists point out that grievances are commonplace in almost all societies at all times. What turns these individual grievances into collective action is, they claim, the availability of resources (Byrne 1997; McCarthy and Zald 1977). They similarly claim that 'new' social movements have come to the fore in times of post-material plenty, and that in order to be successful, SMOs must successfully mobilize resources from the public (McCarthy and Zald 1977). While critics have suggested that this is perhaps a more realistic description of conventional, interest group-type SMOs than it is of unconventional SMOs (Piven and Cloward 1995), a resource-based approach is well suited to explain strategy usage by all types of SMO.

Thus one can argue that SMOs adopt strategies that fit their resources, with resources defined broadly to include not only finances but also factors such as the professional and educational background of personnel (Byrne 1997). Political lobbying is therefore likely to be a realistic strategy only for those with a professional background: policy-makers are less likely to listen to those from unconventional backgrounds who lack the relevant expertise or who are not used to speaking their language. While the actual process of political lobbying could in theory be relatively costless (at least at domestic level), in practice it is associated with payment to a professional lobbying cadre who fit this policy-making mould. Litigation, on the other hand, is potentially doubly financially burdensome: not only — to stand any chance of success — do you have to employ expert, costly lawyers for your own side; but also, if you lose, you are likely to be made to pay your opponents' costs. In addition, litigation is also only likely to be adopted as a strategy where an individual within a SMO or its network has direct experience of the law. It is arguably no coincidence that the SMOs — such as Greenpeace and Compassion in World Farming (CIWF) — that have used the courts relatively frequently, have lawyers on their staff. That leaves the professionally and financially poor with protest as their only realistic course of action. While a basic level of financial capital is obviously also necessary for unconventional protest, social movements can often make up for what they lack in this department with what their close networks possess in terms of social capital (Diani 1997).

Another key framework for explaining new social movement activity is one based on identity politics (Cohen 1985; Hetherington 1998; Laraña et al. 1994; Melucci 1989). In terms of strategy choice, the argument here would be that the type of strategy adopted depends on whether the SMO is instrumental, counter-cultural or sub-cultural in orientation (Koopmans 1995; Kriesi et al. 1995). Taking the environment as an example, instrumental SMOs such as 'Friends of the Earth' (FoE) and Greenpeace are likely to favour whichever strategy will attain the relevant substantive goal sought (such as the non-building of a road). On occasions, this may be protest, but it is increasingly likely to consist of conventional strategies such as lobbying or court proceedings. In contrast, counter-cultural SMOs, such as 'Earth First!', are said to define their identity through confrontational interaction with opponents, while sub-cultural groups such as the Dongas Tribe[5] define their identity through within-group interaction (Doherty 1999; Kriesi et al. 1995). For these counter-cultural and sub-cultural groups, the strategy adopted (direct action) is as much an expression of identity and lifestyle as it is one of seeking an instrumental goal.

Ideas and values are also important factors influencing strategy choice (Rootes 1999a). For example, SMOs such as 'Earth First!', that draw upon anarchist ideas are unlikely to favour the use of state structures, which effectively rules out political lobbying and litigation as strategies. Ideas also influence the strategies employed by the lesbian and gay 'SMO Outrage!': although it adopts lobbying and protest strategies, it consciously avoids rights-based litigation strategies because it regards these as fostering assimilation within heterosexual norms rather than recognizing homosexual difference. Values too play a key part in group strategy. For example, not all SMOs have members who are willing to break the law or engage in violence. For those who value respect for the law and/or non-violence, some forms of protest are likely to be ruled out as a choice of strategy.

What is apparent from the mentioned alternative explanations is that PO/LO should not be seen in isolation: although POs/LOs are undoubtedly an important influence on group strategy, other factors such as those outlined earlier are also significant. Thus, no matter how favourable the PO or LO, if an SMO lacks resources, or is defined by a counter-cultural or sub-cultural identity, or driven by anarchist ideas, it is extremely unlikely to act on it via lobbying or litigation.

Political and Legal Opportunity

Political Opportunity

Political opportunity structure (POS) theories have in recent years been particularly influential in explaining the development of new social movements and their strategy choices (Kitschelt 1986; Kriesi 1995; Tarrow 1994). However, in a cogent critique of such theories, Rootes has pointed out that many include as 'structural', features that are in fact contingent (Rootes 1997, 1999a). Use of the broader notion of 'political opportunity' (PO) avoids this and is therefore preferred in this chapter. It will be used to refer first, to the structural openness or closedness of the political system, and second, to the more contingent receptivity of political élites to collective action.

In looking at openness, there is a tendency to generalize (Byrne 1997; Tarrow 1998). The UK or French political systems as a whole, for example, are often characterized as 'closed' rather than 'open'. While this is understandable in the context of cross-national studies of protest across a wide number of different policy areas (e.g., Kriesi et al. 1995; Koopmans 1996), in relation to longitudinal single county studies, it over-simplifies matters. With the latter, it is necessary not just to move down to examine the openness or closure of the political system in the policy area concerned, but also to proceed further to an examination of the precise sub-area. Thus, although one might conclude that the UK administration is relatively open to environmentalists, it does not necessarily follow that this will be true across all sub-areas of environmental policy.

But even an examination of sub-areas in terms of openness does not take one far enough. PO must be seen not just in terms of openness (in other words access to the administration), but also in terms of political receptivity to the claims being made. After all, in strategy terms, what is essentially being argued is that litigation or protest may arise from lack of success in conventional political arenas. And while access will typically be necessary for success, it is not sufficient. Political élites must also be receptive to the claims being made and willing to change policy accordingly. Hence with an area such as road-building, for example, while environmentalists in the early 1990s may have been granted access to the Department of Transport to make their case in lobbying terms, they did not meet with success because the relevant élites were unreceptive. As we shall see, alternative strategies, including litigation and protest, were thus adopted. In other words, alternative strategies may be adopted despite a favourable political opportunity structure in access or openness terms. And this is because of unfavourable political opportunity in terms of political receptivity to the claims being made.

Legal Opportunity

Most POS theories subsume law within politics. Kitschelt, for example, analyzes POS in terms of open/closed and strong/weak dichotomies — the former relating to the 'input' side of the policy process and the latter relating to a polity's capacity for policy implementation or the 'output' side. In essence, he argues that higher levels of protest can be expected in closed, strong states than in open, weak ones. One of the factors which Kitschelt claims affects strength/weakness or policy effectiveness is the relative independence and authority of the judiciary. As he notes '[p]olicy implementation becomes more hazardous and cumbersome if courts are forums of political arbitration removed from executive branch control' (Kitschelt 1986: 64). Kriesi similarly subsumes law within POS although, unlike Kitschelt, he places judicial strength on the input side as well as on the output side: in other words, a strong judiciary, in providing an alternative access point, can be seen as increasing a polity's openness just as much as it produces implementation weakness (Kriesi 1995).

Both approaches are flawed, however. First, they fall into the trap with law that was observed earlier as a danger with arguments about political access: it is difficult to generalize about judicial strength. Tesoka (1999) illustrates this difficulty when describing the strength of judicial power in the UK. On the one hand, she points to the fact that there is no constitutional review[6] and that there is an absence of a long-standing tradition of judicial control of administrative action — factors which suggest judicial weakness. But, on the other hand, she suggests that the length of Conservative rule turned the courts into arenas where battles over social policies were fought. Her attempt to explain this paradox away by distinguishing between formal judicial weakness and symbolic strength is questionable. Formal judicial strength or activism in the UK is not consistently weak: it varies over time and, as will be seen later, it also varies across policy areas.

From a lawyer's perspective, the second major weakness of the POS theories is that they fail to treat law as a separate variable. Of course, if one tries to separate legal from political opportunity, the question is then what counts as a legal strategy? Should it include participation in planning and licensing decisions, including environmental impact assessment procedures, or only if this takes place in the context of a quasi-judicial public inquiry? And should complaints to the various quasi-political Ombudsmen of the UK and the EU be classed as a legal or political strategy? The position adopted here is that only court-based litigation counts as a legal strategy.

Like political opportunity, legal opportunity consists of both structural and contingent features. On the structural side, one might include relatively stable features relating to access to justice such as laws on standing and the availability of state legal funding. The key contingent feature is judicial receptivity to policy arguments in particular cases: although one might seek to argue that the Conservative political bias of the UK judiciary is structural, political preferences in fact vary considerably — not least, as will be seen later, between different levels of court and tribunal.

The Four Movements Compared

It is only relatively recently that the literature on new social movements has begun to shift its gaze from national PO to consider the effect of transnational (both EU and international) PO on social movement mobilization (Imig and Tarrow 1999; Kriesi 1995; Marks and McAdam 1996; Reising 1998; Tarrow 1995). That such a shift in focus is necessary is borne out by the environmental, animal welfare, lesbian and gay, and women's movements: as will be seen later, the differing strategies adopted by these movements can only be understood in the context of the complex dynamic between national and EU political and legal opportunities.

The Women's Movement

Bearing in mind that opportunity must be seen in terms of both access and receptivity, one of the key reasons for the women's movement adopting a national court litigation strategy was the lack of PO at both national and EU levels. During the late 1970s and early 1980s when this legal strategy took off, the British government was not receptive to moves to broaden the Equal Pay Act 1970 or the Sex Discrimination Act 1975. And the EU at the time was experiencing its famous period of 'Eurosclerosis'. This meant that — despite the pro-women receptivity of the European Parliament and Commission — moves to persuade the Council to broaden existing EU sex discrimination legislation were similarly destined to failure because of the stifling unanimity requirement. In comparison, EU-based national LO was much more favourable (Alter and Vargas 2000; Meehan and Collins 1996). In the UK, the

Equal Opportunities Commission (EOC) was the key orchestrator of the litigation strategy (Barnard 1995). There was little problem with access to the national courts — whether through the EOC supporting individual litigants in industrial tribunals or, latterly, in terms of standing to bring judicial review proceedings in its own name.[7] And success was ensured by the propensity of industrial tribunals to make references to the European Court of Justice (ECJ) under Article 177 EC (now 267 TFEU) (Alter and Vargas 2000; Tesoka 1999). Initial ECJ cases on sex discrimination were activist in nature and tribunals could thus be reasonably sure that the Court's rulings would enable EU law to outflank national policy in the shape of the 1970 and 1975 Acts.[8] However, it was not just a matter of outflanking national policy: the creative, teleological approach to interpretation adopted by the Court enabled it at the same time to extend the scope of EU policy (Barnard 1995). As a number of commentators have noted, the Court's activism at this time can be seen as a direct counterweight to the inactivity of the EU political institutions during their Eurosclerosis period. And given that legal institutional mobilization was successful, there was little need for the women's movement to rely on unconventional strategies.

The Environmental Movement

The environmental movement in the UK was confronted by a different set of political and legal opportunities. UK PO in the early 1990s was rather mixed for the environmental movement: although there were successes in certain areas of environmental policy, development planning was not among them. Despite the presence of access at various points in the administrative process (such as participation in local planning procedures including, in significant cases, public inquiries), the fact that a pro-development Conservative government was in office meant that success proved elusive. The movement was thus driven to adopt a litigation strategy, which involved bringing judicial review proceedings before the English High Court to challenge the decisions to give the go-ahead to developments without conducting a proper environmental impact assessment (EIA) in accordance with EU law. Taking roads as an example, there are various strategies, which come in descending order of desirability. The best opportunity is a political one at the start of the policy process, preventing new roads from being built in the first place. Next comes participation in a planning-type political strategy, which, at best, is likely to offer an opportunity to achieve a change in a road's route away from a site of environmental significance. The legal strategy — EIA-based judicial review — comes very much at the bottom of the pile in terms of conventional institutional strategies, since all it is likely to achieve is a delay while the relevant parties have a second chance to conduct the EIA properly.

However, even the legal opportunity of this latter kind was poor in development planning cases. First, there were problems of formal access to the courts, with environmental groups often being denied standing to bring judicial review proceedings (Hilson and Cram 1996). Even where standing was granted, the chances of success were remote. Unlike the pro-women industrial tribunals, the English High Court was far from receptive to environmental actions. Indeed, given the social background of many of the judges and their ascendance from the planning Bar, one would expect many of them to have shared the Conservative government's pro-development bias. It is thus no surprise that, instead of using Article 177 as a 'sword', they used it as a 'shield' (Golub 1996). Far from referring cases to a pro-environment ECJ in order to outflank UK development policy, they chose to protect it by avoiding referrals and deciding the relevant points of EU law for themselves. Needless to say, their interpretations of EU law never resulted in success for environmental applicants during the period in question (Hilson 1997).

In the case of road development, this failure of legal opportunity led to a splintering of the environmental movement. The turning point was without doubt the construction of a motorway through Twyford Down, a significant piece of English countryside. With the failure of national court action in October 1990,[9] the local Twyford Down Association (TDA) proceeded to try an alternative legal strategy, by lodging a formal complaint with the Commission in November 1990 (Bryant 1996). However, the (eventual) commencement of Article 169 EC (now 258 TFEU) proceedings failed to deter the UK government, which gave instructions for work to start on the motorway in January 1992. It was not long after that protesters were mobilized to take direct action. While this initially involved rather tame protest by members of FoE and the TDA, these groups were soon joined by more radical elements, such as

'Earth First!', and the 'Dongas Tribe', who added more interventionist tactics to the repertoire of contention. It was the perception of the latter groups that the institutionalized wing — in the shape of Greenpeace and FoE — were overly committed to conventional channels and had failed the movement at Twyford Down (Bryant 1996; Byrne 1997; Doherty 1999). This perception may have been misplaced, in that while committed in principle to direct action, the threat of litigation to sequester their assets dissuaded them in practice (Rootes 1999b). Nevertheless, a direct action, anti-roads, sub-movement was arguably born as a result.

Not that Twyford Down saw the end of litigation as a strategy in anti-roads campaigning. Just as direct action at Twyford Down was starting in January 1992, Greenpeace and others brought a High Court challenge of land exchange certificates concerning the proposed East London River Crossing — the approach roads to which would have passed through Oxleas Wood.[10] And in June 1996, FoE and others sought leave for a judicial review of the Secretary of State's decision to continue with the construction of the Newbury bypass while he was at the same time consulting on the designation, under the Habitats Directive, of a Special Area of Conservation to protect a rare snail which was found in the road's path.[11] In so far as these legal actions both failed, the cases resemble Twyford Down. However, the difference is that by this stage the direct action genie was out of the bottle. Twyford Down and other failed development planning-related court cases had cast a shadow on law's ability to deliver, and it subsequently found itself marginalized in comparison with its more potent direct action cousin. The fact that the road through Oxleas Wood was abandoned by the government in 1993 was widely reported as due to a desire to avoid another round of powerful Twyford Down style activism (Doherty 1999).[12] And the legal action in the Newbury case came some time after preferred direct action had been tried and failed in the early part of 1996.

While national political and legal opportunities were poor for the environmental movement, EU PO (Marks and McAdam 1996) was generally good. Access was relatively easy: as numerous studies have pointed out, the environmental movement was among the first to make the most of lobbying opportunities in Brussels. And a degree of success was often assured: the Commission and the Parliament were very pro-environment, and the use of qualified majority voting after the Single European Act (SEA) for environment legislation which could be tied to a single market goal[13] meant that even the Council posed few problems for the passage of environmentalist legislation. Thus, unlike the women's movement, there was simply no need for the environmental movement to rely on a litigation strategy to make up for poor EU PO.

The Animal Welfare Movement

For the animal welfare movement in the mid-1990s, PO was limited, both domestically and at EU level. Domestically, the close links of a Conservative government to farming interests meant that lobbying for expensive animal welfare measures was unlikely to be favourably received. At EU level, there were two problems confronting the movement. First, animal welfare has typically been — if not a uniquely British concern — then certainly a North European one. Unlike the more universal issues surrounding the position of women and the environment therefore, the policy receptivity of the EU institutions was lacking. Second, it has been suggested that the style of lobbying by the animal welfare movement failed to fit in with established ways of doing business at EU level. Kohler-Koch, for example, states that:

> In the mid-90s animal welfare got a very poor reputation among MEPs because their style of lobbying was considered to be 'nerve wrecking' as one Parliamentarian put it. Sending thousands of letters to the EP and monitoring closely voting behaviour was not the kind of 'friendly relation' MEPs would like to entertain with interest groups. Therefore, it is no surprise that key persons in the Commission and the EP rather deal with representatives of the ecological movement, consumer protection, etc. that are socialized to the unwritten code of conduct (sic.) (1997: 7).

Given this closure of PO, it is thus not surprising that the movement turned to alternative strategies. The focus of the campaign in the mid-1990s was the issue of live animal exports, which the movement was seeking to have banned. After successful commercial pressure, two of the principal ferry companies involved in the export trade decided to abandon the shipment of live animals in October 1994. However, animal exporters responded by chartering their own ships and aircraft from various minor seaports and airports. As McLeod (1998) notes, ironically, this produced an intensification of the campaign, with mass protests taking place at many of these departure points from January 1995 onwards.

On this occasion, as with the Newbury roads case, protest came before legal action. And, in fact, the first round of litigation was instituted not by the animal welfare movement (although CIWF was allowed to intervene), but by its adversaries and a local authority in response to the protest activity. Early in 1995, a number of exporters sought judicial review of the decisions of various public authorities which had sought to close down animal exports from their areas because of the disruption being caused by the protesters.[14] And Plymouth City Council — worried about the diversion of police resources — brought a challenge against its own harbour authority for not having closed down the trade.[15] The fact that the judicial review applications by the exporters were successful and the local authority's unsuccessful meant that what the judge disparagingly referred to as 'mob rule' had failed to secure the objective of closing down the various outlets for live animal exports.[16]

Legal action initiated by the animal welfare movement itself came sometime after the main wave of protesting which occurred in the early part of 1995. It was not until the summer of that year that CIWF and the Royal Society for the Prevention of Cruelty to Animals (RSPCA) brought judicial review proceedings against the Minister of Agriculture, Fisheries, and Food, challenging his refusal to restrict the export of veal calves to other member states.[17] And in December 1995, another animal welfare group — the Protesters' Animal Information Network (PAIN) — launched a judicial review action challenging the Minister's failure to take sufficient action to prevent the shipment of live animals in rough seas.[18] For PAIN, legal action was taken, as its website[19] states:

> Out of the belief that conventional protesting had taken us as far as it could and the realization that live animal exports would never stop through the courtesy of government. It made sense, therefore, that protesters from all over the country should join together and create one large and determined vendetta against this unforgivable trade. The only way to do this properly and permanently is through the High Courts, where our gathered strength and new-found power — combined with our limitless information and proof of unbelievable cruelty — can strike at the heart of it all.

PAIN's position is in marked contrast to CIWF's. In interview, CIWF's political and legal director stated that legal action, political lobbying and protest were seen by the organization as complements in an overall campaigning package. There was no sense in which, for CIWF, legal action was taken as a result of the perceived failure of politics and protest. Indeed, legal action might well have been started earlier had the organization not been busy intervening in the cases brought by the exporters and Plymouth City Council; and of course had they started legal action earlier, protest would not have been going on for long enough to be said to have failed.

The Lesbian and Gay Movement

One of the key issues for the lesbian and gay movement in the 1990s was treatment of homosexuals in the workplace, including the armed forces. Domestic PO during Conservative rule was non-existent. A government that introduced Section 28 of the Local Government Act 1988 and consistently refused to lower the age of consent could hardly be described as receptive to gay issues. And domestic legal opportunity was uncharted water. On its face, existing legislation applied only to sex discrimination and not to discrimination on the grounds of sexual orientation and thus it seemed that no 'gay rights' existed in domestic law.

EU PO was no more promising. The lesbian and gay movement came rather late to EU lobbying, with the International Lesbian and Gay Association only starting such activity in 1990 (Bell and Waddington 1996). But even then, receptivity varied among the various political institutions. As Bell and Waddington (1996) point out, the European Parliament was invariably the most receptive to gay issues. The Commission, while seemingly in favour of EU action in the area, adopted a more pragmatic line, seeing little point in proceeding because any proposals on the subject would not meet with Council approval (Bell and Waddington 1996) The reasons for poor PO in the Council are not difficult to discern. As with animal welfare, policy on homosexuality is far from universal across the various member states of the EU. In Kofman's terms, '[t]he Community [EU] has refrained from intervening in what are seen as controversial matters of sexuality and gender relations, often associated with national identity and specificity' (1995: 132).

Given that domestic and EU POs were closed and given the apparent closure of domestic LO stemming from the lack of any substantive domestic gay rights, it is not surprising that the lesbian and gay movement turned to domestic-based EU legal strategies. The catalyst for such a strategy was the *P v. S* case.[20] That case involved a transgendered person who was dismissed on grounds of her gender re-assignment. P subsequently brought a discrimination case before an English industrial tribunal, arguing that her rights under EC sex discrimination law had been breached. The tribunal referred the case to the ECJ under Article 267, which ruled that discrimination on grounds of gender re-assignment amounted to sex discrimination under the Equal Treatment Directive. The case thus appeared to open up EU LO for the lesbian and gay movement: as with the women's movement a decade earlier, here was a decision by an activist ECJ which offered the prospect of outflanking restrictive national and EU policy on discrimination against lesbians and gays. However, hopes were dashed by the ECJ ruling in *Grant v. South-West Trains,* where it was held that EU sex discrimination laws did not extend to discrimination on the grounds of sexual orientation.[21] Given the closure of political and legal opportunity during this period, it is not surprising that the lesbian and gay movement also adopted protest activity in response to unfavourable treatment of homosexuals in the workplace. 'Outrage!' for example — in action far removed from the conventional type supported by groups such as Stonewall (which had backed the *Grant* case) — occupied a Cambridge postal sorting office and the Post Office's national headquarters in response to the harassment being suffered by a gay postal worker.[22]

The Key Arguments Reconsidered

The key arguments made at the beginning were that a lack of political opportunity may influence the adoption of litigation as a strategy in place of lobbying, and that the choice of protest as a strategy may be influenced by poor political and legal opportunities. It is now appropriate to reconsider these arguments in the light of the discussed empirical examples. Both arguments appear to be supported by the examples. In all the examples, domestic PO was poor (not surprising given that the SMO-unreceptive Conservatives were in power) and in all but the environmental movement, EU PO was equally restricted. Litigation strategies were therefore utilized by all the movements under consideration as a means of attempting to outflank one or both levels of restricted PO. Similarly, in the three empirical examples where political and legal opportunities were poor, the movements adopted varying degrees of direct action. Only in the remaining case of the women's movement — where legal opportunity was favourable — was direct action notably absent. One might of course be tempted to conclude that this is because it is more difficult to mobilize protesters around a personal interest case such as employment than it is for public interest cases such as animal welfare and the environment. However, that does not explain why there is at least one example (the Post Office harassment action) where the lesbian and gay movement successfully mobilized protest in a private interest case.

Nevertheless, one should not conclude from these arguments that strategy choice follows a particular temporal or preference-based logic. In other words, movements do not automatically move on a sort of conveyor belt from political strategies to litigation to protest. Certain examples appear to follow a temporal logic (such as Twyford Down), but in a number of others (such as animal welfare), protest precedes rather than follows legal action. Nor do groups necessarily place lobbying, litigation and protest in that order of preference. First, the animal welfare example suggests that some groups regard the various strategies as equally important means for effecting policy change. But, in addition, there are obviously some groups for whom protest will always be the favoured option.

What this points to is the crucial need to distinguish between movements as a whole, and particular groups within the various movements. Thus, the strategies adopted by conventional groups within a movement may well be influenced by prevailing political and legal opportunities. The examples suggest that they (and hence, in a sense, the movement as a whole) do indeed try litigation if the political opportunities presented by lobbying are poor, and that they may adopt protest where PO and LO are unfavourable. However, as was argued earlier in the chapter, unconventional groups such as 'Earth First!' will invariably eschew lobbying and litigation strategies whatever the opportunities. This is in part due to its anarchist-inspired ideas and in part due to the counter-cultural, identity-based nature of protest as its chosen strategy. Similarly, whatever the legal opportunities, an organization like 'Outrage!' is never likely to choose litigation as a strategy because of its critical stance on liberal rights. PO and LO, in other words, can only ever be part of the equation in explaining group strategies. Other factors such as resources, identity, ideas and values also play an important role.

A European Protest Strategy?

What is clear from much of the preceding analysis is that movements have become increasingly adept at using European strategies. For some movements, conventional EU lobbying strategies have been used to further EU policy and to outflank national policy choices. For others, EU law-based litigation strategies have been used to achieve similar results. It should come as no surprise, then, that protest can be analyzed in similar terms. In the period under consideration here, although most protest involved action at domestic level by domestic actors rather than pan-European protest by transnational social movements, much of this domestic protest was European in nature (Imig and Tarrow 1999; Reising 1998; Tarrow 1995). In the case of live animal exports, for example, protest — though located domestically in both spatial and organizational terms — was arguably directed at both domestic and EU targets. Thus, just as a domestically played Euro-law game is capable of outflanking restricted domestic and EU policy, so protesters may hope that their domestic protest will lead to a shift in public policy at both domestic and EU levels.

Conclusion

It is clear from the empirical examples in this chapter that civic exclusion from both political and legal opportunity may be an important factor in explaining protest as a strategy. The EU has in recent years made increasing moves to integrate new social movement actors into the policy process, including those previously excluded such as the lesbian and gay and animal welfare movements. Both movements have won significant concessions in recent years — in the case of the gay movement, the clearest example being the introduction of Article 19 TFEU by the Treaty of Amsterdam, allowing for the introduction of legislation to combat discrimination based on sexual orientation. In the UK, the election of a Labour government in 1997 also created greater PO for many movements. As a result of this broadening of PO, one might expect litigation and protest levels to have decreased. However, this broadening was far from across the board in scope. There remained important policy areas, such as GM crops, where PO was poor. It therefore comes as no surprise that both litigation[23] and protest were used as strategies in that area.

Of course, that is not to say that all protest can be explained by exclusion from the system of governance. On the one hand, inclusion may not prevent protest. Anti-capitalism protests such as May Day in London in 2000 and 2001, Prague in September 2000, and Gothenburg and Genoa in the summer of 2001 are cases in point. While some elements at these protests undoubtedly had a clear policy target, many either lacked any such target or were seeking one which was never likely to be granted (the overthrow of global capitalism). In both of the latter instances, it is difficult to see how any form of inclusion would have prevented protest. And, on the other hand, many groups are excluded from the system, but not all adopt protest as a strategy. To explain this, one has to factor in other variables such as resources, identity, ideas and values. However, while not all protest stems from exclusion, and while exclusion does not always produce protest, the main empirical examples presented in the chapter suggest that exclusion is an important factor in explaining some of the protest activity that does occur.

Notes

* This chapter was earlier published in *Journal of European Public Policy*, 9(2): 238–55, 2002. Reproduced with permission of the publisher (Taylor & Francis Ltd, http://www.tandf.co.uk/journals). Research for this chapter was funded by the ESRC as part of the project 'Strategies of Civic Inclusion in Pan-European Civil Society' (L213 25 2022) under its 'One Europe or Several?' programme. I am grateful to Alex Warleigh, other project members and the two anonymous *JEPP* referees for their comments.

1. This term will be used to refer to all sections of the movement concerned with the welfare and rights of domesticated and farm animals (although there are of course significant differences in strategy and philosophy between animal welfarists and animal rights activists).
2. Such as 'Earth First!' and 'Reclaim the Streets' in the case of the environmental movement and the Animal Liberation Front in the case of animal rights. All of these are highly decentralized and lack any formal structure.

3. Those which tend to adopt more conventional tactics are often referred to as 'interest groups', in contrast with the typically unconventional tactics employed by the 'new social movement organizations'. However, where does that place organizations such as Greenpeace that uses both sets of tactics? Given its institutionalized and professionalized nature and the fact that it increasingly uses conventional tactics, many would label it as an interest group (cf. Byrne 1997). Since the focus of the present chapter is on strategies rather than on organizations or groups, the distinction is not crucial. The term 'new social movement organizations' (SMOs) will thus be used to refer to *all* organizations within a particular social movement — whatever form their tactics take and however institutionalized they may be. For a fuller discussion of the alleged distinction between interest groups and SMOs, see Jordan and Maloney (1997).
4. Thus distinguishing them from ordinary street demonstrations, which are not specifically intended to disrupt a particular form of activity.
5. One of the key groups in the road protest at Twyford Down, discussed later.
6. Though this of course changed with the entry into force of the Human Rights Act 1998.
7. *R* v. *Secretary of State for Employment, ex parte* EOC [1995] 1 AC 1.
8. On 'outflanking', see Rawlings (1993).
9. *Twyford Parish Council* v. *Secretary of State for Transport* (1992) 4 *JEL* 273.
10. (1992) 2 *LMELR* 48; *London Borough of Greenwich and Others* v. *The Secretary of State for the Environment and the Secretary of State for Transport* [1993] Env LR 344.
11. *R* v. *Secretary of State for Transport and Secretary of State for the Environment, ex parte Berkshire, Buckinghamshire and Oxfordshire Naturalists' Trust and Others* [1997] Env LR 80.
12. The danger was real: to avoid the divisions which had taken place over Twyford Down, a number of environmental groups including FoE, WWF and 'Earth First!' formed the Oxleas Alliance to plan for direct action to protect Oxleas Wood.
13. Although the environment Article 130S (now 192 TFEU) still required unanimity post-SEA, the *Titanium Dioxide* case (Case 300/89 *Commission* v. *Council* [1991] ECR I-2867) essentially legitimized the existing practice of attempting to squeeze most environmental legislation into Article 100A (now 114 TFEU), which required only qualified majority voting.
14. *R* v. *Coventry CC, ex parte Phoenix Aviation and other applications* [1995] 3 All ER 37.
15. Ibid.

16. That is not to say that the exporters had everything going their way. A judicial review application brought in 1995 by another exporter against the Chief Constable Sussex for reducing policing to two days a week was unsuccessful (*R* v. *Chief Constable of Sussex, ex parte International Trader's Ferry* [1999] 1 CMLR 1320).
17. Case C-1/96 *R* v. *MAFF, ex parte CIWF* [1998] 2 CMLR 661. The RSPCA ceased to be a party in 1997 when the reference to the ECJ was made.
18. *R* v. *MAFF, ex parte PAIN* (1997) *Current Law* 238.
19. http://www.pain.org.uk/about.htm (accessed 3 October 2013).
20. Case C-13/94 *P* v. *S and Cornwall* CC [1996] ECR I-2143.
21. Case C-249/96 [1998] 1 CMLR 993. See also *R* v. *Secretary of State for Defence, ex parte Perkins* [1998] 2 CMLR 1116.
22. http://www.outrage.cygnet.co.uk/aboutus.htm (accessed 3 October 2013).
23. For example, *R* v. *Secretary of State for Environment and MAFF, ex parte Watson* [1999] Env LR 310.

References

Alter, Karen and Jeannette Vargas. 2000. 'Explaining Variation in the Use of European Litigation Strategies: European Community Law and British Gender Equality Policy', *Comparative Political Studies*, 33: 452–82.

Barnard, Catherine. 1995. 'A European Litigation Strategy: The Case of the Equal Opportunities Commission', in Jo Shaw and Gillian More (eds), *New Legal Dynamics of European Union*. Oxford: Clarendon Press.

Bell, Mark and Lisa Waddington. 1996. 'The 1996 Intergovernmental Conference and the Prospects of a Non-discrimination Treaty Article', *Industrial Law Journal*, 25: 320–36.

Bryant, Barbara. 1996. *Twyford Down: Roads, Campaigning and Environmental Law*. London: E. & F. N. Spon.

Byrne, Paul. 1997. *Social Movements in Britain*. London: Routledge.

Cohen, Jean. 1985. 'Strategy or Identity: New Theoretical Paradigms and Contemporary Social Movements', *Social Research*, 52: 663–716.

Diani, Mario. 1997. 'Social Movements and Social Capital: A Network Perspective on Movement Outcomes', *Mobilization*, 2: 129–47.

Doherty, Brian. 1999. 'Paving the Way: The Rise of Direct Action against Road-building and the Changing Character of British Environmentalism', *Political Studies*, 47: 275–91.

Golub, Jonathan. 1996. 'The Politics of Judicial Discretion: Rethinking the Interaction between National Courts and the European Court of Justice', *West European Politics*, 19: 360–85.

Harlow, Carol and Richard Rawlings. 1992. *Pressure through Law*. London: Routledge.

Hetherington, Kevin. 1998. *Expressions of Identity: Space, Performance Politics*. London: Sage Publications.

Hilson, C. 1997. 'Community Rights in Environmental Law: Rhetoric or Reality?', in Jane Holder (ed.), *The Impact of EC Environmental Law in the United Kingdom*. Chichester: John Wiley & Sons.

Hilson, C. and Ian Cram. 1996. 'Judicial Review and Environmental Law — Is There a Coherent View of Standing?', *Legal Studies*, 16: 1–26.

Imig, Doug and Sidney Tarrow. 1999. 'The Europeanization of Movements? A New Approach to Transnational Contention', in Donatella Della Porta et al. (eds), *Social Movements in a Globalizing World*. Basingstoke: Macmillan.

Jordan, Grant and William Maloney. 1997. *The Protest Business? Mobilizing Campaign Groups*. Manchester: Manchester University Press.

Kitschelt, Herbert. 1986. 'Political Opportunity Structures and Political Protest: Anti-nuclear Movements in Four Democracies', *British Journal of Political Science*, 16: 57–85.

Kofman, Eleonore. 1995. 'Citizenship for some but not for others: Spaces of Citizenship in Contemporary Europe', *Political Geography*, 14: 121–37.

Kohler-Koch, Beate. 1997. 'Organized Interests in the EC and the European Parliament', European Integration Online Papers, 1(9), available at http://eiop.or.at/eiop/texte/1997-009.htm (accessed 14 October 2013).

Koopmans, Ruud. 1995. *Democracy from Below: New Social Movements and the Political System in West Germany*. Boulder, CO: Westview Press.

———. 1996. 'New Social Movements and Changes in Political Participation in Western Europe', *West European Politics*, 19: 28–50.

Kriesi, Hanspeter. 1995. 'The Political Opportunity Structure of New Social Movements: Its Impact on their Mobilization', in J. Craig Jenkins and Bert Klandermans (eds), *The Politics of Social Protest*. Minneapolis: University of Minnesota Press.

Kriesi, Hanspeter, et al. (eds). 1995. 'New Social Movements in Western Europe: A Comparative Analysis'. London: UCL Press.

Larana, Enrique et al. (eds). 1994. 'New Social Movements: From Ideology to Identity'. Philadelphia: Temple University Press.

McCarthy, John and Mayer Zald. 1977. 'Resource Mobilization and Social Movements: A Partial Theory', *American Journal of Sociology*, 82: 1212–41.

McLeod, Rhoda. 1998. 'Calf Exports at Brightlingsea', *Parliamentary Affairs*, 51: 345–57.

Marks, Gary and Doug McAdam. 1996. 'Social Movements and the Changing Structure of Political Opportunity in the European Union', *West European Politics*, 19: 249–78.

Mazey, Sonia and Jeremy Richardson (eds). 1993. *Lobbying in the European Community*. Oxford: Oxford University Press.

Meehan, Elizabeth and Evelyn Collins. 1996. 'Women, the European Union and Britain', *Parliamentary Affairs*, 49: 221–34.

Melucci, Alberto. 1989. *Nomads of the Present: Social Movements and Individual Needs in Contemporary Society*. London: Hutchinson Radius.

Piven, Frances Fox and Richard Cloward. 1995. 'Collective Protest: A Critique of Resource Mobilization Theory', in Stanford Lyman (ed.), *Social Movements: Critiques, Concepts, Case Studies*. Basingstoke: Macmillan.

Rawlings, Richard. 1993. 'The Eurolaw Game: Some Deductions from a Saga', *Journal of Law and Society*, 20: 309–40.

Reising, Uwe. 1998. 'Domestic and Supranational Political Opportunities: European Protest in Selected Countries 1980–1995', European Integration Online Papers, 2(5), available at http://eiop.or.at/eiop/texte/1998-005.htm (accessed 14 October 2013).

Rootes, Chris. 1997. 'Shaping Collective Action: Structure, Contingency and Knowledge', in Rica Edmondson (ed.), *The Political Context of Collective Action: Power Argumentation and Democracy*. London: Routledge.

———. 1999a. 'Political Opportunity Structures: Promise, Problems and Prospects', *La Lettre de la Maison Française d'Oxford*, 10: 75–97.

———. 1999b. 'The Transformation of Environmental Activism: Activists, Organizations and Policy-making', *Innovation: The European Journal of Social Sciences*, 12: 153–73.

Tarrow, Sidney. 1994. *Power in Movement: Social Movements, Collective Action and Politics*. Cambridge: Cambridge University Press.

———. 1995. 'The Europeanization of Conflict: Reflections from a Social Movement Perspective', *West European Politics*, 18: 223–51.

———. 1998. *Power in Movement: Social Movements and Contentious Politics* (2nd edn). Cambridge: Cambridge University Press.

Tesoka, Sabrina. 1999. 'Judicial Politics in the European Union: Its Impact on National Opportunity Structures for Gender Equality', MPIfG Discussion Paper, 99/2. Koln: Max-Planck-Institut fur Gesellschaftsforschung.

Warleigh, Alex. 2000. 'The Hustle: Citizenship Practice, NGOs and "Policy Coalitions" in the European Union — The Cases of Auto Oil, Drinking Water and Unit Pricing', *Journal of European Public Policy*, 7: 229–43.

14

Language of Political Socialization

Language of Resistance

*Janette Habashi**

This chapter argues that the social-political circumstances of life constitute the current language usage of Palestinian children. However, the local meaning and usage of children's language is not an isolated interaction. The local language is a direct result of the dialectic relationship between global and local political discourse. Language discourse follows political power. Global contested power is in every local issue even when a locality is in a remote area. The boundaries of global discourse are undefined; it is elastic and is defused in every local act, whereby locals, including the children must amend to such global/local contests. Therefore, locals' responses are extensively fluid and contingent on the global discourse, and yet local forces are unequal to global ones (Katz 2004). This framework of understanding the relationship between global and local issues explicitly intersects with Fairclough's approach (2001) to language usage and power. Language usage and presentation should not be perceived as merely a medium of communication and expression, but instead be understood as a power structure deployed in social policy and used in shaping the power structure of the new world order. According to Fairclough, language is a power discourse and extensively intersects and renders the meaning of local and global policies and ideologies. Language as power discourse constitutes ideology and policy; thereby the contested usage of language encompasses language meaning. The debates over language as power are observed in social and political domains of language meaning (Gould 2005). The language meaning, whether it is governed by state ideology or collective experience, employs the tension over the power struggle between global and local discourse (Fairclough 2001). The meaning of language explicitly reflects elements of global/local power discourse; additionally it embraces implicit meaning that is ingrained in political structure (Gould 2005).

Falah (2004) illustrated how language as a word-labelling activity employed in the Israeli state power discourse, diluted both perception and reality and thereby established a state of control that the Palestinians (the locals) are conditioned to respond to and struggle against. Furthermore, Forman and Kedar (2004) provided examples in which language as a social and political fabric altered the meaning of land acquisition from the Palestinian people by the Israeli government; effortlessly the Palestinian land claims were subrogated by the language of Israeli legislation. Such legislation turned a 'land-grab' into a legal transfer of real property without the consent of the original owners. Such is the nature of the language power discourse. Language as power discourse is not unique to one incident in the case of the Palestinians. Falah (2004) further illustrated several language usages that eventually benefited Israeli policies. For example the term 'fled' rather than 'expelled' was used by the Israeli government as a word of choice to describe the Palestinian people's experience in 1948 during the Al-Nakba. Some Israeli commentators argued that Palestinians fled as a reaction to the Arab leaders call and challenged the claim that Palestinians were actually expelled in 1948. Choosing the word fled complied with the Israeli state ideology that refused to acknowledge and take responsibility for such coercive action. The power discourse of language according to Fairclough (2001) is transparent in its political ideology and state practices and policies. This perimeter of language power not only alters contemporary reality but also the historical memories where language adds new political meaning to historical events thereby erasing or modifying historical facts (Whitelam 1996; Said 2000). The exercise of language power discourse is further noted in the continuation of language usage as a conscious public policy, as evident in the term 'occupied Palestine' (Falah 2004). Using this occupied Palestine label, the Israeli government succeeded in taming the reality of Palestinian humiliation; the use of this term failed to convey the actual experience of the Palestinian people's degradation and land confiscation. Thus, for Falah, the 'occupied land' phrase denies the Palestinians any real language by which to express their own truth. It would seem that the language of power discourse dictates truth, while simultaneously suppressing all of other voices. Therefore the control of language labelling defines the debate, dictates meaning and imposes consequences. In this context, it denies voices for locals, adding further struggles within the existing oppression.

Socio-political policies intertwined with language meaning added political nuances to reality. Language in this framework is power as well as a tool of power that echoes ideology across time, whereby global and local discourses consistently compete over word meanings as a parallel to the contests of ideologies. The struggle is not exclusive to adults. Children are part of the social-political fabric and are constantly responding to and immersed in the power struggle of language. The challenge here is to illustrate the complexity of such language power discourse as it relates to Palestinian children living in war-like situations and how children's rendering of language meaning is a tool of response to the global ideology and policy. To understand the interdependence of multiple issues for this research, the chapter is divided into four sections: first, a literature review on contemporary views of children's responses to global power discourse; second, a section outlining the different forms of Palestinian children's political resistance, reworking and resilience; third, an explanation of methodology, including participants, context of the study, data analysis, and emerging themes; and the fourth and final section is the conclusion.

Children's Response to Global Power Discourse

Katz's study (2004) illustrated how locals, including children, are pragmatic in their answer to global hegemony and they are innovative in producing and reproducing themselves as needed to counter global discourses. Individuals living in oppressive circumstances produced themselves through resilience, reworking and resistance so as to fight the global power. Some acts, such as resilience, could be observed as an opposition to resistance or one of reworking the system, yet in some instances the act of resilience could be an act of resistance; one is not necessarily a separate entity from the other. Reworking is the ability to respond pragmatically within local resources to global hegemony. These three segments of locals reproducing themselves are a sign of persistent efforts to tackle the global power discourse. These nuances served as insight into the understanding of local processes as well as children's responses to language as power discourse. In addition, these segments would facilitate the understanding over the contested meaning of language in children's own local realities. According to Katz (2004), contesting the global power is no different for children when compared to adults; children participate and engage in power discourse within their localities and the boundaries between being an adult or a child are not precisely defined in the observation of local/global power struggles. The child's language role in this complicated equation of power discourse is illustrated by Bhatia (2000), who shows that the child takes an active role in the social-political processes and in understanding the emerging meaning of the larger society. The meaning of the social group is the result of the non-linear approach of global language and the child's active role in language construction that is deeply intertwined in the local/global discourse. Soto (1997) also affirmed that children's responses to the contested power language as it is filtered and reconstructed within their views of contemporary socio-political circumstances, is a result of the global/local power discourse. The representation of global language disputes is not concerned with the labelling of words only, but also the words that constitute particular meanings as locals create their own meanings. Labov (2001) concluded that the creation of local language responses and language meanings serve as community speech whereby it functions not only as a shared way of talking but also as a survival tool for the community. In this context, community speech serves as a tool to respond to the global power discourse. The juxtaposition is not implicit in language as power, a tool of resilience, reworking or resistance, but in understanding the complexity of assumed meanings while children conveyed the debate of the power discourse of language meaning; in return local language and meaning became tools for survival. This provides inclusive nuances to community speech as an act of disagreement over language meaning and labelling. Local language shed light on community speech and the social-political circumstances of Palestinian children's lives; in the meantime it allows us to comprehend the tension in language expressions. This chapter discusses the language of Palestinian children that seemingly encompassed religious language connotations, but differed substantially in meaning from its original religious script. Therefore, examination of the political language of Palestinian children requires clarification of language as a tool to respond to global hegemony in relation to the construction of meaning. The challenge here is to illustrate the complexity of such language meaning for Palestinian children living in a war-like situation. Palestinian children are constantly responding to global power, however, for the benefit of this research, the chapter will focus on the two Intifada periods.

Forms of Palestinian Children's Political Resistance, Reworking and Resilience

Palestinian children have continually been a part of the Palestinian struggle against Israeli occupation. For several decades, the Palestinian people continued to be under occupation; however, there were many attempted revolts. The most contemporary uprisings are the first and the second Intifada. The first Intifada began in 1987 and lasted until the year 1993 (Finkelstein 1990). The second Intifada started in 2000 and ended in 2005. The purpose of the two Intifadas was to end Israeli occupation; however, the first one resulted in the negotiation of a peace process, not necessarily in a peace settlement. In 1993, both Palestinian and Israeli leaderships signed the Oslo Accord, ensuring the foundation of a two-state solution — Palestine and Israel. The Palestinian authorities from the Diaspora entered the territories and took on an administrative role, ending Israeli governance. However, the existence of the Palestinian Authority (PA) did not ensure freedom nor did it establish a Palestinian state. Israel continued to control Palestinian land and resources while Israeli oppression persisted against the Palestinians (Cook et al. 2004). The Israel persecution included killings, imprisonments, destruction of crops, confiscation of Palestinian land, and the building of more settlements in the West Bank. As the oppression became increasingly more intense, it led to the second uprising, Alaqsa Intifada in 2000 (Kimmerling and Migdal 2003). Within these political developments Palestinian children became part of the political fabric.

Brian (2001) evaluated the impact of Intifada on the wellbeing of Palestinian youth and children from the ecological perspective, one that does not focus primarily on one aspect but also on children's integration into social and political life in the community. He revealed that the Intifada configured social and political realities for Palestinian youth that are immensely integrated into the regional social-political discourse. The integration is not directed at only one dimension in the lives of children and youth, but is ingrained in their daily activities, for example,

> substantial proportions of young people were involved in demonstrations against the occupation (male children 80%, male adolescents 85%, female 50%, female adolescents 65%), and were harassed by opposition soldiers (male children 68%, male adolescents 86%, female children 34%, female adolescents 48%) (Brian 2001: 260).

Palestinian children engaged in resistance and harassment, yet they exercised resilience. According to Kanaana (1990) resilience was manifested in other forms in the Intifada such as humour. Specific humour elements became ingrained within the political reality of the Palestinians. Some popular jokes portrayed youth's reactions to the oppression. Jokes stood in stark contrast to reality but served to facilitate resilience; 'resilient acts are self-reinforcing, and inasmuch as they are fortifying; they offer the possibility of fostering something beyond recuperation' (Katz 2004: 246).

Another example that served as an act of resistance, reworking and resilience is graffiti-writing. Oliver and Steinberg (2005) described that most of the graffiti was done by Palestinian youth and such performances were acts of defiance against the Israel occupation that 'suggested the sense of community and assertiveness of a leadership bound by the common political experience and language' (Peteet 1996: 146). Graffiti functioned as a resistant act as well as an affirmation of the Palestinian identity and also as a reworking project. Katz identified reworking projects as those that are 'driven by explicit recognition of problematic conditions and offer focused often pragmatic, responses to them' (Katz 2004: 247). The reworking of the graffiti was not only an adamant response to the Israeli practice of constantly erasing these works of art, in spite of the Palestinians pragmatic rewriting of the same, but it also succeeded at creating a rift among the Israeli army. 'Some soldiers read them as defiance to be met with violent response. For others their presence and content reaffirmed the sense that it was time to withdraw from the territories' (Peteet 1996: 152).

The sheer ubiquity of resistance, resilience and reworking of the system was also observed in theatre and music. Massad (2003) analyzed the songs in which lyrics served to maintain the collective experience and motivate individuals to resist Israeli occupation; it was a pragmatic way to utilize the entertainment avenue for the Palestinian cause. Some of the lyrics described the Palestinian child's experience under the Israeli oppression. This message also extended to the theatre where plays narrated the journey of the Palestinian people (Nassar 2006). Though by definition theatre is a space of self-expression, in this case it was utilized to intersect resistance, resilience and reworking in the narratives of the locals including the children. In many instances local theatres were targeted by the Israeli Army and were forced to shut down. Recognition of the multiple responses of Palestinians to the Israeli occupation facilitated an understanding of the political stance on language meaning. Therefore, as the data revealed, language comprehension of the global discourse is not merely a domain of communication, but an act of resistance, resilience and reworking the system for the Palestinian children.

Methodology

Participants and the Context of the Study

Data collection developed from the interviews of 12 Palestinian children, conducted during the fall of 2001. The participants ranged from 10 to 13 years old. Four children were interviewed from each of the three different geographical areas: cities, refugee camps and villages in the West Bank and East Jerusalem. All of them were enrolled in school systems in their particular areas and all considered themselves academically competent. The study was divided equally across gender: two males and two females from each area. Each participant was interviewed twice. The recruitment for the interviewees was random and dependent upon the areas. The interview settings varied. In refugee camps, I met with interviewees on the street, in schools and refugee centres. In the city, I met the participants in cultural centres. In the villages, interviews took place in school settings and on the streets.

The overarching questions presented to the interviewees were: Define a Palestinian person. Where did you learn about Palestine? What are the political problems of Palestine? Why are the Palestinians fighting? What do you think about the current political situation and the future? How are the Palestinians fighting? Who are the

Palestinians fighting? Do you think Palestine will have a civil war? All the interviewees were contacted during the second uprising (Intifada) in the occupied territories in the West Bank and East Jerusalem.

Transcription

The interviews were recorded and conducted in Arabic. The interview tapes were transcribed to Arabic and then into English. At this stage, an independent bilingual person served as a reviewer. Another bilingual person was summoned to facilitate in the process where the cultural translation was often considered to be more significant than the literal translation. In most instances, the researchers opted for cultural translation over literal translation in an effort to maintain the integrity of the interviews.

Data Analysis and Emerging Themes

The interview questions were based on an open-ended structure. Interviewees produced thick, rich data that enhanced the understanding of the research statement. The grounded theory method guided the development of the study and data analysis. The purpose of grounded theory is to study social phenomena through the identification of patterns and relationships; coding facilitates such a process. Cross-members checking served to verify the analysis, by utilizing the comparison of coding between data across different interviewees and within the data produced by each interviewee. This element is the foundation of analysis progression. The coding was previewed by independent scholars who double-checked categories and subcategories, after which two core categories were identified, in this case the naming of resistance, and forms of resistance. The two categories intersected in children's responses to resistance, resilience and reworking of the system in language meaning of the local/global discourses. The participants' articulations facilitated the procedure and naming of the themes, as the emerging themes must be generated by the data (Creswell 2003; Glaser 2002). Naming of themes maintained the integrity of the themes while assisting in defining concepts according to participants.

Theme One: Naming of Resistance

The naming of resistance conveyed the response to global discourse that is infused in secular and religious meanings of language.

Responses to language generally vary according to global ideology and children are engaged in this process (Bhatia 2000). This global/local language approach intersects with language as children emerge in the culture (Harvey 2003), in that it contributes to the community speech (Labov 2001). Hence, participants in this study engaged in language meaning not only from the impact of local/global discourse and its relationship to cultural competency, but also from the understanding of the Arabic language structure. This was especially evident in their efforts to define the word 'jihad'. One 12-year-old female from a Balata Refugee camp in Nablus defined the meaning of jihad while talking about her language learning experience in school. She stated, '[s]ometimes [jihad/it] is a name of a girl or a boy, but sometimes [it] is a strong person who defends his homeland'. Schieffelin and Ochs (1986) described the connection of language structure on the construction of meaning. The word jihad in regard to language structure could be a verb, noun, or an adjective and it could be used as a female or male name. However, the literal meaning of jihad in the Arabic language is exertion, to strive, effort, and struggle. The religious meaning of jihad suggests two different characteristics, one is concerned with spiritual growth and the other one is used in relation to holy war and more radical means (Gould 2005). These two different meanings are associated with the local meaning of jihad, while it is reconstructed through a comparison between the term *fedayee* (freedom fighter) and the term martyr. The local meaning for fedayee is a person who is committed to sacrifice himself/herself for his/her homeland. The comparison of the meaning of these two words was eloquently articulated by a 12-year-old female participant, living in Rammallah city who described the transformation of naming as evident in her family history saying, '[m]y parents are fedayeen [freedom fighters], my mother was jailed for six months and my father was jailed for six years'. She continued to define the meaning of fedayee as she narrated family events, saying 'fedayee defends his homeland, he might die, but he is defending his homeland. But if someone got to be a martyr it might have happened by accident.' The issue of an incident being an accident in this context is that an individual is killed without planning to do an act of martyrdom. Participants recognize the parallel intention of jihad and fedayee for liberating Palestine, yet they question the credibility of labelling every person who dies as a martyr regardless of whether he/she committed a liberation act of resistance.

Associating word to meaning did not necessarily translate to credibility but served in the resilience of the community, because the word itself showed that fighting against oppression was part of people's conscience; yet it was questioned. Changing the name of resistance from fedayee to martyr invoked nuances that paralleled the global language discourse as it was embedded in political realities of the Palestinian territories. From the 1950s to 1999, the Palestinian Liberation Organization (PLO) affiliation was a common underground activity. Palestinian people were once arrested by the Israel authority for being a member in the PLO. This was especially prevalent before the establishment of Palestinian Authority in 1993. This political development was transmitted to language meaning. A 13-year-old male participant from Hebron City described his observation of people's political involvement and language, saying, '[w]e call them fedayee, because the PLO was fighting in secrecy. They used to meet in Tunis but now you see those [members] in the street.' The global/local power struggle mirrored the naming of resistance in Palestine from purely secular naming to naming with religious connotations (Assad 2000; Suleiman 2004). The secrecy was associated with fedayee and was no longer necessary. Fighting against Israeli occupation was a public event and it mirrored the evolving global discourse. The contribution of global/local discourse in changing the meaning and naming associated with Palestinian resistance was also discussed, as the 12-year-old female participant from Ramallah city continued reflection on the change of naming:

> Maybe because long time ago people they used to be fedayee but now they are thinking about death; they do not think in terms of sacrifices and resisting; they are thinking in [terms of] dying; they do not have hope. Although they have hope; but the way they go about is not like the way they had before.

The meaning of martyrdom provided hope for people although the act martyrdom itself, in essence, meant the complete loss of hope. In this instance the meaning of martyrdom served the spiritual growth as an act of hope in refusing to give in to the power discourse and fighting against oppression as subscribed in the meaning of jihad (Gould 2005). The word functioned as the embodiment of spiritual and earthly aspirations. The act of martyrdom is the local response to global power and served as community hope and survival. The representation of two characteristic meanings in one act was not exclusive to the term martyr. Participants transferred the religious connotation applied to the terms martyr and fedayee, as a 13-year-old male participant from Nablus city indicated, 'I think fedayee could also go to heaven like the martyr because he fights for his homeland; I do not associate [this] with religion because both of them have the same goal'. The local meaning of jihad served as a heroic resistance against global oppression (Reuben 2002), in this case the Israeli one.

The articulation of jihad indicates that the meaning applied to local reality was not clearly defined as exclusively spiritual or characteristic of holy war. In many situations the overlap was immense because it addressed the local circumstances and concerns of children, as a 12-year-old female participant from Nablus city stated:

> It [jihad] is resistance; the Palestinian jihad is not against Zionism but also to fight the people who are dropping out of school. They should get educated because when you grow up the only thing you could benefit from is education. When we resist, we are defending our homeland of Palestine. We do not give up or give in; this is jihad.

The complex meaning of the term jihad was not absolutely confined within the resistance to Israeli oppression but also within liberation and empowerment of the community and the individual; in return, it maintained the existence and the survival of the community. Rahme (1999) and Gould (2005) illustrated the two levels of jihad — internal and external — and both denote a fight against evil; but the inner jihad is concerned with moral issues and fighting the temptations of life. The external jihad is concerned with fighting and building the Islamic community. This parallels to the two characteristics of meanings in jihad — spiritual and holy war (Gould 2005). Hence, the objective is not to ignore the religious connotation, but to comprehend it as a tool of response to global discourse in an effort to understand its presence in local realities (Fairclough 2001; Katz 2004). This happened while participants deconstructed and questioned the meaning of martyrdom in other countries with similar situations, as a 13-year-old male from Balatah refugee camp in Nablus City stated:

> Resistance is [when] one is trying to resist the dangers and defend any attack on one's country. Jihad is to face the Jewish soldiers face to face. He wants also to be granted martyrdom and liberate Palestine. Jihad for God — and he should be Muslim — and this is all that the word means. Not everyone could be considered a martyr or not even all the Palestinians could be considered martyrs. It [is] only the people who comply with the definition of martyrdom: Muslim and prays. Not everyone who says he is martyr means he is martyr. Even when someone is killed in refugee camp (not by Israeli soldiers) they say he is a martyr, he is not. In Afghanistan they (in TV) call them dead people not martyrs although they are Muslims, and they are not facing the enemy, they are sitting in their houses and the warplanes are above them; they are Muslims and they should be considered martyrs.

Being a Muslim in itself was not sufficient to earn martyrdom; one must be a devoted Muslim. This was not the case for Muslims that are proximately distanced from the participants. The debate was more explicit regarding martyrs in Palestine; participants defined martyr but questioned the basis of assigning the word jihad. Jihad was defined by activity yet it was not assigned identically across geopolitical entities because the local/global power discourse is not the same across countries and therefore the language discourse is different (Fairclough 2001). The construction of the meaning of jihad was tailored by responses to the presence of global discourse. However, this local interpretation creates possibilities for solidarity by using the word jihad. In a way, this addressed the spiritual and moral side of the meaning (Gould 2005). Solidarity in jihad as articulated by the participants was not limited to people under oppression; other individuals from free nations could join the quest, as one 10-year-old male from Dheisheh refugee camp in Bethlehem city indicated, '[j]ihad is only if they abused his land; if not, and he is concerned about other countries he could jihad in these countries'. This again served the two characteristics of the meaning of jihad: the goal of spiritual aspiration through means of fighting.

Fairclough (2001), Silberstein (2002) and Wolin (2002) verified that global language discourse contributes to the construction of local meaning; a local lens deconstructs global reality and creates an incompatibility of meaning. This dialectic notion generated a discussion on the conditions of earning martyrdom status. Participants provided two core elements as requirements for earning martyrdom; first of all, one should be a Muslim and second, he/she should practise life in accordance with Islamic teaching. The juxtaposed view is that religious affiliation did not necessarily reflect devotion; as a 13-year-old male from Hebron city stated, 'I would not consider [them] martyrs because they are Muslim in name'. Acts of resistance did not warrant anyone the heavenly status if he/she was not a faithful Muslim. Participants presented a paradox by claiming that non-Muslim resistors could also be awarded a heavenly status, as one 13-year-old female from Nablus city stated:

> Martyrdom is only for Muslims, but if a Christian resists, it is called defending the homeland. And he has a status in heaven. Resistance is for all people from different religions. He wanted to show his people or [the] Christian community that resistance is not only for Muslims. He wanted to defend his homeland, and his roots; the roots are not only for Muslims.

Acknowledgement of the diversity of resistors complicated the construction of resistance naming, especially for jihad and martyr. The Palestinian community, by definition, is not monolithic in that it assists in weaving the contemporary religious connotation into the meaning of the word jihad. This local meaning of jihad and resistance does not comply with the global language discourse (Faiq 2004); it is a response to the global power discourse (Fairclough 2001). Lack of monolithical characteristics in naming of resistance showed that naming and meaning intersected on the intention of resistance. The intention of jihads, martyrs and fedayees is the liberation of Palestine as well as maintenance of Palestinian community survival. Though the religious connation is present in the naming as a mirror of the global discourse, its local usage was due to the resistance of oppression and served as an act of hope. Religious connation in the naming of resistance provided comfort even while the Palestinian community was in despair. In this context, the juxtaposition of naming functioned in resilience by surviving and reworking the system whereby paradoxes in meaning of naming resistance reflected the pragmatics of Palestinian identity. Also the meaning of different resistance naming served as a way to rework the words — jihad, martyr, fedayee — as much as possible and created a lack of consensus among participants. In this way meanings contributed to the variety of characteristics of jihad and martyr and in turn, created possibilities for redefining the words according to the global/local contested language discourse.

Theme Two: Forms of Resistance

Forms of resistance implicitly mirrored the multifarious and the multifaceted elements of local/global discourse in the naming of resistance whereby it emerged in methods of resistance. The methods were in the two characteristic meanings of jihad, spiritual and holy war, and are illustrated by the two levels of jihad, internal and external (Rahme 1999; Gould 2005). The local nuances in methods of resistance paralleled the political realities of the Palestinian people yet also provided insight into the diversity of methods, conditions and resources of the community. Forms of resistance facilitated the language meaning utilized among Palestinian children. Hence, the most apparent two forms of resistance that the participants apparently agreed on were their faith in liberating Palestine and their education. These two forms were spiritual but also in compliance with the two levels of jihad. In addition, these forms expressed the resistance, resilience and reworking of the system (Katz 2004) as a 13-year-old male participant from Nablus city indicated:

> Yes, through having faith in God, we defend our land. For example if they wanted to evacuate him from his home he should refuse. He should be a martyr before leaving the house. Also through his education; the students through their education they will defend their homeland.

In this respect, the consensus was that every Palestinian is engaged in resistance, by the fact that they are still surviving and attempting to be free through the promotion of education. This was in accordance with the notion of internal jihad as identified by Rahme (1999), but also it was a method of resilience and reworking by ensuring students were in schools for the betterment of the community. According to the participants, it was a struggle to obtain an education that included a long suffering journey to cross the Israeli army checkpoints and an ongoing effort just to keep schools open for students to attend. Schools suffered from Israeli closure during the Intifada and Israeli army checkpoints became obstacles for movement. Whether it was the checkpoints or school closures, the Israeli Army managed to undermine the education system by decreasing the attendance level of teachers and students. Participants recognized the significance of education not only for the short term but for the survival of the community and this recognition served as a form of resilience and unity for the community. As one 12-year-old male from Nablus city stated, '[t]hrough education, when he grows up, he should do something for Palestine, and he could fight for Palestine'. Contribution to the community was a form of resistance and was celebrated and acknowledged as a path for alteration of the political situation. This served the internal and external levels of jihad (Rahme 1999), as another 12-year-old female participant from Nablus city stated:

> By educating is jihad, and thinking about solutions for [the] homeland, [this] is jihad. The physician is majihad [a person who commits jihad]; he is helping injured people; he is helping his people. As one who is helping someone who could not find a piece of bread, this is jihad. Anything you do for your homeland is jihad.

This local meaning of jihad was a heroic resistance against oppression and a form of response to global discourse. The forms of resistance were sophisticated. They addressed innovation in finding resources that were defined in local conditions as equivalent to language discourse (Fairclough 2001). However, these different methods of resistance allowed the participants to dispute the effectiveness of throwing stones as a form of resistance. For example, one 12-year-old female interviewee from Rammallah city eloquently indicated, '[t]he one who [does] jihad is defending his homeland, maybe the one who is throwing stones is jihad but it is not the right way'. Preferring the spiritual path of jihad as a method of resistance acknowledged that throwing stones is not effective, yet the act of throwing stones was a political position and demonstrated that Palestinians were a proud people. It was indeed a response contingent on the global discourse, but it was vastly unequal to it (Katz 2004). As one female participant from Rammallah city stated, '[t]hrowing stones is not effective, but it is a matter of dignity and integrity ... I am telling them [the Israelis] that I would not allow you take more of me'. Communicating the meaning of the local discourse to other countries was another method of resistance (Andoni 1997; Slyomovics 1991).

The participants were also familiar with the modern world possibilities and the power of the pen as a form of resistance, as noted by a 13-year-old male participant from Nablus city, who said '[w]riting something to encourage the Majihad, like writing something in the newspaper'. Another 12-year-old male participant from Hebron city endorsed the writing option not only for the benefit of the local audience but as a way to affect the global discourse. He stated, '[t]he one who has a mind and it could benefit the homeland, he could graduate from journalism. Journalism spreads the news about Palestinians, and moves the feelings of the Arabs . The recognition of the possibility to cross borders to other nations and thereby influence the global discourse about the Palestinian cause reinforced the role of education as a form of resistance. This demonstrated the conscious recognition for the need to compete with the global discourse. Competition is the essence of altering the global hegemony (Katz 2004). However, propagation of the Palestinian cause was merely one dimension of resistance.

Participants also discussed the effectiveness of boycotting Israeli products and encouraging Palestinian manufacturers, as a 12-year-old female from Ramallah city suggested:

> I want to buy candy; if I see any Israeli product that is good and I see beside the same but it is Palestinian product that might not be as good as the Israeli one. I will buy the Palestinian product in order to support the Palestinians; in this way I am fighting. In this way everyone could fight. I am getting my education; I am resisting. The ones who are committing martyr operations are resisting, the ones who are throwing stones are resisting, the ones who are boycotting the Israeli products are resisting . . . Now there is Palestinian product and Israeli product, when we do not buy the Israeli products and buy the Palestinian products we are supporting it. When we buy the Israeli product we give them good economy to buy weapons that they use to kill us.

Boycotting as a method of resistance served as a reworking of the local recourses to benefit the community and also functioned on the spiritual characteristic and internal–external levels of jihad (Gould 2005; Rahme 1999). Participants understood that there are multiple strategies for resistance that benefit their community. Indeed, in this form the participants exemplified resistance, resilience and reworking. Participants' active roles in expressing forms of resistance and local discourse conveyed the representation of the global discourse in their local realities (Katz 2004). In addition, participants realized that forms of resistance fit within each individual's circumstances, as a 12-year-old male participant from Nablus city stated, '[r]esistance, or jihad, has a lot of variety, in money, in tongue and in soul. One old rich person — he could support the Majihad through his money. One, through his tongue, has strength and determination; he could fight'. As presented by Fairclough (2001), individual resistances are involved in ideological discourse that prevails globally, but is defined locally and tempered by local experiences. A 12-year-old male participant from Hebron city expressed his local circumstances as they pertained to forms of resistance, stating '[i]f there is Majihadian in the area I will tell them that the Jews invaded the area; this is the least I could do'. Although children voiced awareness in the diverse forms of resistance, there was a conscious recognition that the methods used were not compatible with the Israeli army's capabilities and its power. As the same participant continued stating, '[w]e want weapons but Western countries support Israel'. Knowing that Israel is more equipped in military resources and the Israeli solider is well-trained did not inhibit the participants' awareness of empowerment within their own means, as a 13-year-old male participant from Nablus city shared, '[f]or example an Israeli soldier had a gun and the two young Palestinian men attacked him with knives, the soldiers ran away; our people are courageous'. Another 12-year-old female from Nablus city commented on this incompatibility between the Israeli army and the Palestinian resistance, by indicating, '[t]he stones would not defeat a tank or a machine gun. We are stronger than the bullets they have, but they have weapons.' The incompatibility between the Israeli army and the liberation movement was recognized not only in weaponry, but also in training: the fight was unequal between locals and global power (Katz 2004). As a 13-year-old male participant from the Dheisheh refugee camp in Bethlehem city stated, '[w]e have weapons in the camp, but not much; even if you resist using weapons, he will not benefit; he should know how to use them, because he does not know how to shoot at the target'. As Katz (2004) stated, the local resistance is contiguous on the global discourse and is not necessarily equivalent.

Restraint from weapon usage was another form of resistance, but was also disputed as participants questioned the effectiveness of weapon usage on both sides. A 12-year-old female participant from Ramallah articulated:

> Like non-violence policy, there is no need for violence, why killing? People should live; we did not create them so to kill them. It is the same that we do not like when they kill us. They do not like when we kill them; maybe there is another way.

Disputing the two characteristics of jihad, as observed in forms of resistance, was a continuous event by the participants. The function of the dispute was significant for the evolvement of the local response to the global discourse. Participants articulated the reasons for resistance that ascribed the historical and contemporary conditions for the Palestinian people (Cohen and Kliot 1992). They made the connection of the historical circumstances and the impact on their lives, as a 12-year-old female participant from Nablus city stated, '[t]he Jews came and colonized us and terrorized us'. Historical consciousness about the Palestinian land and its evolvement across time was present in the participants' realities. Recognition of the historical impact on the Palestinian people indicated an understanding of the global role which evoked a particular meaning as well as forms of resistance. Therefore, in order to capture the dialectic relationship of local and global discourse of both the naming of resistance and forms of resistance, it is vital to understand the global language discourse across time and its function in the process of constructing the meaning in language of resistance. A refusal to recognize this complex web, in essence, ignores participants' complex understanding of their political environment and also dismisses global/local power discourse.

Conclusion

Participants in this research study inherited the political discourse not only from the Palestinian community but also from global interaction and the Israeli oppression. The language meaning facilitated the complexity of the participants' voices and indicates that the meaning of language is implanted in the political circumstances in which children are an interactive entity of the global/local discourse (Katz 2004). In addition, the acceptance of such a notion of language meaning echoes the idea that language itself is a tool of resistance as much as it is a tool for survival. This survival characteristic encompasses the aspect that children's abilities to construct resilience, reworking and resistance and perhaps even their participation in this path ensures that future children will reconstruct meaning in the same way. The construction of meaning of language carries on the local response to global hegemony (Fairclough 2001) and the possibility for change. From a socio-linguistic perspective, the children in this study changed language and meaning to fit the situation of their experiences. This ability supports Labov's idea of 'speech community' (2001), a term describing the fact that people share ways of talking in accordance with community reality. In this research, the children demonstrated that they can reconstruct and modify words common to global discourse in order to create the reality of local discourse and meaning. Thus, using the children's voices or data, reminds us that their peers and the world-at-large can understand that the power discourse of geopolitics is not the only voice to be heard. Even when weaker perspectives are silenced by oppression, the community remains. Children's refusal to be objectified by the global discourse is, in itself, an act of liberation. Global discourse tends to objectify the discourse and create a singular meaning of resistance; on the other hand, children in local settings create shades of meaning that reflect their realities. The paradox in this global/local construction of meaning is ironic in the sense that meaning will lead to liberation as well as hope. Following practices of children themselves, it would seem that preservation of the group's ability to name resistance and to reconstruct local meaning is an act of hopeful resistance throughout the community.

This study has shown only a few examples of how Palestinian children make local meaning by reconstructing global discourse. In the way that meaning changes with political reality, language usage remains a tool of power to interpretation. Meaning of language changes because it must. Users modify meaning to serve their everyday needs and to inform their experiences. To the extent that power discourse attempts to objectify socio-political reality as a tool of domination (Bourdieu 1977), the voices of the children serve as an experiential countermeasure to the power of greater forces operating in their lives. The very acts of living and the making of meaning bear witness to the possibilities of a discourse different from the global, of a world informed by the local.

Note

* This chapter was earlier published in *Children's Geographies*, 6(3): 269–80, 2008. Reproduced with permission of the publisher (Taylor & Francis Ltd, http://www.tandf.co.uk/journals).

References

Andoni, L. 1997. 'Searching For Answers: Gaza's Suicide Bombers', *Journal of Palestinian Studies*, 26(4): 33–45.

Assad, I. 2000. 'Palestinian Educational Philosophy between Past and Present', *Studies in Philosophy and Education*, 19: 387–403.

Bhatia, S. 2000. 'Language Socialization and the Construction of Socio-Moral Meanings', *Journal of Moral Education*, 29(2): 149–66.

Bourdieu, P. 1977. *Outline of a Theory of Practice*. New York: Cambridge University Press.

Cohen, S. and N. Kliot. 1992. 'Place-Names in Israel's Ideological Struggle over the Administered Territories', *Annual of the Association of American Geographers*, 82(4): 653–80.

Cook, C., A. Hanieh and A. Kay. 2004. *Stolen Youth: The Politics of Israel Detention of Palestinian Children*. London: Pluto.

Creswell, J. 2003. *Research Design: Qualitative, Quantitative, and Mixed Methods Approach* (2nd edn). Thousand Oaks, CA: American Psychological Association.

Euben, R. L. 2002. 'Killing (for) Politics: Jihad, Martyrdom, and Political Action', *Political Theory*, 30(1): 4–35.

Faiq, S. 2004. 'The Cultural Encounter in Translating from Arabic', in S. Faiq (ed.), *Cultural Encounters in Translation from* Arabic (26th edn), pp. 1–13. Toronto: Multilingual Matters Ltd.

Fairclough, N. 2001. *Language and Power*. Harlow: Pearson.

Falah, G. 2004. 'Truth at War and Naming the Intolerable in Palestine', *Antipode*, pp. 596–600.

Finkelstein, N. 1990. 'The Ordinary, the Awful, and the Sublime: Beit Sahur in Year II of the Intifada', *Social Text*, 24: 3–30.

Forman, G. and A. Keda. 2004. 'From Arab Land to 'Israel Lands': The Legal Dispossession of the Palestinians Displaced by Israel in the Wake of 1948', *Environment and Planning D: Society and Space*, 22: 809–30.

Glaser, B. 2002. 'Conceptualization: On Theory and Theorizing Using Grounded Theory', *International Journal of Qualitative Methods* 1(2), available at www.ualberta.ca/ijqm (accessed 3 October 2013).

Gould, M. 2005. 'Understanding Jihad', *Policy Review*, 129: 15–32.

Harvey, S. 2003. 'Critical Perspectives on Language(s)', *Journal of Sociolinguistics*, 7(2): 246–59.

Kanaana, S. 1990. 'Humor of the Palestinian "Intifada"', *Journal of Folklore Research*, 27(3): 231–40.

Katz, C. 2004. *Growing up Global: Economic Restructuring and Children's Everyday Lives*. Minneapolis, MN: University of Minnesota Press.

Kimmerling, B. and J. Migdal. 2003. *The Palestinian People: A History*. London: Harvard University Press.

Labov, W. 2001. *Principles of Linguistic Change: Social Factors*. Malden, MA: Blackwell.

Nassar, H. 2006. 'Stories from Under Occupation: Performing the Palestinian Experience', *Theatre Journal*, 58: 15–37.

Massad, J. 2003. 'Liberating Songs: Palestine put to Music', *Journal of Palestine Studies*, 32(3): 21–38.

Oliver, A. and P. Steinberg. 2005. *The Road to Martyrs' Square: A Journey into the World of the Suicide Bomber*. New York: Oxford University Press.

Peteet, J. 1996. 'The Writing on the Walls: The Graffiti of the Intifada', *Cultural Anthropology*, 11(2): 139–59.

Rahme, G. J. 1999. 'Ethnocentric and Stereotypical Concepts in the Study of Islamic and World History', *The History Teacher*, 32(4): 473–94.

Said, E. 2000. 'Invention, Memory, and Place', *Critical Inquiry*, 26(2): 175–92.

Schieffelin, B. and E. Ochs. 1986. 'Language Socialization', *Annual Review of Anthrograpthy*, 15: 163–91.

Silberstein, L. 2002. *War of Words: Language, Politics and 9/11*. New York: Routledge.

Slyomovics, S. 1991. 'To Put one's Fingers in the Bleeding Wound: Palestinian Theatre under Israeli Censorship', *The Drama Review*, 35(2): 18–38.

Soto, L. D. 1997. *Language, Culture and Power: Bilingual Families and the Struggle for Quality Education*. New York: State University of New York Press.

Suleiman, Y. 2004. *A War of Words: Language and Conflict in the Middle East*. London: Cambridge University Press.

Whitelam, K. 1996. *The Invention of Ancient Israel: The Silencing of Palestinian History*. London: Routledge.

Wolin, R. 2002. 'September 11 and the Self-castigating Left', *South Central Review*, 19(2/3): 39–49.

15

Reshaping Social Movement Media for a New Millennium

*Chris Atton**

Towards a New Socio-technical Paradigm

In his challenging empirical analysis of new communication technologies, Paschal Preston convincingly argues that 'the new social order and communication order of informational capitalism' is fundamentally unequal and polarized, and that the neoliberal project of an 'information society' has failed to deliver its promised socio-technical paradigm (Preston 2001: 272). Rather than Information and Communication Technologies (ICTs) holding out the possibility of a radical change in the existing social order, instead they reproduce existing social inequalities. Preston's argument is that new technologies will be overlaid on existing systems, not to replace them but to exist alongside them. This 'long-wave' approach, highlighting economic and social continuities of inequality and exclusion, contradicts the over-optimistic and unrealistic claims of techno-gurus such as Alvin Tofler. Preston emphasizes not technological changes but economic, political and social continuities: of persistent imbalances between the information rich and the information poor, as well as deep-rooted inequalities of education, employment opportunities, access to health care ability to participate in democratic government and access to markets. He finds hope not in technological advances, nor in knowledge or information tout court, but in 'political will and social mobilisation' (ibid.).

He places both the mature and the new social movements at the forefront of this struggle for 'a more egalitarian, inclusive and social "information society"' (Preston 2001: 272, original emphasis). His plea is to history: just as earlier movements (such as the British trades unions) had played a significant part in reshaping production and consumption regimes, from which dominant socio-technical paradigms would be reshaped (through reform and state policy), contemporary social movements have a similar capacity to shift the balance of social power. This is not an anti-technology agenda, nor is it simply about replacing one technological development with another. Instead of viewing 'technology as the end of social development' (Preston 2001: 268) in a competitive, market-driven culture, new social movements — based as they are on notions of equity, inclusivity, social justice and radical notions of democracy — hold out the possibility of transforming the production and consumption capacities of new communication technologies into a new socio-technical paradigm, what Preston terms a 'social holism' (ibid.: 258).

The use of new communication technologies, specifically the Internet, by new social movements can thus be viewed as a double response to informational capitalism and neoliberalism. First, the embedding of Internet practices in a wider socio-economic struggle against the internationalization of capital can be considered as a globalized, radical-democratic struggle against globalized finance. The movement's aims and praxis are fundamentally global in reach, whilst demonstrating the significance of local struggles, not only for those in that locale, but for those who might learn from those struggles, recontextualizing the strategies and tactics of others at the same time as drawing moral, economic and political support from them. Second, the deployment of new communication technologies offers new social movements prefigurative methods of organizing (Downing 2001), in particular through the radicalization of production, to a degree not seen in previous manifestations of social movement media.

The rich and diverse history of social movement media practices does not admit of any easy generalizations: particular configurations of political, social, economic, and cultural forces at specific historical and geographical junctures make this task theoretically and empirically fraught. Historiographical analyses of some two centuries of social movement media in the USA and the UK do reveal, however, some striking common features (Hamilton and Atton 2001). Broadly, the history of social movement media has been one of vanguardism and essentialism. Too often have these media been considered as the political weapons of 'great men', too rarely have they been viewed as the 'voices of the voiceless'. Historical accounts have essentialized these media, divorcing them from historical specificity, seeing them as immanent, structural forces rather than processes of symbolic struggle which are themselves embedded in emerging and continually shifting social and political processes. Such accounts make it difficult to see the realism of social movement media as constellations of symbolic struggle, historically and culturally determined, intimately though not unproblematically connected to the popular forces from which they sprang and which they sought to represent. Rather than accounts of great men, social movement media present the involvement of 'ordinary' people, whose history and aspirations these media seek to reveal and mobilize. This is not to say that these media have been consistently successful, nor that they have not been at times the organs of key individuals.

Whilst internationalism and prefigurative methods of organizing are hardly new phenomena within alternative media projects, the earlier dominance of Leninist models of media production has often prevented these features from becoming much more than ideological desiderata. Attempts by various socialist newspapers to have workers write for them — a significant tactic of prefigurative politics — appear to have failed as a result of those papers' reliance on elite groups and hierarchical methods of organizing. John Downing notes how the narrow range of people involved in producing working-class papers ('authorities in or close to the Communist Party' in the case of the *Morning Star*, whereas *Socialist Worker* and *The Militant* . . . tend only to have the faithful open their mouths') stifles controversy and debate, and ensures the marginality of the papers to their readers' everyday struggles (Downing 1980: 198–99). This problem was recognized by the editorial staff of Socialist Worker from its earliest days. In his history of the paper, Peter Allen notes that, even by the second year of its life, the number of articles written by workers was increasing, but he gives no indication as to the size of the increase or whether it continued (Allen 1985: 211). By the mid-1970s Tony Cliff, the leader of the Socialist Workers' Party, was insisting that '[w]orkers' names will have to appear in the paper . . . more and more often and less and less often the by-lines of the Paul Foots, Laurie Flynns and Tony Cliffs' (cited in Sparks 1985: 145). Allen notes that a general appeal to its worker-readers 'did increase the number of articles written by workers, [but] the increase was neither dramatic nor sustained' (Allen 1985: 220). This clearly caused some anxiety amongst the party's Central Committee, not least to its leader, Tony Cliff. Writing in 1982, he noted that 'to a large extent workers' writing is limited to a small area of the paper'. His solution was to propose that the paper become 'a workers' diary' (ibid.: 216), but Allen provides no evidence to show that the paper evolved even partially along the lines that Cliff was demanding.

Yet there is another discernible tradition of social movement media that has focused on projects that radically reform three key aspects of communication: 'skills, capitalization and controls' (Williams 1980: 54). For the English Radical press (roughly, 1790–1830) this resulted in papers that were characterized by pauper management, where 'journalists saw themselves as activists rather than as professionals' and where there was an interest 'in expos[ing] the dynamics of power and inequality rather than report[ing] "hard news"' (Curran and Seaton 1997: 15). These features reappear at the heart of contemporary social movement media and it is in the continuity of this tradition that we can place the use of new communication technologies by new social movements. Preston's vision of a social information society offers a useful theoretical framework against which we may test the use of ICTs by new social movements. Whereas a Leninist paper such as *Socialist Worker* claimed internationalism as part of its ideology and modelled its organizational form on the former Soviet system, ICTs with global reach present the possibility of a more inclusive, networked socio-technical paradigm. The majority of alternative media examined by Downing (2001) are at bottom local interventions, however committed they may be to international perspectives. Preston's social holism suggests not only a global reach in terms of ideology and media content, but one that seeks an inclusivity, an anti-elitist approach to organization and production that stands in stark contrast to earlier Leninist forms and to those geographically circumscribed forms of social anarchist media examined by Downing. In this respect at least, the notion of social holism, achievable through the radical deployment of ICTs, suggests a development of Downing's notion of prefigurative politics that potentially has a far greater reach. In terms of Internet use, we can locate the beginnings of this approach as a political strategy in the communication methods of the Zapatistas.

The Internet and New Social Movements

The most widely cited example of radical Internet use is that employed by the Zapatistas in their struggle for the Chiapas region of Mexico. This has been considered the 'radical ideal' by alternative media commentators and social scientists alike. Manuel Castells' term for their campaign — 'the first informational guerrilla movement' (1997: 79) — is arguably over-technologized. After all, their struggle remains at its heart, one for land, and for political and cultural recognition, fought in a number of arenas, only one of which is the informational. Yet the significance of the Chiapas movement's deployment of the Internet has had global reverberations. John Downing emphasizes the Zapatistas' 'conception of the public sphere as an arena for dialogic praxis . . . an arena for radical inclusivity' (Ford and Gil 2001: 219, 220). The cross-cultural dialogue that the Zapatistas encouraged through the publishing of their communiqués on the Internet, the support they built up across the world, the visibility their message enjoyed in the mainstream media: all grew out of the deployment of an international communications medium for a project of local resistance. In microcosm, the Zapatistas' struggle represented the burgeoning anti-capitalism movement, itself a development of the holistic tendencies of the environmentalist movement, coming together with groups and movements campaigning for Third World debt relief, human rights (including employment rights) and social justice.

The significance of the Zapatistas' use of the Internet lies in their promotion of dialogical praxis: 'Zapatismo is a living example of how we can open the space, prepare the soil, and through direct democratic dialogue, witness the radical roots going deep' (Jordan 2001: 21). The Internet not only publicized their local struggle but their methods of political communication and organization. Their methods did not proceed from a deployment of the Internet, however; they were embedded in their local struggles. Dialogic praxis effected through the Internet — that is, praxis that sought a 'radical internationalisation' through available technology rather than using the technology to raise awareness of a local praxis — came most significantly from anarchist groups in the West. Inspired by the Zapatistas, hitherto separate groups began not only to act in solidarity with each other, but to act together, publishing and protesting as networked 'affinity groups' (Bookchin 1986), as an anarchist model of organizing.

Where early uses of the Internet by anarchist groups had been more or less fragmented assays into small-scale electronic media production, seeing only small increases in the circulation and reach compared to their print precursors and experiencing chronic difficulties in sustaining their media projects economically (Atton 1996), the development of the McSpotlight Website in 1996 demonstrated a more successful strategy based on international networking, a broadening of the protest agenda and the participation of numerous local groups (Atton 2000). The site provided a non-hierarchic centre for a range of diffuse, only informally connected groups and individuals — Bookchin's affinity groups in action. As the site grew to involve more groups, opportunities arose to expand the interests of the site to cover not only the 'McLibel' trial, but the practices of multinational corporations in all countries, and their links with governments and supra-governmental bodies. Whilst it is not necessary to argue that the current anti-capitalist movement began in McSpotlight, its trajectory may be similarly applied to the development, reach and extent of the latest phase of radical Internet use, the Indymedia network.

The Indymedia Network

The network of Independent Media Centers (IMCs) has become a highly visible feature of the media landscape of the global anti-capitalism movement at the turn of the millennium. The IMCs or Indymedia network came to prominence during the demonstrations in the American city of Seattle against the World Trade Organization summit meeting there on 30 November 1999. The Seattle IMC acted as an independent media focus for the broad coalition of social justice groups, trade unions, anarchists, socialist, communists, environmental groups and others — a coalition that has come to be known as the anti-capitalist movement. In Seattle the Centre had both a physical and a virtual presence. Its virtual presence on the Web enabled its small core staff to distribute streaming audio and video footage of the demonstrations, as well as written reports, across the world. Technically this was achieved through the use of open publishing software, where any independent journalist (any activist, for that matter, though the two were often the same) could upload their reports using a pro-forma on the IMC website. No prior approval was needed from the core group, neither was that group responsible for editing the content of reports in any way. Hundreds of hours of audio and video footage and hundreds of thousands of eyewitness reports, analyses and commentaries became available to activists, supporters, detractors — to 'global citizens' at large.

Such independent accounts provide a powerful counter to the enduring frames of social movement coverage in mainstream media. A study of the framing of the women's movement by US print media (Ashley and Olson 1998) presents what have become standard responses in the mainstream media to social movement actors, their aims and their ideologies. Ashley and Olson found dominant patterns and emphases on surface details, the de-legitimization of feminists and their depiction as disorganized and riven by conflict. Framing devices were used to minimize ideological threats by representing the actors as deviants on the margins of society (a tactic which also exaggerates such threats to the status quo and to 'reasonable' people). These frames are widespread in mainstream coverage of social movements (Gitlin 1980; van Zoonen 1992). The ideologies and practices of social movement actors become simplified and homogenized; rather than exploring the complex, unstable and 'structurally undetermined' components of these protests (K.W. Brand, cited in van Zoonen 1992), mainstream framing devices render deeper explorations of social movement activity unavailable. By homogenizing varieties of dissent the mass media reify protest and instantiate the richness of ideologies and actions, often through a crudely simplified single example, such as we saw during the Genoa protests in July 2001, where a photograph of a masked protester, standing defiantly on an overturned car, was reproduced throughout the mainstream media to represent the entire protest movement. By contrast, social movement ideologies and practices are complex and internally contradictory (or so it seems, with socialists working with greens, anarchists with socialists, the different hue of green politics, organized groups working with grassroots individuals) — social movement activity is a process, not simply a series of events — it is 'a network of active relationships between actors who interact, communicate, influence each other, negotiate, and make decisions' (Melucci 1996: 71).

Since Seattle, the Indymedia network has expanded. At the time of writing (April 2002) there were 78 IMCs in 31 countries. The concentration remains greatest in the USA (36) and Europe (one in each of 17 countries, with two in the UK). Other regions are far less well-represented. There is one IMC in India and only two in Africa (Nigeria and South Africa). The Seattle IMC remains as the network's de facto centre, and it is from its collective that the bulk of technical information about uploading comes, as well as proposals for managing the substantial flow of information the network generates. For example, the network now operates a unique form of editorial control. Whilst reports may be uploaded from or by any source, the editorial group reserves the right to remove contributions judged unsuitable. The 'Publish' page of Indymedia states that: 'The Independent Media Center is a collectively run media outlet for the creation of radical, *accurate*, and passionate tellings of the truth' (author's emphasis). Towards this aim the collective states that 'while we struggle to maintain the news wire as a completely open forum we do monitor it and remove posts'. The large majority of these posts are removed for 'being comments, not news, duplicate posts, obviously false or libelous posts, or inappropriate content [such as hate speech]'. Indymedia does, however, still make these posts available on a separate page titled 'hidden stories' (http://www.indymedia.org/search-process.php3? hidden true). Whilst editing does take place, it does not prevent voices from being heard, nor does it prevent users from accessing that content. Neither does this quasi-editorial function of the core group extend to the editing of individual pieces of work: if they do not breach the criteria set out, as mentioned earlier, then pieces will remain on the 'open' pages of the site. These limitations apart, IMC/Indymedia enable any activists to contribute their work. The use of open source software bypasses the need for an editor or Webmaster to upload contributions: writers and producers may do these themselves, using the pro-forma on the 'Publish' page. The effectiveness of this method has been shown most recently by its approach to the coverage of the events of 11 September and the ensuing Operation Enduring Freedom. '9–11: Peace & Justice' is the title of a feature page on the Seattle site (http://www.indymedia.org/peace) that links to news, analysis and comment posted to many of the 64 IMCs, as well as providing links to news and features appearing on other independent media organizations. These include local radio stations offering streaming audio and independent media monitoring projects such as Fairness and Accuracy in Reporting (FAIR).

Indymedia connects local work to a global struggle, and it is from within this global context that the movement perceives itself. Despite the presence of some editorial control, open source programming erodes any centralization of Indymedia that might otherwise occur. From the perspective of both producers and consumers (often the same people when we are talking about activists), Indymedia functions as a content aggregator of independent journalism, organized by country, issue and medium (text, audio, video, and multimedia). Not only do journalists place original, previously unpublished work there, IMCs themselves will often link to already-broadcast or published reports. To consider Indymedia as an organization is to consider a network of independent, collectively run 'nodes' through which independent journalists may circulate their work, largely unimpeded by the gatekeeping of those collectives.

It is not only the scale (in terms of geographical spread, global reach and volume of material) that makes the Indymedia network an interesting moment for the study of social movement media: it is the most thorough working-out on the Internet of the conditions and processes of radical media projects. The Indymedia network powerfully exemplifies the three core principles of John Downing's model (2001) of radical media organization. First, there is an emphasis on self-management, resulting in small-scale, collectively run projects. Second, the project suggests a 'socialist anarchist angle of vision' which, Downing argues, sets contemporary radical media apart from its Leninist precursors (still alive, of course, in some forms). Despite its revolutionary aims and content, Downing finds in the latter an unwelcome emphasis on vanguardism and party 'correctness'. This is not to claim that self-managed media that reject the Leninist, transmission-belt model will easily and unproblematically be freed from concerns over control and correctness. Jo Freeman's notion of 'the tyranny of structurelessness' (1972) reminds us of how even in avowedly non- or anti-hierarchical structures, hierarchies might still develop. Third, and proceeding from this interest in socialist anarchism as an organizing principle, the project embodies 'prefigurative politics, the attempt to practice socialist principles in the present, not merely to imagine them for the future' (Downing 2001: 71). Downing's emphasis here on socialism need not prevent us from applying these core principles to an organization as politically, culturally and geographically diffuse as the Indymedia network. Downing's vision is that of a democratic, non-corporate media network comprising non-hierarchically run, independent groups and individuals horizontally linked, and where what organization and control does take place is necessarily light. At this general level, at least, the Indymedia network appears to realize his vision.

Yet the features of Indymedia we have examined so far suggest a rather too comfortable fit with Downing's three principles, offering an almost idealized version of alternative media. To explore Indymedia further, however, is to reveal a more complex and apparently contradictory structure that tests Downing's desiderata and Preston's notion of social holism. We shall turn first to the news sources that set Indymedia apart from its Leninist counterparts (and from mainstream news sources) and examine those whose voices are most prominent on the site — the activists who report events from their own engaged, 'amateur' perspective. We shall then turn to other voices on Indymedia — those of intellectuals and other elite groups — whose contributions move us away from Indymedia as an ideal, unproblematic type of alternative media.

Amateur Journalism and Native Reporters

Social movement media have throughout their history privileged amateur journalists who are writing from a position of engagement with the event or process that is their subject. Here I use the term 'amateur' as Edward Said uses it to describe the amateur intellectual, one who is 'unestablished', that is, with no formal relationship to a profession or institution (Said 1994). 'Amateur' here has everything to say about commitment to radical intellectual and social practices; it has nothing to do with the common notion of the amateur as the ignorant, self-deceived dabbler. These amateur journalists — explicitly partisan — report from the 'front line', from the grassroots, from within the movements and communities they thus come to represent. At this more specific level of journalistic practice, the principles of self-management, organizational and ideological independence, and prefigurative politics are played out in what we can think of as 'native reporting':

> Native reporting' can usefully define the activities of alternative journalists working within communities of interest to present news that is relevant to those communities' interests, presented in a manner that is meaningful to them and with their collaboration and support . . . native reporter' also evokes those local grassroots journalists of the South by whom Michael Traber sets so much store, whose value lies not in their role of message-creators for a passive audience, but as members of a community whose work enables the entire community to come together, to 'analyse one's historical situation, which transforms consciousness, and leads to the will to change a situation' (Atton 2002: 112–13; Traber 1985: 3).

In the case of the Genoa protests in July 2001, native reporting provided a powerful counter to the dominant mainstream media coverage of the protests as riots, protesters, and as 'anarchists' (a term that in mass media terms is most often allied with 'terrorist') and as enemies of democracy. In place of these marginalizing and distorting accounts, Indymedia journalists presented accounts of the many peaceful protests that took place (largely unreported by the mainstream press), the heterogeneity of protesters (far from them being all young, male 'anarchists', there was a remarkable diversity of ethnic groups, ages, genders, and backgrounds). The reporters' active, lived presence within these events, whilst no guarantor of impartiality, enabled the production of news that told other stories from those reported in the mainstream: 'our news, not theirs'. This radical process of reporting in which activists become journalists, and where grassroots reporting and analysis from within movements and communities themselves is considered central, is activated through the Indymedia network, leading to a remarkable increase in the 'publicity' of social movement media.

This is a very different notion of publicity and of expertise and authority from that encountered through the activities of the more 'established' social movement experts and movement intellectuals such as George Monbiot and Naomi Klein (author of *No Logo*). Despite their close links to the movements that they support and on which they report (Monbiot, for instance, is a member of the Steering Committee of the Globalize Resistance coalition), their public authority has come from their positioning of themselves and their work in the liberal press (in the UK, primarily in *The Guardian* and its sister paper *The Observer*). By contrast, the work of grassroots activists, whose reports make up the bulk of the content on

Indymedia, exemplifies the passage of native reporters from participants in a demonstration to activist-journalists, whilst remaining positioned as 'rank and file' within those movements.

This relationship between native reporter and community is crucial: many social movement activists are sceptical of the mainstream liberal press' attitudes to social movements, particularly of their dealings with alternative journalists. Jim Carey's account (1998) of how, as an editor of the UK activist newspaper *Squall* he found his work plagiarized by the British mainstream press, offers convincing reasons for such scepticism. For the majority of activists who contribute to Indymedia, however, this is less of a problem. Carey's work and that of *Squall* generally, places a premium on journalistic standards that accord well with those of the mainstream profession. Consequently, the work of Carey and others like him is already tailored to the requirements of the mainstream journalist, in the same way as the professionally written press release or news agency report already accords in terms of structure, sourcing, development and language with the standards of the mainstream media. In short, Carey's work is ripe for plagiarism. By contrast, the partisan, first-person narratives and commentaries of the native reporter inhabit an uneasy terrain. The sustained first-person narrative in the mainstream is typically the province of the senior reporter or the columnist; partisan commentary will also come from the columnist or the op-ed writer: these are roles of significant status. The native reporter, by mainstream criteria, is unauthoritative and marginal, at the bottom of the hierarchy of access. Under the radical conditions of social movement media, and especially as demonstrated by the open publishing approach of Indymedia, these reporters become central: the role and function of the journalist are transformed and hybridized. Further, the demotic approach of the native reporter, whether evinced by the gritty camcorder footage shot in the heat of protest or by the 'public-colloquial' style of textual discourse (Fairclough 1995: 72), emphasizes a radical populism in visual and written language. Peter Golding has argued that 'the demotic and casually convivial tone of the popular press [is] rooted in the evolution of a journalism of the market from a more socially anchored journalism of community or movement' (1999: 51). We might consider the radical populism of native reporting as both an acknowledgement of and a return to the roots of popular journalism (say, in the English Radical press), springing from its location and status as a communication technology for community and movement.

Elite Voices and Hybrid Sources

Indymedia is not only a space for individual, native reporters to place their original, previously unpublished work there. In terms of sources, the site is far more hybridized than that. Indymedia will often link to already-broadcast or published reports. These include the streaming audio output of independent radio stations 'in exile', such as Free Speech Radio News (a production of Pacifica Reporters Against Censorship, made up of reporters boycotting the independent Pacifica Radio for alleged censorship); and the Web-based WBIX ('WBAI Radio in Exile'), comprising production and reporting staff fired from New York City's WBAI Radio. Such stations, for all their radicalness, however, present a hybrid of radical content and news values with mainstream production values, institutional frameworks and professionalized reporting.

In its coverage of the attacks on the USA on 11 September we find Indymedia embracing hybridity even further. In this case we must note the apparent move away from Indymedia's practice of 'open publishing' — the 47 items that comprise its '9–11' pages have been selected by the Indymedia collective in Seattle from various sources. In these pages there is a predominance of elite sources. These are broadly of two types. The first are written by movement intellectuals such as Noam Chomsky, Michael Albert and George Monbiot and are generally linked to the Indymedia site or copied from their original places of publication or broadcast. In the case of Chomsky and Albert, for instance, these sources include Albert's radical online journal site *Znet* (a development of the US Left journal *Z Magazine*) and independent radio stations such as those already noted, whose interviews with Chomsky are available on streaming audio. Despite its international network and international reach, Indymedia's choice of intellectuals is firmly US centred, and Chomsky is pre-eminent. This emphasis has to do with Chomsky's continuing currency within a wide range of both politically aligned and non-aligned radical movements, both in the USA and across the world. In both the radical socialist and anarchist communities Chomsky is a highly favoured author, contributing articles to the socialist and anarchist press (even on occasion to the European liberal press).

Almost two-thirds of the contributions on the Indymedia 9–11 pages are driven by US-based, movement-intellectual concerns: explications and analyses of US foreign policy, anti-war arguments, and economic and political analyses. In this case, Indymedia coverage hardly depends at all on its international network of native reporters — on the few occasions when it does draw on 'native voices' these tend to be drawn from radical groups and collectives, based either in North America or Afghanistan. There is only a partial, limited sense of the globalized reach of the Indymedia network.

We also find commentary from independent, Web-based journalists such as John Tarleton and Pat Holt. Both Tarleton and Holt have histories as professional journalists: Tarleton as a former news and sports reporter, Holt as former book reviews editor for the *San Francisco Chronicle*. Both appear to have become radicalized (Holt describes himself on his site as a human rights activist) and publish exclusively from their own websites. We can also identify contributions from mainstream and official sources. These include links to articles from mainstream news sources such as the BBC, CNN and *Los Angeles Times*, which seem to have been chosen either as evidence of dissent within official political discourse or to offer news that can contribute to a critique of the US position towards Afghanistan, such as the BBC report that the US was planning its attack on the Taliban well in advance of 11 September.

The presence of mainstream sources might come as a surprise, given Indymedia's status as an activist-run news 'agency' staffed by activist or amateur journalists, until we recognize the pluralism that Indymedia is developing in its 9–11 pages. Unlike more radical media practices (such as elements of the anarchist press), Indymedia is not pursuing an ideological purity in the nature of its sources. The highly selective procedure it operates does, however, strongly suggest an ideological focus for the content of the 9–11 pages: the selections from the *Los Angeles Times*, for example, are in line with the arguments made by movement intellectuals such as Chomsky and Albert: here, analyses of US support for the Taliban prior to 11 September are used to argue for the US's hypocrisy in its foreign policy and for the historic predictability of its actions.

Similarly, Colin Powell's address to the international media on 17 May 2001 (taken from US government Web pages) announced '$43 million in new aid to Afghans' — again we see a precise selection of official news to demonstrate inconsistencies in US policy towards Afghanistan.

Reports of events such as those at Seattle and Genoa were considered newsworthy by independent journalists to the degree that they were able to counter the dominant mainstream coverage. Such accounts attempted to take back 'our news' with accounts of peaceful protests, of discussion and debate, and analyses of the complexity and heterogeneity of the various protest groups. In these cases the native reporters typically reported from within the context of their own active, lived presence at an event. By contrast, the 9–11 pages emphasize not direct-action news, nor even hard news about Operation Enduring Freedom, but largely present in-depth, discursive features that seek to understand the wellsprings of the attacks of 11 September and the US government's responses to them. Alternative understandings and explanations are preferred over alternative news reports. These are presented from a much wider array of sources than we would expect from previous studies of alternative media: mainstream sources are more prominent than in most grassroots media projects. It appears that Indymedia s argument is that their readers may obtain 'the news' anywhere — what is more difficult is to see beyond the daily news cycle of events to the various histories of politics and policy that inform these events. The selections on the 9–11 pages provide what Indymedia believes are the appropriate analyses, commentaries and background.

The major features that typify Indymedia's non-hierarchical, collective approach to Web-based reporting and discussion — timeliness; a diversity of voices that emphasizes native reporters; the scope for unlimited postings; a wide range of international sources — are all rendered problematic by an analysis of the 9–11 pages. We find much hybridity that draws equally from alternative and mainstream sources, that includes highly selective polemics from special and sectional interest groups and individuals. This hybridity is underscored by a shared radical–intellectual foundation for its analysis and commentary.

These practices reveal Indymedia as a content aggregator, as a 'reducer' and its activists as editors and diffusers of radical news and opinion. The unusual array and deployment of its selected writer-types and sources (unusual in terms of the idealized practices of alternative media) demonstrate the ability of Internet-based radical media projects to respond flexibly; to propose, through selection and structure, ways of presenting information, stimulating debate and discussion that break with its past. Indymedia demonstrates the evolutionary capacity of radical Internet projects to reconfigure themselves as circumstance and necessity suggest.

Conclusion

This chapter has emphasized the hybridity of social movement media in terms of organization, discourse and most prominently in terms of a hybrid form of media practice in the work of the native reporter or amateur, activist-journalist. This suggests that we must not lose sight of the primary role of media activists: that of political activism. To highlight the intimate linkage of a media formation such as Indymedia with the experience and engagement of protest is not simply to state the obvious: that the subject of the media is the protest. It is to underscore the intimate social, political and technical correspondences that radical use of the Internet enables. It is to envisage a media formation that corresponds with the non-hierarchical, local–global framework of the movement it supports. Finally, it is to acknowledge the prefigurative nature and the radical potential of democratic communication where the hierarchy of access to the media is overturned and where the contest between authoritative and 'illegitimate' news sources is, if not erased, at least rebalanced.

We must also acknowledge the complexity, fluidity and flexibility that a media formation like Indymedia offers. Indymedia's ideological and organizational reach extends well beyond that of Leninist radical media, as well as going beyond Downing's idealized form of alternative media. Its enactment of Preston's social holism is not only concerned with radically democratic journalistic practices of native reporting. Through its inclusion of mainstream, elite and hybrid news sources it challenges the notion of alternative media formations as necessarily 'pure' (whether ideologically, organizationally or productively). Indymedia presents a hybridized form of media which, arguably, could only be possible under the technological conditions of the present.

Note

* This chapter was earlier published in *Social Movement Studies* 2(1): 3–15, 2003. Reproduced with permission of the publisher (Taylor & Francis Ltd, http://www.tandf.co.uk/journals).

References

Allen, P. 1985. '*Socialist Worker* — Paper with a Purpose', *Media, Culture and Society*, 7(2): 205–32.

Ashley, L. and B. Olson. 1998. 'Constructing Reality: Print Media's Framing of the Women's Movement, 1966–1986', *Journalism and Mass Communication Quarterly*, 75(2): 263–77.

Atton, C. 1996. 'Anarchy on the Internet: Obstacles and Opportunities for Alternative Electronic Publishing', *Anarchist Studies*, 4: 115–32.

———. 2000. 'Are there Alternative Media after CMC?', *M/C Reviews*, available at http://www.uq.edu.au/mc/reviews/features/politics/altmedia.html (accessed 12 April 2000).

———. 2002. *Alternative Media*. London: Sage Publications.

Bookchin, M. 1986. 'A Note on Affinity Groups', in M. Bookchin (ed.), *Post-scarcity Anarchism*, 2nd edn, pp. 243–44. Montreal: Black Rose.

Carey, J. 1998. 'Fresh Flavour in the Media Soup: The Story of *SQUALL* Magazine', in G. McKay (ed.), *DiY Culture: Party and Protest in Nineties Britain*, pp. 58–78. London: Verso.

Castells, M. 1997. *The Information Age: Economy, Society and Culture, Vol. II: The Power of Identity*. Oxford: Blackwell.

Curran, J. and J. Seaton. 1997. *Power without Responsibility: The Press and Broadcasting in Britain*, 5th edn. London: Routledge.

Downing, J. 1980. *The Media Machine*. London: Pluto Press.

——— (ed.). 2001. *Radical Media: Rebellious Communication and Social Movements*. Thousand Oaks, CA: Sage Publications.

Fairclough, N. 1995. *Media Discourse*. London: Edward Arnold.

Ford, T. V. and G. Gil. 2001. 'Radical Internet Use', in J. Downing (ed.), *Radical Media: Rebellious Communication and Social Movements*, pp. 201–34. Thousand Oaks, CA: Sage Publications.

Freeman, J. 1972. 'The Tyranny of Structurelessness', *Berkeley Journal of Sociology*, 17: 151–64.

Gitlin, T. 1980. *The Whole World is Watching: Mass Media in the Making and Unmaking of the New Left*. Los Angeles: University of California Press.

Golding, P. 1999. 'The Political and the Popular: Getting the Measure of Tabloidization', in T. Perkins (ed.), *Proceedings of the AMCCS Conference, Sheffield, UK, 1998*, pp. 2–18. Sheffield: Association of Media, Communication and Cultural Studies.

Hamilton, J. and C. Atton. 2001. 'Theorizing Anglo-American Alternative Media: Toward a Contextual History and Analysis of US and UK Scholarship', *Media History*, 7(2): 119–35.

Jordan, J. 2001. 'Zapatismo and the Invisible Icons of Anti-capitalism', *Red Pepper*, September: 19–21.

Melucci, A. 1996. *Challenging Codes: Collective Action in the Information Age*. Cambridge: Cambridge University Press.

Preston, P. 2001. *Reshaping Communications: Technology, Information and Social Change*. London: Sage Publications.

Said, E. 1994. *Representations of the Intellectual: The 1993 Reith Lectures*. London: Vintage.

Sparks, C. 1985. 'The Working-class Press: Radical and Revolutionary Alternatives', *Media, Culture and Society*, 7(2): 133–46.

Traber, M. 1985. *Alternative Journalism, Alternative Media* (Communication Resource, No. 7). London: World Association for Christian Communication.

Williams, R. 1980. 'Means of Communication as Means of Production', in *Problems in Materialism and Culture: Selected Essays*, pp. 50–63. London: Verso.

Zoonen, E. A. van. 1992. 'The Women's Movement and the Media: Constructing a Public Identity', *European Journal of Communication*, 7: 453–76.

About the Editors

Savyasaachi is Professor, Department of Sociology, Jamia Millia Islamia, New Delhi. His research interests include decolonization, sociology of theory, social anthropology of method, political ecology and social production, indigenous and vernacular knowledge, social movements and dissent, crafts and creativity, material culture and conservation architecture and education. A PhD in Sociology from the University of Delhi, his works have been published in various journals and edited volumes.

Ravi Kumar is Associate Professor, Department of Sociology, South Asian University. He is Editor (South Asia) of *Journal of Critical Education Policy Studies*, and Co-editor of *Radical Notes*. He has a PhD in Sociology from Jawaharlal Nehru University. He writes and researches on consequences of neoliberalism on education, social movements, political economy of identity politics and social theory.

Notes on Contributors

Chris Atton is Professor of Media and Culture in the School of Arts and Creative Industries at Edinburgh Napier University, Scotland. His research specializes in alternative media and its audiences, and his books include *Alternative Media* (2002), *An Alternative Internet* (2004) and *Alternative Journalism* (2008). He has made special studies of fanzines, the media of new social movements, new media in Africa, and popular music and its audiences. He is currently researching the ways in which listeners make sense of and gain pleasure from avant-garde music.

Deepankar Basu teaches at University of Massachusetts, Amherst. His areas of interest include applied econometrics with a focus on Marxian political economy, macroeconomics, economic development, and demography. He has published in international journals such as Cambridge Journal of Economics, *Metroeconomica, Economic and Political Weekly* and *Studies in Nonlinear Dynamics and Econometrics*. His publications include *The US Financial Crisis* (2009).

Pratyush Chandra is a labour activist based in Delhi and is associated with *Radical Notes*. He has written and published in various journals on the issues of identities, agrarian question and political economy from a working class perspective. His recent areas of interest include workers' self-organization and the problems of institutionalization within the labour movement.

Maitrayee Chaudhuri teaches Sociology at the Centre for the Study of Social Systems, Jawaharlal Nehru University, New Delhi. She has written and published widely in the areas of gender, culture, globalization and media. Her published works include *Sociology in India* (2010), *Feminism in India* (2004), *The Practice of Sociology* (2003) and *The Women's Movement in India: Reform and Revival* (1993).

Harry Cleaver taught at the University of Texas at Austin (1976–2012). Previously, he taught at the New School for Social Research in New York City (1974–76) and the Université de Sherbrooke in Quebec, Canada (1971–74). He has written and published widely on Marxian theory, on political readings of mainstream economics and policies and on various moments of class struggle. His best known work is *Reading Capital Politically* (2012).

Ana Cecilia Dinerstein is Associate Professor of Sociology at the University of Bath. She is former Editor of *Capital & Class* member of the associate board of Sociology and Corresponding Editor of *Historical Materialism*. She has published extensively on Argentine and Latin American politics and policy, labour and social movements and emancipatory struggles. She is co-editor of *The Labour Debate* (2002, 2006 in Turkish and 2009 in Spanish), co-author of *La ruta de los Piqueteros: Luchas y Legados* (The Piqueteros Road: Struggles and Legacies, 2010).

Arturo Escobar is Professor of Anthropology at the University of North Carolina, Chapel Hill. His main interests include political ecology, the anthropology of development, social movements, and science and technology studies. His most recent publication is *Territories of Difference: Place, Movements, Life, Redes* (2008).

Marieke de Goede is Professor of Political Science at the University of Amsterdam. She has written widely about the cultural and political histories of financial markets and practices of dissent. She is author of *Speculative Security* (2012) and of *Risk and the War on Terror* (2008, co-edited with Louise Amoore). She is also member of the advisory board of the *Journal of Cultural Economy*.

Janette Habashi is Associate Professor in the Department of Human Relations, and teaches graduate and undergraduate-level courses concentrating on local and global human diversity issues and educational developmental theories. Janette actively contributes to the Reconceptualization of Early Childhood Education movement, a dynamic group in the field of childhood, studying and addressing both local and global concerns for children over the last 18 years. She was also honoured with the *Child on the Wing Rockefeller Foundation Resident Fellowship Award* from Johns Hopkins University.

Christopher J. Hilson is Professor of Law and Head of the School of Law at the University of Reading, UK. He was Editor-in-Chief of the *Journal of Environmental Law* (2007–12). His research interests, on which he has published widely, span EU and environmental law and politics, citizenship and rights, risk, and law and social movements. His publications include *Climate Change: Exploring the Legal and Criminological Consequences* (2012).

John Holloway teaches at the Instituto de Ciencias Sociales y Humanidades of the Benemerita, Universidad Autonoma de Puebla in Mexico. His published works include *Crack Capitalism* (2010), *Change the World Without Taking Power* (2010), *Zapatista! Rethinking Revolution in Mexico* (co-edited, 1998) and *Global Capital, National State and the Politics of Money* (1995).

Sangeeta Kamat is Associate Professor at the University of Massachusetts, Amherst, where she teaches courses on social theory, globalisation and education, and NGOs and international development. She completed her PhD in Social and Comparative Analysis of Education from the University of Pittsburgh. Her publications include *Development Hegemony: NGOs and the State in India* (2002).

Jane Mansbridge is the Adams Professor at the Kennedy School of Government. She is the author of *Beyond Adversary Democracy, Why We Lost the ERA* [the Equal Rights Amendment], *Beyond Self-Interest* (edited); *Feminism* (co-edited with Susan Moller Okin), and *Oppositional Consciousness* (co-edited with Aldon Morris).

Gunnar Olofsson is Professor of Sociology, Linnaeus University, Sweden. He has written extensively on Swedish social democracy, labour movements and social movements in general. He has also done research within the field of welfare policies, e.g., housing and older worker/early exit. He is now engaged in research on professions and higher education.

D. L. Sheth is Distinguished Fellow and former Director of the Centre for the Study of Developing Societies, Delhi, and was until recently Editor of the journal *Alternatives: Global, Local, Political.* He publications include *Citizens and Parties* (1975), *Multiverse of*

Democracy (co-edited with Ashis Nandy, 1996) and *Minority Identities and the Nation-State* (co-edited with Gurpreet Mahajan, 1999), and *Satta aur Samaj* (2009). He was previously National Fellow of Indian Council of Social Science Research, New Delhi, and of the Indian Institute of Advanced Study, Shimla.

K. Sivaramakrishnan is Dinakar Singh Professor of India & South Asian Studies, Professor of Anthropology, and Professor of Forestry & Environmental Studies at Yale University. His recent publications include *Ecologies of Urbanism: Metropolitan Civility and Sustainability in India* (co-edited with Anne Rademacher, 2013); *India's Environmental History*, volumes 1 and 2 (co-edited with Mahesh Rangarajan, 2011) and *The State in India after Liberalization: Interdisciplinary Perspectives* (co-edited with Akhil Gupta, 2010).

Index